COLOSSIANS

Society of Biblical Literature

Early Christianity and Its Literature

Series Editor
Gail R. O'Day

Editorial Board
Warren Carter
Beverly Roberts Gaventa
Judith M. Lieu
Joseph Verheyden
Sze-kar Wan

Number 4

COLOSSIANS
Encouragement to Walk in All Wisdom as Holy Ones in Christ

COLOSSIANS

Encouragement to Walk in All Wisdom as Holy Ones in Christ

John Paul Heil

Society of Biblical Literature
Atlanta

COLOSSIANS
Encouragement to Walk in All Wisdom as Holy Ones in Christ

Copyright © 2010 by the Society of Biblical Literature

All rights reserved. No part of this work may be reproduced or transmitted in any form or by any means, electronic or mechanical, including photocopying and recording, or by means of any information storage or retrieval system, except as may be expressly permitted by the 1976 Copyright Act or in writing from the publisher. Requests for permission should be addressed in writing to the Rights and Permissions Office, Society of Biblical Literature, 825 Houston Mill Road, Atlanta, GA 30333–0399, USA.

Library of Congress Cataloging-in-Publication Data

Heil, John Paul.
　　Colossians : encouragement to walk in all wisdom as holy ones in christ / by John Paul Heil.
　　　　p.　cm. — (Society of Biblical Literature early Christianity and its literature ; 4)
　　Includes bibliographical references and index.
　　ISBN 978-1-58983-484-2 (paper binding : alk. paper) — ISBN 978-1-58983-485-9 (electronic library copy)
　　　1. Bible. N.T. Colossians—Criticism, interpretation, etc. I. Title.
　　BS2715.52.H45 2010b
　　227'.7066—dc22   2010007847

Printed on acid-free, recycled paper
conforming to ANSI/NISO Z39.48–1992 (R1997) and ISO 9706:1994
standards for paper permanence.

Contents

Abbreviations..ix

1. Introduction...1

    A. Colossians: Encouragement to Walk in All Wisdom
    as Holy Ones in Christ...1
    B. Authorship...5
    C. Audience...7
    D. Literary-Rhetorical, Audience-Oriented Method.............9
    E. Summary..11

2. The Chiastic Structures of Colossians 13

    A. The Ten Microchiastic Units of the Letter 13
    B. The Macrochiastic Structure of the Letter 32
    C. Overview of the Parallels of the Macrochiasm
    in Colossians..36
    D. Outline of the Macrochiastic Structure of Colossians 37
    E. Summary..37

3. Colossians 1:1–2: Grace from Paul an Apostle by the Will of God 39

    A. Audience Response to Colossians 1:1–2....................39
    B. Summary on Colossians 1:1–2 45

4. Colossians 1:3–14: Thanking God When Praying for You
to Walk in Wisdom..47

    A. Audience Response to Colossians 1:3–14...................47
    B. Summary on Colossians 1:3–14 60

5. Colossians 1:15–23: The Gospel Preached to Every Creature
under Heaven...63

    A. Audience Response to Colossians 1:15–23..................64
    B. Summary on Colossians 1:15–23 80

6. Colossians 1:24–2:5: We Are Admonishing and
Teaching Every Human Being in All Wisdom 83

    A. Audience Response to Colossians 1:24–2:5 84
    B. Summary on Colossians 1:24–2:5 98

7. Colossians 2:6–23: Walk and Live in Christ
with Whom You Have Died and Been Raised.......................... 101

    A. Audience Response to Colossians 2:6–23................. 102
    B. Summary on Colossians 2:6–23 132

8. Colossians 3:1–7: You Died and Were Raised
with Christ from Living as You Once Walked......................... 135

    A. Chiastic Development from
    Colossians 2:6–23 (E) to 3:1–7 (E′) 135
    B. Audience Response to Colossians 3:1–7 136
    C. Summary on Colossians 3:1–7........................... 143

9. Colossians 3:8–16: In All Wisdom Teaching
and Admonishing One Another 145

    A. Chiastic Development from Colossians
    1:24–2:5 (D) to 3:8–16 (D′)................................ 145
    B. Audience Response to Colossians 3:8–16.................. 147
    C. Summary on Colossians 3:8–16.......................... 161

10. Colossians 3:17–4:1: You Have a Master in Heaven.................. 163

    A. Chiastic Development from
    Colossians 1:15–23 (C) to 3:17–4:1 (C′)...................... 163
    B. Audience Response to Colossians 3:17–4:1 164
    C. Summary on Colossians 3:17–4:1 174

11. Colossians 4:2–6: Pray for Us in Thanksgiving
and Walk in Wisdom 177

    A. Chiastic Development from
    Colossians 1:3–14 (B) to 4:2–6 (B′)......................... 177
    B. Audience Response to Colossians 4:2–6................... 178
    C. Summary on Colossians 4:2–6........................... 185

12. Colossians 4:7–18: Assurance in All the Will of God
and Grace from Paul... 187

    A. Chiastic Development from Colossians
    1:1–2 (A) to 4:7–18 (A′) 188

B. Audience Response to Colossians 4:7–18 188
  C. Summary on Colossians 4:7–18 201

13. Summary and Conclusion 203

Bibliography 211

Scripture Index 221

Author Index 225

Abbreviations

AB	Anchor Bible
ABR	*Australian Biblical Review*
AnBib	Analecta biblica
Ang	*Angelicum*
ANTC	Abingdon New Testament Commentaries
AUSS	*Andrews University Seminary Studies*
BDAG	Bauer, W., F. W. Danker, W. F. Arndt, and F. W. Gingrich. Greek-English Lexicon of the New Testament and Other Early Christian Literature. 3d ed. Chicago, 1999
BDF	Blass, F., A. Debrunner, and R. W. Funk. *A Greek Grammar of the New Testament and Other Early Christian Literature.* Chicago, 1961
Bib	*Biblica*
BIS	Biblical Interpretation Series
BJRL	*Bulletin of the John Rylands University Library of Manchester*
BSac	*Bibliotheca sacra*
BT	*The Bible Translator*
BTB	Biblical Theology Bulletin
BZNW	Beihefte zur Zeitschrift für die neutestamentliche Wissenschaft
CBQ	*Catholic Biblical Quarterly*
CBQMS	Catholic Biblical Quarterly Monograph Series
CGTC	Cambridge Greek Testament Commentary
CurTM	*Currents in Theology and Mission*
CTR	Criswell Theological Review
DivThom	*Divus Thomas*
DPL	*Dictionary of Paul and His Letters.* Edited by G. F. Hawthorne and R. P. Martin. Downers Grove, 1993
EBib	*Etudes bibliques*
EDNT	*Exegetical Dictionary of the New Testament.* Edited by H. Balz, G. Schneider. ET. Grand Rapids, 1990–1993

ETL	*Ephermerides theologicae lovanienses*
EvQ	*Evangelical Quarterly*
ExpTim	*Expository Times*
HBT	*Horizons in Biblical Theology*
HvTSt	*Hervormde teologiese studies*
ICC	International Critical Commentary
Int	*Interpretation*
JBL	*Journal of Biblical Literature*
JETS	*Journal of the Evangelical Theological Society*
JJS	*Journal of Jewish Studies*
JSNT	*Journal for the Study of the New Testament*
JSNTSup	Journal for the Study of the New Testament: Supplement Series
JTS	*Journal of Theological Studies*
LNTS	Library of New Tesament Studies
NCB	New Century Bible
Neot	*Neotestamentica*
NICNT	New International Commentary on the New Testament
NIGTC	New International Greek Testament Commentary
NovT	*Novum Testamentum*
NovTSup	Supplements to Novum Testamentum
NTL	New Testament Library
NTS	*New Testament Studies*
RB	*Revue biblique*
ResQ	*Restoration Quarterly*
RevExp	*Review and Expositor*
RRef	*La revue réformée*
SBB	Stuttgarter biblische Beiträge
SBLAbib	Society of Biblical Literature Academia Biblica
SBLDS	Society of Biblical Literature Dissertation Series
SBLMS	Society of Biblical Literature Monograph Series
SBLSCS	Society of Biblical Literature Septuagint and Cognate Studies
ScrTh	*Scripta theologica*
SNT	Studien zum Neuen Testament
SNTSMS	Society for New Testament Studies Monograph Series
SP	Sacra pagina
ST	*Studia theologica*
SUNT	Studien zur Umwelt des Neuen Testaments
SVTQ	*St. Vladimir's Theological Quarterly*
Teol	*Teologia*
TJ	*Trinity Journal*

TLNT	*Theological Lexicon of the New Testament.* C. Spicq. Translated and edited by J. D. Ernest. 3 vols. Peabody, Mass., 1994
TNTC	Tyndale New Testament Commentaries
TynBul	*Tyndale Bulletin*
WMANT	Wissenschaftliche Monographien zum Alten und Neuen Testament
WTJ	*Westminster Theological Journal*
WUNT	Wissenschaftliche Untersuchungen zum Neuen Testament
ZNW	*Zeitschrift für die neutestamentliche Wissenschaft und die Kunde der älteren Kirche*

1

INTRODUCTION

A. COLOSSIANS: ENCOURAGEMENT TO WALK IN ALL WISDOM
AS HOLY ONES IN CHRIST

A close examination of the particular words chosen for the title of this book, "Colossians: Encouragement To Walk in All Wisdom as Holy Ones in Christ," will serve to introduce it. The first word, "Colossians," indicates that this book is concerned in a comprehensive way with the whole of the New Testament document commonly known as Paul's letter to the Colossians. In it I will present an entirely new chiastic structure embracing all of the ten units that comprise this letter. In addition, I will show that within this overall macrochiastic structure each and every one of the letter's ten units likewise exhibits its own individual chiastic structure. These macrochiastic and microchiastic patterns serve as a key to understanding what and how Paul, the implied author of the letter to the Colossians, is communicating to his implied audience.[1]

"Encouragement," the next word in this book's title, indicates its concern to demonstrate that the main thrust of the letter to the Colossians is to encourage or exhort its implied audience. This is suggested, first of all, by the two key occurrences of the verb "encourage" (παρακαλέω) in the letter (2:2; 4:8). In 2:1–3 Paul points to the letter's purpose to encourage its various intended audiences when he states: "For I wish you (that is, those in Colossae; cf. 1:2) to know how great a struggle I am having on behalf of you and those in Laodicea and as many as have not seen my face in the flesh,[2] that their hearts may be encouraged (παρακληθῶσιν) as they

---

1. For similar presentations of the comprehensive chiastic structures in Philemon and Ephesians, see John Paul Heil, "The Chiastic Structure and Meaning of Paul's Letter to Philemon," *Bib* 82 (2001): 178–206; idem, *Ephesians: Empowerment to Walk in Love for the Unity of All in Christ* (Studies in Biblical Literature 13; Atlanta: Society of Biblical Literature, 2007).

2. This does not necessarily mean that Paul was unknown to all in his intended audiences. James D. G. Dunn, *The Epistles to the Colossians and to Philemon* (NIGTC; Grand Rapids: Eerdmans, 1996), 130: " '[A]s many as have not seen my face' (not every believer in the area—he may have passed through Colossae earlier and would probably have come to know some of the Colossian Christians during his time in Ephesus)." Bo Reicke, *Re-Examining Paul's Letters: The History of the Pauline Correspondence* (Harrisburg: Trinity, 2001), 75–76: "[I]ndications found in Acts show that Paul may have actually vis-

are held together in love, and for all richness of the full assurance of understanding, for the knowledge of the mystery of God, Christ, in whom all the treasures of wisdom and knowledge are hidden." The words "as they are held together in love" refer not only to the letter's audiences being united in love generally but also, and more specifically and especially, to their being gathered and held together for the occasion of the public reading of the letter to them so that their hearts may be encouraged as they listen to it.[3]

The verb "encourage" occurs for the second time toward the end of the letter in 4:7-8 when Paul tells his audience: "All things regarding me Tychicus, the beloved brother and faithful minister and fellow slave in the Lord, will make known to you, whom I am sending to you for this very purpose, so that you may know the things concerning us and that he may encourage (παρακαλέσῃ) your hearts." In all probability Paul has sent Tychicus to carry the letter to be read publicly before the Colossians either by Tychicus himself or someone delegated by him.[4] A primary way that Tychicus may encourage their hearts, then, is by his role in the public reading of the letter.[5] That the main thrust of the letter to the Colossians

---

ited Colossae and other cities in the Lycus valley during his third journey, around A.D. 55. Journeying through Galatia and Phrygia (Acts 18:23), he is portrayed as passing through 'the upper parts' of the country before arriving in Ephesus (19:1). From the Ephesian perspective, these upper parts were the valley of the river Maeander and its southern tributary, Lycus, where Colossae was situated. Luke's references to these regions were certainly meant to show that Paul visited congregations already existing there, like the church of Colossae. In his letters to Philemon and Colossians, Paul also mentions several acquaintances in Colossae by name, such as Philemon, Onesimus, Archippus, and Epaphras. . . . Paul clearly had had contact with several believers in Colossae before he dictated the letter in question. Paul also extended his admonitions to people in Colossae who had never seen his face (2:1). This utterance, however, refers to neophytes who had been converted and instructed by Epaphras (1:7) in the four years after Paul's visit to Colossae."

3. That the hearts of the letter's audiences may be encouraged "gibt die Intention des Verfassers an" according to Michael Dübbers, *Christologie und Existenz im Kolosserbrief: Exegetische und semantische Untersuchungen zur Intention des Kolosserbriefes* (WUNT 2/191; Tübingen: Mohr Siebeck, 2005), 169 n. 52. That their hearts "may be encouraged" is ultimately a divine passive, so that God is the agent of the encouragement through the instrumentality of the letter. That the letter to the Colossians is also to be read in the church or assembly of the Laodiceans is indicated in 4:16.

4. E. Randolph Richards, *Paul and First-Century Letter Writing: Secretaries, Composition and Collection* (Downers Grove, Ill.: InterVarsity, 2004), 188, 199-200: "Tychicus carried Paul's letters to the church at Colossae (Col 4:7), and likely to Philemon and the church at Ephesus (Eph 6:22)." Luke Timothy Johnson, *The Writings of the New Testament: An Interpretation: Revised Edition* (Minneapolis: Fortress, 1999), 387: "Tychichus, Onesimus' companion, carries three or four letters: the letter of recommendation for Onesimus [Philemon]; the letter to the Colossian church, which Paul expects will be read aloud at the assembly; another possible letter, perhaps for the local assembly at Laodicea; and the circular letter, Ephesians, which Tychichus will deliver to Hierapolis, Ephesus, and other cities in Asia Minor. At the same time, he brings to these churches personal information concerning Paul's condition in prison. The close proximity of Ephesus, Colossae, and Laodicea makes this thesis especially appealing."

5. Tychicus has the same role to play in Eph 6:21-22, with Eph 6:22 being identical to Col 4:8. Richards, *Paul*, 202: "He [Paul] fully expected his letters to be read publicly. It is even possible that he chose carriers who could read his letter effectively. An informed carrier provided additional informa-

is to encourage its audience is confirmed by the many and various ways Paul directly addresses his audience throughout the letter with words of exhortation or encouragement: 1:9–10, 23; 2:6–8, 16, 18; 3:1–2, 5, 8–9, 12–17, 18–23; 4:1–3, 5–6, 15–18.[6]

The words "To Walk" in the title indicate the conduct to which the letter to the Colossians encourages its implied audience. In both Greek (περιπατέω) and English the verb "to walk" can designate "sphere of activity," "comportment," "mode of living," "habit of conduct," or "behavior."[7] "To walk" was chosen for the title because the Greek verb περιπατέω occurs in each chapter of the letter (1:10; 2:6; 3:7; 4:5) at significant places within the overall chiastic structure, as I will demonstrate in more detail later.

"In All Wisdom," the next words of the title, specify the sphere or realm of conduct within which the audience are to walk. In four of the six occurrences of the word "wisdom" (σοφία) in the letter (1:9; 1:28; 2:3, 23; 3:16; 4:5) it is the object of the preposition "in" (ἐν), and in three of these four instances "wisdom" is modified by the adjective "all" (πᾶς). In the first occurrence of the phrase "in all wisdom" it is closely associated with the verb "to walk": In 1:9–10 Paul and Timothy pray that the audience may be filled with the knowledge of God's will "in all wisdom" (ἐν πάσῃ σοφίᾳ) and Spiritual understanding, "to walk" (περιπατῆσαι) worthy of the Lord. In 1:28 Paul and Timothy state that it is Christ whom they proclaim, admonishing every person and teaching every person "in all wisdom" (ἐν πάσῃ σοφίᾳ). Correspondingly, in 3:16 Paul exhorts the audience to teach and admonish one another "in all wisdom" (ἐν πάσῃ σοφίᾳ). Finally, in 4:5, in what will be seen later as a chiastic correspondence to 1:9–10, Paul exhorts the audience: "In wisdom" (ἐν σοφίᾳ) "walk" (περιπατεῖτε) before those outside, making the most of the opportunity.

"As Holy Ones," the next phrase in the title, characterizes both what the audience now are as believers and what they are still to be at the end of time, namely, separated from the rest of the world and consecrated to God, in continuity with God's "holy" chosen people of old.[8] The audience are addressed as the "holy ones"

---

tion and perhaps also could comment and expound upon the letter. It was advantageous to both Paul and his recipients to have an informed carrier read the letter so as to provide the proper inflections and nuances."

6. For a treatment of Colossians as parenetic theology, see Walter T. Wilson, "The 'Practical' Achievement of Colossians: A Theological Assessment," *HBT* 20 (1998): 49–74.

7. BDAG, 803; Roland Bergmeier, "περιπατέω," *EDNT* 3.75–76.

8. Peter Thomas O'Brien, *Colossians, Philemon* (WBC 44; Waco, Texas: Word, 1982), 3: "The antecedents of this expression are to be found in the OT. Israel was God's holy people (Exod 19:6) chosen by him and appointed to his service. Having been brought into a covenant relationship with him, Israel was to be a holy nation because he is holy (Lev 11:44; 19:2; etc.). Christians are 'saints' because of the new relationship they have been brought into by God through Jesus Christ. They are set apart for him and his service; as the people of his own possession they are the called and elect community of the end-time: they are 'God's chosen ones, holy (ἅγιοι) and beloved' (3:12) whose lives are to be

(ἁγίοις) and faithful brothers in Christ (1:2),[9] who have love for all of their fellow believers as "holy ones" (ἁγίους, 1:4). God has made the audience, as God's chosen ones, "holy" (ἅγιοι) and beloved (3:12), fit for the share of the inheritance of the "holy ones" (ἁγίων) in the light (1:12). Thus, as "holy ones," the audience, along with their fellow believers, share in the inheritance of the people of Israel as God's chosen holy ones of the past.[10] The mystery of Christ has now been manifested to the audience as among the "holy ones" (ἁγίοις, 1:26), and through the death of Christ God has now reconciled the audience to present them as "holy ones" (ἁγίους), without blemish, and blameless before him (1:22) when Christ is manifested again at the end (3:4).

"In Christ," the final phrase of the title, completes the characterization of the audience as holy ones who have been incorporated to live in union with Christ Jesus within a new sphere, realm, or domain of existence determined by what God has done in raising Christ Jesus from the dead and exalting him to the heavenly regions.[11] The audience are initially addressed as the holy ones and faithful brothers within the realm of being "in Christ" (1:2), who have faith within the realm of being "in Christ Jesus" (1:4). It is in union with Christ, that is, "in him," that all believers have redemption, the forgiveness of sins (1:14). Within the realm of Christ ("in him") all the treasures of wisdom and knowledge are hidden (2:3). In union with Christ the audience were "circumcised" with a "circumcision" not made by

---

characterized by godly behavior." See also Horst Balz, "ἅγιος," *EDNT* 1.18; Stanley E. Porter, "Holiness, Sanctification," *DPL*, 397-98.

9. For an unconvincing attempt to translate ἁγίοις in 1:2 as an adjective rather than a noun, see Thomas B. Slater, "Translating Ἅγιος in Col 1,2 and Eph 1,1," *Bib* 87 (2006): 52-54. As O'Brien (*Colossians*, 3) already pointed out, "Because the article is missing before 'faithful brothers' (πιστοῖς ἀδελφοῖς) it has been argued that ἁγίοις should be connected with πιστοῖς as an adjective and rendered 'holy and faithful brothers'. However, ἅγιοι always appears as a noun in the salutations of the letters and in our view this is how it is being employed here; it should therefore be translated 'saints' or 'holy ones.'" "Paul's use of the word in other letters suggests that for him ἅγιοι (in the plural) was almost a technical term," according to Robert McLachlan Wilson, *Colossians and Philemon* (ICC; London: Clark, 2005), 70.

10. Allan R. Bevere, *Sharing in the Inheritance: Identity and the Moral Life in Colossians* (JSNTSup 226; London: Sheffield Academic Press, 2003), 18: "Colossian Christians participate in Israel's distinctive heritage."

11. Winfried Elliger, "ἐν," *EDNT* 1.448: "Ἐν Χριστῷ thus refers not to mystical life in Christ; it serves rather, like the related formula ἐν πίστει, '*in* faith,' as a characterization of one's realm of existence, which is often met in contrast to the worldly realm (ἐν σαρκί, '*in* the flesh')" (Elliger's emphases). See also Friedrich Büchsel, " 'In Christus' bei Paulus," *ZNW* 42 (1949): 141-58; Fritz Neugebauer, "Das Paulinische 'In Christo'," *NTS* 4 (1957-58): 124-38; John A. Allan, "The 'In Christ' Formula in Ephesians," *NTS* 5 (1958-59): 54-62; Michel Bouttier, *En Christ: Étude d'exégèse et de théologie pauliniennes* (Paris: Presses Universitaires, 1962); Alexander J. M. Wedderburn, "Some Observations on Paul's Use of the Phrases 'in Christ' and 'with Christ'," *JSNT* 25 (1985): 83-97; Celia E. T. Kourie, "In Christ and Related Expressions in Paul," *Theologia Evangelica* 20 (1987): 33-43; James D. G. Dunn, *The Theology of Paul the Apostle* (Grand Rapids: Eerdmans, 1998), 396-401; Mehrdad Fatehi, *The Spirit's Relation to the Risen Lord in Paul: An Examination of Its Christological Implications* (WUNT 128; Tübingen: Mohr Siebeck, 2000), 269-74; Mark A. Seifrid, "In Christ," *DPL*, 433-36.

hand (2:11) and were buried and raised from the dead "with him" in baptism (2:12). Indeed, the audience have died "with Christ" (2:20) and were raised "with Christ" (3:1), so that their life is now hidden "with Christ" in God (3:3). Consequently, through the letter to the Colossians Paul and Timothy are admonishing and teaching (thus encouraging) the audience to walk in all wisdom, that they may present them as perfect holy ones within the realm of being "in Christ" (1:28).

B. Authorship

Although the letter to the Colossians presents itself as authored and sent by Paul and Timothy (1:1), with Paul eventually emerging as the primary authorial voice (1:23; 4:18), many scholars in modern times have questioned and/or denied that the historical apostle Paul could have authored Colossians because in their estimation it differs too greatly from the so-called main or undisputed letters of Paul.[12] But an appeal to pseudonymity involves problematical assumptions, so that it is debatable whether any of the NT letters which present Paul as their primary author is pseudonymous.[13] Recent studies in the role of co-authors, co-workers, and secretaries in the composition of the Pauline letters have indicated the complexity involved in the question of their authorship. Paul may have authored his letters in a broader sense of authorizing or directing their composition in collaboration

---

12. See, for example, Walter Bujard, *Stilanalytische Untersuchungen zum Kolosserbrief als Beitrag zur Methodik von Sprachvergleichen* (SUNT 11; Göttingen: Vandenhoeck & Ruprecht, 1973); Mark Kiley, *Colossians as Pseudepigraphy* (The Biblical Seminar 4; Sheffield: JSOT, 1986). Colossians is pseudonymous based on an analysis of its inscription in 1:1-2, according to Pierre Jordaan, "The *Inscriptio* Colossians 1:1-2," *Ekklesiastikos Pharos* 79 (1997): 62-69.

13. E. Earle Ellis, *The Making of the New Testament Documents* (Leiden: Brill, 2002), 324: "The hypothesis of innocent apostolic pseudepigrapha appears to be designed to defend the canonicity of certain New Testament wrtitings that are, at the same time, regarded as pseudepigrapha. It is a modern invention that has no evident basis in the attitude or writings of the apostolic and patristic church and is more an exercise in apologetics than in historical criticism." Terry L. Wilder, *Pseudonymity, the New Testament and Deception: An Inquiry Into Intention and Reception* (Lanham, Md.: University Press of America, 2004), 265 n. 52: "Though the case against the traditional authorship of some of the disputed Pauline letters is sometimes strong, several scholars today believe that no pseudonymous works exist in the NT. Scholars hold this view with good reason because (a) the greatest weakness of pseudepigraphic theories is the number of assumptions upon which they rest, and (b) they have been encouraged by recent studies which focus on Paul's use of a secretary, a co-author, and tradition when writing his letters. A resort to pseudonymity is not necessary." D. A. Carson and Douglas J. Moo, *An Introduction to the New Testament* (Grand Rapids: Zondervan, 2005), 350: "In short, the search for parallels to justify the view that the intended readers of some New Testament documents would have understood them to be pseudonymous, so that no deception took place, has proved a failure. The hard evidence demands that we conclude either that some New Testament documents are pseudonymous and that the real authors intended to deceive their readers, or that the real authors intended to speak the truth and that pseudonymity is not attested in the New Testament." Ben Witherington, *Letters and Homilies for Hellenized Christians Volume 1: A Socio-Rhetorical Commentary on Titus, 1-2 Timothy and 1-3 John* (Downers Grove, Ill.: InterVarsity, 2006), 38: "[A]lthough there may be pseudepigrapha within the New Testament, the burden of proof falls squarely on the shoulders of those who make that claim."

with fellow workers. Furthermore, the different audiences, situations, and times of composition, could also account for many of the differences among the Pauline letters.[14]

With this broader sense of authorship and complexity of composition in mind, then, I follow those scholars who argue that the historical apostle Paul of Tarsus, the Paul who is the primary author of the "undisputed" letters of Paul, is indeed also the primary author of the letter to the Colossians.[15] But even those

---

14. Luther M. Stirewalt, *Paul: The Letter Writer* (Grand Rapids: Eerdmans, 2003); E. Randolph Richards, *The Secretary in the Letters of Paul* (WUNT 42; Tübingen: Mohr Siebeck, 1991); idem, *Paul*. For suggestions regarding the possible roles of Timothy, Epaphras, or Tychicus in the writing of Colossians, see Michael J. Gorman, *Apostle of the Crucified Lord: A Theological Introduction to Paul and His Letters* (Grand Rapids: Eerdmans, 2004), 477-78. Johnson, *Writings*, 269, 273: "The composition of Paul's letters involved a complex process, which affects how we understand his authorship of the various epistles ascribed to him. Paul 'authors' all his letters, in the broad sense that they were composed under his authority and direction. But it is sometimes difficult to determine the exact nature of his role in the writing process. . . . The reader may be surprised at my bias for the authenticity of all the letters. It is based on the persuasiveness of their literary self-presentation, the ability to find plausible places for them in Paul's career, and a conviction that the whole Pauline corpus is one that Paul 'authored' but did not necessarily write." See also Reicke, *Paul's Letters*.

15. For the arguments of those who hold that Paul is the primary author of Colossians, see O'Brien, *Colossians*, xli-xlix; Reicke, *Paul's Letters*, 75-78; Frederick Fyvie Bruce, *The Epistles to the Colossians, to Philemon, and to the Ephesians* (NICNT; Grand Rapids: Eerdmans, 1984), 28-32; Nicholas Thomas Wright, *The Epistles of Paul to the Colossians and Philemon: An Introduction and Commentary* (TNTC; Grand Rapids: Eerdmans, 1986), 31-34; Murray J. Harris, *Colossians & Philemon* (Exegetical Guide to the Greek New Testament; Grand Rapids: Eerdmans, 1991), 3-4; Markus Barth and Helmut Blanke, *Colossians: A New Translation with Introduction and Commentary* (AB 34B; New York: Doubleday, 1994), 114-26; Gordon D. Fee, *God's Empowering Presence: The Holy Spirit in the Letters of Paul* (Peabody, Mass.: Hendrickson, 1994), 636-38; David E. Garland, *Colossians and Philemon: The NIV Application Commentary* (Grand Rapids: Zondervan, 1998), 17-22; Paul E. Deterding, *Colossians* (Concordia Commentary; St. Louis: Concordia, 2003), 3-7; Marianne Meye Thompson, *Colossians & Philemon* (The Two Horizons New Testament Commentary; Grand Rapids: Eerdmans, 2005), 2-5, esp. 4: "I will refer to the author of the letter as Paul because I believe that, in spite of the difficulties, the letter can still best be explained as written or authorized by Paul during his own lifetime." Ian K. Smith, *Heavenly Perspective: A Study of the Apostle Paul's Response to a Jewish Mystical Movement at Colossae* (LNTS 326; London: Clark, 2006), 6-16, esp. 16: "It is concluded that there is insufficient evidence to deny Pauline authorship of Colossians." See also Todd D. Still, "Colossians," in *The Expositor's Bible Commentary: Revised Edition* (vol. 12; ed. Tremper Longman and David E. Garland; Grand Rapids: Zondervan, 2006), 268-70. Gordon D. Fee, *Pauline Christology: An Exegetical-Theological Study* (Peabody, Mass.: Hendrickson, 2007), 289 n. 2: "It remains one of the singular mysteries in NT scholarship that so many scholars reject Pauline authorship of Colossians yet affirm the authenticity of Philemon." On the issue of authorship see also James D. G. Dunn, "Colossians, Letter To," in *The New Interpreter's Dictionary of the Bible A-C Volume 1* (Nashville: Abingdon, 2006) 705; Charles H. Talbert, *Ephesians and Colossians* (Paideia Commentaries on the New Testament; Grand Rapids: Baker, 2007), 7-11; Ben Witherington, *The Letters to Philemon, the Colossians, and the Ephesians: A Socio-Rhetorical Commentary on the Captivity Epistles* (Grand Rapids: Eerdmans, 2007), 100-103; Douglas J. Moo, *The Letters to Colossians and to Philemon* (Pillar New Testament Commentary; Grand Rapids: Eerdmans, 2008), 28-41; Stephen Finlan, *The Apostle Paul and the Pauline Tradition* (Collegeville, Minn.: Liturgical Press, 2008), 151-59.

who maintain that the historical Paul is not the author of Colossians must admit that the letter itself presents Paul as its primary textual or implied author. And it is with this implied author "Paul" that I will be concerned in this investigation of the rhetorical dynamics of the chiastic structures in the letter to the Colossians.

Paul is in prison (4:3, 10, 18; cf. 1:24) when he and Timothy send the letter, so that Colossians is one of the Pauline "captivity" letters, in addition to Philemon, Ephesians, Philippians, and 2 Timothy. Rome, Ephesus, or Caesarea have been suggested as possible locations for Paul's imprisonment while authorizing and directing the composition of Colossians. Although no absolute certainty is possible in this matter, it seems likely that Paul sent Tychicus with the letter to the Colossians from his Caesarean imprisonment with both the letter to Philemon and the letter to the Ephesians. All three of these letters appear to be very closely related.[16] At any rate, that the implied author "Paul" was in prison somewhere for its composition and sending is significant for the interpretation of Colossians.[17]

C. Audience

What does the letter to the Colossians tell us about the character and situation of its implied audience? Paul and Timothy address their audience as fellow believers set apart from the world and consecrated to God: They are "the holy ones and

---

16. Reicke, *Paul's Letters*, 75, 83: "The remarkable correspondence in personal names between Philemon and Colossians supports the conclusion that Colossians was also written during Paul's two-year imprisonment (A.D. 59–60) in Caesarea (Acts 24:27).... Chronologically, Ephesians may have been written somewhat later than Philemon and Colossians since Timothy is not mentioned. But A.D. 59 must still be the year of composition, because Tychicus was expected to take all three letters with him, delivering the letters to Philemon and to the Colossians in Colossae, before continuing on with Ephesians (cf. Col. 4:7—Tychicus with Philemon's servant Onesimus in 4:9, who was returned to Colossae—and Eph. 6:21, where Tychicus is still mentioned but not Onesimus)." See also Bo Reicke, "The Historical Setting of Colossians," *RevExp* 70 (1973): 429–38. On Caesarea as the origin of Colossians, see also John A. T. Robinson, *Redating the New Testament* (London: SCM, 1976), 65–67. With regard to the possibility that Paul sent Colossians while imprisoned in Caesarea, Thompson (*Colossians*, 6) states: "One might note here the interesting, but not complete, overlap between the names of co-workers in Colossians and those who accompanied Paul, particularly as he journeyed towards Jerusalem and subsequent detention in Caesarea (Aristarchus, Acts 19:29; 20:4; 27:2; Timothy and Tychicus, 20:4; see also Acts 12:12, 25; 15:37, 39 for references to Mark; 4:36; 9:27–15:39 *passim* for Barnabas)." See also E. Earle Ellis, *History and Interpretation in New Testament Perspective* (BIS 54; Atlanta: Society of Biblical Literature, 2001), 86; idem, *Making of the New Testament*, 266–75.

17. On the significance of Paul being in prison for the interpretation of Colossians but arguing for an imprisonment in Rome, see Richard J. Cassidy, *Paul in Chains: Roman Imprisonment and the Letters of St. Paul* (New York: Crossroad, 2001), 88–94. For a treatment of Colossians in the context of the Roman Empire, see Brian J. Walsh and Sylvia C. Keesmaat, *Colossians Remixed: Subverting the Empire* (Downers Grove, Ill.: InterVarsity, 2004); Harry O. Maier, "A Sly Civility: Colossians and Empire," *JSNT* 27 (2005): 323–49. And for a discussion of Paul's use of scripture in Colossians in relation to its Roman imperial context, see Sylvia C. Keesmaat, "In the Face of the Empire: Paul's Use of Scripture in the Shorter Epistles," in *Hearing the Old Testament in the New Testament* (ed. Stanley E. Porter; McMaster New Testament Studies; Grand Rapids: Eerdmans, 2006), 198–203.

faithful brothers in Christ in Colossae" (1:2).[18] They have faith in Christ Jesus as well as love for all of their fellow believers, their fellow "holy ones" (1:4; 2:5). They have already heard of the hope reserved for them in heaven through the gospel (1:5) they learned from Epaphras, "our beloved fellow slave, who is a faithful minister of Christ on behalf of you" (1:7).

The audience were probably mainly believers of Gentile origin whom God has made "fit for the share of the inheritance of the holy ones in the light" (1:12). They were once alienated from God and hostile of mind in evil deeds (1:21), "dead" in transgressions and in the "uncircumcision" of their flesh (2:13), indeed, they formerly lived (3:7) in immorality, impurity, passion, evil desire, the greed that is idolatry (3:5), anger, fury, malice, slander, obscene language, and lying (3:8–9), but have now been reconciled through the death of Christ in the body of his flesh (1:22). Yet this audience of former Gentiles seem to be familiar with some of the practices of Jews and probably also included former Jews, as indicated by the references to circumcision (2:11) and sabbaths (2:16).[19]

The implied Colossian audience include husbands and their wives, parents and their children, masters and their slaves (3:18–4:1), a certain "Nympha and the church in her house" (4:15), as well as Archippus, who is to fulfill the ministry he received in the Lord (4:17; cf. Phlm 1:2). Although the primary audience of the letter are the Colossian believers, it is meant to be read also to the believers in Laodicea (4:16; cf. 2:1; 4:13), and possibly by those in nearby Hierapolis as well (4:13), so that it can be considered a kind of circular letter addressed primarily to the Colossians, but relevant also to those in Laodicea and Hierapolis.

These implied audiences of believers are apparently in danger of being captivated "through a philosophy that is of empty deceit" (2:8). There has been much discussion about the precise nature of this "philosophy," with a great divergence of resulting theories and opinions.[20] I am persuaded by those who argue that this

---

18. Colossae, together with the nearby cities of Laodicea and Hierapolis (cf. 4:13), was located in the Lycus river valley in the region of Phrygia in Asia Minor. The archaeological site now located in modern Turkey remains unexcavated. For a recent discussion of Colossae, see Wilson, *Colossians*, 3–6.

19. Smith, *Heavenly Perspective*, 5: "It would appear that the Christian church in Colossae was made up of both Jews and Gentiles. The Jewish influence within the congregation can be seen by references to circumcision (2.11) and to Sabbath (2.16). There are also allusions to a Gentile background for other members of the congregation. In 1.12, 21; 2.13 there are indications of outsiders being brought into the company of the people of God." See also Christopher A. Beetham, *Echoes of Scripture in the Letter of Paul to the Colossians* (BIS 96; Leiden: Brill, 2008).

20. See, for some recent examples, H. Wayne House, "Doctrinal Issues in Colossians. Part 1 (of 4 Parts): Heresies in the Colossian Church," *BSac* 149 (1992): 45–59; Jerry L. Sumney, "Those Who 'Pass Judgment': The Identity of the Opponents in Colossians," *Bib* 74 (1993): 366–88; Alexander J. M. Wedderburn, "The Theology of Colossians," in *The Theology of the Later Pauline Letters* (ed. James D. G. Dunn; New Testament Theology; Cambridge: Cambridge University Press, 1993), 3–71; Harold W. Attridge, "Becoming an Angel: Rival Baptismal Theologies at Colossae," in *Religious Propaganda and Missionary Competition in the New Testament World: Essays Honoring Dieter Georgi* (ed. Lukas Bormann et al.; NovTSup 74; Leiden: Brill, 1994), 481–98; Richard E. DeMaris, *The Colossian Controversy: Wisdom in Dispute at Colossae* (JSNTSup 96; Sheffield: JSOT, 1994); Clinton E. Arnold, *The Colossian*

"philosophy" is not really a heresy,[21] but rather refers to the erroneous viewpoints and practices of some Jews in the local synagogues in the area of Colossae and/or of some Jewish Christians influenced by them.[22]

D. Literary-Rhetorical, Audience-Oriented Method

Colossians is a letter written to be read publicly, most likely in a liturgical assembly, as an oral performance substituting for the personal presence of the imprisoned Paul.[23] I will employ a literary-rhetorical method that treats Colossians as a let-

---

Syncretism: The Interface Between Christianity and Folk Belief at Colossae (WUNT 77; Tübingen: Mohr Siebeck, 1995); Michael D. Goulder, "Colossians and Barbelo," *NTS* 41 (1995): 601–19; L. Hartman, "Humble and Confident: On the So-Called Philosophers in Colossae," *ST* 49 (1995): 25–39; Troy W. Martin, *By Philosophy and Empty Deceit: Colossians as Response to a Cynic Critique* (JSNTSup 118; Sheffield: Sheffield Academic Press, 1996); H. Van Broekhoven, "The Social Profiles in the Colossian Debate," *JSNT* 66 (1997): 73–90; J. H. Roberts, "Jewish Mystical Experience in the Early Christian Era as Background to Understanding Colossians," *Neot* 32 (1998): 161–89; Gregory E. Sterling, "A Philosophy According to the Elements of the Cosmos: Colossian Christianity and Philo of Alexandria," in *Philon d'Alexandrie et le langage de la philosophie: Actes du colloque international organisé par le Centre d'études sur la philosophie hellénistique et romaine de l'Université de Paris XII-Val de Marne (Créteil, Fontenay, Paris, 26-28 octobre 1995)* (ed. Carlos Lévy; Turnhout, Belgium: Brepols, 1998), 349–73; Paolo Garuti, "L' eresia di Colossi, l'antanaclasi e la storia della redazione: Qualche considerazione a proposito di Col 2,6–23," *Ang* 79 (2002): 303–26; Robert M. Royalty, "Dwelling on Visions: On the Nature of the So-Called 'Colossians Heresy,'" *Bib* 83 (2002): 329–57; Wilson, *Colossians*, 35–58.

21. Morna D. Hooker, "Were There False Teachers in Colossae?" in *Christ and Spirit in the New Testament: Essays in Honour of Charles Francis Digby Moule* (ed. Barnabas Lindars and Stephen S. Smalley; Cambridge: Cambridge University Press, 1973), 315–31.

22. Fred O. Francis, "Humility and Angelic Worship in Col 2:18," in *Conflict at Colossae: A Problem in the Interpretation of Early Christianity Illustrated by Selected Modern Studies: Revised Edition* (ed. Fred O. Francis and Wayne A. Meeks; Sources for Biblical Study 4; Missoula, Mont.: Scholars Press, 1975), 163–95; idem, "The Christological Argument of Colossians," in *God's Christ and His People: Studies in Honour of Nils Alstrup Dahl* (ed. Jacob Jervell and Wayne A. Meeks; Oslo: Universitetsforlaget, 1977), 192–208; Stanislas Lyonnet, "Paul's Adversaries in Colossae," in *Conflict at Colossae: A Problem in the Interpretation of Early Christianity Illustrated by Selected Modern Studies: Revised Edition* (ed. Fred O. Francis and Wayne A. Meeks; Sources for Biblical Study 4; Missoula, Mont.: Society of Biblical Literature, 1975), 147–61; Craig A. Evans, "The Colossian Mystics," *Bib* 63 (1982): 188–205; Wright, *Colossians*, 23–30; Thomas J. Sappington, *Revelation and Redemption at Colossae* (JSNTSup 53; Sheffield: JSOT, 1991), 17–22; Daniel J. Harrington, "Christians and Jews in Colossians," in *Diaspora Jews and Judaism: Essays in Honor of, and in Dialogue with, A. Thomas Kraabel* (ed. J. Andrew Overmann and Robert S. MacLennan; South Florida Studies in the History of Judaism 41; Atlanta: Scholars Press, 1992), 153–61; James D. G. Dunn, "The Colossian Philosophy: A Confident Jewish Apologia," *Bib* 76 (1995): 153–81; idem, *Colossians*, 29–35; Garland, *Colossians*, 23–32; Bevere, *Sharing*; Thompson, *Colossians*, 6–9. See also the recent treatments by Christian Stettler, "The Opponents at Colossae," in *Paul and His Opponents* (ed. Stanley E. Porter; Pauline Studies 2; Leiden: Brill, 2005), 169–200; Smith, *Heavenly Perspective*. Jerry L. Sumney, *Colossians: A Commentary* (NTL; Louisville: Westminster John Knox, 2008), 10–12.

23. For treatments of the oral performance of NT documents, see: Whitney Taylor Shiner, *Proclaiming the Gospel: First Century Performance of Mark* (Harrisburg: Trinity, 2003); Holly E. Hearon, "The Implications of Orality for Studies of the Biblical Text," in *Performing the Gospel: Orality, Mem-*

ter with a rhetorical strategy of persuading its implied audience to the viewpoint of Paul, the primary implied author. I use the term "rhetorical" in its broadest and most general sense. Rather than applying the categories of either ancient Greco-Roman rhetoric or the modern "new rhetoric" to Colossians, the rhetorical method I will follow is entirely and rigorously text-centered. I will determine Paul's rhetorical or persuasive strategy by carefully and closely listening to the chiastic structures of the text of the letter to the Colossians.[24]

My method is "audience-oriented" in that it is concerned to determine how the implied audience are meant to respond to Paul's rhetorical strategy as it unfolds in the progression of the chiastically arranged textual units of the letter to the Colossians. Paul as the primary implied author presupposes a certain competency on the part of his implied audience. Within the rhetorical strategy of the letter Paul utilizes a number of various traditions—Jewish, Christian, and Gentile, assuming his audience are familiar with them.[25] This would accord with an implied audience consisting mainly of converts of Gentile origin who are now in danger of being influenced by Jews in the area. Our focus, then, is upon how this implied audience are being encouraged to conduct their lives in all the wisdom they have as holy ones in union with Christ.[26]

---

ory, and Mark: Essays Dedicated to Werner Kelber (ed. Richard A. Horsley et al.; Minneapolis: Fortress, 2006), 3–20; Bridget Gilfillan Upton, *Hearing Mark's Endings: Listening to Ancient Popular Texts Through Speech Act Theory* (BIS 79; Leiden: Brill, 2006); William David Shiell, *Reading Acts: The Lector and the Early Christian Audience* (BIS 70; Boston: Brill, 2004), 209: "Paul's letters also give examples of the kinds of documents that need to be discussed in light of delivery. How were they performed, and what vocal inflection would have been used?" On the public performance of Paul's letters, see Pieter J. J. Botha, "The Verbal Art of the Pauline Letters: Rhetoric, Performance and Presence," in *Rhetoric and the New Testament: Essays from the 1992 Heidelberg Conference* (ed. Stanley E. Porter and Thomas H. Olbricht; JSNTSup 90; Sheffield: JSOT, 1993), 409–28; Stirewalt, *Paul*, 13–18; Richards, *Paul*, 202. On oral patterns in Paul's letters, but which unfortunately does not include a discussion of Colossians, see John D. Harvey, *Listening to the Text: Oral Patterning in Paul's Letters* (Grand Rapids: Baker, 1998). On the liturgical context and worship dimensions of Colossians, see Gerald L. Borchert, *Worship in the New Testament: Divine Mystery and Human Response* (St. Louis: Chalice, 2008), 146–51.

24. For a text-centered approach to the rhetoric of another Pauline letter, see D. Francois Tolmie, *Persuading the Galatians: A Text-Centered Rhetorical Analysis of a Pauline Letter* (WUNT 190; Tübingen: Mohr Siebeck, 2005).

25. George E. Cannon, *The Use of Traditional Materials in Colossians* (Macon, Ga.: Mercer University Press, 1983). See also Johannes Lähnemann, *Der Kolosserbrief: Komposition, Situation und Argumentation* (SNT 3; Gütersloh: Gerd Mohn, 1971).

26. For more on the audience-oriented method to be used in this investigation, see Warren Carter and John Paul Heil, *Matthew's Parables: Audience-Oriented Perspectives* (CBQMS 30; Washington: Catholic Biblical Association, 1998), 8–17; John Paul Heil, *The Meal Scenes in Luke-Acts: An Audience-Oriented Approach* (SBLMS 52; Atlanta: Society of Biblical Literature, 1999), 2–4; idem, *The Transfiguration of Jesus: Narrative Meaning and Function of Mark 9:2–8, Matt 17:1–8 and Luke 9:28–36* (AnBib 144; Rome: Biblical Institute, 2000), 22–24; idem, *The Rhetorical Role of Scripture in 1 Corinthians* (Studies in Biblical Literature 15; Atlanta: Society of Biblical Literature, 2005), 5–10; idem, *Ephesians*, 9–10.

E. Summary

1. In this book I will propose and demonstrate new chiastic structures for the entire letter to the Colossians as a key to understanding it as a means of encouraging its implied audience(s) to walk in all wisdom as holy ones in Christ.

2. Although it is debated whether the historical apostle Paul composed Colossians, this investigation follows those who argue that he did, at least in the broad sense of authorizing and directing the writing of it. At any rate, according to the text of Colossians, Paul, imprisoned somewhere, is the primary implied author (together with Timothy) who sent Tychicus to carry the letter to its destination in Colossae.

3. Although the letter is sent primarily to believers in Colossae, it is also to be read to the believers in Laodicea, and possibly in Hierapolis as well, to encourage them not to be unduly influenced by local Jewish synagogues in the area.

4. In this investigation I will employ a text-centered, literary-rhetorical and audience-oriented method concerned with demonstrating how the implied audience are persuaded and encouraged by the dynamic progression of the letter's chiastic structures to conduct themselves according to all the wisdom now at their disposal as holy ones in union with Christ.

2

The Chiastic Structures of Colossians

A. The Ten Microchiastic Units of the Letter

To be absolutely convincing the determination of an extended chiastic structure should be based upon a methodology with very rigorous criteria. It must be clear that the chiasm has not been subjectively imposed upon the text but actually subsists and operates objectively within the text. Our investigation will be guided by the following list of nine criteria for detecting an extended chiasm:

1. There must be a problem in perceiving the structure of the text in question, which more conventional outlines fail to resolve.
2. There must be clear examples of parallelism between the two "halves" of the hypothesized chiasm, to which commentators call attention even when they propose quite different outlines for the text overall.
3. Verbal (or grammatical) parallelism as well as conceptual (or structural) parallelism should characterize most if not all of the corresponding pairs of subdivisions.
4. The verbal parallelism should involve central or dominant imagery or terminology important to the rhetorical strategy of the text.
5. Both verbal and conceptual parallelism should involve words and ideas not regularly found elsewhere within the proposed chiasm.
6. Multiple sets of correspondences between passages opposite each other in the chiasm as well as multiple members of the chiasm itself are desirable.
7. The outline should divide the text at natural breaks which would be agreed upon even by those proposing very different structures to account for the whole.
8. The central or pivotal as well as the final or climactic elements normally play key roles in the rhetorical strategy of the chiasm.
9. Ruptures in the outline should be avoided if at all possible.[1]

---

1. For a slightly different and more detailed version of this list as well as an example of an extended biblical chiasm, see Craig L. Blomberg, "The Structure of 2 Corinthians 1–7," *CTR* 4 (1989):

One of the most distinctive features of this investigation is that all of the proposed chiasms are based on precise verbal parallels found objectively in the text, rather than on thematic or conceptual parallels, which can often be subjective. Indeed, the main criterion for the establishment of chiasms in this investigation is the demonstration of these verbal parallels. I will seek to determine how the subsequent occurrence(s) of a paralleled word or phrase develops the first occurrence after a central unparalleled element or central parallel elements serve as a pivot from the first to the second half of the chiasm.

Since they are based strictly on verbal parallels, some of the proposed chiasms may or may not exhibit a balance in the length of the various parallel elements or units—one parallel element or unit may be much longer or much shorter than its corresponding parallel. This may seem odd to a modern audience, but an ancient audience would presumably be attuned to the key verbal parallels that are heard rather than the balance of length between the elements or units of a given chiasm. The main presupposition of this investigation is that if there are demonstrable verbal parallels with a pivotal section between them, then a chiasm is operative regardless of a certain lack of balance between various elements or units.

Furthermore, some of the verbal parallels involve what might be considered by a modern audience as rather ordinary or trivial words, unlikely to be key words in chiastic parallels. But it should be kept in mind that what may seem to be insignificant words or phrases on the surface to a modern audience may have been very significant indeed to the particular situation of the original audience as they listened to the entire oral performance of the letter to the Colossians. In some cases the parallels are between cognates or between synonyms, antonyms, and/or alliterative terms. And in some cases an identical grammatical form of a word determines the chiastic parallel.

Not all of the proposed chiasms have the same number of elements or units. Some chiasms may exhibit a single unparalleled central element, e.g. A-B-C-B'-A', while others may exhibit dual, parallel central or pivotal elements, e.g. A-B-C-C'-B'-A'. Nevertheless, both of these types operate as chiasms in the ears of the implied audience, since they both involve a pivot from the first to the second half of the chiasm. In one type a central unparalleled element serves as the pivot,

---

4–8. And for more discussion of criteria and more biblical examples of extended chiasms, see Wayne Brouwer, *The Literary Development of John 13–17: A Chiastic Reading* (SBLDS 182; Atlanta: Society of Biblical Literature, 2000). See also Joachim Jeremias, "Chiasmus in den Paulusbriefen," *ZNW* 49 (1958): 145–56; John W. Welch, "Chiasmus in the New Testament," in *Chiasmus in Antiquity: Structures, Analyses, Exegesis* (ed. John W. Welch; Hildesheim: Gerstenberg, 1981), 211–49; idem, "Criteria for Identifying and Evaluating the Presence of Chiasmus," in *Chiasmus Bibliography* (ed. John W. Welch and Daniel B. McKinlay; Provo, Utah: Research, 1999), 157–74; Ian H. Thomson, *Chiasmus in the Pauline Letters* (JSNTSup 111; Sheffield: Sheffield Academic Press, 1995), 13–45; Mark Wilson, *The Victor Sayings in the Book of Revelation* (Eugene, Oreg.: Wipf and Stock, 2007), 3–8; David A. DeSilva, "X Marks the Spot? A Critique of the Use of Chiasmus in Macro-Structural Analyses of Revelation," *JSNT* 30 (2008): 343–71.

whereas in the other type two parallel elements together serve as the pivot to the second half of parallel elements. In addition, it may often be more accurate to speak of the central element or elements as the pivotal point of the chiasm and the final A´ element as the climax. This is important to keep in mind, lest one think that chiastic patterns are a type of circular or merely repetitive argument, rather than exhibiting an ongoing, dynamic progression.

Chiastic patterns serve to organize the content to be heard and not only aid the memory of the one delivering or performing a document, but also make it easier for the implied audience to follow and remember the content. A chiasm works by leading its audience through introductory elements to a central, pivotal point or points, and then reaching its conclusion by recalling and developing, via the chiastic parallels, aspects of the initial elements that led to the central, pivotal point or points. Since chiasms were apparently very common in ancient oral-auricular and rhetorical cultures,[2] the original ancient audience may and need not necessarily have been consciously identifying or reflecting upon any of these chiastic structures in themselves as they heard them. They unconsciously experienced the chiastic phenomenon as an organizing dynamic, which had a subtle but purposeful effect on how they perceived the content.[3]

But I would suggest that a discovery, delineation, and bringing to consciousness of the chiastic structures of ancient documents can greatly aid the modern audience to a more proper and precise interpretation of them. The illustration of the various chiastic structures provide us with a visual guide to what the audience hear. They enable us to experience the rhythm and flow of the rhetorical argument. More specifically, they indicate the key pivotal and climactic words within units as an aid to more precise exegesis.[4]

In what follows, then, I will first demonstrate how the text of Paul's letter to the Colossians naturally divides itself into ten distinct literary units based upon their microchiastic structures as determined by very precise verbal parallels found objectively in the text. Where applicable I will point out how other linguistic and grammatical features often confirm the integrity of these units. Secondly, I will demonstrate how these ten units form a macrochiastic pattern based upon very precise verbal parallels found objectively in the text between the chiastically paired units.[5] Thirdly, I will point out the various transitional words that connect a unit

---

2. For some of the evidence of this see Brouwer, *Literary Development*, 23–27.

3. On chiasms as an aid to both listener and performer, see Joanna Dewey, "Mark as Aural Narrative: Structures as Clues to Understanding," *Sewanee Theological Review* 36 (1992): 50–52.

4. John Breck, *The Shape of Biblical Language: Chiasmus in the Scriptures and Beyond* (Crestwood, NY: St. Vladimir's Seminary Press, 1994).

5. On the interpretive significance of chiastic structures, see Ronald E. Man, "The Value of Chiasm for New Testament Interpretation," *BSac* 141 (1984): 146–57; Augustine Stock, "Chiastic Awareness and Education in Antiquity," *BTB* 14 (1984): 23–27; John Breck, "Biblical Chiasmus: Exploring Structure for Meaning," *BTB* 17 (1987): 70–74. For a discussion of chiasm in relation to chain-link interlock, see Bruce W. Longenecker, *Rhetoric at the Boundaries: The Art and Theology of the New Testament Chain-Link Transitions* (Waco, Texas: Bayler University Press, 2005), 16–17, 22–23. For examples

to the unit that immediately precedes it. These various transitional words, which occur at the conclusion of one unit and at the beginning of the following unit, indicate that the chiastic units are heard as a cohesive sequence. These various transitional words are capitalized in the translations of the units below.

1. Grace from Paul an Apostle by the Will of God (1:1–2)
To Holy Ones and Faithful Brothers in Christ[6]

    A: [1:1a] Paul, apostle of Christ Jesus through the will of God (θεοῦ),
        B: [1b] and Timothy the brother (ἀδελφός)
            C: [2a] to those in Colossae,
        B′: [2b] holy ones and faithful brothers (ἀδελφοῖς) in Christ,
    A′: [2c] grace to you and peace from GOD (θεοῦ) our FATHER.[7]

Directed to "those in Colossae," as "holy ones and faithful brothers in Christ," the opening address and greeting of "grace to you and peace *from* God our Father" in Col 1:1–2 is grammatically set off from the thanksgiving that begins in 1:3, which is directed *to* the God and Father of our Lord Jesus Christ.[8] The integrity of this first unit is further secured by its A-B-C-B′-A′ chiastic structure. The only occurrences in this unit of the genitive singular of "God"—"through the will of God (θεοῦ)" in 1:1a and "peace from God (θεοῦ) our Father" in 1:2c—establish the parallelism of the A and A′ elements of the chiasm. The only occurrences in this unit of the word for "brother"—"Timothy the brother (ἀδελφός)" in 1:1b and "faithful brothers (ἀδελφοῖς)" in 1:2b—establish the parallelism of the B and B′ elements and further distinguish this first unit from the second unit (1:3–14), which does not contain the word "brother."[9] The central, unparalleled C element (1:2a) of the chiasm, "to those in Colossae," is the only reference to Colossae not only in this first unit (1:1–2) but in the entire letter.

---

of chiastic structures of other Pauline letters, see A. Boyd Luter and Michelle V. Lee, "Philippians as Chiasmus: Key to the Structure, Unity and Theme Questions," *NTS* 41 (1995): 89–101; Stanley E. Porter and Jeffrey T. Reed, "Philippians as a Macro-Chiasm and Its Exegetical Significance," *NTS* 44 (1998): 213–31; Murray J. Harris, *The Second Epistle to the Corinthians: A Commentary on the Greek Text* (NIGTC; Grand Rapids: Eerdmans, 2005), 110–14; Heil, "Philemon"; idem, *Ephesians*. For a structural-thematic outline of Colossians based on discouse analysis, see Ernst R. Wendland, "Cohesion in Colossians: A Structural-Thematic Outline," *Notes on Translation* 6 (1992): 28–62. For a recent proposal of a comprehensive chiastic structure for the letter to the Hebrews, see Gabriella Gelardini, "*Verhärtet eure Herzen nicht*": *Der Hebräer, eine Synagogenhomilie zu Tischa be-Aw* (BIS 83; Leiden: Brill, 2007).

6. The main heading of each unit is intended to summarize the unit as it relates to its parallel unit within the overall macrochiastic structure of the letter, while the sub-heading of each unit is intended to summarize or characterize the microchiastic dimension of each unit.

7. The translation of this and all subsequent units of the letter is my own, striving to be as literal as possible to the Greek text for the purpose of clarifying the exegesis.

8. Although Epaphras and Tychicus are each described as a "faithful" (πιστός) minister (1:7; 4:7) and Onesimus as a "faithful" (πιστῷ) and beloved brother (4:9), this is the only time in the letter that the audience as a whole are referred to as "faithful" (πιστοῖς, 1:2) brothers.

9. The word for "brother" (ἀδελφός) does not occur again in the letter until 4:7, 9, 15.

2. Thanking God When Praying for You to Walk in Wisdom (1:3–14)
Bearing Fruit and Growing in the Knowledge of God

A: ³ We thank (εὐχαριστοῦμεν) GOD the FATHER (πατρί) of our Lord Jesus Christ always when praying for you, ⁴ having heard of your faith in Christ Jesus and the love (ἀγάπην) which you have (ἔχετε) for all the holy ones (ἁγίους)

B: ⁵ because of the hope laid up for you in the heavens, which you have heard before in the word of the truth of the gospel ⁶ that has come to you, as indeed in all (παντί) the world it is bearing fruit and growing (καρποφορούμενον καὶ αὐξανόμενον), so also among you, from the day you heard (ἀφ' ἧς ἡμέρας ἠκούσατε) and came to know (ἐπέγνωτε) the grace of God (θεοῦ) in truth,

C: ⁷ as you learned it from Epaphras our beloved fellow slave, who is a faithful minister of Christ on behalf of you,[10] ⁸ who also has informed us of your love in the Spirit.

B': ⁹ Therefore we also, from the day we heard (ἀφ' ἧς ἡμέρας ἠκούσαμεν), do not cease praying on behalf of you and asking that you may be filled with the knowledge (ἐπίγνωσιν) of his will in all wisdom and Spiritual understanding,[11] ¹⁰ to walk worthy of the Lord for every desire to please, in every (παντί) good work bearing fruit and growing (καρποφοροῦντες καὶ αὐξανόμενοι) with regard to the knowledge (ἐπιγνώσει) of God (θεοῦ), ¹¹ in all power empowered according to the might of his glory for all endurance and patience.

---

10. For the choice of the reading "you" (ὑμῶν) here rather than "us" (ἡμῶν), see Bruce Manning Metzger, *A Textual Commentary on the Greek New Testament: Second Edition* (Stuttgart: Deutsche Bibelgesellschaft, 1994), 552–53. Although many scholars and translations opt for the "us" reading, which also has good manuscript support, there are internal reasons for choosing the "you" reading. There are five other occurrences in Colossians of the preposition ὑπέρ with ὑμῶν (1:9, 24; 2:1; 4:12, 13) but none with ἡμῶν. Furthermore, the choice of the "us" reading would involve a connotation of "in place of us" for the preposition ὑπέρ, a connotation which does not occur elsewhere in Colossians. Rather, in Colossians ὑπέρ always has the connotation of "for the sake or benefit of." See also Wolf-Henning Ollrog, *Paulus und seine Mitarbeiter: Untersuchungen zu Theorie und Praxis der paulinischen Mission* (WMANT 50; Neukirchen-Vluyn: Neukirchener Verlag, 1979), 101.

11. According to Dunn (*Colossians*, 54), 1:3-9 "falls naturally into a chiastic pattern" (Garland [*Colossians*, 45] presents a similar chiasm for 1:4-8). But the linguistic basis for such a chiasm is not explained; it appears as if "bearing and growing fruit" in 1:6 is at the center of this alleged chiasm, thus neglecting its obvious parallelism with the same participial pair in 1:10, as indicated by the chiasm for 1:3-14 that we are proposing. With regard to the meaning of πνευματική in 1:9, "Unless there is strong contextual evidence to the contrary, this word should ordinarily be understood as the adjective for 'the Spirit' . . . it has a kind of 'possessive' sense to it: something is πνευματικός in the sense that it properly and essentially belongs to the sphere of the Spirit," according to Fee, *God's Empowering Presence*, 641. Dunn, *Colossians*, 70: "The spiritual source and character of this knowledge is reinforced by the qualifying phrase, 'in all wisdom and spiritual understanding,' which could equally well be rendered 'in all spiritual wisdom and understanding,' or 'with all the wisdom and understanding that his Spirit gives.'"

A´: With joy[12] [12] thanking (εὐχαριστοῦντες) the Father (πατρὶ) who has made you fit for the share of the inheritance of the holy ones (ἁγίων) in the light.[13] [13] HE has rescued us from the authority of the darkness and has transferred us into the kingdom of the Son of his love (ἀγάπης), [14] in whom we have (ἔχομεν) redemption, the forgiveness of sins.

The words "God (θεῷ) the Father (πατρί)" in the expression "We thank God the Father" that introduces this unit in 1:3 recall "from God" (θεοῦ) our Father (πατρός)" in the greeting "grace to you and peace from God our Father" in 1:2 that concludes the preceding unit. These occurrences of "God" and "Father" thus serve as the transitional words linking the first unit (1:1–2) to the second unit (1:3–14).

An A-B-C-B´-A´ chiastic pattern secures this second unit's (1:3–14) integrity and distinctness. The only occurrences in this unit of the verb for "thanking" with God the "Father" as object—"we thank (εὐχαριστοῦμεν) God the Father (πατρί)" in 1:3 and "(you) thanking (εὐχαριστοῦντες) the Father (πατρὶ)" in 1:12,[14] the occurrences of the word "love"—"the love (ἀγάπην) which you have" in 1:4 and "of the Son of his love (ἀγάπης)" in 1:13,[15] the only occurrences in this unit of the verb "have"—"the love which you have (ἔχετε)" in 1:4 and "in whom we have (ἔχομεν) redemption" in 1:14, as well as the only occurrences in this unit of the word "holy ones"—"for all the holy ones (ἁγίους)" in 1:4 and "the inheritance of the holy ones (ἁγίων)" in 1:12, provide the parallelisms between the A (1:3–4) and A´ (1:12–14) elements of this unit's chiasm.

A literary inclusion between verbs for "hearing" in the second person plural aorist—"of which you have heard before (προηκούσατε)" in 1:5 and "from the day you heard (ἠκούσατε)" in 1:6—secures the integrity of the B (1:5–6) element of this second unit's chiasm, distinguishing it from both the A (1:3–4) and C (1:7–8) elements.[16]

The five occurrences of the adjective "all" or "every"—"in all (πάσῃ) wisdom"

---

12. On taking the phrase "with joy" (μετὰ χαρᾶς) with the following participle in 1:12 rather than with what precedes in 1:11, see O'Brien, *Colossians*, 25; Dunn, *Colossians*, 67 n. 3; Deterding, *Colossians*, 36; Wilson, *Colossians*, 110; Ingrid Maisch, *Der Brief an die Gemeinde in Kolossä* (Theologischer Kommentar Zum Neuen Testament 12; Stuttgart: Kohlhammer, 2003), 64. For the alternative argument for taking "with joy" with what precedes in 1:11, see J. H. Roberts, "Die sintaktiese binding van μετὰ χαρᾶς in Kolossense 1:11: 'n Strukturele motivering," *HvTSt* 57 (2001): 187–209.

13. For the variant readings in 1:12, see Metzger, *Textual Commentary*, 553.

14. This same verbal clause occurs again in 3:17: "giving thanks (εὐχαριστοῦντες) to God the Father (πατρὶ) through him." The noun for "thanksgiving" occurs in 4:2: "In prayer persevere, being watchful in it with thanksgiving (εὐχαριστίᾳ)."

15. The word "love," however, also occurs in the central C element of this chiastic unit in 1:8: "your love (ἀγάπην) in the Spirit."

16. An aorist verb for "hearing" occurs also in the A element, but as an active plural masculine nominative participle—"having heard (ἀκούσαντες) of your faith" (1:4)—rather than as a second person plural indicative as in the B element. This verbal form for "hearing" occurs elsewhere in Colossians only in 1:23.

in 1:9, "for every (πᾶσαν) desire" in 1:10, "in every (παντί) good work" in 1:10, "with all (πάσῃ) power" in 1:11, and "for all (πᾶσαν) endurance" in 1:11—secure the integrity of the B′ (1:9-11) element of this second unit's chiasm, distinguishing it from both the C (1:7-8) and A′ (1:12-14) elements, which contain no occurrences of the adjective "all" or "every."

The only occurrences in this unit as well as in the entire letter of the participial pair "bearing fruit and growing" preceded by the use of the adjective "all" or "every"—"in all (παντί) the world it is bearing fruit and growing (καρποφορούμενον καὶ αὐξανόμενον)" in 1:6 and "in every (παντί) good work bearing fruit and growing (καρποφοροῦντες καὶ αὐξανόμενοι)" in 1:10, the only occurrences in this unit and in the letter of the phrase "from the day" followed by the verb for "hearing"— "from the day you heard (ἀφ' ἧς ἡμέρας ἠκούσατε)" in 1:6 and "from the day we heard (ἀφ' ἧς ἡμέρας ἠκούσαμεν)" in 1:9, and the only occurrences in this unit of the words for "knowledge" with "God" or an attribute of God as object—"came to know (ἐπέγνωτε) the grace of God (θεοῦ)" in 1:6 and "with the knowledge (ἐπίγνωσιν) of his (God's) will" in 1:9 as well as "in the knowledge (ἐπιγνώσει) of God (θεοῦ)" in 1:10, establish the parallelisms between the B (1:5-6) and B′ (1:9-11) elements of this second unit's (1:3-14) chiasm.

The central and unparalleled C (1:7-8) element contains the only focus on Epaphras in this unit's chiasm.[17] In addition, the C element contains the letter's only occurrence of the verb for "learning"—"as you learned (ἐμάθετε) it from Epaphras" in 1:7—and of the verb for "informing"—"who also has informed (δηλώσας) us of your love in the Spirit" in 1:8.

3. The Gospel Preached to Every Creature under Heaven (1:15-23)
God Has Reconciled You in the Body of the Flesh of Christ

A: [15] HE is the image of the invisible God, the firstborn of all creation (πάσης κτίσεως), [16] for in him were created all things in the heavens (οὐρανοῖς) and on the earth, the visible and the invisible, whether thrones or dominions or principalities or authorities; all things through him and to him have been created. [17] And he alone is before all things and all things in him hold together.[18]

B: [18] And he alone is the head of the body (σώματος), the church. He is the beginning, the firstborn from the dead, that he alone might become in all things preeminent, [19] for in him all the fullness chose to dwell, [20a] and through him to reconcile (ἀποκαταλλάξαι) all things to him,[19]

---

17. The only other explicit reference to Epaphras is at the end of the letter in 4:12.
18. On the translation of αὐτός here and 1:18 as the emphatic "he alone," Harris (*Colossians*, 46) states that "here and in v. 18a the wider context indicates that the word is clearly emphatic: 'he himself,' 'he and no other.'" Wilson, *Colossians*, 143: "αὐτός is clearly emphatic, as in v. 18 below."
19. According to Wilson (*Colossians*, 154), "the sense seems to require the reading εἰς αὐτόν, with a rough breathing. The older mss were written without accents or breathings, and an editor is therefore free to choose;" see also Metzger, *Textual Commentary*, 554. But, as Dunn (*Colossians*, 83 n. 3) points out, such a reflexive reading, that is, "to himself (God)" rather than "to him (Christ)," "would break

C: ²⁰ᵇ making peace through the blood of his cross, through him,²⁰ whether the things on the earth or the things in the heavens.²¹

B′: ²¹ And you, once being alienated and enemies in mind in works that are evil, ²² he has now reconciled (ἀποκατήλλαξεν) in the body (σώματι) of his flesh through death to present you holy and unblemished and blameless before him,²²

A′: ²³ if indeed you persevere in the faith, having been established and steadfast and not shifting from the hope of the gospel which you heard, which was proclaimed in all creation (πάσῃ κτίσει) that is under heaven (οὐρανόν), of which I BECAME, I, PAUL, A MINISTER.

The Greek relative pronoun ὅς, translated as "he" in the assertion that introduces this unit in 1:15, "he is the image of the invisible God," recalls the same relative pronoun, again translated as "he" in the assertion that "he has rescued us" toward the the conclusion of the preceding unit in 1:13. These occurrences of "he" in reference to Christ thus serve as the transitional words linking the second unit (1:3–14) to the third unit (1:15–23).

An A-B-C-B′-A′ chiastic pattern secures this third unit's (1:15–23) integrity and distinctness. The three occurrences of "all things" in the nominative case as the subject of verbs—"in him were created all things (τὰ πάντα)" in 1:16a, "all things (τὰ πάντα) through him and for him have been created" in 1:16b, and "all things (τὰ πάντα) in him hold together" in 1:17—establish the unity of the A element (1:15–17).²³ The only occurrences in this unit of verbs in the second person plural—"if indeed you remain (ἐπιμένετε) in the faith" in 1:23a and "the gospel

---

the triple parallel of 'in him,' 'through him,' 'to him' (1:16/1:19–20)." See also L. Hartman, "Universal Reconciliation (Col 1,20)," *Studien Zum Neuen Testament und Seiner Umwelt* 10 (1985): 109–21; Jean-Noël Aletti, *Saint Paul Épitre aux Colossiens: Introduction, traduction et commentaire* (EBib 20; Paris: Gabalda, 1993), 111.

20. Dunn, *Colossians*, 83 n. 4: "The manuscript attestation is equally weighty for omission as for inclusion of 'through him' (δι αὐτοῦ). It could have been included by scribal reflex in view of the repeated use of the phrase in 1:16 and 20 or omitted by accident (the scribe's eye jumping directly from the immediately preceding αὐτοῦ) or design (because it is so awkward for the sense). The presence of the phrase must count as the more difficult reading and so it should probably be included." See also Metzger, *Textual Commentary*, 554; Wilson, *Colossians*, 154–55.

21. For an attempt to read 1:13–20 as a nine-part chiastic structure, see J. Behr, "Colossians 1:13–20: A Chiastic Reading," *SVTQ* 40 (1996): 247–64. And for a treatment of 1:15–20 as a chiasmus, see Steven M. Baugh, "The Poetic Form of Col 1:15–20," *WTJ* 47 (1985): 227–44. For other proposed chiastic and structural elements in 1:15–20, see Wayne McCown, "The Hymnic Structure of Colossians 1:15–20," *EvQ* 51 (1979): 156–62; Luis Carlos Reyes, "The Structure and Rhetoric of Colossians 1:15–20," *Filología Neotestamentaria* 12 (1999): 139–54.

22. For the text-critical preference of the reading of the aorist active, "he has reconciled" (ἀποκατήλλαξεν), rather than the variant in the aorist passive, "you have been reconciled" (ἀποκατηλλάγητε), see Dunn, *Colossians*, 105 n. 1; Wilson, *Colossians*, 159–60.

23. "All things" (τὰ πάντα) occurs in 1:20a of the B element, but in the accusative case as the object of the verb.

which you heard (ἠκούσατε)" in 1:23b—as well as in the first person singular—"of which I became (ἐγενόμην), I, Paul, a minister" in 1:23d—establish the unity of the A′ (1:23) element. The only occurrences in the letter of the word "creation"—"the firstborn of all creation (πάσης κτίσεως)" in 1:15 and "proclaimed in all creation (πάσῃ κτίσει)" in 1:23, as well as occurrences of the word for "heaven(s)"—"in the heavens (οὐρανοῖς)" in 1:16 and "under heaven (οὐρανόν)" in 1:23—establish the parallelisms between the A and the A′ elements of the chiasm in this third unit.[24]

The literary inclusion formed by the occurrence of the third person singular masculine pronoun at the beginning—"And he (αὐτός) is the head of the body" in 1:18—and end—"to reconcile all things to him (αὐτόν)" in 1:20a—indicates the unity of the B (1:18-20a) element. The only occurrences in this unit of the second person plural pronoun "you" in the accusative case—"And you (ὑμᾶς) . . . he has now reconciled" in 1:21-22a and "to present you (ὑμᾶς)" in 1:22b—indicate the unity of the B′ (1:21-22) element. The only occurrences in this unit of the word "body"—"the head of the body (σώματος)" in 1:18 and "in the body (σώματι) of his flesh" in 1:22, as well as the only occurrences in the letter of the verb "reconcile"—"and through him to reconcile (ἀποκαταλλάξαι) all things to him" in 1:20a and "he has now reconciled (ἀποκατήλλαξεν)" in 1:22—determine the parallelisms between the B and the B′ elements of this third unit's chiasm.

The chiasm's central and unparalleled C (1:20b) element is distinguished by containing the letter's only occurrences of the words "making peace" (εἰρηνοποιήσας) and "blood" (αἵματος).

4. We Are Admonishing and Teaching Every Human Being in All Wisdom (1:24–2:5)
In Christ Are All the Treasures of Wisdom and Knowledge Hidden

A: [24] Now I am rejoicing (χαίρω) in the sufferings on behalf of you and I am filling up what is lacking of the afflictions of the Christ in my flesh (τῇ σαρκί) on behalf of his body, which is the church, [25] of which I BECAME A MINISTER according to the plan of God given to me to fulfill for you the word (λόγον) of God,

B: [26] the mystery (μυστήριον) that has been hidden (ἀποκεκρυμμένον) from the ages and from the generations. But now it has been manifested to his holy ones, [27] to whom God wished to make known what is the richness (πλοῦτος) of the glory of this mystery (μυστηρίου) among the Gentiles, which is Christ among you, the hope of the glory. [28] Him we proclaim, admonishing every human being and teaching every human being in all wisdom (σοφίᾳ), that we may present every human being complete in Christ.

---

24. The phrase "in the heavens (οὐρανοῖς)" also occurs in the central C (1:20b) element of the chiasm in this third unit but not in the context of an explicit reference to "all creation" as in the A and A′ elements.

C: ²⁹ᵃ For this I also labor, struggling (ἀγωνιζόμενος)
　　D: ²⁹ᵇ according to his working (ἐνέργειαν)
　　D´: ²⁹ᶜ that is working (ἐνεργουμένην) in me in power.
C´: ²:¹ For I wish you to know how great a struggle (ἀγῶνα) I am having on behalf of you and those in Laodicea and as many as have not seen my face in the flesh,
B´: ² that their hearts may be encouraged as they are held together in love, and for all richness (πλοῦτος) of the full assurance of understanding, for knowledge of the mystery (μυστηρίου) of God, Christ,²⁵ ³ in whom are all the treasures of wisdom (σοφίας) and knowledge hidden (ἀπόκρυφοι).
A´: ⁴ This I speak (λέγω), that no one may speak contrary to you with persuasive speech. ⁵ For even if in the flesh (τῇ σαρκί) I am absent, yet in the Spirit I am with you,²⁶ rejoicing (χαίρων) at seeing your good order and the firmness of your faith in CHRIST.²⁷

Paul's statement at the beginning of this unit in 1:25, "of which I became a minister (ἐγενόμην ἐγὼ διάκονος)," recalls his climatic proclamation that "I became, I, Paul a minister" (ἐγενόμην ἐγὼ Παῦλος διάκονος) at the conclusion of the preceding unit in 1:23. The occurrences of these similar assertions by Paul thus serve as the transitional words linking the third unit (1:15–23) to the fourth unit (1:24–2:5).

An A-B-C-D-D´-C´-B´-A´ chiastic pattern secures this fourth unit's (1:24–2:5) integrity and distinctness. The only occurrences in the letter of the verb "rejoice"—"Now I am rejoicing (χαίρω)" in 1:24 and "rejoicing (χαίρων) at seeing your good order" in 2:5, the only occurrences in the letter of the phrase "in the flesh" with the article in the Greek—"in my flesh (τῇ σαρκί)" in 1:24 and "in the flesh (τῇ σαρκί)" in 2:5,²⁸ and the correlation between the only occurrences in this unit of the noun "word" and its cognate verb "say"—"the word (λόγον) of God" in 1:25 and "This I speak (λέγω)" in 2:4, establish the parallels between the A (1:24–25) and A´ (2:4–5) elements of this fourth unit's chiasm.

The only occurrences in this unit of the word "mystery"—"the mystery

---

25. Metzger, *Textual Commentary*, 555: "Among what at first sight seems to be a bewildering variety of variant readings, the one adopted for the text is plainly to be preferred (a) because of strong external testimony and (b) because it alone provides an adequate explanation of the other readings as various scribal attempts to ameliorate the syntactical ambiguity of τοῦ θεοῦ, Χριστοῦ." As Harris (*Colossians*, 82) notes, understanding Χριστοῦ as an epexegetical genitive—"God's mystery, which is Christ"—is supported by Col 1:27.

26. For the translation and meaning of "in the Spirit" (τῷ πνεύματι) here, see Fee, *God's Empowering Presence*, 345–46.

27. On translating χαίρων καὶ βλέπων not literally as "rejoicing and seeing" but as a hendiadys, "rejoicing at seeing," see Harris, *Colossians*, 87.

28. The phrase "in the flesh" (ἐν σαρκί) occurs in the C´ element of this unit in 2:1, but without the article in the Greek. The word "flesh" (σάρξ) occurs elsewhere in the letter in 1:22; 2:11, 13, 18, 23; 3:22, but not, as in 1:24 and 2:5, in the dative case with the article.

(μυστήριον) that has been hidden" in 1:26 together with "the glory of this mystery (μυστηρίου)" in 1:27 and "knowledge of the mystery (μυστηρίου)" in 2:2,[29] the only occurrences in the letter of the verb and adjective for "hidden"—"the mystery that has been hidden" (ἀποκεκρυμμένον) in 1:26 and "in him are all the treasures of wisdom and knowledge hidden (ἀπόκρυφοι)" in 2:3, the only occurrences in the letter of the word "richness"—"what is the richness (πλοῦτος)" in 1:27 and "for all richness (πλοῦτος)" in 2:2, as well as the only occurences in this unit of the word "wisdom"—"in all wisdom (σοφίᾳ)" in 1:28 and "all the treasures of wisdom (σοφίας)" in 2:3, determine the parallels between the B (1:26-28) and the B′ (2:2-3) elements of the chiasm in this fourth unit.

The only occurrences in this unit of a word for "struggle"—"For this I also labor, struggling (ἀγωνιζόμενος)" in 1:29a and "how great a struggle (ἀγῶνα)" in 2:1—establish the parallelism between the C (1:29a) and C′ (2:1) elements of this fourth unit's chiasm.[30]

Finally, the only occurrences in this unit of words for "working"—"according to his working (ἐνέργειαν)" in 1:29b and "that is working (ἐνεργουμένην) in me in power" in 1:29c—determine the parallelism between the central D (1:29b) and D′ (1:29c) elements of the chiasm in this fourth unit.[31]

5. Walk and Live in Christ with Whom You Have Died and Been Raised (2:6–23) Why Let Yourselves Be Subjected to Decrees as if Living in the World?

A: [6] As (ὡς) then you received the CHRIST, Jesus the Lord,[32] in him go on walking, [7] having been rooted and being built up in him and being confirmed in the faith as you were taught, abounding in thanksgiving. [8] See to it that there will not be anyone who is captivating you through the philosophy (φιλοσοφίας) which is empty deceit,[33] according to the tradition of human beings (κατὰ τὴν παράδοσιν τῶν ἀνθρώπων), according to the elemental forces of the world (τὰ στοιχεῖα τοῦ κόσμου), and not according to Christ.

---

29. The word "mystery" (μυστήριον) occurs elsewhere in the letter in 4:3.
30. "Struggling" (ἀγωνιζόμενος) occurs elsewhere in the letter in 4:12.
31. The noun "working" (ἐνέργεια) occurs elsewhere in the letter in 2:12.
32. With regard to the translation "the Christ, Jesus the Lord," Harris (*Colossians*, 89) states: "The whole expression appears to be a combination of two early christological confessions, ὁ Χριστὸς Ἰησοῦς, 'Jesus is the Messiah' (Acts 18:5, 28; cf. 2:36; 9:22; 17:3), and κύριος Ἰησοῦς, 'Jesus is Lord (Rom. 10:9; 1 Cor. 12:3; cf. Phil. 2:11), with the one common element and proper name being anar[throus]. (Ἰησοῦν) and the two titular elements being art[icular]. and (here) not pred[icative]. (τὸν Χριστὸν . . . τὸν κύριον)."
33. On the translation "through the philosophy which is empty deceit" (διὰ τῆς φιλοσοφίας καὶ κενῆς ἀπάτης) Harris (*Colossians*, 92) explains: "The single prep[osition]. and art[icle]. qualifying both nouns suggest that one conceptual entity, not two, is being named and therefore that καί is epex[egetical]. 'through a philosophy which is empty deceit,' 'through hollow and deceptive philosophy.' By the term φιλοσοφία, thus qualified, Paul means neither philosophy in general nor classical G[ree]k. philosophy specifically but so-called philosophy, what is falsely termed philosophy (cf. 1 Tim. 6:20), 'philosophy' that has the mere 'appearance of wisdom' (cf. 2:23)."

B: ⁹ For in him dwells all the fullness of the deity bodily (σωματικῶς), ¹⁰ and you are in him having been and being filled, who is the head (κεφαλή) of every principality (ἀρχῆς) and authority (ἐξουσίας).

C: ¹¹ In whom indeed you were circumcised with a circumcision not made with hands (ἀχειροποιήτῳ) in the removal of the body of the flesh (σαρκός), in the circumcision of the Christ, ¹² having been buried with (συνταφέντες) him in the baptism, in whom indeed you were raised with him (συνηγέρθητε) through faith in the working of God who raised him from the dead (νεκρῶν).[34]

C′: ¹³ And you, being dead (νεκρούς) in transgressions and in the uncircumcision of your flesh (σαρκός), he brought you to life along (συνεζωοποίησεν) with (σύν) him, having forgiven us all our transgressions, ¹⁴ having obliterated the handwritten charge (χειρόγραφον) against us with its decrees, which was opposed to us, and this he has taken from our midst, having nailed it to the cross,

B′: ¹⁵ having removed the principalities (ἀρχάς) and the authorities (ἐξουσίας), he exposed them in public, leading them away in triumph in him.[35] ¹⁶ Let then no one judge you in food and in drink or in regard to a festival or new moon or sabbaths, ¹⁷ which things are a shadow of the things that were to come, but the body (σῶμα) belongs to the Christ. ¹⁸ Let no one condemn you,[36] delighting in humility and worship of the angels, going into detail about what things he had seen, vainly being made arrogant by the mind of his flesh, ¹⁹ not holding to the head (κεφαλήν), from whom the whole body (σῶμα), supported and held together through ligaments and bonds, grows with the growth that is from God.[37]

A′: ²⁰ IF YOU DIED WITH CHRIST from the elemental forces of the world (τῶν στοιχείων τοῦ κόσμου), why let yourselves be subjected to decrees as if (ὡς) living in the world (κόσμῳ)? ²¹ "Do not touch, do not taste, do not handle"— ²² which things are all destined for destruction in being consumed—according to the commandments and teachings of human beings (κατὰ τὰ ἐντάλματα καὶ διδασκαλίας τῶν ἀνθρώπων); ²³ such (decrees) have indeed a reputation

---

34. For the reasons to understand ἐν ᾧ καί in 2:12 as referring to Christ and translating "in whom also" rather than as referring to baptism and translating "in which also," see O'Brien, *Colossians*, 118–19; Dunn, *Colossians*, 160–61.

35. Dunn, *Colossians*, 145 n. 4: "ἐν αὐτῷ could be taken as 'in it,' referring to the cross. But it is more appropriate to read it as a final chord of the 'in him' theme."

36. For the preference of translating καταβραβευέτω not as "disqualify" but rather as "condemn," "injure," or "take advantage of," see Kent L. Yinger, "Translating καταβραβευέτω ['Disqualify' NRSV] in Colossians 2:18," *BT* 54 (2003): 138–45.

37. For an unconvincing attempt to construe 2:6–19 as a chiasm, see Thomson, *Chiasmus*, 152–80. According to Dübbers (*Christologie*, 198 n. 10), Thomson's proposed chiasm "orientiert sich dagegen zu sehr an formalen Beobachtungen und kann insgesamt nicht überzeugen." For a discourse analysis of 2:16–3:17 within a chiastic framework, see G. T. Christopher, "A Discourse Analysis of Colossians 2:16–3:17," *Grace Theological Journal* 11 (1990): 205–20.

of wisdom (σοφίας) in self-chosen worship and humility and severe treatment of the body,[38] not of value to anyone against self-indulgence of the flesh.

The word "Christ" in the statement that "as then you received the Christ" at the beginning of this unit in 2:6 recalls "Christ" in the phrase "the firmness of your faith in Christ" at the conclusion of the preceding unit in 2:5. These occurrences of "Christ" thus serve as the transitional words linking the fourth unit (1:24–2:5) to the fifth unit (2:6–23).

An A-B-C-C′-B′-A′ chiastic pattern secures this fifth unit's (2:6–23) integrity and distinctness. The only occurrences in this unit of the conjunction "as"—"As (ὡς) then you received the Christ, Jesus the Lord" in 2:6 and "as (ὡς) if living in the world" in 2:20, the only occurrences in this unit of words containing the Greek root for "wisdom"—"through the philosophy (φιλο-σοφίας)" in 2:6 and "a reputation of wisdom (σοφίας)" in 2:23, the only occurrences in the letter of the genitive plural of the word for "human being" modifying a prepositional phrase beginning with "according to"—"according to the tradition of human beings (κατὰ τὴν παράδοσιν τῶν ἀνθρώπων)" in 2:8 and "according to the commandments and teachings of human beings (κατὰ τὰ ἐντάλματα καὶ διδασκαλίας τῶν ἀνθρώπων)" in 2:22, and the only occurrences in the letter of the phrase "elements of the world"—"according to the elemental forces of the world (τὰ στοιχεῖα τοῦ κόσμου)" in 2:8 and "from the elemental forces of the world (τῶν στοιχείων τοῦ κόσμου)" as well as the added occurrence of "living in the world (κόσμῳ) in 2:20, establish the parallels between the A (2:6–8) and A′ (2:20–23) elements of the chiasm in this fifth unit.[39]

The only occurrences in this unit of terms referring to the "body" of which Christ is the head—"in him dwells all the fullness of the deity bodily (σωματικῶς)" in 2:9 and "the body (σῶμα) belongs to the Christ" in 2:17, as well as "the head, from whom the whole body (σῶμα) . . . grows with the growth that is from God" in 2:19,[40] the only occurrences in this unit of the word "head"—"who is the head

---

38. Dübbers, *Christologie*, 278 n. 363: "Das Relativum ἅτινα ist im Sinne von 'solches' auf die gegnerischen Forderungen zu beziehen." On the retention of the variant reading "and" (καί) after "humility" here, see Metzger, *Textual Commentary*, 556–57.

39. A literary inclusion formed by the only occurrences in this unit of the word "Christ" in the accusative singular—"as then you received Christ (Χριστόν) Jesus" in 2:6 and "not according to Christ (Χριστόν)" in 2:8—indicates the unity of this chiasm's A (2:6–8) element. The word "Christ" occurs in this unit also in 2:11, 17, 20, but not in the accusative case.

40. The term "body" occurs twice elsewhere in this unit but not as a reference to the "body" of Christ and not in close association with the term "head" in reference to Christ. In 2:11 the term "body" in the phrase "the removal of the body (σώματος) of the flesh" refers to the physical body of the audience. In 2:23 the term "body" in the phrase "severe treatment of the body (σώματος)" likewise refers to a physical, "fleshly" body. In both 2:11 and 2:23 the term "body" is used not in close association with the term "head" in reference to Christ but in close association with the term "flesh" in reference to the physical nature of the human body. Furthermore, both references to "body" in 2:11 and 2:23 are in the genitive case, whereas the references to "body" in 2:17 and 2:19 are in the nominative case, while the reference in 2:9 is an adverb.

(κεφαλή)" in 2:10 and "not holding to the head (κεφαλήν)" in 2:19,[41] as well as the only occurrences in this unit of the word pair "principalities and authorities"—"every principality (ἀρχῆς) and authority (ἐξουσίας)" in 2:10 and "having removed the principalities (ἀρχάς) and the authorities (ἐξουσίας)" in 2:15,[42] determine the parallelisms between the B (2:9-10) and B´ (2:15-19) elements of this fifth unit's chiasm.

The only occurrences in this unit of terms involving something done with human hands—"with a circumcision not made with hands (ἀχειροποιήτῳ)" in 2:11 and "handwritten charge" (χειρόγραφον) in 2:14, the only occurrences in this unit of the word "flesh" in reference to the flesh of the audience—"In him also you were circumcised with a circumcision not made with hands in the removal of the body of the flesh (σαρκός)" in 2:11 and "in the uncircumcision of your flesh (σαρκός)" in 2:13,[43] occurrences of the prefix and preposition "with" to express the audience's union with the dead and risen Christ—"having been buried with (συνταφέντες) him in baptism, in him also you were raised with him (συνηγέρθητε)" in 2:12 and "he brought you to life along (συνεζωοποίησεν) with (σύν) him" in 2:13,[44] and the only occurrences in this unit of the word for "the dead"—"God who raised him from the dead (νεκρῶν)" in 2:12 and "you, being dead (νεκρούς) in transgressions," in 2:13,[45] constitute the parallelisms of the central C (2:11-12) and C´ (2:13-14) elements of the chiasm in the fifth unit.[46]

6. You Died and Were Raised with Christ from Living as You Once Walked (3:1-7)
Put to Death Then the Parts That Are upon the Earth

A: **3:1 IF THEN (οὖν) YOU WERE RAISED WITH THE CHRIST**, seek (ζητεῖτε) the things above, where the Christ is (ἐστιν), seated at the right hand of God (θεοῦ).[47] 2 Think of the things above, not the things upon the earth (τὰ ἐπὶ τῆς γῆς),

---

41. The word "head" (κεφαλή) occurred previously in the letter in 1:18.
42. "Principalities or authorities" (ἀρχαὶ εἴτε ἐξουσίαι) occurred previously in the letter in 1:16.
43. The word "flesh" (σάρξ) occurs elsewhere in this unit but not in specific reference to the flesh of the audience—"the mind of his flesh (σαρκός)" in 2:18 and "gratification of the flesh (σαρκός)" in general in 2:23.
44. "If you have died with (σύν) Christ" occurs also in this unit in 2:20.
45. The word for "the dead" (νεκρός) occurred previously in the letter in 1:18.
46. The integrity of the C element is secured by the only occurrences in this unit of the prepositional phrase with the relative pronoun, "in him" (ἐν ᾧ), that is, "in Christ" in 2:11 and 2:12. And the integrity of the C´ element is secured by the only occurrences in this unit of the first person plural pronoun—"having forgiven us (ἡμῖν) in 2:13 and "against us (ἡμῶν)" as well as "opposed to us (ἡμῖν)" in 2:14.
47. According to Harris (*Colossians*, 137), "given the word-order, it is preferable to tr[anslate] 'where Christ is, seated . . .' Paul is making two distinct affirmations—Christ is resident in 'the realm above'; and he is enthroned there at God's right hand."

B: ³ for you died and your life (ἡ ζωὴ ὑμῶν) has been hidden with (σύν) the Christ (Χριστῷ) in God.

B': ⁴ Whenever the Christ (Χριστός), your life (ἡ ζωὴ ὑμῶν),[48] is manifested, then you also with (σύν) him will be manifested in glory.

A': ⁵ Put to death then (οὖν) the parts that are upon the earth (τὰ ἐπὶ τῆς γῆς): unlawful sex, impurity, passion, evil desire, and the covetousness, which is (ἐστὶν) idolatry, ⁶ on account of which things the wrath of God (θεοῦ) is coming upon the sons of disobedience.[49] ⁷ Among whom YOU ALSO walked once, when you lived (ἐζῆτε) in these.

The statement "if then you were raised with the Christ" (εἰ οὖν συνηγέρθητε τῷ Χριστῷ) that begins this unit in 3:1 resonates with the statement "if you died with Christ" (εἰ ἀπεθάνετε σὺν Χριστῷ) toward the conclusion of the preceding unit in 2:20. These similar statements thus serve as the transitional words linking the fifth unit (2:6-23) to the sixth unit (3:1-7).

An A-B-B'-A' chiastic pattern secures this sixth unit's (3:1-7) integrity and distinctness. The only occurrences in this unit of the coordinating conjuncion "then"—"If then (οὖν) you were raised with the Christ" in 3:1 and "Put to death then (οὖν) the parts" in 3:6,[50] the alliteration in Greek between the verb "seek" (ζητεῖτε) in 3:1 and the verb "you lived" (ἐζῆτε) in 3:7, the only occurrences in this unit of the verb "is"—"where the Christ is (ἐστιν)" in 3:1 and "which is (ἐστὶν) idolatry" in 3:5, the only occurrences in this unit of the word "God" in the genitive case (it occurs in the dative case in 3:3)—"at the right hand of God (θεοῦ)" in 3:1 and "the wrath of God (θεοῦ)" in 3:6, and the only occurrences in this unit of the phrase "the things upon the earth"—"not the things upon the earth (τὰ ἐπὶ τῆς γῆς)" in 3:2 and "the parts that are upon the earth (τὰ ἐπὶ τῆς γῆς)" in 3:5,[51] establish the parallelisms between the A (3:1-2) and the A' (3:5-7) elements of the chiasm in this sixth unit.

The only occurrences in the letter of the phrase "your life"—"for you have died and your life (ἡ ζωὴ ὑμῶν) has been hidden" in 3:5 and "Whenever the Christ, your life (ἡ ζωὴ ὑμῶν), is manifested" in 3:4, as well as the only occurrences in this unit of the preposition "with" having Christ as object—"with the Christ (σὺν τῷ Χριστῷ)" in 3:3 and "with (σύν) him," that is, "the Christ (ὁ Χριστός) in 3:4, determine the parallelisms of the central B (3:3) and B' (3:4) elements of the sixth unit's chiasm.

---

48. On the preference for the reading "your" (ὑμῶν) rather than "our" (ἡμῶν) here, see Metzger, *Textual Commentary*, 557; Harris, *Colossians*, 140.

49. On the retention of the reading "upon the sons of disobedience" here, see Metzger, *Textual Commentary*, 557.

50. The conjunction "then" (οὖν) occurs elsewhere in the letter in 2:6, 16; 3:12.

51. The phrase "the things upon the earth" (τὰ ἐπὶ τῆς γῆς) occurred previously in the letter in 1:20.

7. In All Wisdom Teaching and Admonishing One Another (3:8–16)
Let the Peace of Christ Rule in Your Hearts

> A: [8] But now YOU ALSO (καὶ ὑμεῖς) must put them all away: anger, rage, malice, slander, obscene talk from your (ὑμῶν) mouth. [9] Do not lie to one another (ἀλλήλους), having removed the old human being with its practices
> > B: [10] and having put on (ἐνδυσάμενοι) the new which is being renewed for knowledge according to the image of the one who created it,
> > > C: [11] wherein there is not Greek and Jew, circumcision and uncircumcision, barbarian, Scythian, slave, free, but Christ is all and in all.
> > B′: [12] Put on (ἐνδύσασθε) then, as God's chosen ones, holy and beloved, heartfelt compassion, kindness, humility, gentleness, patience,
> A′: [13] bearing with one another (ἀλλήλων) and forgiving each other if anyone has a complaint against someone; just as the Lord forgave you, so must you also (καὶ ὑμεῖς). [14] And over all these love, that is the bond of completeness. [15] And let the peace of Christ rule in your (ὑμῶν) hearts, to which indeed you were called in one body. And be thankful. [16] Let the word of Christ dwell in you richly, in all wisdom teaching and admonishing each other with psalms, hymns, and Spiritual songs, in grace singing in your (ὑμῶν) hearts to GOD.[52]

The words "you also" (καὶ ὑμεῖς) in Paul's directive to the audience that "now you also must put them all away" at the beginning of this unit in 3:8 recall the same words "you also" (καὶ ὑμεῖς) in Paul's reminder to the audience that "among whom you also once walked" at the conclusion of the preceding unit in 3:7. These occurrences of the phrase "you also" thus serve as the transitional words linking the sixth unit (3:1–7) to the seventh unit (3:8–16).

An A-B-C-B′-A′ chiastic pattern secures this seventh unit's (3:8–16) integrity and distinctness. The only occurrences in this unit of the phrase "you also"—"But now you also (καὶ ὑμεῖς)" in 3:8 and "so must you also (καὶ ὑμεῖς)" in 3:12, the only occurrences in this unit of the genitive second person plural pronoun "your"—"from your (ὑμῶν) mouth" in 3:8 and "in your (ὑμῶν) hearts" in 3:15, 16, and the only occurrences in the letter of the word "one another"—"Do not lie to one another (ἀλλήλους)" in 3:9 and "bearing with one another (ἀλλήλων)" in 3:13—establish the parallelism between the A (3:8–9) and the A′ (3:13–16) elements of the chiasm in this seventh unit. The only occurrences in the letter of the word "put on"—"having put on (ἐνδυσάμενοι) the new" in 3:10 and "put on (ἐνδύσασθε) then, as God's chosen ones" in 3:12—determine the parallelism between the B (3:10) and B′ (3:12) elements of the chiasm. The unparalleled central C (3:11) ele-

---

52. For the basis of this translation of 3:16, see Fee, *God's Empowering Presence*, 648–57. Note that the integrity and distinctiveness of the A′ element is secured by the literary inclusion formed by the only two occurrences in the letter of the reflexive pronoun, "each other"—"forgiving each other (ἑαυτοῖς)" in 3:13 and "teaching and admonishing each other (ἑαυτούς)" in 3:16.

ment of the chiasm is distinguished by containing the letter's only occurrences of the words "Greek," "Jew," "barbarian," "Scythian," and "free."

8. You Have a Master in Heaven (3:17–4:1)
Work as for the Lord and Not Human Beings

> A: [17] And all, whatever you do (ὅ τι ἐὰν ποιῆτε) in word or in work (ἔργῳ), do all things in the name of the Lord Jesus, thanking GOD the Father through him.
>> B: [18] Wives, submit to your husbands as is fitting in the Lord. [19] Husbands, love your wives and do not become bitter toward them. [20] Children, obey (ὑπακούετε) your parents in all things (κατὰ πάντα), for this is pleasing in the Lord. [21] Fathers, do not provoke your children, so that they do not become discouraged.
>> B′: [22] Slaves, obey (ὑπακούετε) in all things (κατὰ πάντα) those who are your masters according to the flesh, not with eye service as human-pleasers, but with sincerity of heart, fearing the Lord.
> A′: [23] Whatever you do (ὃ ἐὰν ποιῆτε), from your soul work (ἐργάζεσθε) as for the Lord and not human beings, [24] knowing that from the Lord you will receive the reward of the inheritance; to the Lord Christ be slaves. [25] For the wrongdoer will be paid back for the wrong he has done, and there is no partiality. [4:1] Masters, what is just and fair grant to the slaves, knowing that YOU ALSO have a Master in heaven.

The word "God" (τῷ θεῷ) in Paul's description of the audience as "thanking God the Father" that introduces this unit in 3:17 recalls the word "God" (τῷ θεῷ) in Paul's description of the audience as "singing in your hearts to God" that concludes the preceding unit. These occurrences of the word "God" thus serve as the transitional words linking the seventh unit (3:8–16) to the eighth unit (3:17–4:1).

An A-B-B′-A′ chiastic pattern secures this eighth unit's (3:17–4:1) integrity and distinctness. The only occurrences in the letter of the clause "whatever you do"—"And all, whatever you do (ὅ τι ἐὰν ποιῆτε)" in 3:17 and "Whatever you do (ὃ ἐὰν ποιῆτε)" in 3:23, as well as the only occurrences in this unit of words for "work"—"in word or in work (ἔργῳ)" in 3:17 and "work (ἐργάζεσθε) from your soul as for the Lord" in 3:23,[53] establish the parallelisms between the A (3:17) and A′ (3:23–4:1) elements of the chiasm in this eighth unit.

The unity of the B (3:18–21) element is constituted by the only occurrences in this unit of the prepositional phrase "in the Lord"—"as is fitting in the Lord (ἐν κυρίῳ)" in 3:18 and "this is pleasing in the Lord (ἐν κυρίῳ)" in 3:20, and by the only occurrences in this unit of the particle "not" (μή) negating a verb—"do not (μή) become bitter toward them" in 3:19 and "do not (μή) provoke your children,

---

53. The noun for "work" (ἔργον) occurred previously in the letter in 1:10, 21.

lest (μή) they become discouraged" in 3:21.[54] The only occurrences in the letter of the verb "obey"—"Children, obey (ὑπακούετε) your parents" in 3:20 and "Slaves, obey (ὑπακούετε)," in 3:22, as well as the only occurrences in the letter of the phrase "in all things"—"in all things (κατὰ πάντα)" in 3:20 and "in all things (κατὰ πάντα)" in 3:22, determine the parallelisms between the central B (3:18–21) and B′ (3:22) elements of this unit's chiasm.

9. Pray for Us in Thanksgiving and Walk in Wisdom (4:2–6) That God May Open for Us a Door for the Word about the Mystery of Christ

> A: ² In prayer persevere, being watchful in it in thanksgiving, ³ᵃ praying at the same time ALSO FOR US, that God may open to us a door for the word (λόγου)
>> B: ³ᶜ to speak (λαλῆσαι) the mystery of the Christ,
>>> C: ³ᵈ on account of which indeed I have been bound,
>> B′: ⁴ that I may manifest it as it is necessary for me to speak (λαλῆσαι).
> A′: ⁵ In wisdom walk toward those outside, making the most of the opportunity. ⁶ Let your word (λόγος) always be in grace, seasoned with salt, to know how it is necessary for you to answer each one.

The phrase "also for us" (καὶ περὶ ἡμῶν) that occurs at the beginning of this unit in 4:3 recalls the similar phrase "you also" (καὶ ὑμεῖς) at the conclusion of the preceding unit in 4:1. These similar phrases thus serve as the transitional words linking the eighth unit (3:17–4:1) to the ninth unit (4:2–6).

An A-B-C-B′-A′ chiastic pattern secures this ninth unit's (4:2–6) integrity and distinctness. The only occurrences in this unit of "word"—"that God may open to us a door for the word (λόγου)" in 4:3a and "Let your word (λόγος) always be in grace" in 4:6—establish the parallelism between the A (4:2–3a) and A′ (4:5–6) elements of the chiasm in this ninth unit.[55] The only occurrences in the letter of the verb "speak"—"to speak (λαλῆσαι) the mystery of Christ" in 4:3c and "as it is necessary for me to speak (λαλῆσαι)" in 4:4—determine the parallelism between the B (4:3c) and B′ (4:4) elements of this unit's chiasm. The central C (4:3d) element of the chiasm is distinguished by containing the only occurrence in the letter of the verb "bind" in the passive voice—"on account of which I have been bound (δέδεμαι)."[56]

---

54. The particle "not" (μή) negates a prepositional phrase—"not (μή) with eye service"—rather than a verb in the B′ element in 3:22.

55. These are the last two occurrences of "word" (λόγος) in the letter; it occurred previously in 1:5, 25; 2:23; 3:16, 17.

56. A form of this verb occurs in the active voice (δει, "it is necessary"), however, in 4:4.

10. Full Assurance in All the Will of God and Grace from Paul (4:7–18)
Greet the Brothers and Fulfill the Ministry in the Lord

A: ⁷ All the things regarding me Tychicus, the beloved brother (ἀδελφός) and faithful minister (διάκονος) and fellow slave in the Lord (ἐν κυρίῳ), will make known to you, ⁸ whom I am sending to you for this very purpose, that you may know the things concerning us and that he may encourage your hearts, ⁹ with Onesimus, the faithful and beloved brother (ἀδελφῷ), who is one of you. They will make known to you all the things that are happening here.

B: ¹⁰ Aristarchus, my fellow prisoner, greets you (ἀσπάζεται ὑμᾶς), also Mark, the cousin of Barnabas (concerning whom you have received instructions; if he comes to you, receive him), ¹¹ also Jesus who is called Justus, who are the only ones of the circumcision who are fellow workers for the kingdom of God, who have become to me a comfort. ¹²ᵃ Epaphras, who is one of you, a slave of Christ Jesus, greets you (ἀσπάζεται ὑμᾶς),

    C: ¹²ᵇ always struggling on behalf of you (ὑπὲρ ὑμῶν) in the prayers,

        D: ¹²ᶜ that you may stand complete and fully assured in all the will of God.

    C′: ¹³ For I testify for him that he is having much labor on behalf of you (ὑπὲρ ὑμῶν) and those in Laodicea and those in Hierapolis.

B′: ¹⁴ Luke, the beloved physician, greets you (ἀσπάζεται ὑμᾶς), and Demas.

A′: ¹⁵ Greet the brothers (ἀδελφούς) in Laodicea also Nympha and the church at her house. ¹⁶ And when the letter has been read among you, make sure that it is read also in the church of the Laodiceans, and that you also read the one from Laodicea. ¹⁷ And say to Archippus, "Look to the ministry (διακονίαν) which you received in the Lord (ἐν κυρίῳ), that you fulfill it." ¹⁸ The greeting in my own hand, of Paul: Keep on remembering my chains. Grace be with you.

The address to "you" (ὑμῖν) in the statement "will make known to you" at the beginning of this unit in 4:7 recalls the reference to "you" (ὑμᾶς) in the statement "to know how it is necessary for you to answer each one" at the conclusion of the preceding unit in 4:6. These occurrences of "you" in reference to the audience thus serve as the transitional words linking the ninth unit (4:2–6) to the tenth unit (4:7–18).

An A-B-C-D-C′-B′-A′ chiastic pattern secures this tenth and final unit's (4:7–18) integrity and distinctness. The only occurrences in this unit of the word "brother"—"Tychicus, the beloved brother (ἀδελφός)," in 4:7, "Onesimus, the faithful and beloved brother (ἀδελφῷ)," in 4:9, and "Greet the brothers (ἀδελφούς) in Laodicea" in 4:16,⁵⁷ the only occurrences in this unit of a word referring to "minister" or "ministry"—"faithful minister (διάκονος)" in 4:7 and "fulfill the ministry

---

57. The word "brother" (ἀδελφός) occurred previously in the letter in 1:1, 2.

(διακονίαν)" in 4:17,[58] the only occurrences in this unit, and the final occurrences in the letter, of the phrase "in the Lord"—"fellow slave in the Lord (ἐν κυρίῳ)" in 4:7 and "which you received in the Lord (ἐν κυρίῳ)" in 4:17,[59] establish the parallelisms between the A (4:7-9) and the A′ (4:15-18) elements of the chiasm in this tenth unit.

The only occurrences in the letter of the clause "greets you"—"Aristarchus, my fellow prisoner, greets you (ἀσπάζεται ὑμᾶς)" in 4:10a, "Epaphras, who is one of you, a slave of Christ Jesus, greets you (ἀσπάζεται ὑμᾶς)" in 4:12a, and "Luke, the beloved physician, greets you (ἀσπάζεται ὑμᾶς)" in 4:14, determine the parallelisms between the B (4:10-12a) and the B′ (4:14) elements of this unit's chiasm. Furthermore, the occurrences of "greets you" in 4:10a and 4:12a serve as a literary inclusion sealing the integrity of the B element.

The only occurrences in this unit, and the final occurrences in the letter, of the phrase "on behalf of you"—"always struggling on behalf of you (ὑπὲρ ὑμῶν)" in 4:12b and "he has much labor on behalf of you (ὑπὲρ ὑμῶν)" in 4:13—constitute the parallelism between the C (4:12b) and C′ (4:13) elements of the chiasm.[60] The central and unparalleled D (4:12c) element of this final unit's chiasm is distinguished by containing the only occurrences in the letter of the verbs "stand" (σταθῆτε) and "fully assured" (πεπληροφορημένοι).

B. The Macrochiastic Structure of the Letter

Having illustrated the various microchiastic structures operative in the ten distinct units of the letter to the Colossians, I will now demonstrate how these ten main units form an A-B-C-D-E-E′-D′-C′-B′-A′ macrochiastic structure embracing the entire letter.

A: Grace from Paul an Apostle by the Will of God (1:1-2)
A′: Full Assurance in All the Will of God and Grace from Paul (4:7-18)

Repetitions of significant words indicate the parallelism between the opening A unit (1:1-2) and the closing A′ unit (4:7-18) within the macrochiastic structure of the letter to the Colossians. The occurrence of the name "Paul" (Παῦλος) at the beginning of the letter in 1:1a of the A unit parallels its occurrence at the conclusion of the letter in the final greeting written in the hand of "Paul" (Παύλου) in 4:18 of the A′ element.[61] The introductory description of Paul as an apostle of Christ Jesus through "the will of God" (θελήματος θεοῦ) in 1:1a of the A unit

---

58. The word "minister" (διάκονος) occurred previously in the letter in 1:7, 23, 25; the word "ministry" (διακονία) occurs in the letter only in 4:17.
59. The phrase "in the Lord" (ἐν κυρίῳ) occurred previously in the letter in 3:18, 20.
60. The phrase "on behalf of you" (ὑπὲρ ὑμῶν) occurred previously in the letter in 1:7, 9, 24; 2:1.
61. The only other occurrence in the letter of the name "Paul" is in 1:23.

parallels Paul's explanation that Epaphras is struggling on behalf of the Colossian audience so that they may be complete and fully assured in all "the will of God" (θελήματι τοῦ θεοῦ) in 4:12c, the central D element of the A´ unit. That these are the only two occurrences in the letter of the phrase "will of God" enhances the significance of this parallel.[62]

The designations of Timothy as the "brother" (ἀδελφός) in 1:1b and of the Colossians as holy ones and faithful "brothers" (ἀδελφοῖς) in 1:2b of the A unit parallel the designations of Tychicus as the beloved "brother" (ἀδελφός) in 4:7 and of Onesimus as the faithful and beloved "brother" (ἀδελφῷ) in 4:9, as well as the reference to those in Laodicea as "brothers" (ἀδελφούς) in 4:15 of the A´ unit. That these are the only occurrences in the letter of the word "brother" likewise enhances the significance of these parallels.

The description of the Colossians as "faithful" (πιστοῖς) brothers in 1:2b of the A unit parallels the description of Tychicus as a "faithful" (πιστός) minister in 4:7 as well as of Onesimus as the "faithful" (πιστῷ) and beloved brother in 4:9 of the A´ unit.[63] And finally, the greeting of "grace (χάρις) to you" in Paul's opening address to his audience in 1:2c of the A unit parallels his greeting of "grace (χάρις) be with you" at the close of the letter in 4:18 of the A´ unit, thus serving as a literary inclusion enveloping the entire letter.[64]

B: Thanking God When Praying for You to Walk in Wisdom (1:3–14)
B´: Pray for Us in Thanksgiving and Walk in Wisdom (4:2–6)

The expressions of thanksgiving to God—"We thank (εὐχαριστοῦμεν) God the Father" in 1:3 and "thanking (εὐχαριστοῦντες) the Father" in 1:12—in the B unit parallel the expression of thanksgiving in the B´ unit—"In prayer persevere, being watchful in it with thanksgiving (εὐχαριστίᾳ)" in 4:2.[65] Paul and Timothy's "praying (προσευχόμενοι) for you" in 1:3 and "praying (προσευχόμενοι) on behalf of you" in 1:9 of the B unit parallel and are complemented by Paul's exhortation to the audience, "In prayer (προσευχῇ) persevere, being watchful in it with thanksgiving, praying (προσευχόμενοι) at the same time also for us," in 4:2–3a of the B´ unit.[66]

"In the word (λόγῳ) of the truth of the gospel" in 1:5 of the B unit parallels "a door for the word (λόγου)" in 4:3a and "Let your word (λόγος) always be in grace"

---

62. The phrase "his will" (θελήματος αὐτοῦ) in 1:9 refers to the will of God, but uses the pronoun rather than noun for the name of God.
63. The adjective "faithful" (πιστός) occurs in only one other place in the letter—in the description of Epaphras in 1:7.
64. The word "grace" (χάρις) occurs elswhere within the body of the letter in 1:6, 3:16, and 4:6.
65. The verb "thank" (εὐχαριστέω) occurs elswhere in the letter only in 3:17, while the noun "thanksgiving" (εὐχαριστία) occurs eleswhere in the letter only in 2:7.
66. These are the only occurrences in the letter of the verb "pray" (προσεύχομαι), while the noun "prayer" (προσευχή) occurs elsewhere in the letter only in 4:12.

in 4:6 of the B´ unit.⁶⁷ Finally, "In all wisdom (σοφίᾳ) and Spiritual understanding, to walk (περιπατῆσαι) worthy of the Lord" in 1:9–10 of the B unit parallels "In wisdom (σοφίᾳ) walk (περιπατεῖτε) toward those outside" in 4:5 of the B´ unit.⁶⁸

C: The Gospel Preached to Every Creature under Heaven (1:15–23)
C´: You Have a Master in Heaven (3:17–4:1)

"For in him were created all things in the heavens (οὐρανοῖς)" in 1:16, "the things in the heavens (οὐρανοῖς)" in 1:20b, and "the gospel which you heard, which has been proclaimed in all creation under heaven (οὐρανόν)" in 1:23 of the C unit parallel "knowing that you also have a Master in heaven (οὐρανῷ)" in 4:1 of the C´ unit.⁶⁹ "All things through him (δι' αὐτοῦ) and to him have been created" in 1:16 and "through him (δι' αὐτοῦ) to reconcile all things to him, making peace through the blood of the cross, through him (δι' αὐτοῦ)" in 1:20 in the C unit parallel "thanking God the Father through him (δι' αὐτοῦ)" in 3:17 of the C´ unit.⁷⁰ "In works (ἔργοις) that are evil" in 1:21 of the C unit parallels "whatever you do in word or in work (ἔργῳ)" in 3:17 and "work (ἐργάζεσθε) from your soul as for the Lord" in 3:23 of the C´ unit.⁷¹ And finally, "in the body of his flesh (σαρκός)" in 1:22 of the C unit parallels "your masters according to the flesh (σάρκα)" in 3:22 of the C´ unit.⁷²

D: We Are Admonishing and Teaching Every Human in All Wisdom (1:24–2:5)
D´: In All Wisdom Teaching and Admonishing One Another (3:8–16)

"On behalf of his body (σώματος)" in 1:24 of the D unit parallels "to which indeed you were called in one body (σώματι)" in 3:15 of the D´ unit. "The word (λόγον) of God" in 1:25 of the D unit parallels "the word (λόγος) of Christ" in 3:16

---

67. These represent the first and last occurrences in the letter of "word" (λόγος); it occurs elsewhere in 1:25; 2:23; 3:16, 17.
68. These are the first and last occurrences in the letter of "wisdom" (σοφία), which occurs elsewhere in 1:28; 2:3, 23; 3:16. And these are the first and last occurrences in the letter of the verb "walk" (περιπατέω), which occurs elsewhere in 2:6 and 3:7.
69. These represent the last four of the five occurrences of the word "heaven" (οὐρανός) in the letter; it occurred for the first time in 1:5.
70. That these are the only occurrences in the letter of the prepositional phrase "through him" (δι' αὐτοῦ) enhances the significance of this parallelism.
71. These represent the last two of the three occurrences of the noun "work" (ἔργον) in the letter, which first occurred in 1:10, while this is the only occurrence of the verb "work" (ἐργάζομαι) in the letter.
72. These represent the first and last occurrences of the word "flesh" (σάρξ) in the letter, which occurs elsewhere in 1:24; 2:1, 5, 11, 13, 18, 23.

of the D´ unit. And "to his holy ones (ἁγίοις)" in 1:26 of the D unit parallels "as God's chosen ones, holy (ἅγιοι) and beloved" in 3:12 of the D´ unit.[73]

"Admonishing (νουθετοῦντες) every human being and teaching (διδάσκοντες) every human being in all wisdom (ἐν πάσῃ σοφίᾳ)" in 1:28 of the D unit parallels "in all wisdom (ἐν πάσῃ σοφίᾳ) teaching (διδάσκοντες) and admonishing (νουθετοῦντες) each other" in 3:16 of the D´ unit.[74] While "admonishing every human being (ἄνθρωπον) and teaching every human being (ἄνθρωπον) in all wisdom, that we may present every human being (ἄνθρωπον)" in 1:28 of the D unit parallels "having removed the old human being (ἄνθρωπον)" in 3:9 of the D´ unit.[75] And "that we may present every human being complete (τέλειον)" in 1:18 of the D unit parallels "the bond of completeness (τελειότητος)" in 3:14 of the D´ unit.[76]

"As they are held together in love (ἀγάπῃ)" in 2:2 of the D unit parallels "And over all these things love (ἀγάπην)" in 3:14 of the D´ unit.[77] And finally, "for the knowledge (εἰς ἐπίγνωσιν) of the mystery of God" in 2:2 of the D unit parallels "having put on the new which is being renewed for knowledge (εἰς ἐπίγνωσιν) according to the image of the one who created it" in 3:10 of the D´ unit.[78]

E: Walk and Live in Christ with Whom You Have Died and Been Raised (2:6–23)
E´: You Died and Were Raised with Christ from Living as You Once Walked (3:1–7)

"As then you received Christ Jesus the Lord, in him walk (περιπατεῖτε)" in 2:6 of the E unit parallels "Among whom you also walked (περιεπατήσατέ) once" in 3:7 of the E´ unit. "You were raised with him (συνηγέρθητε)" in 2:12 of the E unit parallels "If then you were raised (συνηγέρθητε) with Christ" in 3:1 of the E´ unit, the only two occurrences in the letter of this verb form.

"He (God) brought you to life along with him (σὺν αὐτῷ)," that is, with Christ,

---

73. These represent the last two of the six occurrences of the word "holy" (ἅγιος) in the letter, which occurred previously in 1:2, 4, 12, 22.
74. These represent the last two of the three occurrences in the letter of the phrase "in all wisdom" (ἐν πάσῃ σοφίᾳ), which occurred for the first time in 1:9. These are the only occurrences in the letter of the pairing of the verb "admonish" (νουθετέω), which occurs only in these units in the letter, with the verb "teach" (διδάσκω), which occurs elsewhere in the letter only in 2:7.
75. These represent the only occurrences in the letter of the word "human being" (ἄνθρωπος) in the singular; it occurs in the plural in 2:8, 22; 3:23.
76. This is the only occurrence in the letter of the noun "completeness" (τελειότης), while the adjective "complete" (τέλειος) occurs also in 4:12.
77. These represent the last two of the five occurrences in the letter of the word "love" (ἀγάπη), which occurred previously in 1:4, 8, 13.
78. These are the only occurrences in the letter of the phrase "for knowledge" (εἰς ἐπίγνωσιν) and represent the last two of the four occurrences of the word "knowledge" (ἐπίγνωσις), which occurred previously in 1:9, 10.

in 2:13 of the E unit parallels "Whenever Christ, your life, is manifested, then you also will be manifested with him (σύν αὐτῷ) in glory" in 3:4 of the E´ unit, the only two occurrences in the letter of this particular prepositional phrase. "If you died (ἀπεθάνετε) with Christ (σὺν Χριστῷ)" in 2:20 of the E unit parallels "for you have died (ἀπεθάνετε) and your life has been hidden with Christ (σύν τῷ Χριστῷ)" in 3:3 of the E´ unit, the only two occurrences in the letter of this verb form as well as of this particular prepositional phrase.[79] And finally, "as if living (ζῶντες) in the world" in 2:20 of the E unit parallels "when you lived (ἐζῆτε) in these" in 3:7 of the E´ unit, the only two occurrences in the letter of this verb form.

C. Overview of the Parallels of the Macrochiasm in Colossians

A 1:1-2: will of God (θελήματος θεοῦ, v. 1a)–brother (ἀδελφός, v. 1b)–faithful (πιστοῖς, v. 2b)–brothers (ἀδελφοῖς, v. 2b)–grace (χάρις, v. 2c)
A´ 4:7-18: brother (ἀδελφός, v. 7)–faithful (πιστός, v. 7)–faithful (πιστῷ, v. 9)–brother (ἀδελφῷ, v. 9)–will of God (θελήματι τοῦ θεοῦ, v. 12c) brothers (ἀδελφούς, v. 15)–grace (χάρις, v. 18)

B 1:3-14: we thank (εὐχαριστοῦμεν, v. 3)–praying (προσευχόμενοι, v. 3)–word (λόγῳ, v. 5)–praying (προσευχόμενοι, v. 9)–wisdom (σοφίᾳ, v. 9)–walk (περιπατῆσαι, v. 10)–thanking (εὐχαριστοῦντες, v. 12)
B´ 4:2-6: prayer (προσευχῇ, v. 2)–thanksgiving (εὐχαριστίᾳ, v. 2)–praying (προσευχόμενοι, v. 3a)–word (λόγου, v. 3a)–wisdom (σοφίᾳ, v. 5)–walk (περιπατεῖτε, v. 5)–word (λόγος, v. 6)

C 1:15-23: heavens (οὐρανοῖς, v. 16)–heavens (οὐρανοῖς, v. 20b)–through him (δι' αὐτοῦ, v. 16)–works (ἔργοις, v. 21)–flesh (σαρκός, v. 22)–heaven (οὐρανόν, v. 23)
C´ 3:17-4:1: work (ἔργῳ, v. 17)–through him (δι' αὐτοῦ, v. 20, twice)–flesh (σάρκα, v. 22)–heaven (οὐρανῷ, v. 1)

D 1:24-2:5: body (σώματος, v. 24)–word (λόγον, v. 25)–holy ones (ἁγίοις, v. 26)–admonishing (νουθετοῦντες, v. 28)–human being (ἄνθρωπον, v. 28)–teaching (διδάσκοντες, v. 28)–human being (ἄνθρωπον, v. 28)–in all wisdom (ἐν πάσῃ σοφίᾳ, v. 28)–human being (ἄνθρωπον, v. 28)–complete (τέλειον)–love (ἀγάπη, v. 2)–for knowledge (εἰς ἐπίγνωσιν, v. 2)
D´ 3:8-16: human being (ἄνθρωπον, v. 9)–for knowledge (εἰς ἐπίγνωσιν, v. 10)–holy (ἅγιοι, v. 12)–love (ἀγάπην, v. 14)–completeness (τελειότητος, v. 14)–body (σώματι, v. 15)–word (λόγος, v. 16)–in all wisdom (ἐν πάσῃ σοφίᾳ, v. 16)–teaching (διδάσκοντες, v. 16)–admonishing (νουθετοῦντες, v. 16)

---

79. The only difference being that the phrase in 3:3 includes the article before "Christ."

E 2:6–23: walk (περιπατεῖτε, v. 6)–you have been raised with (συνηγέρθητε, v. 12)–with him (σὺν αὐτῷ, v. 13)–you died (ἀπεθάνετε, v. 20)–with Christ (σὺν Χριστῷ, v. 20)–living (ζῶντες, v. 20)

E′ 3:1–7: you have been raised with (συνηγέρθητε, v. 1)–you died (ἀπεθάνετε, v. 3)–with Christ (σὺν τῷ Χριστῷ, v. 3)–with him (σὺν αὐτῷ, v. 4)–walked (περιεπατήσατέ, v. 7)–lived (ἐζῆτε, v. 7)

D. Outline of the Macrochiastic Structure of Colossians

A: 1:1–2: Grace from Paul an Apostle by the Will of God
  B: 1:3–14: Thanking God When Praying for You to Walk in Wisdom
    C: 1:15–23: The Gospel Preached to Every Creature under Heaven
      D: 1:24–2:5: We Are Admonishing and Teaching Every Human in All Wisdom
        E: 2:6–23: Walk and Live in Christ with Whom You Have Died and Been Raised
        E′: 3:1–7: You Died and Were Raised with Christ from Living as You Once Walked
      D′: 3:8–16: In All Wisdom Teaching and Admonishing One Another
    C′: 3:17–4:1: You Have a Master in Heaven
  B′: 4:2–6: Pray for Us in Thanksgiving and Walk in Wisdom
A′: 4:7–18: Full Assurance in All the Will of God and Grace from Paul

E. Summary

1. There are ten distinct units in the letter to the Colossians with each exhibiting its own microchiastic structure.

2. The ten units comprising Colossians operate as a macrochiastic structure with five pairs of parallel units and with the pivot of this macrochiastic structure occurring in the progression from the E unit in 2:6–23 to the E′ unit in 3:1–7.

3
Colossians 1:1–2

Grace from Paul an Apostle by the Will of God (A)

To holy ones and faithful brothers in Christ
A: [1:1a] Paul, apostle of Christ Jesus through the will of *God*,
   B: [1b] and Timothy the *brother*
      C: [2a] to those in Colossae,
   B': [2b] holy ones and faithful *brothers* in Christ,
A': [2c] grace to you and peace from *God* our Father.[1]

A. Audience Response to Colossians 1:1–2

1. Col 1:1a (A): Paul, Apostle of Christ Jesus through the Will of God

In the opening A (1:1a) element of the chiasm that commences the letter the audience are addressed by an author-sender who identifies himself as "Paul, apostle of Christ Jesus."[2] That Paul is an "apostle" (ἀπόστολος) means that he has been "sent out" or authorized to be a delegate or representative to deliver a message on behalf of the one who sent him.[3] That Paul is an apostle "of Christ Jesus" tells the audience not only that Paul has been sent by and speaks with the authority of Christ Jesus, but that he is in service or allegiance to Christ Jesus to whom he

---

1. For the establishment of Col 1:1–2 as a chiasm, see ch. 2.
2. Dunn, *Colossians*, 43: "[T]he Colossian recipients of the letter would have no doubt that the Paul named at the head of the letter was the famous/infamous missionary who had brought the message of a Jewish Messiah/Christ so effectively to Gentiles."
3. Paul K. Moser ("Apostle," *Eerdmans Dictionary of the Bible* [ed. David Noel Freedman; Grand Rapids: Eerdmans, 2000] 78) defines "apostle" as "'One sent out,' generally to proclaim a message. NT use is continuous with the OT idea of a special messenger from God." Jan-Adolf Bühner, "ἀπόστολος," *EDNT* 1.143: "Paul employs the concept ἀπόστολος in the service of an emphatically dignified and authoritative self-introduction . . . With this word he describes his task of proclaiming the gospel: he is authorized, as a messenger and representative of the crucified and risen Lord, to bring the gospel to the churches of the Gentile Christians." Dunn, *Colossians*, 44: "[T]he authority of the apostle lay behind the letter, and that would be sufficient to ensure that the letter was treasured by the Colossians and/or other of the other churches to which the letter was circulated (cf. 4:16), subsequently to be included in the earliest collection(s) of Paul's letters."

belongs as an apostle.[4] This introductory phrase, then, attunes the audience to hear what Christ Jesus himself is going to communicate to them through his devoted apostle Paul in the letter to follow.[5]

It is "through the will of God" that Paul is an apostle of Christ Jesus. This communicates three things to the audience: First, Paul is an apostle of Christ Jesus not because of his own initiative, merit, or accomplishment but because he has been chosen, appointed, and thus graced by God.[6] Second, as an apostle Paul speaks with an authority that comes not only from Christ Jesus but through the very "will" (θελήματος)—the salvific purpose or plan—of God himself.[7] And third, as

---

4. Bühner, "ἀπόστολος," 143–44: "The meaning of ἀπόστολος is tied to the peculiar character the word has attained as a result of popular-juridical usage which has drawn on its Hebrew equivalent, *šālîaḥ*. Already according to pre-NT legal practice, which the rabbinic sources merely fix in written form, the *šālîaḥ* is the direct representative of the one who sends him and can in that person's place act in a way that is authoritative and legally binding. He is obligated to strict obedience and to act in all matters in the best interests of the one who sends him. The linking of the term 'apostle' with legal titles which point to the perpetual bond to the one who sends and the task given by him to the Church corresponds to the custom of masters who appointed deputies as their representatives in charge of the household. One must add, finally, the countless observations which testify that not only Paul's calling but also his understanding of his mission as a whole is to be understood from the perspective of the OT prophets: in post-biblical Judaism the prophet was also called a *šālîaḥ* of God." See also Francis H. Agnew, "The Origin of the NT Apostle-Concept: A Review of Research," *JBL* 105 (1986): 75–96; Paul W. Barnett, "Apostle," *DPL*, 45–51; Deterding, *Colossians*, 21–22. Dunn, *Colossians*, 44: "But as always in Paul's claims for his own apostleship, the claim is that his commission and authorization came directly from Christ Jesus. It is as a representative of and spokesman for Christ Jesus, therefore, that Paul would lay claim to a hearing—not simply as spokesman for some agreed tradition or some church council. And for Paul that meant a commission and authorization equal in weight to that of the earliest and most prominent Christian leadership (1 Cor. 15:1–11; 2 Cor. 12:11–12; Gal. 2:7–9). In other words, the added phrase is not merely a matter of providing fuller identification, as though the name 'Paul' was insufficient. It is also and still more a claim to authority and respect."

5. Dunn, *Colossians*, 45: "Behind the two words 'Christ Jesus,' therefore, we must understand a whole body of preaching and teaching about Christ Jesus, on which the Colossian congregation was founded and which could be summed up in these two words."

6. O'Brien, *Colossians*, 2: "There is no suggestion of high-handedness on Paul's part when he styles himself as 'apostle'; as such he belongs to Christ Jesus and has been called to this ministry 'through the will of God,' an expression that is tantamount to a declaration of God's unmerited grace, as well as a renunciation of personal worth."

7. Margaret Y. MacDonald, *Colossians and Ephesians* (SP 17; Collegeville, Minn.: Liturgical Press, 2000), 191: "To state that Paul is an apostle 'by the will of God' is to stress Paul's apostolic authority." Dunn, *Colossians*, 46–47: "It is characteristic of the opening paragraphs of Paul's letters that he takes care to provide what we might call balancing mentions of Christ and God (cf. Rom. 1:1, 7–8; Gal. 1:1; Phil. 1:3–4; 1 Thess. 1:1–3). Christ Jesus is nowhere thought of as an authority independent of God. . . . but the phrase ['through the will of God'] rounds out a mutually reinforcing mesh of authority: Paul as apostle of Christ Jesus, Jesus as Christ owned and authorized by God, and God as the one God of Israel through whose Messiah and apostle good news is extending to the nations." Deterding, *Colossians*, 22–23: "As also in the salutation of 1 and 2 Corinthians, Ephesians, and 2 Timothy, Paul here identifies himself as one who is an apostle 'through the will of God.' This prepositional phrase indicates that the apostolic office is not one that a man takes upon himself. It must be bestowed on him by another, namely, God in Christ Jesus."

an apostle of Christ Jesus Paul is playing an important role in accord with God's salvific "will" or "purpose" that demands his obedience and the audience's attention.[8] The audience are thus poised to hear what Christ Jesus has sent Paul to communicate to them that is in accord with the authority of the decisive and purposeful will of God.

2. Col 1:1b (B): And Timothy the Brother

The letter is sent not only by Paul but by someone named "Timothy" and designated as "the brother" (1:1b).[9] The mention of Timothy along with Paul as a sender of the letter indicates to the audience that the content of what is to follow comes not just from Paul, as an authoritative apostle, but also from one who is a close associate and co-worker of Paul, indeed one who can be considered as a "brother" to Paul.[10] In addition, that Timothy is designated as *the* brother (ὁ ἀδελφός)—not simply "my" brother or "your" brother or even "our" brother—means that the letter comes from Paul, an apostle, and not only from one who is a "brotherly" co-worker of Paul but from one who is a fellow believer along with the Colossians, from one to whom both Paul and the audience can relate to as a fellow,

---

8. Wright, *Colossians*, 46: "The supporting claim, that this apostleship came about *by* (literally, 'through') *the will of God*, is not merely an indication of the ultimate source of this authority, but a linking of Paul's task to the over-arching divine plan of salvation which, prepared in the Old Testament and brought to a climax in the life, death and resurrection of Jesus Christ, was now being put into effect through the world-wide mission in which Paul had been allotted a key initiating role." Dunn, *Colossians*, 47: "Here not least is evoked the characteristic Jewish understanding of time and history as a process working out in accordance with a predetermined purpose of God, with the further particularly Christian inference that Messiah Jesus is the climax of that purpose and Paul his eschatological emissary."

9. Garland, *Colossians*, 40–41: "Timothy appears as the cosender in five other letters: 2 Corinthians, Philippians, and Philemon, and with Silvanus in 1 and 2 Thessalonians. According to Acts 16:1–2, Paul met this young man during his ministry in Derbe or Lystra. Because Timothy's mother was Jewish, Paul made his status as a Jew official by circumcising him (Acts 16:3). Timothy joined Paul on his missionary travels, and Paul extolled him as a devoted son (1 Cor. 4:17; Phil. 2:22) and trusted him as a faithful emissary, sending him to various churches to help assuage anxious converts or to put out fires of conflict (1 Cor. 4:17; Phil. 2:19; 1 Thess. 3:2, 6). Although Timothy was not an apostle, Paul affirms him as one who carries on the same work (1 Cor. 16:10) and the same preaching task (2 Cor. 1:19). . . . His inclusion also makes clear that what follows is not Paul's peculiar opinion. Paul is no maverick and does not stand alone on these issues. He works with a team of ministers, and this letter reflects the consensus of those who are with him (see 4:10–14)."

10. O'Brien, *Colossians*, 3: "Of all who were associated with the apostle's mission none held a more honored place than Timothy. He is here described as a 'brother' (ἀδελφός; cf. 2 Cor 1:1; 1 Thess 3:2; Phlm 1), which in this context means not so much 'fellow-Christian' (though Timothy was obviously this, and the term has this meaning at v 2) as 'co-worker' or 'helper'. . . .the mention of Timothy alongside Paul would be a useful buttress to his own teaching position and a denial that the letter was simply an expression of his own ideas." Wilson, *Colossians*, 69: "The point of the reference to Timothy here, as in the other letters, is to indicate that Paul is not writing merely on his own account; his fellow-workers also share his concern for the well-being of the addressees."

"brotherly" believer in Christ Jesus.[11] Nevertheless, Timothy, mentioned after Paul as "the brother," remains secondary to Paul, the primary author and sender of the letter as an "apostle of Christ Jesus through the will of God" (1:1a).[12]

3. Col 1:2a (C): To Those in Colossae

The chiastic structure of this first unit reaches its central element with the mention of those to whom the letter is sent, the addressees or implied audience of the letter. Paul, an apostle of Christ Jesus through the will of God, and Timothy the brother are sending the letter to an urban audience in a specific geographical location in the Lycus river valley in the region of Phrygia in Asia Minor, namely, "to those in Colossae" (1:2a).

4. Col 1:2b (B´): Holy Ones and Faithful Brothers in Christ

Within the chiasm of this first unit the central and unparalleled C (1:2a) element ("to those in Colossae") serves as a pivotal point in the transition from the B (1:1b) element with its mention of "brother" (ἀδελφός) to the B´ (1:2b) element with its parallel mention of "brothers" (ἀδελφοῖς). The B´ element thus develops not only the C element by further specifying "those in Colossae" as "holy ones and faithful brothers in Christ" but also the B element in progressing from the description of Timothy as "the brother" to the description of the audience as faithful "brothers" in Christ.[13]

---

11. On the meaning of ἀδελφός as "brother" Johannes Beutler ("ἀδελφός," *EDNT* 1.30) states: "The prevailing sense in Paul is that of *fellow Christian*, the foundational statement being Rom 8:29: the redeemed are conformed to Christ, the 'first-born among many brethren.'" Andrew D. Clarke, "Equality or Mutuality? Paul's Use of 'Brother' Language," in *The New Testament in Its First Century Setting: Essays on Context and Background in Honour of B. W. Winter on His 65th Birthday* (ed. P. J. Williams et al.; Grand Rapids: Eerdmans, 2004), 164: "It is brotherly love which holds together the relationship between brothers . . . Brotherly love is concerned with mutuality, rather than equality." See also Reidar Aasgaard, "'Role Ethics' in Paul: The Significance of the Sibling Role for Paul's Ethical Thinking," *NTS* 48 (2002): 513–30; idem, *"My Beloved Brothers and Sisters!": Christian Siblingship in Paul* (JSNTSup 265; London: Clark, 2004); Alanna Nobbs, "'Beloved Brothers' in the New Testament and Early Christian World," in *The New Testament in Its First Century Setting: Essays on Context and Background in Honour of B. W. Winter on His 65th Birthday* (ed. P. J. Williams et al.; Grand Rapids: Eerdmans, 2004), 143–50; Philip A. Harland, "Familial Dimensions of Group Identity: 'Brothers' (Ἀδελφοί) in Associations of the Greek East," *JBL* 124 (2005): 491–513. Dunn, *Colossians*, 47–48: "It is not surprising, therefore, that 'brother' had become a title of respect ('the brother') and that Paul should so speak of several of his colleagues or particular Christians. As such the term indicates warmth of fraternal feeling and common (spiritual) kinship rather than a title or office restricted to a few special individuals."

12. David M. Hay, *Colossians* (ANTC; Nashville: Abingdon, 2000), 38: "Though Timothy may in fact have had a major hand in the composition of Colossians, the letter itself makes no such claim for him. The salutations of several other Pauline letters mention Timothy's name immediately after Paul's. Still, the emphasis of the letter is on the apostle Paul as author, not on Timothy, and the letter-writer will soon shift from 'we' (1:3–4, 7–9) to the Pauline 'I' (predominant in 1:24–2:5; 4:3–4, 7–18)."

13. On the Greek term "brothers" (ἀδελφοῖς) here Wilson (*Colossians*, 72) notes: "This word, already applied above to Timothy, was a common term for Christians, and the plural here would include the female members of the community; the masculine form could be taken to include women,

By describing "those in Colossae" as "holy ones" (ἁγίοις), Paul is making his audience aware that God has set them, like his chosen people of Israel of old, apart from other people—those not only in Colossae but in the world—and consecrated them for special benefits from and service to God.[14] The audience are to realize that whereas Paul has been set apart through the will of God to be an apostle of Christ Jesus (1:1a), God has also set them apart to be "holy ones" consecrated to God.[15]

That the audience are not only holy ones but "faithful brothers" affirms their status as Christian believers. The prepositional phrase "in Christ" expresses not so much the object of their faith as their location within a new sphere or realm of existence by being closely united with Christ through their faith.[16] While they are physically located "in Colossae," as faithful brothers they are spiritually located "in Christ."[17] That they are faithful "brothers" in Christ further attunes the audience to

---

and repetition of the word with only minor changes in termination was felt unnecessary, unless there were special reasons."

14. Dunn, *Colossians*, 48: "The substantive ('the holy ones') derives from the cultic idea of holiness as a being 'set apart from everyday usage, dedicated to God.' That idea of holiness was familiar in Hellenistic cults, but otherwise it is a characteristic and overwhelmingly Jewish category.... What is striking, therefore, is that Paul felt able to incorporate into this distinctively Jewish self-description small gatherings of predominantly Gentile believers in Christ Jesus. The important inference is that Paul understood these Gentiles to have been incorporated into Israel, the people of God, through faith in and baptism in the name of Messiah Jesus—that is, without becoming Jewish proselytes (by being circumcised)." See also Wilson, *Colossians*, 70–71.

15. Garland, *Colossians*, 41: "As God has made Paul his own as Christ's apostle, so God has made the Colossians as his covenant people in Colossae."

16. O'Brien, *Colossians*, 4: "While πιστός ('faithful') is used several times by Paul in Colossians to draw attention to the absolute reliability of his co-workers (1:7; 4:7, 9), here it has the sense of 'believing,' of being Christian. The Colossians have placed their wholehearted trust in Jesus as Son of God, Lord and Savior. The expression 'in Christ,' however, does not point to him as the one in whom they have believed so much as the one in whom they, as brothers, have been brought together into a living fellowship." Deterding, *Colossians*, 20–21: "When used of those 'in Christ' (Col 1:2), the term [πιστός] denotes those who believe and are faithful. Sometimes the latter meaning is predominant (Col 1:7; 4:7, 9). At other times, as here, the emphasis is that the faithful have saving faith (see also 2 Cor 6:15; Gal 3:9; 1 Tim 4:10; 6:2; Titus 1:6). Saving faith also involves the desire to exhibit faithfulness toward God, and faithfulness in the Christian life is possible only with saving faith; hence, neither emphasis is entirely lacking when the term is used of believers." See also Wilson, *Colossians*, 72–73.

17. Wright, *Colossians*, 47: "The two phrases 'in Christ' and 'in Colossae' are nicely balanced in the Greek... This encourages us to take 'in Christ' in a locative sense, i.e. neither merely as a synonym for 'Christian' nor in a sense of 'mystical absorption', but as referring to the Messiah, the anointed King, *in whom* the true people of God find their identity. To be described as 'in Christ' and 'in Colossae' is to be located with precision in the purposes of God, as a member both of his true people and of that particular earthly community where one is called to service and witness." See also Garland, *Colossians*, 42. Dunn, *Colossians*, 50: "[A]t the root of the phrase ['in Christ'] there seems to be a sense of intimate and existential relationship with Christ, as the phrase 'with Christ' also suggests—that is, with Christ as a living personality, risen from the dead. And ἐν seems to indicate an integration of personal (and social) identity with this Christ (in some real sense 'in' Christ; cf. Gal. 2:20), as the correlated phrase 'into Christ' and the image of 'the body of Christ' also imply." See also Deterding, *Colossians*, 23–25.

listen to what is to follow as sent not only by Paul, an "apostle" of Christ Jesus, but also by Timothy, "the brother" (1:1b).

5. Col 1:2c (A´): Grace to You and Peace from God Our Father

With its mention of "God" the A´ element of the chiasm—"Grace to you and peace from *God* (θεοῦ) our Father" (1:2c)—parallels the A element—"through the will of *God* (θεοῦ)" (1:1a). Paul's greeting of God's "grace" to "you," his audience, expresses his prayer-wish that God, who has already graced the audience in making them holy ones and believers in Christ, will grant them yet further "grace" (χάρις)—God's gracious, generous, and freely given favor.[18] This concept of the "grace" or "favor" of God is thus not only a gift from God but carries with it a connotation of divine empowerment or enablement.[19] God's grace has empowered the audience to become holy ones and will empower them to live as holy ones who are in Colossae (1:2a); it has empowered them to become believers and will empower them to live as believers who are in Christ (1:2b).

Coupled with God's grace that Paul prays to be given to his audience is "peace" (εἰρήνη)—a state of overall well-being or harmony.[20] Paul prays that with the grace of God his audience may live in peace with God, with one another as believers who are in Christ (1:2b), and, as holy ones and faithful brothers who are in Christ and in Colossae, with non-believers who are not in Christ but in Colossae (1:2a).[21]

In a progressive development of the A element of the chiasm in this first unit,

---

18. A. Boyd Luter, "Grace," *DPL*, 374: "[T]he Pauline letters all begin and end by sounding a note of grace. It is not unlikely that the apostle intended all of his writings to be viewed within the all-encompassing framework of divine grace, from beginning to end." O'Brien, *Colossians*, 5: "Paul's use of χάρις in his greetings indicates a deep prayerful concern (the element of intercession is present in the greetings) for the readers. He desires that the Colossians may apprehend more fully the grace of God in which they already stand." Garland, *Colossians*, 43: "The letter itself is intended to be a means of grace, and the word reappears in the concluding wish in Colossians 4:18."

19. James R. Harrison, *Paul's Language of Grace in Its Graeco-Roman Context* (WUNT 172; Tübingen: Mohr Siebeck, 2003), 243: "It is worth remembering that Paul links χάρις with the language of glory, wealth, mystery, and power." See also John Nolland, "Grace as Power," *NovT* 28 (1986): 26–31.

20. Ceslas Spicq, "εἰρενεύω," *TLNT* 1.424–38. Dunn, *Colossians*, 51: "The richness of the Jewish greeting 'peace' should not be lost sight of since it denotes not simply cessation of war but all that makes for well-being and prosperity in the absence of war, and not simply individual or inner peace, but also the social wholeness of harmonious relationships."

21. Judith M. Lieu, "'Grace to You and Peace': The Apostolic Greeting," *BJRL* 68 (1985): 161–78. Wright, *Colossians*, 48: "'Grace' sees Christian life and growth as the free gift of God; 'peace', with the overtones of the Hebrew word *shālôm*, encompasses not merely personal 'peace' of mind and heart, but all the wider blessings of belonging to God's covenant family. The scene is set for a letter through which Paul intends by his writing, to be a means of that grace, and so to bring about that rich and mature peace (see, e.g., 3:15)." Dunn, *Colossians*, 51: "Paul seems deliberately to have adapted the regular Greek greeting, χαίρειν ('hail, greeting'), by replacing it with χάρις ('grace') and to have linked it with the characteristic Jewish greeting, *šalom* = εἰρήνη ('peace'). The more common Jewish association was 'mercy' with 'peace.'" See also Klaus Berger, "Apostelbrief und apostolische Rede: Zum Formular frühchristlicher Briefe," *ZNW* 65 (1974): 190–231.

which mentions simply the unadorned term "God" (1:1a), Paul's prays in the A′ element for the bestowal on his audience of the grace and peace that come from "God our Father" (1:2c). The God who decisively willed and thus graced Paul to be an apostle of Christ Jesus (1:1a) is the God who is the source of grace and peace for the audience as well. By referring to God as "our *Father*," Paul alerts his audience to their sharing not only with Paul and Timothy, "the brother" (1:1b), but with all the holy ones and believers in a communal, familial, and personal relationship to God as "Father" (πατήρ).[22] Paul has thus made his audience aware that as the "you" (ὑμῖν), who have been divinely graced to be holy ones and believing "brothers" in Christ (1:2b), they are part of the "we"—Paul, Timothy, and all the holy ones and believers who live under the fatherhood of God as "*our* (ἡμῶν) Father" (1:2c).[23]

B. Summary on Colossians 1:1–2

1. In the opening elements of the chiasm in 1:1–2 Paul indicates that he has not only received God's grace in being designated an authoritative apostle of Christ Jesus through the purposeful, salvific will of God (1:1a), but responds to God's grace by exercising his apostleship in writing and sending, together with Timothy, "the brother" (1:1b), this letter to "those in Colossae" (1:2a).

2. The Colossian audience are addressed by Paul as those who have also received God's grace and the empowerment to respond to it as both "holy ones"— those set apart and consecrated by God for special benefits from and service to God—and "faithful brothers in Christ"—believing fellow Christians now within the realm of being "in Christ" (1:2b) while also in Colossae (1:2a).

3. Paul's introductory prayer-wish in the concluding elements of the chiasm in 1:1–2 that continued grace as well as peace be granted to his audience from God our Father (1:2c) prepares the audience to further receive and experience, by their listening to what Christ Jesus himself is going to communicate to them in this letter from his authorized apostle Paul and Timothy the brother, the empowerment that comes from the grace and peace that are special gifts from God as "our Father"—the Father of all brotherly believers.

---

22. On the background of the concept of God as Father, see Otto Michel, "πατήρ," *EDNT* 3.53–57.
23. Dunn, *Colossians*, 52: "What is striking here . . . is that a relationship claimed particularly by Israel for itself and for the righteous within Israel is appropriated also by Gentile believers: 'our God.' Paul's implicit claim is that by accepting the gospel of Christ and his Spirit Gentiles were incorporated into Israel/the family of God." Wilson, *Colossians*, 75: "The salutation is conventional, but not merely formal and remote. There is as yet nothing to indicate that the addressees are unknown to the author. They are addressed as brothers and sisters in Christ, fellow-members of the Christian society."

4
COLOSSIANS 1:3–14

Thanking God When Praying for You to Walk in Wisdom (B)

Bearing fruit and growing in the knowledge of God
A: ³ *We thank* God the *Father* of our Lord Jesus Christ always when praying for you, ⁴ having heard of your faith in Christ Jesus and the *love* which you *have* for all the *holy ones*
    B: ⁵ because of the hope laid up for you in the heavens, which you have heard before in the word of the truth of the gospel ⁶ that has come to you, as indeed in *all* the world it is *bearing fruit and growing*, so also among you, *from the day you heard* and *came to know* the grace of *God* in truth,
        C: ⁷ as you learned it from Epaphras our beloved fellow slave, who is a faithful minister of Christ on behalf of you, ⁸ who also has informed us of your love in the Spirit.
    B′: ⁹ Therefore we also, *from the day we heard*, do not cease praying on behalf of you and asking that you may be filled with the *knowledge* of his will in all wisdom and Spiritual understanding, ¹⁰ to walk worthy of the Lord for every desire to please, in *every* good work *bearing fruit and growing* with regard to the *knowledge* of *God*, ¹¹ in all power empowered according to the might of his glory for all endurance and patience,
A′: with joy ¹² *thanking* the *Father* who has made you fit for the share of the inheritance of the *holy ones* in the light. ¹³ He has rescued us from the authority of the darkness and has transferred us into the kingdom of the Son of his love, ¹⁴ in whom *we have* redemption, the forgiveness of sins.[1]

A. Audience Response to Colossians 1:3–14

1. Col 1:3–4 (A): The Love You Have for All the Holy Ones

After his prayer-wish that his audience further experience the grace and peace that come "*from* God our Father" (1:2b), Paul along with Timothy immediately

---

1. For the establishment of Col 1:3–14 as a chiasm, see ch. 2.

give thanks *to* God at the beginning of this chiasm's A element (1:3-4):² "We thank the God and Father of our Lord Jesus Christ" (1:3a).³ Paul thus thanks the God and Father of Jesus Christ, who is "our" Lord, that is, the Lord not only of Paul and Timothy but of the audience and all believers. That God is not only "our" (ἡμῶν) Father (1:2b) but the Father of "our" (ἡμῶν) Lord Jesus Christ (1:3a) prepares the audience for what the Lord Jesus Christ's relationship to God as his Father means for the audience's relationship not only to God as "our" Father but to Jesus Christ as "our" Lord.⁴ When the audience hear the words "God (θεῷ) the Father (πατρί)," they hear the transitional words that link this unit (1:3-14) with the previous one (1:1-2), which concluded with the greeting of "grace to you and peace from God (θεοῦ) our Father (πατρός)" (1:2).

The prayer report that Paul and Timothy thank the God and Father of our Lord Jesus Christ "always when praying for you (ὑμῶν) " (1:3b) reinforces the previous prayer-wish that "grace and peace from God our Father be with you (ὑμῖν)" (1:2c).⁵ It further strengthens the bond between the senders and audience of the

---

2. A sustained alliteration of words beginning with "p" (π) in each of the clauses in 1:3-4 contributes to the unity of this A element—πατρί-πάντοτε περί-προσευχόμενοι-πίστιν-πάντας—and distinguishes it from the B element in 1:5-6, whose first clause (1:5a) lacks the letter "p." The preposition περί ("for," "concerning") may have been employed here rather than the variant reading ὑπέρ ("on behalf of") for the sake of the alliteration. On the issue of whether the plural "we thank" (εὐχαριστοῦμεν) is a real or an "epistolary" plural—that is, whether it includes both Paul and Timothy (real) or only refers to Paul (epistolary)—Wilson (*Colossians*, 81) states: "In Col., as already noted, after using plurals at vv. 3, 7 and 9 the author switches to the singular at 1.23 and uses it consistently to the end of the letter. This suggests that the plural here should be taken as a real plural."

3. On the introductory thanksgiving here, see Paul Schubert, *Form and Function of the Pauline Thanksgiving* (BZNW 20; Berlin: Töpelmann, 1939); Peter Thomas O'Brien, *Introductory Thanksgivings in the Letters of Paul* (NovTSup 49; Leiden: Brill, 1977); Terrence Y. Mullins, "The Thanksgivings of Philemon and Colossians," *NTS* 30 (1984): 288-93.

4. With regard to the phrase "the Father of our Lord Jesus Christ" here Dunn (*Colossians*, 55-56) comments: "Contained in it is the implicit Christian claim that God, the one God made known to Israel, is now to be understood no longer simply as Father of Israel, but most clearly as the Father of Jesus Christ, and only as such 'our Father', Father of Gentiles as well as Jews.... it is important to recognize that Paul and Timothy begin by reminding their readers... that God is the *God* and Father of our *Lord* Jesus Christ. From the outset, therefore, Paul and Timothy wish it to be understood that the high christology to be enunciated shortly is kept within the constraints of Jewish monotheism. God the Father is the one to whom prayer should properly be ordered, just as he is the ultimate source ('Father') of all creation and all being, including the dignity and authority of Jesus' Messiahship and Lordship." Wilson, *Colossians*, 83: "What is central to talk of God as Father is not any mere masculinity but the kindness, graciousness, tolerance and mercy, and other attributes which characterize the ideal father."

5. The adverb "always" (πάντοτε) should be construed with the preceding verb "we thank" (εὐχαριστοῦμεν) rather than with the succeeding participle "praying" (προσευχόμενοι). Wilson, *Colossians*, 83: "[W]here a πάντοτε occurs in the formula in other letters (1 Cor., 1 Thess., 2 Thess.; the structure in Phil. is different), it clearly belongs with εὐχαριστῶ (cf. also Eph. 5.20), which suggests that here too it should be taken with εὐχαριστοῦμεν and not with προσευχόμενοι." With regard to the significance of the adverb "always" here O'Brien (*Colossians*, 10) points out that it does not refer "to unceasing thanksgiving. To speak of prayer by this and similar terms (e.g. 'continually,' 'at all times,' 'day

letter, making the Colossians aware not only of Paul and Timothy's appreciative gratitude but prayerful concern for them.⁶

Paul and Timothy's "having heard of your faith (πίστιν) in Christ Jesus" (1:4a) further affirms and underlines the status of the Colossians as "faithful (πιστοῖς) brothers (and sisters) in Christ" (1:2b).⁷ "In Christ Jesus" once again expresses not the object of their faith but the realm or "lordship" in which they exist in union with Christ, as indicated by the previous reference to our "Lord" Jesus Christ (1:3a).⁸ That Paul and Timothy have heard also of "the love you have for all the holy ones" (1:4b) affirms the strong bond of love that links the Colossians as "holy ones" (ἁγίοις, 1:2b) to all of their fellow believers, all of the "holy ones" (ἁγίους, 1:4b) throughout the world.⁹

In the A (1:3–4) element of this second unit's chiasm, then, the audience are assured of Paul and Timothy's loving care and concern in always thanking God as the Father of our Lord Jesus Christ when they pray for the audience (1:3). The faith that the audience have within the realm of their being in Christ Jesus and the love they have for all the holy ones is affirmed (1:4), thus establishing a close bond of love between the audience and not only Paul and Timothy but all other holy ones, all other fellow believers.

2. Col 1:5–6 (B): *In All the World the Gospel You Heard Is Bearing Fruit and Growing*

The motivation for the love the Colossian audience has for all the holy ones as well as the faith they have in God within the realm of their being in union with

---

and night') was part and parcel of the style of ancient letters, being a Jewish practice as well as a pagan one. A measure of hyberbole is also to be noted in these expressions."

6. Gordon P. Wiles, *Paul's Intercessory Prayers: The Significance of the Intercessory Prayer Passages in the Letters of St. Paul* (SNTSMS 24; Cambridge: Cambridge University Press, 1974), 156: "At the beginning of most of his letters, in the formal thanksgiving period, the apostle assures his readers not only of his continual thanksgivings for them, but also of his constant intercessions on their behalf, and he indicates briefly some of the contents of his prayers." Dunn, *Colossians*, 56: "The use of περί ('concerning') rather than ὑπέρ ('on behalf of') is sufficient to indicate that Paul saw his prayers not as a substitute for their own prayers but as a natural expression of Christian love and concern."

7. On the meaning of "faith" here Wilson (*Colossians*, 86) points out: "It is fundamentally a believing and trusting response to the revelation of God in Christ, with the obedience which such a response entails. This faith is the basis of the Christian life, the source and inspiration of Christian love and charity."

8. O'Brien, *Colossians*, 11: "This faith is 'in Christ Jesus' (ἐν Χριστῷ Ἰησοῦ), an expression which does not denote the object to which their faith is directed but rather indicates the sphere in which 'faith' lives and acts. The Colossian Christians live under the lordship of Christ Jesus for they have been incorporated into him." See also Bruce, *Colossians*, 41; Wilson, *Colossians*, 86–87.

9. According to Dunn (*Colossians*, 58) "love" (ἀγάπη) here refers to "an active concern for one another among the Colossian Christians which did not stop short of self-sacrifice of personal interests—and not just for one another, if the 'all the saints' is to be taken seriously." Wilson, *Colossians*, 87: "Christians chose a word that was not widely used, and gave it a new depth of meaning. . . . This love is a human response to the love of God revealed in Christ, and knows no bounds."

Christ Jesus (1:4) is expressed at the beginning of this chiasm's B element (1:5-6): "because of the hope laid up for you in the heavens" (1:5a).[10] The future object of the hope that the audience may with full confidence look forward to is a certainty "laid up" (ἀποκειμένην) by God (divine passive) and reserved as a destiny safe and sure for them in the divine, transcendent realm of the heavens.[11] Such a divinely assured hope has inspired not only their faith in God as Christians but their love for all of their fellow believers, the holy ones.[12]

The audience heard about this assured hope when they first heard the word of the gospel preached to them and became believers: "which you have heard before in the word of the truth of the gospel" (1:5b). The employment of the word "truth" (ἀληθείας) in the phrase "the word of the truth of the gospel" alerts the audience to the possibility that they have heard of another word of falsehood not in accord with the truth of the gospel they originally heard.[13]

---

10. The integrity and distinctiveness of 1:5-6 as the B element within the chiasm in 1:3-14 is secured by the only occurrences in this unit of the second person plural pronoun in the dative case—"laid up for you (ὑμῖν)" in 1:5a and "so also among you (ὑμῖν)" in 1:6b, the only occurrences in this unit of a form of the verb "to hear" in the indicative aorist active second person plural—"of which you have heard before (προηκούσατε)" in 1:5b and "from the day you heard (ἠκούσατε)" in 1:6c, and the only occurrences in the entire letter of the noun "truth"—"the truth (ἀληθείας) of the gospel" in 1:5b and "the grace of God in truth (ἀληθείᾳ)" in 1:6c.

11. For the argument that there is more futurist eschatology in Colossians than is commonly held and that there is less variance between the eschatological perspective of Colossians and the other letters of Paul than is typically recognized, see Todd D. Still, "Eschatology in Colossians: How Realized is It?" *NTS* 50 (2004): 125-38.

12. Garland, *Colossians*, 48: "A sure hope is the source of faith and love. What is interesting in this formulation is that hope is not grounded in faith, but the reverse—faith is grounded in hope. 'Hope,' therefore, does not refer to the 'subjective attitude of expectation.' Rather, it refers to the thing hoped for. Paul does not clarify what that hope precisely is except that it is stored up in heaven." O'Brien, *Colossians*, 11-12: "It [hope] already lies prepared (ἀποκειμένην) for them in the heavens, a phrase from common parlance denoting certainty. The Colossian Christians are assured that everything contained in their hope is kept for them in its right place—in heaven where no power, human or otherwise, can touch it." Dunn, *Colossians*, 58-60: "Given the fact that faith and love have already been given prominent mention, it should occasion no surprise that the third member of the characteristic Christian trio, ἐλπίς ('hope'), should immediately appear in close connection. For the linking of the three is another distinctive feature of Pauline teaching. 'Hope' itself is almost as distinctively a Pauline feature in the New Testament (36 of 53 occurrences).... The plural form 'heavens' should not be ignored, since it is hardly found in nonbiblical Greek and therefore reflects the common Jewish view that the heavenly realm above had a number of regions, if not many. If the usual topography is in mind here, the implication would be that the lower reaches of heaven were populated by (normally hostile) 'principalities and powers,' with God and his angels in the upper regions or beyond all the heavens. The hope, then, would be for a destiny that outmaneuvers and defeats these powers and reaches right into the presence of God."

13. Deterding, *Colossians*, 29: "The aorist tense of 'heard about beforehand' (προηκούσατε) refers to the readers' initial coming to faith through the 'Word.' The 'Word' is here indicated as that which gives hope (see also 1:23) and consequently also bestows faith and love. Paul uses 'truth' (see also 1:6) to designate facticity and reliability." Dunn, *Colossians*, 61: "[I]mplicit in the language is the emphatic Pauline claim that the gospel is for Gentiles also, without requiring them to become proselytes... there

The Colossian audience are then made aware of their place within the ongoing fruitfulness and growth of this gospel throughout the whole world: "(the gospel) that has come to you, as indeed in all the world it is bearing fruit and growing, so also among you, from the day you heard and came to know the grace of God in truth" (1:6).[14] The parallel powerful effect that the preaching of the word of truth of the gospel has on both the whole world and the audience is indicated by a more strictly literal translation and by the a-b-a´-b´ structure of 1:6b, in which the b´ element is a grammatical ellipsis:

a: as also in all the world (καθὼς καὶ ἐν παντὶ τῷ κόσμῳ)
b: it is bearing fruit and growing (ἐστὶν καρποφορούμενον καὶ αὐξανόμενον)
a´: as also in you (καθὼς καὶ ἐν ὑμῖν)
(b´: it is bearing fruit and growing [ἐστὶν καρποφορούμενον καὶ αὐξανόμενον])

This somewhat unusual grammatical structure has its rhetorical purpose. It makes the audience aware, on the one hand, that what has been going on elsewhere with regard to the gospel has reached, embraced, and incorporated even them who are in Colossae—"that has come to you" (1:6a), so that they by no means should feel left out of this world-wide phenomenon. It also makes the audience aware, on the other hand, that what has happened among them with regard to the gospel is not a phenomenon isolated or limited to Colossae, so that they should consider themselves somehow unique, but something happening throughout the whole world of which they are an integral part.

The word order—"bearing fruit and growing"—rather than a more expected "growing and bearing fruit" gives the impression of the continual, ongoing, and open-ended growth of the gospel throughout the world—it does not merely grow and bear fruit, but continues to grow even after the bearing of fruit.[15] In accord with the biblical tradition in which all agricultural growth and fruit-bearing has its origin in God as Creator (cf. Gen 1–2, etc.), the metaphorical "bearing fruit and growing" of the gospel is due not to any human achievement but to the creative power of God. This creative power of God has an automatic, independent,

---

is probably a further implication that this is a truth that has to be stoutly maintained against teachings that deny or diminish the eschatological thrust of the gospel's emphasis on hope."

14. With regard to "in all (παντί) the world" here, "The universal scope of the apostolic gospel appears . . . in the letter's extensive use of formulations with πᾶς, πᾶσα, πᾶν—over thirty of them," according to Walter T. Wilson, *The Hope of Glory: Education and Exhortation in the Epistle to the Colossians* (NovTSup 88; Leiden: Brill, 1997), 73.

15. Joseph Barber Lightfoot, *The Epistles of St Paul: Colossians and Philemon* (London: Macmillan, 1875), 133: "The Gospel is not like those plants which exhaust themselves in bearing fruit and wither away. The external growth keeps pace with the reproductive energy." Garland, *Colossians*, 40: "The gospel, however, continues to produce harvest after harvest." Hay, *Colossians*, 43: "The use of the terms 'bearing fruit' and 'growing' is the first instance of a major stylistic feature of Colossians, the use of repetitious phrasing for emphasis."

and inevitable dimension to it, as connoted by the middle voice of the participle "bearing fruit" (καρποφορούμενον), that is, bearing fruit of itself or automatically (by God), and the passive voice of the participle "growing" (αὐξανόμενον), which may be considered to function as a divine passive even though it has an active, intransitive meaning.[16]

The agricultural metaphor of the gospel "bearing fruit and growing" among the audience in Colossae as well as in the whole world is open to referring both to the continual, ongoing, and extensive increase in the number of those who are becoming believers and to the continual, ongoing, and intensive spiritual and/or moral development within the believers themselves.[17]

"From the day you heard and came to know the grace of God in truth" (1:6c) reinforces, intensifies, and develops "which (hope) you have heard before in the word of the truth of the gospel" (1:5b). "From the day," that is, from the very first time, immediately and without hesitation or delay, "you," the audience, "heard" (ἠκούσατε) and came to know the grace of God in truth, which includes the hope "you heard before" (προηκούσατε) in the word of the truth of the gospel, that very gospel has been bearing fruit and growing among the audience. That the audience have not only heard but come to know—not only intellectually but experientially—the grace of God is indicated by the gracious gifts given them already by God—their faith, love, and hope (1:4–5a).[18] That they have already come to know the "grace" (χάριν) of God reinforces the previous prayer-wish that "grace" (χάρις) continue to be given to them from God our Father (1:2c). That the audience have come to know the grace of God "in truth" (ἐν ἀληθείᾳ) means that they have experienced the grace of God within the realm or sphere of existence established and dominated by the "truth" (ἀληθείας) of the gospel (1:5b).

The B (1:5–6) element of this second unit's chiasm reminds the audience of the motivation for their faith and love—the hope laid up for them by God in the heavens, which hope they heard about in the word of the truth of the gospel (1:5). The audience are assured that they have been part of the world-wide and remarkable "bearing fruit and growing" of the gospel from the very day they heard it and experienced the grace of God within the realm of being "in truth" (1:6), thus alerting the audience to the possibility that they have heard of another word, a word of falsehood not in accord with the truth of the gospel they originally heard.

---

16. BDAG, 151, 510; Harris, *Colossians*, 19–20.

17. Dunn, *Colossians*, 62: "[B]oth ideas may be implied—the success of the gospel in producing so many mature and moral people."

18. Wolfgang Hackenberg, "ἐπιγινώσκω," *EDNT* 2.24: "*Know* means here (as in the OT and Jewish tradition) not primarily an intellectual event, but rather acceptance of the electing love of the Father." That "hope" is a specific grace given by God is indicated by the divine passive—"because of the hope laid up (ἀποκειμένην) for you (by God) in the heavens" (1:5a). Maisch, *Gemeinde in Kolossä*, 61: "Das Hören und Akzeptieren der Verkündigung war aber nicht menschliche Leistung—weder des Missionars noch der Bekehrten—, sondern das Gnadengeschenk Gottes."

3. Col 1:7–8 (C): Epaphras Has Informed Us of Your Love in the Spirit

The audience are then assured that they have learned this gospel from a very reliable source: "as you learned it from Epaphras our beloved fellow slave, who is a faithful minister of Christ on behalf of you" (1:7).[19] The audience have not only "heard" and "come to know" (1:6c) what is involved in the gospel—the grace and truth of the gospel—but "learned" (ἐμάθετε) it, suggesting that they have been carefully taught so that they have a firm foundation of knowledge with regard to the gospel.[20]

That Epaphras, the one from whom the audience have learned the gospel, is described as "our beloved fellow slave" establishes him in an endearing relationship to both the authors and audience of the letter.[21] That Epaphras is our "beloved" (ἀγαπητοῦ) fellow slave further motivates the audience, who have "love" (ἀγάπην) for all the holy ones (1:4), to extend that love to Epaphras in a special way. The audience are to realize that Epaphras, as "our fellow slave"—the fellow slave of Paul and Timothy under the lordship of our Lord Jesus Christ (1:3)—has the same authoritative concern for them as Paul and Timothy.[22]

The audience, who are themselves "faithful" (πιστοῖς) brothers in Christ (1:2b), are to appreciate that Epaphras is likewise "faithful" (πιστός) with regard to Christ—a faithful minister of Christ on behalf of or for the sake of "you," thus further endearing Epaphras to the audience. He is the faithful minister of the Christ in union with whom the audience are faithful brothers. Whereas Paul and Timothy are always praying "for you" (περὶ ὑμῶν, 1:3), Epaphras is a faithful minister of Christ "on behalf of you" (ὑπὲρ ὑμῶν, 1:7), further assuring the audience of his authoritative and reliable concern in having taught them the word of the truth of the gospel (1:5).[23]

---

19. For the choice of the variant reading "on behalf of you" rather than on "behalf of us," see ch. 2 n. 5.

20. Deterding, *Colossians*, 30: "The aorist tense of 'you learned,' like the aorists ἠκούσατε and ἐπέγνωτε in 1:6, refers to the readers' initial coming to faith." O'Brien, *Colossians*, 15: "The term 'learned' (ἐμάθετε) probably indicates that Epaphras had given them systematic instruction in the gospel rather than some flimsy outline and that these Colossians had committed themselves as disciples to that teaching." Dunn, *Colossians*, 64: "The verb used ('as you learned') may imply that Epaphras had seen his task in Colossae not simply as winning them to faith but as instructing them in the traditions and parenesis without which they would have no guidelines in translating their faith into daily living."

21. Dunn, *Colossians*, 63 n. 13: "Epaphras is a shortened from of Epaphroditus, but it is most unlikely that Epaphras is to be identified with the Epaphroditus named in Phil. 2:25 and 4:18, who is as much identified with Philippi as Epaphras is with Colossae." Garland, *Colossians*, 51: "Paul's close association with Epaphras and Epaphras's close association with the Colossians is the mutual bond that allows the apostle to write this friendly letter to them filled with instructions."

22. Dunn, *Colossians*, 64–65: "Implicit in the designation [slave], therefore, is the readiness to hand over one's life completely to a master, but to a master (Christ Jesus) whose power and authority were greater than that in any other master-slave relation." Garland, *Colossians*, 50: "He [Paul] does not view Epaphras as one of his underlings but treats him as his collaborator and clarifies that both serve Christ. Epaphras does not have two masters, Christ and Paul. He has only one—Christ."

23. Dunn, *Colossians*, 65: "At this stage the word [διάκονος-'minister'] seems to be still descriptive of an individual's sustained commitment and not yet the title of a clearly defined office."

That Epaphras "also has informed us of your love (ἀγάπην) in the Spirit" (1:8) reinforces the senders' having already heard of "the love (ἀγάπην) you have for all the holy ones" (1:4). But in this case the object of their love is left unexpressed, allowing it to include the audience's love not only for all the holy ones in general but implicitly and more specifically for Paul and Timothy as well as for Epaphras.[24] Not only are the audience faithful brothers "in Christ" (ἐν Χριστῷ, 1:2b)—within the realm of their being in union with Christ, and not only have they come to know the grace of God "in truth" (ἐν ἀληθείᾳ, 1:6c)—within the realm of truth established by the gospel, but the love they have for all the holy ones, including Paul, Timothy, and Epaphras, is "in the Spirit" (ἐν πνεύματι, 1:8)—within the realm determined by the Spirit.

The central C (1:7-8) element of this second unit's chiasm reminds the audience that they learned the gospel from Epaphras, a beloved associate of Paul and Timothy and a reliable minister of Christ for the sake of the audience (1:7). That Epaphras has informed Paul and Timothy of the audience's love within the realm of being in the Spirit (1:8) further endears not only Epaphras but Paul and Timothy to the audience, establishing a loving receptivity on the part of the audience for the authoritative care and concern—the love—they can expect to receive from Paul and Timothy as they listen to the rest of the letter.

4. Col 1:9-11 (B´): Bearing Fruit and Growing in the Knowledge of God

Within the chiasm of this second unit the central and unparalleled C (1:7-8) element serves as a pivotal point in the transition from the B (1:5-6) element to its progressive parallels in the B´ (1:9-11) element. "From the day you heard (ἀφ' ἧς ἡμέρας ἠκούσατε*) and came to know the grace of God in truth" in 1:6c of the B element progresses, by way of the chiastic parallel, to "Therefore we also," that is, "we" for our part,[25] the "we," Paul and Timothy, whom Epaphras informed of the audience's love in the Spirit (1:8) in the pivotal C element, "from the day we heard (ἀφ' ἧς ἡμέρας ἠκούσαμεν), do not cease praying on behalf of you" in 1:9a of the B´ element. Whereas *from the very day* the audience heard of the grace of God in truth—in the word of the truth of the gospel (1:5-6)—the gospel has been bearing fruit and growing among them (1:6b), correspondingly, *from the very day* Paul and Timothy heard of the audience's faith and love (cf. "having heard [ἀκούσαντες]" in 1:4) motivated by hope (1:4-5, 8), they do not cease praying on behalf of the audience, thus reinforcing the loving care and concern that closely unites Paul and Timothy with the audience.[26]

That Paul and Timothy do not cease "praying (προσευχόμενοι) on behalf of

---

24. Fee, *God's Empowering Presence*, 639: "Thus their 'love for all the saints,' mentioned already in v. 4, is now acknowledged as specifically directed toward Paul as well."

25. For this meaning see the discussion in Wilson, *Colossians*, 99.

26. Dunn, *Colossians*, 69: "'From the day we heard' is perhaps a deliberate echo of the same phrase already used in 1:6: as they were fruitful from the very day they heard the gospel, so Paul and Timothy have been prayerful from the very day they heard of their response to the gospel."

you (ὑπὲρ ὑμῶν)" (1:9) develops their previous statement about thanking the God and Father of our Lord Jesus Christ always when "praying (προσευχόμενοι) for you (περὶ ὑμῶν)" (1:3). Whereas Epaphras is a faithful minister of Christ "on behalf of you (ὑπὲρ ὑμῶν)" in 1:7b of the C element of the chiasm, Paul and Timothy do not cease praying "on behalf of you (ὑπὲρ ὑμῶν)" in 1:9a of the B´ element, thus further strengthening the loving care and concern that closely unites not only Epaphras but Paul and Timothy with the audience.

Paul and Timothy's prayer "that you may be filled with the knowledge (ἐπίγνωσιν) of his will in all wisdom and Spiritual understanding" in 1:9b of the B´ element develops, by way of the chiastic parallel, the statement that the audience "have come to know (ἐπέγνωτε) the grace of God in truth" in 1:6c of the B element.[27] With regard to the theme of knowledge, Paul and Timothy pray that the audience's experiential knowledge of the grace of God in truth progresses to their being filled by God (divine passive) with the knowledge of God's will in all wisdom and the understanding that comes from the Spirit.[28] They thus pray that the audience, who are faithful brothers (and sisters) within the realm of being "in Christ" (1:2b), who have come to know the grace of God within the realm of being "in truth" (1:6c) established by the truth of the gospel (1:5b), and who have love within the realm of being "in the Spirit" (1:8), may progress to being filled with the knowledge of God's will within the realm of being "in all wisdom and Spiritual understanding" (1:9b).[29] The audience who have love in the "Spirit" (πνεύματι, 1:8) are also to have "Spiritual" (πνευματικῇ, 1:9b) understanding.[30]

The purpose of the prayer, that the audience "walk worthy of the Lord for

---

27. O'Brien, *Colossians*, 21: "In fact, because the Colossians had *come to know* God's grace when they were converted (ἐπέγνωτε is probably an inceptive aorist), they might now be expected to grow in 'knowledge.'" Dunn, *Colossians*, 69: "No doubt the knowledge prayed for here included the teachings that follow in the letter, but hardly need be limited to that."

28. O'Brien, *Colossians*, 20: "The motif of 'fullness' recurs frequently in this epistle (note the different terms used at 1:19, 24, 25; 2:2, 3, 9, 10; 4:12, 17)."

29. Wright, *Colossians*, 58: "The three terms 'knowledge', 'wisdom' and 'understanding', so important elsewhere in Paul, are therefore best understood against their Old Testament and Jewish background, in which they regularly denote aspects of that character which God seeks to inculcate in his people." Dunn, *Colossians*, 70–71: "[T]he combination of 'wisdom and understanding' is a repeated feature of Jewish writings. Here, too, the wisdom in particular is understood as given through the law, but it is equally recognized that such wisdom can come only from above (as in Wis 9:9–10). And particularly to be noted is the recognition that wisdom and understanding come only from the Spirit (Exod. 31:3; 35:31; Isa. 11:2; Wis. 9:17–19; Sir 39:6; Philo, *De gigantibus* 22–27; 4 Ezra 14:22, 39–40). It is certainly this thought that is taken up here ('spiritual' as given by and manifesting the Spirit—cf. 1 Cor. 2:12–13; 12:1, 4; 14:1–2)." Wilson, *Colossians*, 102: "The two adjectives ['all' and 'Spiritual'] should probably be taken as qualifying both nouns—the wisdom as well as the understanding is wrought by the Spirit, and the author's prayer is that his readers may be endowed with both in full measure (cf. 1.28; 3.16, where the reference is to instruction 'in all wisdom', but without the qualification 'spiritual')."

30. "Spiritual" (πνευματικῇ) in 1:9b "is emphatic because of its position; this is no ordinary human wisdom or understanding, but wrought by the Spirit," according to Wilson, *Colossians*, 104.

every desire to please,³¹ in every (ἐν παντί) good work bearing fruit and growing (καρποφοροῦντες καὶ αὐξανόμενοι) with regard to the knowledge (ἐπιγνώσει) of God (θεοῦ)" in 1:10 of the B´ element further develops, by way of the chiastic parallelism, the statement that "as indeed in all (ἐν παντί) the world it is bearing fruit and growing (καρποφορούμενον καὶ αὐξανόμενον), so also among you, from the day you heard and came to know (ἐπέγνωτε) the grace of God (θεοῦ) in truth" in 1:6 of the B element. As the gospel *in all* the world is *bearing fruit and growing*, from the time the audience *came to know* the grace of *God* in truth, so, the prayer is, *in every* good work the audience may be *bearing fruit and growing* with regard to the *knowledge* of *God*.³² Regarding the theme of knowledge, the prayer is that the audience, who "have come to know" the grace of God in truth (1:6) may be filled by God with the "knowledge" of God's will (1:9b), so that they may bear fruit and grow with regard to the "knowledge" of God (1:10).³³

The B´ element's fivefold emphasis on "all" or "every" reaches its climax in 1:11. The audience are to be filled with the knowledge of God in "all" (πάσῃ) wisdom (1:9b) for "every" (πᾶσαν) desire to please (1:10a), in "every" (παντί) good work bearing fruit and growing with regard to the knowledge of God, "in all (πάσῃ) power empowered according to the might of his glory for all (πᾶσαν) endurance and patience" (1:11).³⁴ The prayer is thus that the audience may be gifted and equipped by God in a comprehensive way, so that they are not lacking in anything they may need with regard to their conduct and way of life.³⁵ It alerts

---

31. O'Brien, *Colossians*, 22-23: "Paul often characterizes the life and behavior of the Christian by this verb 'walk' and in this he is indebted to the OT. . . . There is no doubt that in the context of this intercessory prayer, and in the light of the apostle's use of the cognate verb, ἀρεσκεία refers to pleasing the Lord." Deterding, *Colossians*, 35: " 'Walk' here, as often in both testaments, refers to ethical conduct in Christian faith, one's 'way of life.' "

32. On 1:10 Dunn (*Colossians*, 72) states: "The imagery of 'bearing fruit and increasing' echoes 1:6, but this time clearly in reference to moral maturity."

33. O'Brien, *Colossians*, 23: "Since the participles which define the walking worthily are all in the present tense and stress the notion of progress, it is probably right to conclude that the Colossian Christians would receive further knowledge as they were obedient to the knowledge of God they had already received." On "knowledge" (ἐπιγνώσει) in 1:10 Dunn (*Colossians*, 72) notes: "Repetition of the same possibly intensive form (ἐπίγνωσις) as in 1:9 doubles the insistence that such conduct can only grow from such knowledge. The term here includes 'knowledge of his will,' but is much larger in scope, including knowledge of God's grace. Another characteristic Jewish theme, 'knowledge of God,' includes experience of God's dealings and acknowledgment of God in appropriate action."

34. Dunn, *Colossians*, 73: "[T]he Semitic doubling ('empowered with all power') is sufficient indication that the thought world here is still preeminently Jewish. . . . Still more characteristically Jewish is the talk of divine glory (δόξα) . . . . Like Hebrew *kabod*, it denotes the awesome radiance of deity that is the visible manifestation of God in theophany." Deterding, *Colossians*, 36: "In so far as they can be distinguished from one another, 'power' (δύναμις) denotes capacity or ability, while 'strength' (κράτος) has more the sense of might or force."

35. "In all power" in 1:11 "implies all the spiritual resources necessary to their Christian life," according to Wilson, *Colossians*, 108.

the audience to their need for all endurance and patience in the face of possible opposition.[36]

In the B´ (1:9–11) element of the second unit's chiasm the audience experience the loving care and concern of Paul and Timothy as they hear their prayer that the audience, who have "come to know" the grace of God within the realm of truth (1:6), may be filled by God with the "knowledge" of God's will within the realm of being in *all* wisdom and understanding that comes from the Spirit (1:9), so that they may "walk," that is, conduct themselves and live, for *every* desire to please the Lord, in *every* good work bearing fruit and growing with regard to the "knowledge" of God (1:10), empowered within the realm of *all* power according to the might of God's glory for *all* endurance and patience (1:11).

5. Col 1:12–14 (A´): Thanking the Father for a Share of the Inheritance of the Holy Ones

Paul and Timothy's announcement, "We thank (εὐχαριστοῦμεν) God the Father (πατρί) of our Lord Jesus Christ always when praying for you, having heard of your faith in Christ Jesus and the love which you have for all the holy ones (ἁγίους)" in 1:3–4 of the A element of this unit's chiasm progresses, by way of the chiastic parallels, to their description of the audience for whom they are praying in 1:12 of the A´ element: "With joy thanking (εὐχαριστοῦντες) the Father (πατρί) who has made you fit for the share of the inheritance of the holy ones (ἁγίων) in the light."[37] The senders' *thanking* of God as the *Father* in regard to the audience's love for all other believers—all the *holy ones*—progresses to the audience themselves joyfully *thanking* the *Father* who has made them fit for the share of the inheritance together with all other believers—the *holy ones* in the light.[38]

Paul and Timothy's prayer, then, is for the audience to be joyfully thanking God the Father for having made them, as composed mainly of Gentiles, fit or worthy for the share of the inheritance originally meant for the chosen people of Israel but now destined for all the holy ones as the new people of God, believing Jews and

---

36. On "all endurance and patience" Dunn (*Colossians*, 74) comments: "The two nouns are near synonyms. Both are included not so much because of their distinctive meanings but to reinforce the point that hope of heavenly glory in the future requires patience and endurance now (not least in the face of alternative religious claims) and that both the present patience and the future transformation are the outworking of the same glorious might."

37. On taking the phrase "with joy" with 1:12 rather than 1:11, see ch. 2 n. 7. "Holy ones in the light" here refers, as in 1:2, 4, to believers, and not to both believers and angels as suggested by Pierre Benoit, "'Ἅγιοι en Colossiens 1.12: hommes our anges?" in *Paul and Paulinism: Essays in Honour of Charles Kingsley Barrett* (ed. Morna D. Hooker and Stephen G. Wilson; London: SPCK, 1982), 83–101. See also, Bruce, *Colossians*, 49–50; O'Brien, *Colossian*, 26; Dunn, *Colossians*, 76–77; Garland, *Colossians*, 66 n. 13; Bevere, *Sharing*, 144; Dübbers, *Christologie*, 136. Barth and Blanke, *Colossians*, 186: "As in the OT, the word [ἁγίων–'holy ones' in 1:12] is used to designate the covenant people of Israel, in whose inheritance the 'former outsiders' are now entitled participants."

38. Deterding, *Colossians*, 36: "The apostle enjoins his readers to imitate his example of thankfulness ('we give thanks,' 1:3)."

Gentiles alike. God has privileged the audience, who have love of all the holy ones (1:4), to join with them for the share of the inheritance (1:12), a further description in Jewish biblical terms of the hope that has been laid up for them by God in the heavens (1:5a).[39] The audience, then, who are faithful brothers (and sisters) within the realm of being "in Christ" (1:2b), who have come to know the grace of God within the realm of being "in truth" (1:6c), who have love within the realm of being "in the Spirit" (1:8), and for whom it is prayed that they be filled with the knowledge of God's will within the realm of being "in all wisdom and Spiritual understanding" (1:9b), God has made fit for the share of the inheritance of the holy ones within the salvific realm of being "in the light" (1:12).[40]

The audience, the "you" (ὑμᾶς) whom the Father has made fit (1:12), are now part of the "us" (ἡμᾶς)—not only Paul and Timothy but all believers—whom the Father has rescued from the authority of the "darkness" (1:13a),[41] so that they are now among the holy ones, the new Jewish and Gentile people of God, within the salvific realm of being in the "light" (1:12).[42] That the Father has transferred all of

---

39. Dunn, *Colossians*, 75-76: "Paul and his Gentile converts understood their coming to faith in Christ Jesus as an act of divine grace whereby they were 'qualified or made fit' (ἱκανώσαντι) to share in an inheritance for which they had previously been unqualified, that is, an inheritance thought to be exclusively Israel's. Certainly the phrase 'the share of the inheritance of the saints' is unmistakably Jewish in character. And for anyone familiar with the Jewish scriptures it would immediately evoke the characteristic talk of the promised land and of Israel as God's inheritance. Particularly notable is the way the language could be transferred to the eschatological hope of share in the resurrection and/or life beyond death in the eternal life of heaven." Bevere, *Sharing*, 143: "The authors addressing the Gentile Christians in this very Jewish way, reaffirm what the Colossians must have been told when the gospel was first preached to them: they have a share in the inheritance of God's people.... The authors appropriate this image and use it in reference to the church, which includes both Jews and Gentiles. The Gentiles now share in the inheritance given to Israel *by God's grace*. They are to be numbered among those who are called 'saints'.... The affirmation of 1.12 implies that the inheritance of the people of God given by grace is no longer the privilege of one race, but has now expanded to include those not of Jewish background (Bevere's emphasis)." Deterding, *Colossians*, 37: "The terms Paul uses here for 'inheritance' (κλῆρος) and to a lesser extent 'share' (μερίς) are used in the Septuagint for Palestine as the land which was to be apportioned to the people of Israel. The promised land of OT times was a prophecy in type of the resurrection of the body to eternal life in heaven (the new heavens and new earth)." See also Wright, *Colossians*, 61-63; O'Brien, *Colossians*, 26; Dübbers, *Christologie*, 134-35; Fee, *Pauline Christology*, 295-98; idem, "Old Testament Intertextuality in Colossians: Reflections on Pauline Christology and Gentile Inclusion in God's Story," in *History and Exegesis: New Testament Essays in Honor of Dr. E. Earle Ellis for His 80th Birthday* (ed. Sang-Won Son; London: Clark, 2006), 201-21, esp. 202-7.

40. O'Brien, *Colossians*, 27: "The point is that the inheritance for which the all-powerful Father had fitted them was in the realm of the light of the age to come."

41. Deterding, *Colossians*, 37: "The meaning of ἐξουσία, 'authority,' here is 'the sphere in which power is exercised, *domain*' (BDAG, 6), with the modifier 'darkness,' giving the expression an evil connotation." Dunn, *Colossians*, 78: "The weight of ἐξουσία should also be noted. It denotes an executive authority, in this case a domination of darkness. The implication, therefore, is not so much that the darkness has been already stripped of all its power and banished. Rather, the darkness can be legitimately and authoritatively resisted, as having had its license revoked."

42. Wilson, *Colossians*, 115-16: "The change to the first person plural is perfectly natural: in v. 12 the reference is to the readers, predominantly Gentiles, who have been accorded the privilege of

us believers, all of us holy ones, into the kingdom of the Son of his "love" (ἀγάπης) in 1:13b of the A′ element develops, by way of the chiastic parallel, the "love" (ἀγάπην) of the audience for all the holy ones in 1:4 of the A element. The audience who have extended their *love* to all of the holy ones, all of their fellow believers, are, along with all of those fellow holy ones, also beneficiaries of the *love* God the Father has extended to his Son. Indeed, God the Father has transferred them into the kingdom of the Son of his *love*.[43]

It is "in him" (ἐν ᾧ)—within the salvific realm of being in union with the Son of the Father's love—that all of us believers now have the redemption, the forgiveness of sins (1:14). The love that "you," the audience, "have" (ἔχετε) for all the holy ones in 1:4 (cf. 1:8) of the A element thus progresses, by way of the chiastic parallel, to the redemption, the forgiveness of sins that all of "us"—all believers including the audience— now "have" (ἔχομεν) as beneficiaries of the love of God the Father for his Son in 1:14 of the A′ element.[44]

---

admission into God's holy people; here the author includes himself, and indeed all Christians, among those who have been delivered." Dunn, *Colossians*, 77–78: "The antithesis between 'light' and 'darkness' is made explicit. In this context it is not simply the obvious moral antithesis familiar in Jewish wisdom, but the eschatological dualism of apocalyptic. . . . Presumably the language was not intended to imply that deliverance from the power of darkness was complete and that transfer to the kingdom had been fully carried out. They were not yet in heaven! There is no hint in Colossians of any awareness of the danger of an overrealized eschatology. The language is rather the exaggerated expression of rich spiritual experience and full confidence (hope) that what had already been done (aorist tense) would be completed without fail."

43. O'Brien, *Colossians*, 27–28: "The inheritance for which the Colossians had been fitted was in the realm of light, a complete contrast to that tyranny under which they had once lived prior to their conversion. Like a mighty king who was able to remove peoples from their ancestral homes and to transplant them into another realm, God had taken the Colossians from the tyranny of darkness, where evil powers rule and where Satan's authority is exercised, transferring them to the kingdom in which his beloved Son held sway." Dunn, *Colossians*, 79–80: "This is the only time in the letter that Christ is explicitly described as God's Son, and in the unusual formula, 'Son of his love,' a Semitic form equivalent to 'beloved son.' . . . The usage reflects something of the range of relationship to God that could be expressed by this category, including especially Israel, Israel's king, or the righteous. That is to say, the metaphor of sonship to God denoted different degrees of closeness to God or favor and acknowledgement given by God with the added 'beloved' indicating a further degree of closeness." Fee, *Pauline Christology*, 297: "In Paul's sentence the unusual phrase 'the Son of his love' is perhaps deliberately ambiguous. On the one hand, it is a Semitism for 'beloved Son' and thus initially says something about the relationship of Father and Son: the Son himself is loved by the Father. At the same time, and probably more to Paul's immediate point, the Son who redeems through his own blood is the ultimate expression of God's love for us."

44. Dunn, *Colossians*, 80–82: "Given the clear echo of the settlement of the promised land in 1:12, the compound word [ἀπολύτρωσις–'redemption'] would probably evoke thought of Israel's ransom from slavery in Egypt and from captivity in Babylon, which were usually described with the uncompounded verb λυτροῦν. In that case the great acts of Israel's redemption are being understood typologically as foreshadowing the eschatological redemption of Gentile as well as Jew to share in the new promised land ('the kingdom of God's beloved Son'). . . . it is the possibility of Gentiles being 'in Christ' that brings them within the sphere of God's gracious forgiveness. 'In Christ' is the key to all." Stephen Finlan, *The Background and Content of Paul's Cultic Atonement Metaphors* (SBLAbib 19;

In sum, in the A′ (1:12–14) element of the second unit's chiasm Paul and Timothy's prayer embraces a noteworthy past, present, and future dimension. Their prayer is for the audience, who presently "have" faith and *love* for all the "holy ones" motivated by hope (1:4–5a), to imitate Paul and Timothy by joyfully thanking (cf. 1:3) God the Father for what he has done in the past not only for the audience in having made them fit (1:12a), but for all of us believers in having rescued us from the authority of the darkness and transferred us into the kingdom of the Son of his *love* (1:13), so that the audience along with all the other "holy ones" within the salvific realm of being in the light may look forward to the future "share of the inheritance" promised to the "holy ones" as God's chosen people (1:12b), the hope laid up for them by God in the heavens (1:5a), even while the audience as part of all of us believers are assured that we presently "have" the redemption, the forgiveness of sins (1:14).[45]

B. Summary on Colossians 1:3–14

1. The audience are assured of Paul and Timothy' loving care and concern in always thanking God as the Father of our Lord Jesus Christ when they pray for the audience (1:3). The faith that the audience have within the realm of their being in Christ Jesus and the love they have for all the holy ones is affirmed (1:4), thus establishing a close bond of love between the audience and not only Paul and Timothy but all other holy ones, all other fellow believers.

2. The audience are reminded of the motivation for their faith and love—the hope laid up for them by God in the heavens, which hope they heard about in the word of the truth of the gospel (1:5). The audience are assured that they have been

---

Atlanta: Society of Biblical Literature, 2004), 226: "The term commonly used for the purchase or manumission of slaves, ἀπολύτρωσις, describes salvation in Rom 3:24; 1 Cor 1:30; and Col 1:14. Redemption is easily conflated with sacrifice, since payment is one of the notions underlying Hebrew sacrifice... However, sacrifice is only sometimes conceived as being a kind of payment; it has a purifying function, with the implied correlate of forgiveness."

45. O'Brien, *Colossians*, 26: "The aorist tenses point to an eschatology that is truly realized (i.e. God had *already* qualified the Colossians to share in the inheritance, he had *already* delivered them from this alien power and had *already* transferred them to his Son's kingdom), while by contrast, the present tense of verse 14, 'we have' stresses the continued results of the redemption wrought in the past." Wright, *Colossians*, 63: "[T]he 'forgiveness of sins' here is... one of the specific blessings of the new covenant spoken of in Jeremiah 31:31ff. and Ezekiel 36:16–36. This idea belongs within the wider Jewish belief that God's purposes for Israel were part of his plan to rid the world of evil entirely. It is this plan that he has now put into effect." Wilson, *Colossians*, 121–22: "One point to be noted is that here ἀπολύτρωσις ['redemption'] is immediately defined by the following words, which stand in apposition, as ἄφεσις τῶν ἁμαρτιῶν, the forgiveness of sins.... v. 14 reaches something of a climax with its reference to the redemption." See also Gary S. Shogren, "Presently Entering the Kingdom of Christ: The Background and Purpose of Col 1:12–14," *JETS* 31 (1988): 173–80; Thomas Witulski, "Gegenwart und Zukunft in den eschatologischen Konzeptionen des Kolosser- und Epheserbriefes," *ZNW* 96 (2005): 213–15.

part of the world-wide and remarkable "bearing fruit and growing" of the gospel from the very day they heard it and experienced the grace of God within the realm of being "in truth" (1:6), thus alerting the audience to the possibility that they have heard of another word, a word of falsehood not in accord with the truth of the gospel they originally heard.

3. The audience are reminded that they learned the gospel from Epaphras, a beloved associate of Paul and Timothy and a reliable minister of Christ for the sake of the audience (1:7). That Epaphras has informed Paul and Timothy of the audience's love within the realm of being in the Spirit (1:8) further endears not only Epaphras but Paul and Timothy to the audience, establishing a loving receptivity on the part of the audience for the authoritative care and concern—the love—they can expect to receive from Paul and Timothy as they listen to the rest of the letter.

4. The audience experience the loving care and concern of Paul and Timothy as they hear their prayer that the audience, who have "come to know" the grace of God in truth (1:6), may be filled by God with the "knowledge" of God's will within the realm of being in *all* wisdom and understanding that comes from the Spirit (1:9), so that they may "walk," that is, conduct themselves and live, for *every* desire to please the Lord, in *every* good work bearing fruit and growing with regard to the "knowledge" of God (1:10), in *all* power empowered according to the might of God's glory for *all* endurance and patience (1:11). This prayer thus alerts the audience to their need for all endurance and patience in the face of possible opposition to the word of the truth of the gospel that they have heard (1:5) and carefully learned from Epaphras (1:7).

5. Paul and Timothy's prayer is for the audience, who presently "have" faith and *love* for all the "holy ones" motivated by hope (1:4–5a), to imitate Paul and Timothy by joyfully thanking (cf. 1:3) God the Father for what he has done in the past not only for the audience in having made them fit (1:12a), but for all of us believers in having rescued us from the authority of the darkness and transferred us into the kingdom of the Son of his *love* (1:13), so that the audience along with all the other "holy ones" within the salvific realm of being in the light may look forward to the future "share of the inheritance" promised to the "holy ones" as God's chosen people (1:12b), the hope laid up for them by God in the heavens (1:5a), even while the audience as part of all of us believers are assured that we presently "have" the redemption, the forgiveness of sins (1:14).

5
Colossians 1:15–23

The Gospel Preached to Every Creature under Heaven (C)

God has reconciled you in the body of the flesh of Christ
A: [15] He is the image of the invisible God, the firstborn of *all creation*, [16] for in him were created all things in the *heavens* and on the earth, the visible and the invisible, whether thrones or dominions or principalities or authorities; all things through him and to him have been created. [17] And he alone is before all things and all things in him hold together.
   B: [18] And he alone is the head of the *body*, the church. He is the beginning, the firstborn from the dead, that he alone might become in all things preeminent, [19] for in him all the fullness chose to dwell, [20a] and through him to *reconcile* all things to him,
      C: [20b] making peace through the blood of his cross, through him, whether the things on the earth or the things in the heavens.[1]

---

1. For recent treatments of the hymnic section in 1:15–20, in addition to works already cited, see Nicholas Thomas Wright, "Poetry and Theology in Colossians 1.15–20," *NTS* 36 (1990): 444–68; Larry R. Helyer, "Recent Research on Colossians 1:15–20," *Grace Theological Journal* 12 (1991): 51–67; Larry L. Helyer, "Cosmic Christology and Col 1:15–20," *JETS* 37 (1994): 235–46; Jerome Murphy-O'Connor, "Tradition and Redaction in Col 1:15–20," *RB* 102 (1995): 231–41; Claudio Basevi, "Col 1,15–20: Las posibles fuentes del 'himno' cristológico y su importancia para la interpretación," *ScrTh* 30 (1998): 779–802; idem, "La doctrina cristológica del 'himno' de Col 1:15–20," *ScrTh* 31 (1999): 317–44; Jeffrey S. Lamp, "Wisdom in Col 1:15–20: Contribution and Significance," *JETS* 41 (1998): 45–53; P. Jones, "L'Évangile pour l'âge du verseau: Colossiens 1:15–20," *RRef* 50 (1999): 13–23; Tomás Otero Lázaro, *Col 1,15–20 en el contexto de la carta* (Tesi Gregoriana, Serie Teologia 48; Rome: Editrice Pontificia Università Gregoriana, 1999); Christian Stettler, *Der Kolosserhymnus: Untersuchungen zu Form, traditionsgeschichtlichen Hintergrund und Aussage von Kol 1,15–20* (WUNT 2/131; Tübingen: Mohr Siebeck, 2000); Paolo Garuti, "Il Primogenito, immagine del Dio invisibile: Qualche spunto di cristologia da *Col* 1,15–20 ed *Ef* 2,14–18," *DivThom* 28 (2001): 119–37; Otfried Hofius, "'Erstgeborener vor aller Schöpfung'—'Erstgeborener aus den Toten': Erwägungen zu Struktur und Aussage des Christushymnus Kol 1, 15–20," in *Auferstehung—Resurrection: The Fourth Durham-Tübingen Research Symposium: Resurrection, Transfiguration and Exaltation in Old Testament, Ancient Judaism and Early Christianity (Tübingen, September, 1999)* (ed. Friedrich Avemarie and Hermann Lichtenberger; WUNT 135; Tübingen: Mohr Siebeck, 2001), 185–203; George H. van Kooten, *Cosmic Christology in Paul and the Pauline School: Colossians and Ephesians in the Context of Graeco-Roman Cosmology, with*

B′: ²¹ And you, once being alienated and enemies in mind in works that are evil, ²² he has now *reconciled* in the *body* of his flesh through death to present you holy and unblemished and blameless before him,

A′: ²³ if indeed you persevere in the faith, having been established and steadfast and not shifting from the hope of the gospel which you heard, which was proclaimed in *all creation* that is under *heaven*, of which I became, I, Paul, a minister.²

A. Audience Response to Colossians 1:15–23

1. Col 1:15–17 (A): Firstborn of All Creation in Whom Were Created All in the Heavens

After the statement that God has rescued us believers from the authority of darkness and has transferred us into the kingdom of the Son of his love, in whom we have redemption, the forgiveness of sins (1:13–14), the audience hear a further hymnic description of the Son of God's love: "He is the image of the invisible God, the firstborn of all creation" (1:15). When the audience hear the word "he" (ὅς) here they hear the word that links this unit (1:15–23) with the previous one (1:3–14), which concluded with the occurrence of "he" in the assertion that "he (ὅς) rescued us" (1:13). That Christ, the Son of God's love, is the "image" (εἰκών) of the invisible God tells the audience that he has a likeness to the invisible God that transcends the realm of the created world and that is preexistent and preeminent over it.³ That he is the "firstborn" (πρωτότοκος) of all creation reinforces his

---

a New Synopsis of the Greek Texts (WUNT 2/171; Tübingen: Mohr Siebeck, 2003), 115–21; Stefano Romanello, "*Col* 1,15–20: la posta in gioco di una cristologia singolarmente pregnante," *Teol* 30 (2005): 13–48; Michael Trainor, "The Cosmic Christology of Colossians 1:15–20 in the Light of Contemporary Ecological Issues," *ABR* 53 (2005): 54–69; Matthew E. Gordley, *The Colossian Hymn in Context: An Exegesis in Light of Jewish and Greco-Roman Hymnic and Epistolary Conventions* (WUNT 228; Tübingen: Mohr Siebeck, 2007); Ulrich Luz, "Bild des unsichtbaren Gottes—Christus: Der Kolosserhymnus (Kol 1,15–20)," *BK* 63 (2008): 13–17.

2. For the establishment of Col 1:15–23 as a chiasm, see ch. 2.

3. Dübbers, *Christologie*, 95: "Der Ausdruck εἰκὼν τοῦ θεοῦ bezeichnet im Kontext des Hymnus wie auch des Kolosserbriefes nicht eine lediglich defizitäre Abbildung Gottes, sondern die Gotteseikon Christus hat (auch gegenwärtig) an dem als ἀόρατος qualifizierten Wesen Gottes teil, das den Bereich der geschaffenen Welt transzendiert und ihm kategorial übergeordnet ist." Horst Kuhli, "εἰκών," *EDNT* 1.390: "In Col 1:15 it is not revelatory function (though it is present here) but Christ's cosmological significance that stands in the foreground.... What εἰκών means in the Colossians hymn must therefore be asked as a question concerning the relationship of Christ to cosmos." As the "image," Christ is the physical, visual embodiment of God according to Jarl E. Fossum, "Colossians 1.15–18a in the Light of Jewish Mysticism and Gnosticism," *NTS* 35 (1989): 188. As the "image" (εἰκών) of the invisible God, then, Christ is the "image" of God according to which (κατ' εἰκόνα) mankind was created in LXX Gen 1:26–27. Dübbers, *Christologie*, 94: "Christus ist die εἰκών, die dem geschaffenen Menschen auf Seiten des Schöpfergottes gegenübersteht." On the wisdom theme in Col 1:15–20, see Jean-Noel Aletti, *Colossiens 1:15–20: Genre et exégèse du texte: Fonction de la thématique sapientielle* (AnBib 91; Rome: Biblical Institute, 1981). But, on the issue of a Wisdom christology in Colossians and the other Pauline letters, see Fee (*Pauline Christology*, 317–25, 595–619), who concludes: "In light of the evidence, therefore,

temporal priority and superior status over all of the cosmos.[4]

The hymnic description continues with the role of Christ as the locus, mediator, and goal of the creaton over which he is the firstborn: "for in him were created all things in the heavens and on the earth, the visible and the invisible, whether thrones or dominions or principalities or authorities; all things through him and to him have been created" (1:16). The audience hear this verse as a mini-chiasm elaborating why Christ is the image of the invisible God and the firsborn of all creation (1:15):

a: for in him (αὐτῷ) were created (ἐκτίσθη)
   b: all things (τὰ πάντα)
      c: in the heavens (οὐρανοῖς)
         d: and on the earth (γῆς)
         d′: the visible (ὁρατά)
      c′: and the invisible (ἀόρατα) whether thrones or dominions or principalities or authorities
   b′: all things (τὰ πάντα)
a′: through him (αὐτοῦ) and to him (αὐτόν) have been created (ἔκτισται)

---

both in Paul's letters and in the Wisdom literature, we must conclude that Wisdom Christology is *not* found in Paul's letters and thus has no role in the reconstruction of Paul's christology" (p. 619). Smith, *Heavenly Perspective*, 161–62: "Paul therefore uses terms that were current in first-century Judaism, that are reflective of the invisible world of God and the invisible world of creation, and applies them to Christ, thereby taking them to new heights. The term εἰκὼν τοῦ θεοῦ would certainly attract the attention of Paul's readers if the opponents in Colossae were propagating some form of Jewish mysticism. The identification of the εἰκὼν τοῦ θεοῦ with the one who *descended* to earth would show the folly of religious ritual to gain a heavenly *ascent*. God has revealed himself through his image, and this revelation is sufficient."

4. In LXX Exod 4:22 God declares that "Israel is my firstborn (πρωτότοκός) son" and in LXX Ps 88:28 God declares about the Davidic king that "I will make him firstborn (πρωτότοκον), high over the kings of the earth." Maisch, *Gemeinde in Kolossä*, 108–9: "Der Ausdruck 'Erstgeborener' hat bereits in der hebräischen Bibel, dann auch im griechisch-jüdischen Schriftum die Verbindung zur Vorstellung des Zeugens und Gebärens und damit das zeitliche Moment weitgehend verloren und wird meist im übertragenen Sinn gebraucht. Er bezeichnet einen hoheitlichen Rang, der in der besonderen *Beziehung* des Genannten *zu Gott* begründet ist (Ex 4,22 LXX von Israel); in Verbindung mit anderen Sohnesbezeichnungen wird er zum Synonym für den Geliebten, Einziggeborenen, Auserwählten (vgl. PsSal 13,9; 18,4; 4 Esr 6,58). Daneben bezeichnet er die hervorragende *Stellung* des so Genannten *gegenüber anderen* (Ps 88,28 LXX David bzw. der messianische König)." Hugolinus Langkammer, "πρωτότοκος," *EDNT* 3.190: "[T]he *firstborn* stands in a relationship to creation as its mediator. Hence this is not a matter of a purely temporal priority of the preexistent Christ, but rather of a superiority in essence.... Christ, as the mediator of creation, is not a part of creation himself, but stands rather in a unique relationship to God, the 'invisible.'" See also Larry R. Helyer, "Arius Revisited: The Firstborn Over All Creation (Col 1:15)," *JETS* 31 (1988): 59–67; Tom Holland, "Firstborn and the Colossian Hymn," *Trinity Theological Journal* 12 (2004): 22–53. Smith, *Heavenly Perspective*, 163: "As the πρωτότοκος Christ has priority and primacy. His dominion is even greater than that of the first Adam because he is separated from creation: he is the creator. His dominion extends even to cosmic beings." According to Fee (*Pauline Christology*, 301) "firstborn" here means "both heir and sovereign with regard to creation."

The only occurrences in this mini-chiasm of the third person singular pronoun "him" referring to Christ—"in him (αὐτῷ)" in 1:16a and "through him (αὐτοῦ) and for him (αὐτόν)" in 1:16h—as well as of the verb "create"—"were created (ἐκτίσθη)" in 1:16a and "have been created (ἔκτισται)" in 1:16h—establish a verbal parallelism between the "a" and "a'" sub-elements. The only occurrences in this mini-chiasm of the noun "all things" referring to the cosmos—"all things (τὰ πάντα)" in 1:16b and "all things (τὰ πάντα)" in 1:16g—establish a verbal parallelism between the "b" and "b'" sub-elements. "In the heavens" in 1:16c and the synonymous elaboration of what is in the heavens—"the invisible" in 1:16f—establish a conceptual parallelism between the "c" and "c'" sub-elements. "On the earth" in 1:16d and the synonymous elaboration of what is on the earth—"the visible" in 1:16e—establish a conceptual parallelism between the central "d" and "d'" sub-elements.[5] Noteworthy is the emphatic fourfold elaboration of "the invisible" —"whether thrones or dominions or principalities or authorities"—in the "c'" sub-element of the mini-chiasm.

In the "a" and "b" sub-elements (1:16ab) of the mini-chiasm the audience hear in an emphatic position before the verb that it was "in him," that is, in Christ—within the spatial sphere or realm established by the Christ event—that all things were created by God (divine passive).[6] The "c" and "d" sub-elements (1:16cd) function together as a rhetorical merism, that is, opposites to express totality, to further explain the cosmic expanse of what is meant by all things—all the things "in the heavens and on the earth." Then the "d'" and "c'" sub-elements (1:16ef) function together as another merism to further specify what is meant by all the things in the heavens and on the earth, namely, all the things that are "visible"—the things on the earth, as well as all the things that are "invisible"—the things in the heavens.

But there is an emphatic fourfold elaboration in the "c'" sub-element delineating examples of the kinds of invisible, angelic beings or supernatural powers that

---

5. Wilson, *Colossians*, 140: "τὰ ὁρατά [the visible] must surely be the things on earth, τὰ ἀόρατα [the invisible] the things in heaven." *Contra* Deterding (*Colossians*, 56) for whom the visible and the invisible are both in the heavens and on the earth.

6. Although some maintain that ἐν αὐτῷ should be translated "by him" as an expression of instrumentality (for a recent example, see Dübbers, *Christologie*, 97–98), it is better to translate it "in him" as an expression of locality. Garland, *Colossians*, 88: "It is better, however, to read it [ἐν αὐτῷ] as a dative of sphere (locative), 'in him.' Paul frequently uses 'in Christ' or 'in him' in this sense. Since the last part of the verse states that all things have been created through him (διά), it is unlikely that the apostle intends to repeat the idea of Christ's agency in creation." The prepositional phrase ἐν αὐτῷ, "in him," means that Christ was "the location from whom all came into being and in whom all creation is contained," according to H. Wayne House, "Doctrinal Issues in Colossians. Part 2 (of 4 Parts): The Doctrine of Christ in Colossians," *BSac* 149 (1992): 182. Harris, *Colossians*, 44–45: "'All things in heaven and on earth' were created *in* God's beloved Son (v. 13), not in the sense that he was the preexistent or ideal archetype of creation but in the sense that creation occurred 'within the sphere of' Christ. In his person resided the creative energy that produced all of creation; in the work of creation God did not act apart from Christ." This coheres with the meaning of ἐν αὐτῷ in 1:19 where it surely has the sense of location—"for in him (ἐν αὐτῷ) all the fullness was pleased to dwell." And in 1:17 a meaning of location also seems to be most appropriate—"in him (ἐν αὐτῷ) all things hold together."

are included among all the invisible things in the heavens that were created by God in Christ—"whether thrones or dominions or principalities or authorities" (1:16f). This impresses upon the audience that not only all the visible and invisible things in the cosmos but also, and most especially, the invisible powers, be they beneficent or menacing, were created in Christ, so that the audience are to realize that Christ has a cosmic power vastly superior to all other powers in the universe.⁷

With the "b′" and "a′" sub-elements (1:16gh) the audience hear not only an emphatic reinforcement but a deliberate development of the assertion that all things in the cosmos were created by God in Christ. Not only were all things created in the sphere of Christ ("a" sub-element in 1:16a), but all things have been created "through him" (1:16h), that is, through the agency or instrumentality of Christ, and all things have been created "to him" (1:16h), that is, all created things have their present orientation toward and ultimate destiny and fulfillment in Christ. This thus completes a rhetorical triplet of prepositional phrases—"in him" (ἐν αὐτῷ), "through him" (δι αὐτοῦ), and "to him" (εἰς αὐτόν)—to impress upon the audience the cosmic, comprehensive expanse of Christ's role and preeminent position in all of creation. The audience are to realize that Christ is the original locus, means, and goal of the creation of the entire universe.⁸

---

7. Garland, *Colossians*, 89: "The invisible things are identified as the 'thrones . . . powers . . . rulers . . . authorities' and perhaps refer to heavenly host. They may be good or evil, that is, mediators of divine knowledge or malevolent foes in league with the power of darkness (1:13) . . . The point Paul celebrates is that Christ has majesty and power over all of them." Harris, *Colossians*, 45: "'Things invisible' are now defined in a typical but not exhaustive list of four classes of supernatural powers or spiritual beings . . . By metonymy θρόνοι are probably angelic occupants of heavenly thrones, while κυριότητες, ἀρχαί, and ἐξουσίαι are supernatural potentates who exercise (respectively) 'dominion,' 'rule,' and 'authority' in heavenly realms." Deterding, *Colossians*, 45: "These terms are all attested in Jewish intertestamental literature as names for angels. In his letters, Paul uses these names for angels without any distinction in meaning between them." The four terms used here, "far from conveying to the Colossians the idea of hostile forces of the universe or malevolent spirits, would have at most described beings whose status was neutral, requiring definite signs from the context to be interpreted in an evil sense," according to Wesley A. Carr, *Angels and Principalities: The Background, Meaning and Development of the Pauline Phrase* Hai Archai Kai Hai Exousiai (SNTSMS 42; Cambridge: Cambridge University Press, 1981), 52. According to O'Brien (*Colossians*, 46–47), the four terms "probably represent the highest orders of the angelic realm. Whether the list is complete or the powers are arranged in a particular order is beside the point. From the highest to the lowest, all alike are subject to Christ." Smith, *Heavenly Perspective*, 166: "By listing these angelic beings, each introduced by the same word, εἴτε, Paul is pointing out that even within a developed angelology, with different grades of heaven and different classes of supernatural beings, whether evil or good, Christ is the creator of all, and therefore pre-eminent. All cosmic powers, whether good or bad, are subject to him."

8. For similar "metaphysical" uses of prepositions, see Gregory E. Sterling, "Prepositional Metaphysics in Jewish Wisdom Speculation and Early Christian Liturgical Texts," in *Wisdom and Logos: Studies in Jewish Thought in Honor of David Winston* (ed. David T. Runia and Gregory E. Sterling; Studia Philonica Annual 9; Atlanta: Scholars Press, 1997), 219–38; van Kooten, *Cosmic Christology*, 122–25. Ralph P. Martin, *Colossians and Philemon* (3d ed.; NCB; Grand Rapids: Eerdmans, 1981), 58: "No Jewish thinker ever rose to these heights in daring to predict that Wisdom was the ultimate goal of all creation." Dunn, *Colossians*, 92 n. 21: "That the hymn goes beyond previous talk of Wisdom should make us hesitate before simply identifying Christ with Wisdom."

The audience also hear a concerted development from the aorist tense of the verb create in the "a" sub-element (1:16a)—"were created" (ἐκτίσθη)—to the perfect tense in the "a′" sub-element (1:16h)—"have been created" (ἔκτισται). This chiastic progression underscores for the audience that all things in the cosmos not only were once created by God in Christ but also are still presently being sustained as entities created by God through Christ and to Christ. In sum, then, this mini-chiasm in 1:16 takes the audience from the past creation in Christ of all things in the cosmos, through an emphatic assertion that all heavenly, invisible powers were also created in the sphere of Christ, and climactically concluding that all things in the cosmos not only have been created but still are existing as created entities through and to Christ.[9]

The A element (1:15–17) concludes with a continuation of the hymnic description of Christ and a return to Christ as the grammatical subject, as in 1:15, after "all things" was the subject in 1:16:[10] "And he alone is before all things and all things in him hold together" (1:17). With an emphatic "he himself" or "he alone" (αὐτός) the hymn proclaims that Christ "is" (ἐστιν) even now, presently, "before" (πρό), that is, prior in time to as well as preeminent in position to, all things in the cosmos (1:17a), reinforcing the assertion that Christ is the "firstborn of all creation" (1:15).[11]

With a return to "all things" as the grammatical subject in 1:17b the audience hear the climactic conclusion of the rhetorical triplet of "all things" in the nominative case within the A element. "All things" (τὰ πάντα) were created by God in Christ (1:16ab) and "all things" (τὰ πάντα) through him and to him have been created by God (1:16h), so that "all things" (τὰ πάντα) now "in him"—in the sphere or realm of the Christ event—hold together (1:17b). The phrase "in him" (ἐν αὐτῷ) in emphatic position before the verb at the beginning of the triplet—"*in him* were created all things" (1:16ab)—is thus reinforced by the "in him" (ἐν αὐτῷ) in emphatic position before the verb at the conclusion of the triplet—"all things *in him* hold together" (1:17b). The A element (1:15–17) thus climactically concludes with the verb "hold together" (συνέστηκεν) in the perfect tense—all things *in him* presently and continually hold together, that is, all things in the cosmos, rather

---

9. Bruce, *Colossians*, 64 n. 118: "The tense of 'were created' (ἐκτίσθη) at the beginning of v. 16 is aorist, referring to the act of creation as such, the tense of 'have been created' (ἔκτισται) at the end of the verse is perfect, referring to the enduring result of the creative act." Harris, *Colossians*, 45: "The pf. here emphasizes the state resulting from the past event of creation, pointing not to continuous acts of creation but to the permanent 'createdness' of creation. All things have been created, and remain in their created existence, through Christ and for him."

10. Dübbers, *Christologie*, 102 n. 75.

11. Harris, *Colossians*, 46–47: "πρό may denote time ('before'), status ('supreme over'), or both.... While πρό does not often denote priority of importance, it would seem unwise to exclude here this notion of supremacy of status, given the use of πρωτότοκος in v. 15 and of πρωτεύων in v. 18." See also Dunn, *Colossians*, 93 n. 24; Smith, *Heavenly Perspective*, 166–67.

than disintegrating into chaos, in Christ as the operating principle controlling all of creation, constantly and continually remain held together in existence.¹²

2. Col 1:18–20a (B): All Things Reconciled to Christ as Head of the Body, the Church

Echoing and developing the emphatic uses of the third person singular pronoun referring to Christ that conclude the A element, the B element begins: "And he alone is the head of the body, the church. He is the beginning, the firstborn from the dead, that he alone might become in all things preeminent" (1:18). The audience hear a progression from the emphatic assertion, "and *he alone* is (καὶ αὐτός ἐστιν) before all things," in 1:17a of the A element to the emphatic assertion, "and *he alone* is (καὶ αὐτός ἐστιν) the head of the body, the church," in 1:18a of the B element. And the emphatic assertion that "all things *in him* (ἐν αὐτῷ) hold together" in 1:17b of the A element progresses to the emphatic assertion "that *he alone* (αὐτός) might become in all things preeminent" in 1:18c of the B element.¹³

That Christ and no other is "head" of the "body" which is the church (1:18a) gives expression to a metaphorical head-body relationship between Christ and the church connoting both that Christ is in a position of supremacy over the "body" of the church as its authoritative "head" and that Christ is the "head" of the "body"

---

12. Harris, *Colossians*, 47: "He [Christ] is the source of the unity (συν-, together) and cohesiveness or solidarity (συν-ίστημι, cohere) of the whole universe." O'Brien, *Colossians*, 47: "Not only was the universe created in the Son as the sphere, by him as the divine agent, and for him as the goal; it was also established permanently 'in him' alone, as the second affirmation, 'in him all things are held together,' asserts. He is the sustainer of the universe and the unifying principle of its life. Apart from his *continuous* sustaining activity (note the perfect tense συνέστηκεν) all would disintegrate." Garland, *Colossians*, 89–90: "Christ has precedence over all things in terms of time and status and is a kind of divine glue or spiritual gravity that holds creation together.... The verb 'hold together' can imply that they have their existence in him. Christ is more than the force that preserves the orderly arrangement of the cosmos; he is its rationale, its rhyme and reason.... He is the basic operating principle controlling existence." Fred B. Craddock, "'All Things in Him': A Critical Note on Col. i. 15–20," *NTS* 12 (1965): 79: "He is not in all things for all things are in him. The Logos of the Stoics gave unity, order, and meaning to all things because it permeated all things as *dia*-existent principle, the Colossian hymn praises him in whom all things begin, continue, and conclude because they are in, through, and unto him as a *pre*-existent being." Wilson, *Colossians*, 144: It is, however, difficult to be certain that our author is *directly* dependent on any one set of ideas ... It may rather be a question of ideas which were 'in the air', in more or less general circulation, which could be drawn upon by an author to suit his own ends. In any case, if our author has adopted any concepts, from whatever source, he has also adapted them to give expression to his faith in the supremacy and sufficiency of Christ." Smith, *Heavenly Perspective*, 172: "Christ is shown as not only the creator of the cosmic realm, but also the one who maintains it (συνέστηκεν-v. 17). The present existence of all cosmic powers, whether heavenly or demonic, depends on him. Therefore when tragedy or natural disasters, such as earthquakes, floods and volcanoes occur, these are not beyond Christ's control. Focusing on demonic powers to prevent such tragedy is futile."

13. Harris, *Colossians*, 49: "As in vv. 17a and 18a αὐτός is emphatic: 'he alone became preeminent.'"

of the church as its origin of life and source of provision.[14] Although in antiquity the cosmos was sometimes depicted as a living body,[15] the church as "body" here refers not just to a local assembly or even group of several assemblies but to the universal, world-wide church—the assembly of all the holy ones (cf. 1:2, 4, 12), all believers both on earth and in the heavens.[16]

What it means that Christ alone is the head of the body, the church, in the context of this hymn is then elaborated: "He is the beginning, the firstborn from the dead" (1:18b). That Christ is the "beginning" (ἀρχή) means that as the first to rise from the dead he not only inaugurates the general resurrection from death but holds a position of supremacy over all the dead who will arise, as confirmed by the next phrase—"the firstborn from the dead." As Christ is the "firstborn" (πρωτότοκος) of all creation (1:15), indicating that he has both a temporal priority and superior status over all of creation, so Christ is the "firstborn" (πρωτότοκος) from the dead, indicating that he has a temporal priority and superior status over all who will rise from the dead.[17]

---

14. On the meaning of "head" (κεφαλή) in the Pauline letters, see Stephen Bedale, "The Meaning of *Kephale* in the Pauline Epistles," *JTS* 5 (1954): 211-15; Wayne A. Grudem, "Does *Kephalē* ('Head') Mean 'Source' or 'Authority Over' in Greek Literature? A Survey of 2,336 Examples," *TJ* 6 (1985): 38-59; idem, "The Meaning of Κεφαλή ('Head'): A Response to Recent Studies," *TJ* 11 (1990): 3-72; Richard S. Cervin, "Does Κεφαλή Mean 'Source' or 'Authority Over' in Greek Literature? A Rebuttal," *TJ* 10 (1989): 85-112. Wilson, *Colossians*, 145: "κεφαλὴ means in the first place the actual head of a person, but can also be used metaphorically of a leader or ruler, the head of a tribe; from this it is not a long step to the idea of superiority." Garland, *Colossians*, 91: " '[H]ead' can also indicate source or origin. Christ is the source of the church's life. The metaphor 'head' designates him both as supreme over the church and as the source of the church's life. In the image of a living body, the head not only directs and governs the body, it gives it life and strength." Clinton E. Arnold, "Jesus Christ: 'Head' of the Church (Colossians and Ephesians)," in *Jesus of Nazareth: Lord and Christ. Essays on the Historical Jesus and New Testament Christology* (ed. Joel B. Green and Max Turner; Grand Rapids: Eerdmans, 1994), 360: "In the first place, Christ alone is *the leader* of the church. He alone possesses authority over his people.... Secondly, Christ is *the source of provision* for the church. It is from him that the entire church draws its nourishment for growth." See also Fee, *Pauline Christology*, 306.

15. Wilson, *Colossians*, 146: "Here the body is not the cosmos but, as the text says, the Church. If our author has in fact made use of the concept of the cosmos as a body, he has subjected it to a radical reinterpretation."

16. On the significance of "church" (ἐκκλησία) here, Wilson (*Colossians*, 147) states: "In the New Testament it refers to the Christian community, but here there are nuances and shades of meaning which require to be noted: it can refer (1) to the totality of Christians living in one place (e.g. Jerusalem, Acts 8.1; 11.22); or (2) to house churches such as those in the house of Philemon (Philem. 2) or Nymphas (Col. 4.15) or Aquila and Priscilla (Rom. 16.5); or (3) to the Church universal as here." Smith, *Heavenly Perspective*, 169, 172: "The Colossian Christians therefore have dual citizenship of an earthly church and of a heavenly church.... what Paul is referring to in Col. 1.18 is the church as it gathers around Christ in heaven. Earthly assemblies are to be reflections of this heavenly reality.... It is through this assembly that God is present with his people when they gather in earthly manifestations of this assembly. There is no need to seek a special heavenly ascent or revelation."

17. As Dunn (*Colossians*, 97 n. 32; cf. O'Brien, *Colossians*, 50) points out, in Gen 49:3 LXX "beginning" and "firstborn" are used synonymously: "Reuben, my firstborn (πρωτότοκος), you are my strength and beginning (ἀρχή) of my children." According to Langkammer ("πρωτότοκος," 190) in

Both the divine purpose and consequence of Christ being the beginning and the firstborn from the dead is "that he alone might become in all things preeminent" (1:18c). It is his resurrection from the dead that enables the Christ, who "is" (ἐστιν) the image of the invisible God (1:15a), who "is" (ἐστιν) before all things (1:17a), and who "is" (ἐστιν) the head of the body, the church (1:18a), to "become" (γένηται) in all things preeminent. Not only is Christ the firstborn of "all" (πάσης) creation (1:15b), not only were "all things" (τὰ πάντα) created in Christ (1:16ab), not only through him and for him have "all things" (τὰ πάντα) been created (1:16gh), not only is he alone before "all things" (πάντων, 1:17a), and not only are "all things" (τὰ πάντα) in him held together (1:17b), but he alone has become in "all things" (πᾶσιν), that is, in all spheres and realms, preeminent. Not only is Christ the "firstborn" (πρωτότοκος) of all creation (1:15b), not only is he alone "before" (πρό) all things (1:17a), and not only is he the "firstborn" (πρωτότοκος) from the dead (1:18b), but he alone has become in all things "preeminent" (πρωτεύων).[18]

1:18b "Christ is 'the beginning' of a new series (cf. 1 Cor 15:20, 23; Acts 3:15; 5:31). As such he is the 'firstborn' from the dead' (cf. Acts 26:23).... The resurrection overcomes death once and for all. Though this also implies temporal priority, it probably refers first to the resurrection of Christ as the basis for the general resurrection." Harris, *Colossians*, 48: "[N]ot only is Jesus the cause of the Church's existence and the origin of its vitality (ἀρχή); he is also the pioneer and guarantor of a resurrection from death to immortality. Whereas in v. 15b πρωτότοκος may refer to both time and status, here only temporal priority is signified, since the word is followed by ἐκ τῶν νεκρῶν, and not simply τῶν νεκρῶν. Yet this primacy in time implies superiority in rank." O'Brien, *Colossians*, 50: "The term ἀρχή ('beginning') has basically to do with primacy, whether in a temporal sense or with reference to authority and sovereignty." Dunn, *Colossians*, 97–98: "As with the preceding use of πρωτότοκος [in 1:15], but more clearly, the word has a double force. For it echoes the earlier Pauline talk both of Christ's resurrection as temporally prior to the resurrection of all in Christ, first in order, firstfruits (1 Cor. 15:23; cf. Acts 26:23), and of Christ as the πρωτότοκος among many brothers, eldest in a family destined to share his archetypal image (Rom. 8:29). In both senses it nicely encapsulates what appears to have been the earliest Christian understanding, namely, that with Christ's resurrection the end-time resurrection itself had begun."

18. Harris, *Colossians*, 49: "[I]n relation to the universe Christ is and always was supreme, but in relation to the Church he became supreme by his resurrection to immortality.... Πρωτεύων summarizes the principal emphasis of this christological 'hymn'—the supremacy of Christ, which is sole (cf. αὐτός) and universal (cf. ἐν πᾶσιν, 'in all things'). It is possible that πᾶσιν is masc[uline]., referring back to τῶν νεκρῶν, 'among the dead'; but as in v. 17a this use of anar[throus]. πᾶς is almost certainly neut[er]., 'in all spheres,' 'in every realm,' the natural creation and the spiritual creation, the universe and the Church." O'Brien, *Colossians*, 51: "Because Christ is the 'beginning' and the 'firstborn' in resurrection as well as in creation he has therefore become (note the aorist γένηται) preeminent in all things. This was the divine intention as the purpose clause (ἵνα) makes plain. The words 'be the first' (πρωτεύω) resume the double reference to 'firstborn' (πρωτότοκος, vv 15 and 18), as well as the phrase 'he is before all things' (v 17), while the expression 'in all' (ἐν πᾶσιν) is linked with the frequently mentioned 'all things' (τὰ πάντα). The hymn had previously asserted Christ's primacy in creation; it now mentions his primacy in resurrection. In both new creation and old the first place belongs to him alone. He *has become* preeminent 'in everything'" (O'Brien's emphasis). Dunn, *Colossians*, 98: "[T]he immediate outcome of the resurrection is 'that he might be in all things preeminent' (πρωτεύων, the only occurrence in the New Testament). And we should also note that the clause is introduced with ἵνα, indicating that the purpose of Christ's resurrection from the dead was precisely that he might become

A further hymnic acclamation explains why Christ has become in all things preeminent: "For in him all the fullness chose to dwell" (1:19). The reason Christ is the firstborn of all creation (1:15b)—"for in him (ὅτι ἐν αὐτῷ) were created all things in the heavens and on the earth (1:16a) progresses now to the reason Christ has become in all things preeminent—"for in him (ὅτι ἐν αὐτῷ) all the fullness chose to dwell." This continues the emphatic uses of the prepositional phrase "in him" (ἐν αὐτῷ) to refer to the sphere or realm constituted by Christ: "*in him* were created all things" (1:16a), "all things *in him* hold together" (1:17b), and "*in him* all the fullness chose to dwell" (1:19). Christ is the firstborn of "all" (πάσης) creation (1:15b), in him were created "all things" (τὰ πάντα, 1:16a), "all things" (τὰ πάντα) through him and to him have been created (1:16gh), he alone is before "all things" (πάντων, 1:17a), "all things" (τὰ πάντα) in him hold together (1:17b), and he alone has become in "all things" (πᾶσιν) preeminent (1:18c), because in him "all" (πᾶν) the fullness chose to dwell (1:19).

The alliterative "all the fullness" (πᾶν τὸ πλήρωμα), in which "all" functions as a rhetorical redundancy to intensify "fullness," expresses a comprehensive, absolute, and total fullness, that is, a fullness that can only be a divine fullness and that thus serves appropriately and poignantly in this cosmic hymn as a circumlocution for God, meaning God in all of God's divine fullness that embraces the universe.[19] That "all the fullness" is a rhetorically potent way of referring to God in 1:19 accords with the fact that often in both the OT and NT God is the subject of the verb "chose" (εὐδόκησεν).[20] The audience may even recall a scriptural text with remarkably similar terminology:

LXX Ps 67:17: the mountain that God chose (εὐδόκησεν) to dwell (κατοικεῖν) in it (ἐν αὐτῷ)

Col 1:19: in him (ἐν αὐτῷ) all the fullness chose (εὐδόκησεν) to dwell (κατοικῆσαι)

Whereas God previously chose to dwell on Mount Zion (LXX Ps 67:17), now God, in all of God's cosmic fullness, chose to dwell in Christ alone (Col 1:19).[21]

(γένηται, aorist) preeminent.... Christ's primacy over all things is the consequence, the divinely intended outcome of his resurrection, a becoming firstborn beyond (the other end of) time."

19. O'Brien, *Colossians*, 52: "[T]he phrase *all the* fullness' is tautologous.... the 'fullness' is not a 'fullness' if it does not mean a totality." Harris (*Colossians*, 50) construes "all the fullness" in 1:19 as "'God in all his fullness.' Πᾶν τό signifies 'all the (fullness),' with no part excepted." See also David Tripp, "ΚΑΤΟΙΚΗΣΑΙ, ΚΑΤΟΙΚΕΙ (Colossians 1:19, 2:9): Christology, or Soteriology Also?" *ExpTim* 116 (2004): 78–79. The use of πλήρωμα in the NT is not related to or influenced by Gnosticism, according to P. D. Overfield, "Pleroma: A Study in Content and Context," *NTS* 25 (1979): 384–96.

20. Simon Légasse, "εὐδοκέω," *EDNT* 2.75; O'Brien, *Colossians*, 52. On the preference of translating εὐδόκησεν here as "chose" rather than "was pleased," see BDAG, 404; Fee, *Pauline Christology*, 308 n. 47.

21. O'Brien, *Colossians*, 53: "He [Christ] is the 'place' (note the emphatic position of ἐν αὐτῷ) in whom God in all his fullness was pleased to take up his residence (the verb is the aorist infinitive

The explanation of why Christ alone has become in all things preeminent (1:18c) continues: "and through him to reconcile all things to him" (1:20a). "All the fullness," that is, God in all of God's cosmic fullness, not only chose to dwell in Christ alone (1:19), but also through Christ to reconcile all things in the universe to Christ (1:20a). That "all things (τὰ πάντα) through him (δι' αὐτοῦ) and to him (εἰς αὐτόν) have been created" by God (1:16gh) now progresses to "through him" (δι' αὐτοῦ) God reconciled "all things" (τὰ πάντα) "to him" (εἰς αὐτόν) (1:20a). Just as Christ is the locus ("in him," 1:15a), means ("through him," 1:16h), and goal ("to him," 1:16h) of the creation of the entire cosmos, so Christ is not only the locus ("in him,") where God in all God's fullness chose to dwell (1:19), but the means ("through him") and goal ("to him") of the reconciliation of the entire cosmos (1:20a). God in all God's fullness chose to reconcile through and to Christ, and thus restore to cosmic harmony all the things in the universe that have been divided, estranged, and at enmity due to "the authority of the darkness" (1:13).[22]

In sum, in the B element (1:18-20a) the audience experience a series of hymnic assertions involving emphatic uses of the third person masculine singular pronoun referring to Christ, beginning with his exalted position in relation to the church and ending with him as the orientation, goal, and destiny of a cosmic reconciliation: *He himself* (αὐτός) is the head of the body, the church, and the beginning, the firstborn from the dead, that *he himself* (αὐτός) might become in all things preeminent (1:18), for in *him* (αὐτῷ) all the fullness chose to dwell (1:19) and through *him* (αὐτοῦ) to reconcile all things to *him* (αὐτόν) (1:20a).

κατοικῆσαι)." Dunn, *Colossians*, 101: "[T]he importance of the language is to indicate that the completeness of God's self-revelation was focused in Christ, that the wholeness of God's interaction with the universe is summed up in Christ." Garland, *Colossians*, 93: "The 'fullness' is a circumlocution for God. God pleases to dwell fully and permanently only in Christ."

22. Helmut Merkel, "ἀποκαταλλάσσω," *EDNT* 2.263: "[I]t does not concern the reconciliation of the world of humanity to God, but instead involves the reconciliation between the parts of the universe. In the background of this statement stands 'the feeling, widespread throughout the Hellenistic world, of living in a world that is breaking up, in which the struggle of everything against everything else characterizes the whole of nature' (Eduard Schweizer, *The Letter to the Colossians: A Commentary* [Minneapolis: Augsburg, 1982], 81). These natural powers are now reconciled once for all." Harris, *Colossians*, 51: "Τὰ πάντα is the dir[ect]. obj[ect]. of ἀποκαταλλάξαι [to reconcile] and means 'the universe.' Here it embraces inanimate nature (cf. v. 20c; Rom. 8:19-22), the world of humankind (cf. vv. 20c, 21, 22; 2 Cor 5:19a), and those angelic powers that were at variance with God (cf. vv. 16, 20c)." O'Brien, *Colossians*, 56: "The cosmic reconciliation has to do with τὰ πάντα, including everything in its scope. The reconciliation of the principalities and powers is in mind." Dunn, *Colossians*, 102-3: "The act of reconciliation is described in the uniquely compounded verb ἀποκαταλλάσσω, which is used in literary Greek only here, in 1:22, and in Eph. 2:16 and was therefore quite possibly coined by Paul. Like the simpler form, καταλλάσσω (Rom. 5:10; 1 Cor. 7:11; 2 Cor. 5:18-20), it presumes a state of estrangement or hostility.... there is presupposed an unmentioned event or state, that is, presumably the falling of the cosmos under the domination of the heavenly powers created as part of τὰ πάντα (1:16), the state already spoken of in 1:13 ('the power of darkness')." See also Smith, *Heavenly Perspective*, 171-72.

3. Col 1:20b (C): Making Cosmic Peace through the Blood of His Cross through Him

Christ as the means of cosmic reconciliation is then elaborated and emphasized in the central C element of the chiasm. God in all of God's fullness chose to reconcile all things through and to Christ (1:19–20a), "making peace through the blood of his cross, through him, whether the things on the earth or the things in the heavens" (1:20b). God in all of God's fullness reconciled all things through and to Christ precisely by "making peace" (εἰρηνοποιήσας), that is, by bringing about a right and harmonious relationship among all things in the cosmos,[23] "through" (διά) the sacrificial blood shed by Christ during his suffering and death on his cross, that is, "through him" (δι' αὐτοῦ), an emphatic intensification that it was "through him" (δι' αὐτοῦ), through Christ, that God reconciled and made peace among all things (1:20a).[24]

The cosmic embrace of "all things" is then further specified—"whether the things on the earth or the things in the heavens," echoing that it was in Christ that all things "in the heavens and on the earth" were created by God (1:16ab). The audience thus realize that all things on the earth and in the heavens, especially the invisible, heavenly powers, were not only created (1:16) but also reconciled and made peaceful in, through, and to Christ (1:19–20), especially *through* Christ, as expressed by the triple occurrence of the prepositional phrase "*through him*" (δι' αὐτοῦ), in which the first two occurrences (1:16h, 20a) are emphatically and climactically reinforced by the third occurrence, after it has intensified that this cosmic peace was established "through" (διά) the sacrificial blood of the death of Christ on his cross (1:20b).[25]

---

23. BDAG, 288. Wilson, *Colossians*, 156: "This word [εἰρηνοποιήσας] occurs only here in the New Testament, but the elements of which it is composed appear at the end of Eph. 2.15."

24. Harris, *Colossians*, 51: "There were not two separate actions (reconciliation, making peace) but only one (reconciliation) whose mode of accomplishment is then specified ('by making peace'), so that the reconciliation is related to the 'pacification' as fact to method.... God's reconciliation was achieved through Christ—specifically by God's making of peace through Christ's blood. Αἷμα ['blood'] in this context denotes life offered up sacrificially and voluntarily in death." Garland, *Colossians*, 94: "Blood refers to death by violence; the cross refers to humility and shame. The head of the church is the one who was shamefully crucified.... Paul also uses 'blood' to refer to the work of Christ's atoning sacrifice. The cross establishes a new relationship between God and humans, which overcomes the rupture created by sin—estangement from God, estrangement from other humans, and estrangement from created things. That peace can only be found now in his body. It is not yet an accomplished fact in the cosmos, but God's 'purpose, means, and manner' of making peace have already been established."

25. According to Harris (*Colossians*, 52) the phrase "through him" (δι' αὐτοῦ) in 1:20b "is not so much resumptive ('through him, *I say*,' RV) as an emphatic repetition from v. 20a ('through him alone,' NEB), comparable in effect to αὐτός in vv. 17a, 18a, 18c. Forms of αὐτός are used eleven times in vv. 15–20 in ref. to Christ." Dunn, *Colossians*, 104: "What is being claimed is quite simply and profoundly that the divine purpose in the act of reconciliation and peacemaking was to restore the harmony of the original creation, to bring into renewed oneness and wholeness 'all things,' 'whether things on the earth or things in the heavens'. That the church has a role in this is implied in the correlation of 1:18a with 1:20.... it is by its gospel living (1:10) and by its gospel preaching (1:27) that the cosmic goal of recon-

4. Col 1:21-22 (B´): God Has Now Reconciled You in the Body of Christ's Flesh

The Colossian audience now learn that God's cosmic reconciliation through Christ includes them: "And you, once being alienated and enemies in mind in works that are evil, he has now reconciled in the body of his flesh through death to present you holy and unblemished and blameless before him" (1:21-22). In the B element the audience heard that it was through Christ, who is the head of the "body" (σώματος) which is the church (1:18a), that God "reconciled" (ἀποκαταλλάξαι) all things to Christ (1:20a). And now, in the B´ element, by way of the chiastic parallelism, the audience hear that God has now also "reconciled" (ἀποκατήλλαξεν) them to Christ in the "body" (σώματι) of "his," that is, Christ's flesh, so that God might present them as holy and unblemished and blameless before "him," that is, Christ (1:22).[26]

Just as there was an implicit necessity for all things in the cosmos to be reconciled by God to Christ (1:20a) and thus restored to their proper relationship to Christ as the goal and destiny for which they were created (1:16), so also there was a necessity for the audience, introduced with an emphatic "and you" or "you also" (καὶ ὑμᾶς), to be reconciled by God to Christ, since they were once "alienated"

---

ciled perfection will be achieved (1:28)." Wilson, *Colossians*, 157-58: "The implication may be that the deficiency lies, in the author's view, in a less than adequate appreciation of the significance of Christ, and he seeks to remedy it by his proclamation of the Son's absolute supremacy, in the cosmos and in the Church. As first-born of all creation he is superior to all the powers that may exist, in heaven and on earth.... His readers have nothing to fear from hostile powers, and no need of assistance from other celestial beings." On the relationship of Colossians to Paul's theology of the cross, see Rudolf Hoppe, *Der Triumph des Kreuzes: Studien zum Verhältnis des Kolosserbriefes zur paulinischen Kreuzestheologie* (SBB 28; Stuttgart: Katholisches Bibelwerk, 1994).

26. There are various ways in which interpreters have construed the grammar of Col 1:22; for the discussion, see Wilson, *Colossians*, 164-65. Some take Christ rather than God, that is, God in all of God's fullness (1:19), as the subject of the verb "reconciled." But there is no grammatical indication of a change in the subject of the verbs in 1:19-22, as noted by Wilson, *Colossians*, 164: "[T]he flow of the Greek suggests the same subject for all the verbs in v. 19 to v. 22, i.e. πᾶν τὸ πλήρωμα ['all the fullness']." Many, whether they take God or Christ to be the subject of "reconciled," take God rather than Christ to be the referent in the prepositional phrase "before him" (κατενώπιον αὐτοῦ) at the end of 1:22. This is most unlikely for two reasons: First, if God is understood to be the referent of the pronoun "his" (αὐτοῦ), it would be an abrupt and confusing change after the previous thirteen occurrences of the same third person singular pronoun in 1:16-22a, each and every one of which, with several in emphatic positions, refers to Christ. This includes the immediately preceding occurrence in 1:22a, as noted by Wilson, *Colossians*, 164: "[T]he αὐτοῦ following κατενώπιον ['before'] must have the same referent as the first in the verse, ἐν τῷ σώματι τῆς σαρκὸς αὐτοῦ ['in the body of his flesh'], and hence refer to the Son." Secondly, "before him" as a reference to Christ in 1:22b appropriately corresponds to the previous conceptions of Christ as the cosmic goal and destiny not only of the creation ("all things have been created to him" in 1:16) but also of the reconciliation ("to reconcile all things to him" in 1:20a) of all things in the universe. In other words, God is "to present you holy and unblemished and blameless before him" (1:22b), that is, before the Christ to whom all things were created and reconciled. See also Aletti, *Colossiens*, 124-25.

from and "enemies" of God and Christ "in mind in works that are evil" (1:21).²⁷ They were once separated from and hostile toward and thus not at peace with God and Christ in both their internal attitude and external conduct.²⁸ But the audience are now to realize that the cosmic peace God made both on the earth and in the heavens "through" (διά) the sacrificial blood of the cross of Christ, that is, (emphatically) *"through"* (δι') *him* (1:20b), includes them. God has now reconciled and thus made peace with them in the body of the sacrificial flesh of Christ "through" (διά) his death (1:22a). Christ is both the means "through" whom (1:20ab, 22a) as well as the goal and destiny "to" (1:20a) and "before" whom (1:22b) they have been reconciled by God.

That God has now reconciled the audience in the body of the sacrificial "flesh" of Christ through his death (1:22a) complements God's having made peace with the entire cosmos through the sacrificial "blood" of the cross of Christ (1:20b). The consequence is that God might present "you" (ὑμᾶς, 1:22b), the audience, the "you" (ὑμᾶς, 1:22a) who were once alienated and enemies, as now holy and unblemished and blameless before Christ.²⁹ That God might present the audience as "holy" (ἁγίους) recalls and reinforces that as the "holy ones" (ἁγίοις) in Colossae

---

27. Harris, *Colossians*, 57: "Whether καὶ ὑμᾶς introduces a consequence ('and so you. . . ,' 'you also') or a new point ('moreover, you . . .'), vv. 21-22 indicate that reconciliation is personal as well as cosmic in its effects." O'Brien, *Colossians*, 65: "The opening words, 'and you,' stand in an emphatic position in Paul's sentence as he indicates that the central purpose in Christ's reconciling work has to do with the Christian readers at Colossae. It is not simply that what has occurred on a cosmic scale just happens to relate to them by way of application. Rather, this congregation is designated as the 'goal' toward which the event encompassing heaven and earth is directed. It has special reference to them, designed to reconcile those who were once alienated and at enmity with God."

28. On the perfect passive participle, "being alienated" (ὄντας ἀπηλλοτριωμένους), O'Brien (*Colossians*, 66) comments: "The Colossians were once continuously and persistently out of harmony with God, a statement that could only describe former Gentiles." Dunn, *Colossians*, 105-6: "The verb which the participle is from, ἀπαλλοτριόω ('estrange, alienate'), appears only here and in Eph. 2:12 and 4:18, but the passive (used in all three cases) would be familiar in reference to human estangement, and to alienation from God by sin and idolatry. That human guilt and hostility are in view, and not nameless fate or inscrutable destiny, is clear from the supplementary description: 'enemies in mind' and 'in works that are wicked.' . . . In this case διάνοια has the force of 'mind (as a kind of thinking), disposition, thought,' hence 'hostile in attitude.' . . . Consequently the 'deeds' which such an attitude produces are 'wicked,' where the stronger adjective πονηρός ('wicked, evil') is used rather than κακός ('bad')." Garland, *Colossians*, 96: "The word 'alienated' (1:21) implies isolation, loneliness, and a deep sense of not belonging. The phrase 'from God' is not in the Greek text but fits a Jewish perspective that all Gentiles by definition lived apart from the one true God." Deterding, *Colossians*, 66: "The periphrastic construction with the two participles ὄντας ἀπηλλοτριωμένους denotes that alienation from God is the continual state of those without Christ. In the NT, ἐχθρός is used mostly, if not exclusively, to describe one who hates rather than one who is hated. Hence those without Christ are 'hostile' toward God." Wilson, *Colossians*, 161: "τῇ διανοίᾳ indicates that it is not a literal hostility that is in view: it is a question rather of attitude, of heart and mind."

29. Dunn, *Colossians*, 109: "The repetition of 'you' underscores how personalized was the divine condecension; of course, it does not mean 'you alone' but 'you' among all the other 'you's, all of whom could count themselves the beneficiaries of personally characterized and directed grace."

(1:2), who have love for all the other "holy ones" (ἁγίους) in their faith in Christ Jesus (1:4), God has made them fit for the share of the inheritance of the "holy ones" (ἁγίων) in the light (1:12). The audience are to realize then that it is as "holy ones" that they are part of the "body" (σώματος), the church, of which Christ is the "head" (1:18a), that is, the authoritative origin and source, before whom God is to present them, as those he has reconciled in the "body" (σώματι) of the flesh of Christ, so that Christ is also their goal and destiny (1:22).[30]

That God might present the audience as "holy" (ἁγίους) and "unblemished" (ἀμώμους) and "blameless" (ἀνεγκλήτους) before Christ (1:22b) functions as an alliterative rhetorical triplet within a combination of cultic and juridical imagery,[31] as indicated by the terminology of "presenting" someone "before" Christ, that is, presenting one as an acceptable sacrificial offering for approval before Christ, as well as presenting one deemed to be completely innocent and worthy before the judgment of Christ.[32] This rhetorically rich combination impresses upon the audience, first of all, in accord with the cultic side of the imagery, that the sacrificial offering of Christ through his death on the cross has graciously transformed them likewise into a sacrificial offering—indeed, one that is "holy and unblemished and blameless" before Christ himself.

Secondly, in accord with the juridical side of the imagery, the audience are to realize that the sacrificial death of Christ has empowered them to live as morally "holy" and "unblemished" and "blameless" ones both now and for the final judg-

---

30. Dunn, *Colossians*, 107-8: "This is the second occurrence of σῶμα ('body') in the letter (after 1:18a), the second of one of the most fascinating kaleidoscopes of usage that we can imagine in a key Pauline category. Here it clearly denotes the human body of Christ on the cross, though the 'in' may be locative and not merely instrumental, denoting, that is, not merely the means of identification but also that identification with Christ which is at the heart of Paul's 'in Christ' and 'suffering with Christ' motif.... the σῶμα with which Christ achieved his act of reconciliation was merely that of one single frail human being. 'Of flesh' ensures that this σῶμα could never be confused with the σῶμα of 1:18. The negative here, then, would be the sharpness of the antithesis between glorious cosmic body and individual human frame stretched out in the agonizing humility of crucifixion."

31. As Harris (*Colossians*, 59) remarks, the repeated καί ("and") in this triplet suggests "three distinct descriptions, one positive ('holy') and two negative with the negating α-privative ('free from blemish and beyond accusation')."

32. Harris (*Colossians*, 59) notes that in 1:22 the verb "to present" (παραστῆσαι) "may have legal overtones or a sacrificial setting." O'Brien, *Colossians*, 68: "Cultic terminology is employed in this statement. So the words 'holy' (ἅγιος) and 'blameless' (ἄμωμος) are used to describe the unblemished animals set apart for God as ΟΤ sacrifices. Futhermore, the verb παραστῆσαι ('to present') was, on occasion, employed in presenting a sacrifice.... The last term 'irreproachable' (ἀνέγκλητος) ... was a judicial word denoting a person or thing against which there could be no ἔγκλημα and which was 'free from reproach,' 'without stain.' Likewise the verb παραστῆσαι ('to present') was often employed in legal language with the meaning 'to bring another before the court.'" Dunn, *Colossians*, 109: "The imagery is drawn from cult and law court and reflects the degree to which these two powerful features of daily life in classical society were interwoven. Παρίστημι ('present') here signifies a formal bringing before and presentation in the implied hope of acceptance and acknowledgment. Thus it could be used both of offering a sacrifice and of bringing someone before a judge."

ment before Christ.³³ This means that, as those whom God has reconciled and with whom God has made peace through Christ, the audience need no longer conduct themselves in works that are evil (1:21), but can and must behave as those whom God, both now and ultimately, is to present as "holy and unblemished and blameless" before Christ (1:22b).³⁴

In sum, the B′ element (1:21-22) impresses upon the audience that as members of the "body" of Christ, the church (1:18), God's reconciliation and making of peace with the cosmos (1:20) embraces also and especially them, as those who were once alienated from and enemies of God (1:21), but are now reconciled by God in the "body" of the sacrificial flesh of Christ through his death, so that God might present them as totally acceptable and worthy before Christ (1:22).

5. Col 1:23 (A′): The Gospel Proclaimed in All Creation under Heaven

God's reconciliation of, making peace with, and presentation of the Colossian audience as fully acceptable before Christ (1:20-22) carries with it a condition, as indicated in the climactic A′ element of the chiasm: "if indeed you persevere in the faith, having been established and steadfast and not shifting from the hope of the gospel which you heard, which was proclaimed in all creation that is under heaven, of which I became, I, Paul, a minister" (1:23). In the A element (1:15-16) the audience heard that Christ is the firstborn of "all creation" (πάσης κτίσεως), for in him were created all the invisible things in the "heavens" (οὐρανοῖς). And now, by way of the chiastic parallelism, in the A′ element they hear that the gospel has been proclaimed in "all creation" (πάσῃ κτίσει) that is under "heaven" (οὐρανόν).³⁵ Thus, the focus in the A element on the invisible things of all creation "in" (ἐν) the heavens—"whether thrones or dominions or principalities or authorities"—progresses in the A′ element to a focus on the gospel proclaimed in all creation that is "under" (ὑπό) heaven, under the invisible cosmic powers.

With the conditional clause, "if indeed you persevere in the faith (πίστει)"

---

33. Deterding, *Colossians*, 67: "[T]he entire infinitive clause here ('to present ... before him') refers to our Lord's role as eschatological judge of the living and the dead.... 'Before him' refers to Christ's presence, especially in the final judgment, when he will come as judge of the living and the dead."

34. Dunn, *Colossians*, 109-10: "There is implicit, then, an interplay between the idea of Christ's death as sacrifice (1:20) and the presentation of those who are as unblemished as a sacrifice to God. In other words, there is an echo of the Pauline idea of sacrificial interchange, where the spotless sacrifice by dying as a sin offering is somehow interchanged with the blameworthy sinner and its spotlessness transferred to the sinner. This has been taken up in the imagery of formal presentation to judge or king or emperor, where it is the irreproachable character of those presented that guarantees their acceptance. But it is clearly implicit that this acceptability has been made possible and guaranteed by the death of Christ." Garland, *Colossians*, 97: "Paul emphasizes that Christ has accomplished this perfection for us, it does not come from our own striving. But God's goal of making us a holy and blameless people in Christ is still a work in progress, and it requires some response on our part. Christians need to recognize that they have been reconciled to God to live a life that God approves."

35. It is noteworthy for the establishment of the chiasm that these are the only two occurrences in the entire letter of the phrase "all creation."

(1:23), the audience learn that Paul expects them to continue, to persist, to persevere in their "faith" (πίστιν) in Christ Jesus of which Paul and Timothy have heard (1:4).[36] The rhetorical triplet that describes the audience as "having been established and steadfast and not shifting" (1:23) complements the previous rhetorical triplet—"holy and without blemish and blameless," as it specifies the conditions for which they are responsible if God is to reconcile them and present them as totally acceptable and worthy before Christ (1:22).[37] That the audience, who "have been established" (the perfect passive participle τεθεμελιωμένοι) by God (divine passive) and are thus to continue to be steadfast and not shifting "from the hope (ἐλπίδος) of the gospel (εὐαγγελίου) which you heard (ἠκούσατε)" (1:23) recalls the "hope" (ἐλπίδα) laid up for them in the heavens, which "you have heard before" (προηκούσατε) in the word of the truth of the "gospel" (εὐαγγελίου) (1:5).[38] And that the gospel was proclaimed in "all" (πάσῃ) creation that is under heaven (1:23) recalls that in "all" (παντί) the world the gospel is bearing fruit and growing, as it is also among the Colossian believers (1:6).[39]

With an emphatic "I" in the statement about the gospel "of which I became, I (ἐγώ), Paul, a minister" (1:23), the audience's attention is now focused solely on Paul, as distinct from Timothy, the other co-sender of the letter (1:1). That Paul

---

36. Harris, *Colossians*, 60: "[T]his condition is neither a hypothesis or simply a hope but a condition that Paul is confident or assumes will be fulfilled: 'if you continue—and I am confident/I am assuming that you will.'" Wright, *Colossians*, 84: "The verb 'continue' (ἐπιμένειν) often has the sense, in constructions like this, of remaining in a place or locality. It makes good sense here to take it in this way, and to see 'the faith' as a 'place' (perhaps, as we say, 'the Christian faith') where Christians must 'remain' rather than just the activity of believing. 'The faith' includes that activity, but goes beyond it to indicate the content of what is believed, and perhaps also the whole Christian way of life." Dunn, *Colossians*, 111: "It is probably the faith by which the Colossians first received the gospel which is referred to here: without that same basic conviction and openness to the grace of God they would be unable to persist."

37. Dunn, *Colossians*, 111: "'Established' (τεθεμελιωμένοι) uses the image of a 'foundation' (θεμέλιος). The verb occurs only here and in Eph. 3:17 in the Pauline corpus, but Paul liked to think of himself as a master builder laying a foundation of the gospel or of faith in Christ (Rom. 15:20; 1 Cor. 3:10-12)." Harris, *Colossians*, 60: "If the architectural symbolism behind ... τεθεμελιωμένοι was preserved in general usage, the sense is 'with your foundation established and your structure immovable (ἑδραῖοι).' But both terms are more probably related to the πίστις Paul has just mentioned.... Paraphrase: 'if indeed you continue exercising faith—faith in which you were once (implied by the pf. tense) firmly founded and now should be steadfast' (ἑδραῖοι resuming the thought of perseverance found in ἐπιμένετε)."

38. Bruce, *Colossians*, 79: "The language used may suggest that the readers' first enthusiasm was being dimmed, that they were in danger of shifting from the fixed ground of Christian hope." Deterding, *Colossians*, 70: "The emphasis here is more on the objective content of the Christian faith and hope, although not without including the (subjective) faith by which Christians believe and hope, for the necessary fact of believing and hoping rests on the objective certainty of the content of the Christian faith and hope."

39. Harris, *Colossians*, 61-62: "Like v. 6 ('all over the world'), this statement is hyperbolic, highlighting the proclamation of the good news not to every person on earth without exception but to every type of person in every place."

became a "minister" (διάκονος) of the gospel places him along side of and in continuity with Epaphras, a faithful "minister" (διάκονος) of Christ on behalf of the audience, from whom they first learned the gospel (1:7). The audience are now poised to hear what Paul alone, the authoritative apostle of Christ Jesus by the will of God (1:1), has to say to them as one who is also a minister of the gospel, the gospel about God's creation and reconciliation of the cosmos in, through, and to Christ (1:15–23).[40]

To sum up, through its chiastic progression, the letter's third unit (1:15–23) impresses upon the audience that God's reconciliation of and making of peace with the entire cosmos after God's creation of it in, through, and to Christ (1:15–20) extends to them, so that God is to present them as holy and unblemished and blameless before Christ, if they continue to persevere in the faith and hope of the gospel they first learned from Epaphras (1:7), but of which Paul himself has become a minister (1:21–23).[41] At this point the audience are poised to hear what Paul as a minister of this gospel has to say to them, so that they may indeed persevere in the faith and hope of the gospel.

B. Summary on Colossians 1:15–23

1. The mini-chiasm in 1:16 takes the audience from the past creation in Christ of all things in the cosmos, through an emphatic assertion that all heavenly, invisible powers were also created in the sphere of Christ, and climactically concluding that all things in the cosmos not only have been created but still are existing as created entities through and to Christ.

2. The A element (1:15–17) of the chiasm in 1:15–23 climactically concludes with the verb "hold together" in the perfect tense—all things *in him* presently and continually hold together, that is, all things in the cosmos, rather than disintegrating into chaos, in Christ, as the operating principle controlling all of creation, constantly and continually remain held together in existence.

---

40. Bruce, *Colossians*, 80: "In a letter of joint authorship the locution 'I Paul' indicates that at this point the apostle himself takes direct responsibility for what is said." O'Brien, *Colossians*, 71: "Having begun his thanksgiving report at verse 3 with the plural '*we* give thanks'—so writing on behalf of Timothy and perhaps others as well as himself—Paul now wishes to emphasize his own ministry as closely bound up with God's gracious plan for the world and so he emphatically turns to the singular: 'of which (*sc.* gospel) I, Paul, became a minister'.... Paul appears to be making a different point in this context, namely that the message which focuses on the lordship of Christ and the reconciliation wrought by him is the mighty gospel of which he has been privileged to become a servant. He of all people has become a minister of that gospel." Wilson, *Colossians*, 167: "For the first time, the author uses a first person singular rather than the plural he has hitherto employed, and indeed with a certain emphasis: ἐγὼ Παῦλος.... What is striking here is that no claim is made for any special status or authority: Paul has become a διάκονος of the gospel, a word applied in v. 7 to Epaphras."

41. On the warning contained in 1:21–23, see C. C. Bing, "The Warning in Colossians 1:21–23," *BSac* 164 (2007): 74–88.

3. In the B element (1:18–20a) the audience experience a series of hymnic assertions involving emphatic uses of the third person masculine singular pronoun referring to Christ, beginning with his exalted position in relation to the church and ending with him as the orientation, goal, and destiny of a cosmic reconciliation: *He himself* is the head of the body, the church, and the beginning, the firstborn from the dead, that *he himself* might become in all things preeminent (1:18), for in *him* all the fullness chose to dwell (1:19) and through *him* to reconcile all things to *him* (1:20a).

4. In the central C element (1:20b) the audience realize that all things on the earth and in the heavens, especially the invisible, heavenly powers, were not only created (1:16) but also reconciled and made peaceful in, through, and to Christ (1:19–20), especially *through* Christ, as expressed by the triple occurrence of the prepositional phrase "*through him*," in which the first two occurrences (1:16h, 20a) are emphatically and climactically reinforced by the third occurrence, after it has intensified that this cosmic peace was established "through" the sacrificial blood of the death of Christ on his cross (1:20b).

5. The B′ element (1:21–22) impresses upon the audience that as members of the "body" of Christ, the church (1:18), God's reconciliation and making of peace with the cosmos (1:20) embraces also and especially them, as those who were once alienated from and enemies of God (1:21), but are now reconciled by God in the "body" of the sacrificial flesh of Christ through his death, so that God might present them as "holy ones" (1:2, 12) who are totally acceptable and worthy before Christ (1:22).

6. The letter's third chiastic unit (1:15–23) impresses upon the audience that God's reconciliation of and making of peace with the entire cosmos after God's creation of it in, through, and to Christ (1:15–20) extends to them, so that God is to present them as holy and unblemished and blameless before Christ, if they continue to persevere in the faith and hope of the gospel they first learned from Epaphras (1:7), but of which Paul himself has become a minister (1:21–23). At the point of the climactic A′ element (1:23) of the chiasm the audience are poised to hear what Paul as a minister of this gospel has to say to them, so that they may indeed persevere in the faith and hope of the gospel.

6

Colossians 1:24–2:5

We Are Admonishing and Teaching Every Human Being in All Wisdom (D)

In Christ are all the treasures of wisdom and knowledge hidden
A: [24] Now I am *rejoicing* in the sufferings on behalf of you and I am filling up what is lacking of the afflictions of the Christ in my *flesh* on behalf of his body, which is the church, [25] of which I became, I, a minister according to the plan of God given to me to fulfill for you the *word* of God,
    B: [26] the *mystery* that has been *hidden* from the ages and from the generations. But now it has been manifested to his holy ones, [27] to whom God wished to make known what is the *richness* of the glory of this *mystery* among the Gentiles, which is Christ among you, the hope of the glory. [28] Him we proclaim, admonishing every human being and teaching every human being in all *wisdom*, that we may present every human being complete in Christ.
        C: [29a] For this I also labor, *struggling*
            D: [29b] according to his *working*
            D′: [29c] that is *working* in me in power.
        C′: [2:1] For I wish you to know how great a *struggle* I am having on behalf of you and those in Laodicea and as many as have not seen my face in the flesh,
    B′: [2] that their hearts may be encouraged as they are held together in love, and for all *richness* of the full assurance of understanding, for knowledge of the *mystery* of God, Christ, [3] in whom are all the treasures of *wisdom* and knowledge *hidden*.
A′: [4] This I *speak*, that no one may speak contrary to you with persuasive speech. [5] For even if in the *flesh* I am absent, yet in the Spirit I am with you, *rejoicing* at seeing your good order and the firmness of your faith in Christ.[1]

---

1. For the establishment of 1:24–2:5 as a chiasm, see ch. 2.

A. Audience Response to Colossians 1:24–2:5

1. Col 1:24–25 (A): Paul Is Rejoicing in the Sufferings of His Flesh

After climactically and emphatically singling himself out with the words, "of which (gospel) I became, I, Paul, a minister" (1:23), Paul elaborates on his ministry: "Now I am rejoicing in the sufferings on behalf of you and I am filling up what is lacking of the afflictions of the Christ in my flesh on behalf of his body, which is the church, of which I became a minister according to the plan of God given to me to fulfill for you the word of God" (1:24–25). Previously Paul indicated to the audience that despite their need "for all endurance and patience" (1:11a), which implies their own sufferings and afflictions as believers, they may have joy—"with joy (χαρᾶς) thanking the Father who has made you fit for the share of the inheritance of the holy ones in the light" (1:11b–12). As a minister of the gospel, Paul similarly has joy in the midst of his sufferings: "Now I am rejoicing (χαίρω) in the sufferings on behalf of you" (1:24a).

At this point the audience hear a development regarding individuals acting on their behalf. They learned the gospel from Epaphras, who is a faithful minister of Christ "on behalf of you" (ὑπὲρ ὑμῶν, 1:7). Paul and Timothy do not cease praying "on behalf of you" (ὑπὲρ ὑμῶν, 1:9). And now Paul informs the audience that as a minister of the gospel he is rejoicing in his sufferings "on behalf of you" (ὑπὲρ ὑμῶν, 1:24a).[2] But the audience then learn that it is as members of the church that they have benefited by Paul's sufferings, as he goes on to explain that he is filling up what is lacking of the afflictions of the Christ in his flesh "on behalf of" (ὑπέρ) his body, which is the church (1:24b).

That Paul is filling up what is lacking of the afflictions of the Christ in his "flesh" (σαρκί) on behalf of the "body" (σώματος) of Christ, which is the church (1:24b), recalls for the audience that God reconciled them, who were once alienated from and enemies of God (1:21), in the "body" (σώματι) of the "flesh" (σαρκός) (1:22) of Christ, who is head of the "body" (σώματος), the church (1:18a).[3] The audience are to realize that by "filling up what is lacking," that is, by making present what is absent or completing what is remaining,[4] of the "afflictions of the Christ," the af-

---

2. On Paul's "sufferings" (παθήμασιν) here, Jacob Kremer ("πάθημα," *EDNT* 3.1) explains: "In several instances τὰ παθήματα clearly indicates the *sufferings* to which Christians and esp. the apostles are subject in this world and which result primarily from persecution ... Christians experience this suffering in fellowship with Christ" (Kremer's emphasis).

3. Dunn, *Colossians*, 117: "[W]e should not ignore the further interplay with 1:22: the act of reconciliation took place ἐν τῷ σώματι τῆς σαρκὸς αὐτοῦ; Paul fills up what is lacking of the afflictions of Christ ἐν τῇ σαρκί μου ὑπὲρ τοῦ σώματος αὐτοῦ. There is a degree of continuity between Christ's body of flesh and Paul's flesh for Christ's body."

4. Terminology very similar to "I am filling up" (ἀνταναπληρῶ) "what is lacking" (τὰ ὑστερήματα) in Col 1:24 that occurs elsewhere in the Pauline corpus helps to clarify this expression. In 1 Cor 16:17 Paul rejoices in the arrival of Stephanas, Fortunatus, and Achaicus, because "they fulfilled" (ἀνεπλήρωσαν) your "lacking" (ὑστέρημα), that is, they made up for your absence, they represented

flictions experienced by believers in union with Christ, in his "flesh" on behalf of the "body" of Christ, which is the church,[5] Paul is playing his role in actualizing and bringing to completion for the Colossian believers the reconciliation that God has effected in the "body" of the "flesh" of Christ for the sake of the "body," the church. In other words, by his sufferings on behalf of his Colossian audience Paul is making present and completing for them in his own flesh the afflictions of the Christ that have enabled them, whom God has reconciled in the body of the flesh of Christ, to become members of the body of Christ, the church.[6]

This is confirmed as Paul goes on to inform his Colossian audience that he

---

you or made you present. In Phil 2:30 Paul says that Epaphroditus risked his life that he might "fill up" (ἀναπληρώσῃ) what was "lacking" (ὑστέρημα) in your service for me, that is, he made up for their absence, he represented them or made them present. Whether there is an added nuance to the extra prefix in ἀνταναπληρῶ in Col 1:24 as opposed to ἀναπληρῶ, the form in 1 Cor 16:17 and Phil 2:30 is debatable; see Jerry L. Sumney, "'I Fill Up What Is Lacking in the Afflictions of Christ': Paul's Vicarious Suffering in Colossians," *CBQ* 68 (2006): 676–77. Thus, in Col 1:24 Paul "is filling up" in the sense of making present or completing "what is lacking," that is, what is absent or remaining of the afflictions of the Christ in his flesh. See also Garland, *Colossians*, 122.

5. Harris, *Colossians*, 66: "Paul regarded his sufferings as a servant of the gospel as part of what still remained of the sufferings due to all who are united with Christ . . . Any suffering endured by the servant of Christ in the service of Christ and for the benefit of his Church is part of 'the afflictions of Christ.'" With regard to Paul's "filling up what is lacking of the afflictions of the Christ" here, Gorman (*Apostle*, 484) remarks: "In the context of this letter that exalts the completeness of Christ's person and work, this claim cannot mean that Christ's passion was somehow deficient. Rather, it suggests that because Christ's suffering and death were definitive of God's self-revelation and activity in the world, they must be continued in the life of the apostle." Frank J. Matera, *New Testament Theology: Exploring Diversity and Unity* (Louisville: Westminster John Knox, 2007), 217 n. 27: "Paul, of course, does not mean that his personal sufferings are redemptive in the way that Christ's sufferings are. Nor is he implying that there was something lacking in Christ's redemptive work. The expression 'Christ's afflictions' refers to the afflictions the church must endure on behalf of Christ, before the completion of all things, rather than to Christ's own afflictions or sufferings. It is these afflictions on behalf of Christ that the apostle endures for the sake of the church, the body of Christ."

6. Garland, *Colossians*, 122: "What is lacking is Christ's bodily presence. Paul's physical suffering as a member of Christ's body represents Christ's continuing suffering for the world through his servants. . . . He suffers as the representative of Christ . . . 'What is lacking' has nothing to do with some measure that must be filled but is an idiom for representing Christ bodily (see Phil 1:20). Paul's suffering for the cause of Christ is emblematic of his ministry . . . He presents himself as an example of the indwelling mystery of Christ's cross working itself out in a human life, and he makes the astonishing claim that he is suffering for them as Christ would suffer were he present bodily." According to Sumney ("Paul's Vicarious Suffering," 679), Paul's sufferings in Colossians "serve two important functions. First, they contribute to the letter's construction of a persuasive ethos for Paul. His willingness to suffer for the readers' sake shows how much he cares for them and so builds goodwill with them by demonstrating that he has their best interest at heart. . . . The second function of Paul's sufferings is mimetic; they are exemplary in a sense that goes beyond the rote copying of enduring persecution. The readers are to imitate his faithful endurance of suffering by striving to obey faithfully the commands he gives in the letter. In this way his sufferings are vicarious." See also Andrew C. Perriman, "The Pattern of Christ's Sufferings: Colossians 1:24 and Philippians 3:10–11," *TynBul* 42 (1991): 62–79; Jacob Kremer, "Was an den Bedrängnissen des Christus mangelt: Versuch einer bibeltheologischen Neuinterpretation von Kol 1,24," *Bib* 82 (2001): 130–46.

became a minister of the church according to the plan of God given to him to fulfill or complete for them the word of God (1:25).[7] The purpose of Paul's "filling up" (ἀνταναπληρῶ) what is lacking of the afflictions of the Christ in his flesh on behalf of the body of Christ, which is the church (1:24b), is for him to "fulfill" (πληρῶσαι) or bring to completion for his Colossian audience the "word" (λόγον) of God (1:25), that is, the "word" (λόγῳ) of the truth of the gospel (1:5).[8] Paul rejoices in his sufferings on behalf of his audience (1:24a) because they have enabled the word of the gospel to come to them (1:6a) with its message of God's reconciliation of them in the body of the flesh of Christ (1:21–22) that has made it possible for them to become members of the body of Christ, which is the church (1:18a, 24b). It is thus for the sake of bringing his Colossian audience (and other Gentiles), who have been reconciled by God, into the body of Christ that Paul is filling up what is lacking of the afflictions of the Christ in his flesh on behalf of the body of Christ, which is the church.[9]

Paul reminded his audience that they learned the word of the gospel from Epaphras, who is a faithful "minister" (διάκονος) of Christ on behalf of them (1:7). But with an emphatic "I," Paul insisted that "I became, *I*, Paul, a minister" (ἐγενόμην ἐγὼ Παῦλος διάκονος) of the gospel (1:23). And now, with another emphatic "I," the audience hear that "I became, *I*, a minister" (ἐγενόμην ἐγὼ διάκονος) of the church to fulfill the word of God, the gospel, for the Colossian audience (1:25). These emphatic statements about Paul as minister thus serve as the transitional words linking this unit (1:24–2:5) with the previous one (1:15–23). It is by his sufferings on behalf of his audience that Paul, the minister of the gospel and of the church, fills up what is lacking of the afflictions of the Christ in his flesh on behalf of the body of Christ, which is the church (1:24), in order to make effective and bring to completion the word of God, the gospel, for his audience, enabling them to become members of the body of Christ, the church, of which Christ is the "head" (1:18a) and Paul the preeminent minister (1:25).

---

7. On the meaning of "God's plan" for οἰκονομίαν τοῦ θεοῦ here, O'Brien (*Colossians*, 81) points out: "At Colossians 1:25 this nuance of God's plan, which is administered by him [Paul], is most likely for the following reasons: (a) οἰκονομία τοῦ θεοῦ had this general sense in the Hellenistic world, (b) the genitive τοῦ θεοῦ which is subjective supports this interpretation, and (c) κατά ('according to') suggests the notion of a plan in this context."

8. On the parallelism between Paul's "filling up" (ἀνταναπληρῶ) what is lacking of the afflictions of the Christ in his flesh and "to fulfill" (πληρῶσαι) the word of God for his Colossian audience, see Michael Cahill, "The Neglected Parallelism in Colossians 1,24–25," *ETL* 68 (1992): 142–47. On "word" as a term for "gospel," particularly for Paul, see Michael W. Pahl, "The 'Gospel' and the 'Word': Exploring Some Early Christian Patterns," *JSNT* 29 (2006): 211–27.

9. Garland, *Colossians*, 122–23: "Paul's suffering, unlike Christ's death on the cross, does not save them from their sins. Instead, it is connected to his Gentile mission and comes as the byproduct of preaching the gospel to a hostile, pagan world. Paul was in prison because he proclaimed the gospel (see Eph 3:1), and that struggle on their behalf (2:1) has brought the benefits of the gospel to them. These sufferings did not hinder the proclamation of the gospel but were part of furthering it (see Phil 1:12–14)."

2. Col 1:26–28 (B): The Richness of the Glory of the Mystery in All Wisdom

The word of God that Paul is to bring to completion as a minister of the gospel (1:23) and of the church (1:25) Paul further explains as "the mystery that has been hidden from the ages and from the generations. But now it has been manifested to his holy ones" (1:26). The "mystery" that is the gospel and the word of God is God's secret plan of salvation that has long been hidden by God (divine passive) from the ages of past times as well as from the generations of past peoples.[10] But now in the present time it has been manifested by God (divine passive) to God's "holy ones" (ἁγίοις), that is, all those who believe in Christ. These "holy ones" then include the Colossian audience themselves, who are "holy ones" (ἁγίοις) and faithful brothers in Christ (1:2), as well as all the other "holy ones"(ἁγίους) for whom the Colossian holy ones have love (1:4), the "holy ones" (ἁγίων) with whom God has made the Colossian holy ones fit to share the inheritance (1:12).

Paul then explains what this mystery entails and how it embraces the holy ones to whom God has manifested it: "to whom God wished to make known what is the richness of the glory of this mystery among the Gentiles, which is Christ among you, the hope of the glory" (1:27).[11] The audience hear as a mini-chiasm what God "wished" or "willed" to make known to them as those included within God's holy ones:[12]

a: what is the richness of the glory (τῆς δόξης)[13]

---

10. On the meaning of "mystery" (μυστήριον) here Harris (*Colossians*, 68) explains: "In Pauline usage, it denotes in general a divine truth, unknowable by humankind apart from revelation and once hidden but now disclosed in the gospel era as embodied in the person of Christ. More specifically it refers to God's secret plan of salvation involving the admission of the Gentiles into the freshly constituted people of God and into the benefits of the new covenant on equal terms with the Jews." On the two prepositional phrases, "from (ἀπό) the ages and from (ἀπό) the generations," Harris (*Colossians*, 69) states that "it is possible to take the first ἀπό temp[orally]. and the second locally—'through all past ages and from all mankind.'" According to Wilson (*Colossians*, 177), following Aletti (*Colossiens*, 139), "the phrase should not be regarded as merely temporal ... it includes reference to the people in past ages and generations from whom the mystery has been concealed."

11. The reason for translating Χριστὸς ἐν ὑμῖν as "Christ among you" rather than "Christ in you" (as in many translations) is to preserve the intended and emphatic parallel with "this mystery among the Gentiles" (τοῦ μυστηρίου τούτου ἐν τοῖς ἔθνεσιν). Maisch, *Gemeinde in Kolossä*, 141: "Den Adressaten aus den Heidenvölkern wird *nach Gottes Willen* das volle Geheimnis enthüllt, nämlich, '*Christus unter euch*.' Die Übersetzung 'unter euch bzw. bei euch' entspricht dem vorangehenden 'unter den Völkern bzw. bei den Völkern'; gemeint ist nicht eine mystische Innerlichkeit (=Christus in euch), sondern dass die Botschaft von Christus wie *zu den Völkern* so auch *zu euch*, den Christen und Christinnen in Kolossä, gekommen ist" (Maisch's emphasis). Wright, *Colossians*, 92: "This could be taken as 'Christ among you' (the 'you' is plural), its emphasis being that of the immediately preceding phrase, 'among the Gentiles.'"

12. On the verb ἠθέλησεν here Dunn (*Colossians*, 121) notes: "[T]he aorist tense indicates more of a decision made, so 'willed, resolved, chose.'"

13. O'Brien, *Colossians*, 86: "Here at Colossians 1:27 'riches' and 'glory' are used together to point to the immense greatness of the mystery (the two terms are often mentioned together in the OT; cf.

b: of this mystery among (ἐν) the Gentiles,
   b′: which is Christ among (ἐν) you,
  a′: the hope of the glory (τῆς δόξης)

At the middle of this mini-chiasm (b and b′) the audience hear a pivot from the "mystery" that is "among" the Gentiles to the "Christ" who is "among" you. Thus, the audience hear not only that the mystery is identified as Christ himself, but that this mystery which is Christ is not only among the Gentiles in general, but is specifically and especially among "*you*"—Paul's audience, the believing Gentiles at Colossae.

From the beginning (a) to the end (a′) of the mini-chiasm in 1:27 the audience hear a progression involving "the glory" of this mystery. What is "the richness" of "the glory" of this mystery which is Christ among not only the Gentiles but the audience progresses to "the hope" of "the glory." Thus, the audience hear the "richness" of the glory further described as the "hope" of the glory, as well as the mystery which is Christ further identified as the "hope" of the glory. The "hope" (ἐλπίς) of the glory recalls for the audience the "hope" (ἐλπίδος) of the gospel they heard (1:23), the "hope" (ἐλπίδα) laid up for them in the heavens (1:5).[14] The audience are to realize, then, that as those Gentiles among whom is the mystery which is Christ, they also have the hope identified and represented by Christ himself, the hope of sharing in the richness of God's own "glory" (δόξης; see "the might of his," that is, God's, "glory [δόξης]" in 1:11), the divine glory awaiting them in the heavens.[15]

Reverting to the first person plural and thus speaking not only for himself, as a minister of the gospel and of the church (1:23, 25), but for the co-sender of the letter, Timothy (1:1), and for his other co-workers as well, such as Epaphras (1:7), Paul points to the goal of this gospel ministry, which begins and ends with Christ: "Him we proclaim, admonishing every human being and teaching every human being in all wisdom, that we may present every human being complete in

---

LXX Gen 31:16; 1 Kings 3:13; 1 Chron 29:28; etc)." Dunn, *Colossians*, 121: "Τὸ πλοῦτος τῆς δόξης ('the wealth/riches of the glory') has something of a liturgical ring and again heightens the sense both of divine condescension and that what has been revealed is itself a manifestation of the heavenly majesty of God." Wilson, *Colossians*, 178: "The phrase πλοῦτος τῆς δόξης occurs not only in Eph. 1.18 and 3.16, but also in Rom. 9.23."

14. Harris, *Colossians*, 71: "Ἐλπίς refers to an assured hope, not a vague possibility or even merely an expectation."

15. Garland, *Colossians*, 126: "What made this so mysterious to many Jews was their conviction that the 'adoption as sons . . . the divine glory, the covenants, the receiving of the law . . . and the promises' belonged to Israel and to Israel alone (Rom. 9:4). The 'Christ' also belonged to the race of Israel (9:5), and most took for granted that his purpose in coming was to restore glory and privilege to Israel (see Acts 1:6). Christ among the Gentiles and for the Gentiles seriously undermined most Jewish expectations. . . . The mystery revealed to Paul was that God intended to save the Gentiles *from the beginning* (Garland's emphasis). Christ 'among the Gentiles' was not Plan B after the gospel had been rejected by Jews. Rather, it was God's eternal purpose."

Christ" (1:28).¹⁶ Within this declaration the audience hear a progressive rhetorical triplet involving "every human being."¹⁷ The proclaiming of Christ by Paul and his co-workers is elaborated, first, as simply "admonishing *every human being* (πάντα ἄνθρωπον)," and then, secondly, progresses to "teaching *every human being* (πάντα ἄνθρωπον)," with the addition of the phrase "in all wisdom." Thirdly and finally, the triplet climaxes with the goal of this proclamation—"that we may present *every human being* (πάντα ἄνθρωπον) complete in Christ," thus progressing from every human being taught "in (ἐν) all wisdom" to every human being presented complete "in (ἐν) Christ."

That the proclamation of Christ includes teaching every human being "in all wisdom" (ἐν πάσῃ σοφίᾳ, 1:28) recalls and develops the previous prayer by the senders of the letter, Paul and Timothy, that their Colossian audience may be filled with the knowledge of God's will "in all wisdom" (ἐν πάσῃ σοφίᾳ), that is, within the realm of all the wisdom given by the Spirit (1:9). The prayer for the *audience* to be filled with the knowledge of God's will "in all wisdom" thus progresses to the proclamation of Christ that teaches *every human being*, thus including the audience, "in all wisdom." The goal of the proclamation is thus to fulfill the prayer for not only the audience but for every human being to be taught "in all wisdom." That the teaching of every human being "in (ἐν) all wisdom" is to result in the presentation of every human being as complete "in (ἐν) Christ" thus indicates to the audience the close, parallel correspondence between "all wisdom" and "Christ." Indeed, since the teaching of every human being "in all wisdom" is part of the proclamation of Christ, for every human being to be taught "in all wisdom" is synonymous to being taught "in Christ."¹⁸

That by proclaiming Christ Paul and his co-workers might "present"

---

16. Wilson, *Colossians*, 180: "The 'we' is probably not an editorial 'we', but a recognition that others also have shared in the proclamation of the gospel, at least it includes the apostles and evangelists, and Paul's co-workers, but it could have an even wider reference, 'we Christians.'" O'Brien, *Colossians*, 87–88: "The first verb 'proclaim' (καταγγέλλω) is a weighty one occurring only in Acts and Paul becoming almost a technical term for missionary preaching since it was normally used of the gospel itself or some element in it.... The verb νουθετέω ('admonish,' 'warn,' 'instruct'), together with its cognate noun νουθεσία ('admonition'), had to do with setting the mind of someone in proper order, correcting him or putting him right." Dunn, *Colossians*, 123–24: "Καταγγέλλω is not simply a variation of εὐαγγελίζομαι ('preach the gospel') and κηρύσσειν ('proclaim,' 1:23). From its usage elsewhere, it carries overtones of a solemn intimation, as in the proclamation of a sacred festival or of imperial rule. Hence the use in 1 Cor. 2:1 and 9:14; and hence the use here, appropriate in speaking of a divine mystery which spans both space and time.... Νουθετέω and διδάσκω are near synonyms, both meaning 'instruct.' The former carries the implication of exhortation, warning, and correction, hence 'admonish, warn'... The latter, διδάσκω, more characteristically refers to the skill of the teacher in imparting practical and theoretical knowledge to the pupil."

17. The three occurrences of "every human being" not only emphasize the universality of the gospel, but as O'Brien (*Colossians*, 88) points out: "The singular is used to show that each person individually (ἄνθρωπος is generic) was the object of the apostle's care."

18. Dunn, *Colossians*, 124: "The warning and teaching in all wisdom is also the proclamation of Christ."

(παραστήσωμεν) every human being as "complete," "perfect," or "mature" (τέλειον) within the realm of being in union with Christ—"in Christ" (1:28), and thus as a member of the body of Christ, which is the church (1:18, 24)—leads the audience to realize that this universal proclamation of Christ complements God's reconciliation of them through the death of Christ to "present" (παραστῆσαι) them as holy and unblemished and blameless before Christ (1:22).[19] God's presentation of the *audience* as holy and unblemished and blameless before Christ is thus complemented by the presentation by Paul and his co-workers of *every human being*, thus including the audience, as "complete," as believing human persons within the body of Christ who are totally and perfectly mature, "in Christ."[20]

In sum, the audience are to realize that the mystery long hidden by God from past ages and past generations of human beings God has now manifested to them as among the holy ones, all believers (1:26). To them God wished to make known the lavish richness of the glory of this mystery that is among the Gentiles, which is Christ himself, who is among not only the Gentiles but the Colossian audience and who represents for them the assured hope of their participation in the glory of God in the heavens (1:27). In their extensive proclamation of Christ Paul and his co-workers admonish every human being and teach every human being "in all wisdom," that they might present every human being, and thus including the audience, as totally complete and mature persons within the realm of their being "in Christ;" their having been taught "in all wisdom," then, the wisdom that is part of the proclamation of Christ, results in their being presented as perfect "in Christ" (1:28).

3. Col 1:29a (C): In This Labor Paul Is Struggling

Returning to the use of the first person singular, Paul focuses on his own difficulties in the ministry of proclaiming Christ: "For this I also labor, struggling" (1:29a). While he proclaims Christ along with his co-workers and other Christians, Paul draws the attention of his audience to himself, who, as a minister of the

---

19. Dunn, *Colossians*, 125–26: "The desired state for those to be thus presented is described in a rich word, τέλειος: (1) In wider Greek usage this word could denote the quality of sacrificial victims, entire and without blemish, and is so used of the Passover lamb in Exod. 12:5. In view of the similar imagery in 1:22 such overtones are probably present here as well. (2) By natural extension it can denote the equivalent quality of moral character, of which blameless Noah was a classic example (Gen. 6:9; Sir. 44:17; Philo, *De Abrahamo* 34). . . . (3) The word is also prominently used of someone whose instruction is 'complete,' one who has advanced to 'maturity' and become 'perfect' in mastery of subject or craft. . . . This is probably the principal note here. Here again there may be a gentle reminder that any of the Colossian recipients tempted to look elsewhere for a 'fuller' experience and wisdom need to look, and should look, no further than Christ for their 'completion.'"

20. Harris, *Colossians*, 73: "Here ἐν Χριστῷ means either '(as a mature individual) in union with Christ' or '(as a mature member) of Christ's body,' the individual and corporate senses (respectively) of this phrase, rather than '(made perfect) through Christ.'" O'Brien, *Colossians*, 89: "God's work of reconciliation in Christ and Paul's active ministry have the same end in view, namely, the perfection of each man in Christ on the final day."

gospel and of the church (1:23, 25), is having a particularly arduous experience. Paul is not only "laboring" (κοπιῶ), with its connotation of an exhausting and wearisome exertion,[21] but in this strenuous labor of proclaiming Christ he is also "struggling" (ἀγωνιζόμενος), with its connotation of engaging in a fight, battle, or athletic contest.[22]

4. Col 1:29b (D): According to the Working of Christ

Paul's arduous labor in proclaiming Christ, in which he is strenuously struggling (1:29a), is "according to his working" (1:29b). More than simply "in correspondence to" or "in proportion to," "according to" (κατά) here means "because of" or "relying upon."[23] "His working" (ἐνέργειαν αὐτοῦ) refers to the working or energy generated by Christ, the Christ whom Paul is proclaiming (1:28), the Christ who is among the Colossian audience and who represents the richness of the glory of this mystery now manifested to the audience as God's holy ones (1:26–27).[24] In sum, it is the working or energy generated by Christ that Paul is relying upon as he struggles in his labor of proclaiming Christ.

5. Col 1:29c (D´): That Is Working in Paul in Power

The working or energy generated by Christ that Paul is relying upon as he struggles in his labor of proclaiming Christ (1:29ab) is the energy "that is working in me in power" (1:29c). At this point the audience hear the pivot at the center of the chiasm from the noun "working" (ἐνέργειαν) in the D element (1:29b) to its cognate verbal form, "is working" (ἐνεργουμένην), in the D´ element. With this D´ element the audience hear a very artful and rhetorically potent alliteration involving a threefold occurrence of the preposition "in" (ἐν)—"in-working" (ἐν-εργουμένην) "in" (ἐν) me "in" (ἐν) power—to emphasize how the energy generated by Christ works interiorly within Paul placing him within a realm of divine

---

21. BDAG, 358; "κοπιάω," EDNT 2.307; Ceslas Spicq, "κοπιάω," TLNT 2.328; Deterding, Colossians, 69: "κοπιάω, 'to labor,' can refer to strenuous physical exertion." O'Brien, Colossians, 90: "[I]n Colossians 1:29 the emphasis is on the great effort expended by one who labors unceasingly for the congregation's welfare." Wilson, Colossians, 182: "κοπιῶ conveys the sense of strenuous effort, of toil amid trouble and difficulty."

22. BDAG, 17; Gerhard Dautzenberg, "ἀγωνίζομαι," EDNT 1.26: "In Colossians ἀγωνίζομαι in conjunction with κοπιάω (1:29; cf. Phil 2:16) is intended to characterize the labor, effort, and sufferings (cf. 1:24) of the apostle which he takes upon himself for the sake of the proclamation of Christ and the winning of all humanity for Christ (1:28)." Deterding, Colossians, 69: "ἀγωνιζόμενος-ἀγωνίζομαι, 'to struggle,' is used of the efforts of athletic competition or other conflict." According to O'Brien (Colossians, 90), ἀγωνίζομαι "could denote a physical conflict in which weapons were used and an athletic contest."

23. Harris, Colossians, 74: "Κατά here denotes not simply correspondence ('in accordance with') or proportion ('in proportion to') but either cause ('because of') or, better, means ('using'; 'in reliance upon')."

24. Although many take the "his" that modifies "working" in 1:29 as a reference to God, as Harris (Colossians, 74) points out: "αὐτοῦ refers to Christ, the nearest explicit referent." See also Deterding, Colossians, 69, 81.

power that empowers and strengthens him for the arduous labor of proclaiming Christ, in which he is struggling so strenuously.²⁵

Previously Paul and Timothy assured the audience that they do not cease praying (1:9) that the audience may be empowered "within" (ἐν) a realm of all "power" (δυνάμει) "according to" (κατά) the might of God's glory for all endurance and patience (1:11), as they in every good work are bearing fruit and growing with regard to the knowledge of God (1:10). Now, similarly, Paul is being empowered "according to" (κατά) the energy generated by Christ that is working interiorly within him "within" (ἐν) a realm of divine "power" (δυνάμει), as he struggles in his work of proclaiming Christ (1:29). The audience are thus to realize that it is because the energy generated by Christ is working in Paul "in power" (ἐν δυνάμει) that he is empowered interiorly, as he struggles in the work he shares with others of proclaiming Christ, to teach every human being "in all wisdom" (ἐν πάσῃ σοφίᾳ) that Paul and his co-workers may present every human being complete "in Christ" (ἐν Χριστῷ) (1:28).²⁶

6. Col 2:1 (C´): This Great Struggle of Paul Is on Behalf of His Audiences

Paul then relates his struggling in the work of proclaiming Christ, for which he is being interiorly empowered by the energy generated within him by Christ (1:29), directly to his Colossian audience as well as other potential audiences: "For I wish you to know how great a struggle I am having on behalf of you and those in Laodicea and as many as have not seen my face in the flesh" (2:1).²⁷ At this point the audience hear a development, by way of the chiastic parallelism, from the general "struggling" (ἀγωνιζόμενος) of Paul in the work of proclaiming Christ to every human being in the C element (1:29a) to the great "struggle" (ἀγῶνα) Paul is having in the work of proclaiming Christ that is, as he assures them, specifically and pointedly on their behalf in the C´ element (2:1).²⁸

---

25. Dübbers, *Christologie*, 168 n. 45: "Diese Aussage ist durch die Alliteration mit ἐν- bzw. ἐ sowie die verwandten Ausdrücke ἐνεργεια und ἐνεργουμένη (*figura etymologica*) rhetorisch hervorgehoben."

26. Fee, *Pauline Christology*, 332: "Thus this rather complex sentence (vv. 26–29) is another moment of shared prerogative with God the Father. To be sure, the language of ἐνεργέω/ἐνέργεια (*powerful working*) can be attributed to inanimate realities (love, God's word, etc.), but when elsewhere Paul has attributed it directly to divine activity, the one at work is either God the Father (as in Col 2:12; cf. 1 Cor 12:6; Gal 2:8; Phil 2:13) or the Holy Spirit (1 Cor 12:11). Here that same powerful divine working is attributed to Christ" (Fee's emphasis).

27. Harris, *Colossians*, 79: "'To see somone's face' is a circumlocution for 'to see someone'.... Since to 'see' (ἑόρακαν) was not simply to 'look at,' it is also appropriate to render the whole clause 'all who have not met me personally' or 'all who do not know me personally.'" Dunn, *Colossians*, 129: "The metaphor of 'seeing someone's face' naturally expresses the immediacy of personal encounter."

28. O'Brien, *Colossians*, 92: "Paul's conflict is not to be limited to his inner struggles for the sake of his readers, whether it be his intercessory prayers on their behalf, or his inner turmoil of some kind. Rather, this expenditure of his energies—through his concerns, his prayers and by his letters—are to be understood within the wider struggle for the spread of the gospel and of the faith. His inner conflicts and concerns, then, are part of that wider ἀγών itself." Dunn, *Colossians*, 129: "The metaphor of the

The audience are to realize that the sufferings of Paul "on behalf of you" (ὑπὲρ ὑμῶν), in which Paul is now rejoicing (1:24), are those incurred in Paul's great struggle "on behalf of you" (ὑπὲρ ὑμῶν, 2:1), as he struggles in the work of proclaiming Christ to every human being (1:28-29).[29] Paul's struggle is not only on behalf of his Colossian audience but on behalf of "those in Laodicea," that is, those believers in a city nearby Colossae in the Lycus river valley. And since the proclamation of Christ is intended for the purpose of presenting every human being as complete in Christ (1:28), Paul's struggle, as he informs his Colossian audience, is also on behalf of "as many as have not seen my face in the flesh" (2:1). That there are those who have not yet seen Paul's face in the "flesh" (σαρκί) makes the audience aware that there are still those who have not benefited from Paul's "filling up what is lacking of the afflictions of the Christ in my flesh (σαρκί)" for the sake of making every human being a member of the body of Christ, which is the church (1:24).[30]

In sum, Paul wants his Colossian audience to know that the great struggle he is undergoing in proclaiming Christ is especially on their behalf, but not only on their behalf but on behalf of their fellow believers in Laodicea as well as on behalf of all those other human beings (1:28) who have become believers but who have not yet seen Paul in the "flesh" (2:1), and thus have not yet witnessed and benefited from Paul's afflictions of the Christ in his "flesh" for the sake of the body of Christ, the church (1:24).

7. Col 2:2-3 (B'): All the Richness of the Mystery of Christ in Whom Is All Wisdom

Paul continues to express his great concern for the believers in Laodicea as well as all other believers whom he has not personally met, but for whose sake he is struggling in the work of proclaiming Christ (1:28-2:1): "that their hearts may be encouraged as they are held together in love, and for all richness of the full assurance of understanding, for knowledge of the mystery of God, Christ, in whom are all the treasures of wisdom and knowledge hidden" (2:2-3).[31]

The audience now hear a progression, by way of the chiastic parallels, from the "richness" (πλοῦτος) of the glory of this "mystery" (μυστηρίου) (1:27), the "mystery" (μυστήριον) that has long been "hidden" (ἀποκεκρυμμένον) but now manifested to God's holy ones (1:26), whose proclamation includes teaching every human being in all "wisdom" (σοφίᾳ) (1:28), in the B element (1:26-28) to all

---

athletic contest (ἀγών) is continued from the preceding verse—an image which Paul and his circle used to express the concentrated and sustained effort that his ministry demanded."

29. O'Brien, *Colossians*, 92: "[W]hen he [Paul] refers to his 'struggle on your behalf' this is akin to his statement of verse 24 about his 'sufferings for your sake.'"

30. Deterding, *Colossians*, 81: "Here 'flesh' does not have the more distinctively Pauline sense of the sinful nature of man in hostile opposition against God (as in 2:11, 18, 23)."

31. Bruce, *Colossians*, 91 n. 12: "The phrase 'treasures of wisdom' (θησαυροὶ τῆς σοφίας) appears in Sir 1:25."

"richness" (πλοῦτος) for knowledge of the "mystery" (μυστηρίου) of God, Christ (2:2), in whom are all the treasures of "wisdom" (σοφίας) and knowledge "hidden" (ἀπόκρυφοι) (2:3) in the B′ element (2:2-3). What is made clear for the audience with the B′ element is that the "mystery" which includes the "richness" of "all wisdom" is explicitly identified as the "mystery" of God, which is Christ, and Christ is explicitly identified as the one in whom are hidden "all" the treasures, the "richness," of "wisdom and knowledge."[32]

That the hearts of the believers in Laodicea and those who have not seen Paul may be encouraged as they are held together in "love" (ἀγάπη) (2:2) reminds the audience that Paul and Timothy affirmed the "love" (ἀγάπην) the Colossian audience have for all the holy ones (1:4), and thus serves as an implicit reminder of the audience's love for the holy ones in Laodicea as well as those who have not seen Paul. It also reminds the audience that Epaphras told Paul and Timothy of the audience's "love" (ἀγάπην) in the Spirit (1:8), which refers not only to their love for all the holy ones in general but their love especially for Paul and Timothy, a love Paul reciprocates by struggling on their behalf (1:29-2:1). Finally, it reminds the audience that God has transferred them to the kingdom of the Son of his "love" (ἀγάπης) (1:13), implying that they, like the Son, are recipients of God's love. Thus, the audience are to realize that for the believers in Laodicea and those who have not seen Paul to be held together "in love" means for them to be held together within the realm of being "in love," that is, in the realm constituted by their being loved by God, by fellow holy ones, and by Paul.

In 1:9-10 Paul and Timothy assured the audience of their continual praying for them that they may be filled with the "knowledge" (ἐπίγνωσιν) of God's will in all "wisdom" (σοφίᾳ) and Spiritual "understanding" (συνέσει), and that in every good work they may bear fruit and grow with regard to the "knowledge" (ἐπιγνώσει) of God. And now, in 2:2-3, Paul informs his audience that his great struggle in proclaiming Christ is that the hearts of the believers in Laodicea and of those who have not seen Paul may be encouraged for all richness of the full assurance of "understanding" (συνέσεως),[33] for "knowledge" (ἐπίγνωσιν) of the

---

32. O'Brien, *Colossians*, 95: "'Wisdom' (σοφία) and 'knowledge' (γνῶσις), conjoined under the one definite article (τῆς), are virtually regarded as a single entity, as they are elsewhere in Jewish literature." For this reason plus a concern to more precisely parallel and bind together γνώσεως with σοφίας by keeping both words at three syllables may be why the form γνώσεως rather than ἐπιγνώσεως, the form found elsewhere in Colossians (1:9, 10; 3:10), is employed here. Markus N. A. Bockmuehl, *Revelation and Mystery in Ancient Judaism and Pauline Christianity* (WUNT 2/36; Tübingen: Mohr, 1990), 188: "We expect the term μυστηρίον τοῦ θεοῦ to be synonymous with Paul's gospel message: and if this identification holds, the appositional Χριστοῦ comes as much less of an innovation. Paul can use the terms εὐαγγέλιον and Χριστός almost interchangeably."

33. O'Brien, *Colossians*, 94: "Here he [Paul] goes out of his way to emphasize the abundant fullness of this σύνεσις ('insight' or 'understanding' implies, as at 1:9, the capacity to distinguish the true from the false) by connecting the words 'riches' (πλοῦτος) and 'fullness' (πληροφορίας). The latter term can mean 'full assurance,' 'certainty.'" Note also the strong alliteration involving especially the "p" and "s" sounds that closely binds together the words in the phrase εἰς πᾶν πλοῦτος τῆς πληροφορίας τῆς

mystery of God, Christ, in whom are all the treasures of "wisdom" (σοφίας) and "knowledge" (γνώσεως) hidden.

The audience are to realize then that the knowledge of God and of God's will, with which they are to be filled in all wisdom and understanding (1:9-10), is more specifically the knowledge of the mystery of God, that is, of Christ himself (2:2). And that in Christ, who is the mystery of God, are "hidden" (ἀπόκρυφοι) all the richness of understanding, all the treasures of wisdom and knowledge (2:3), that are now available not only for the believers in Laodicea and those who have not seen Paul, but also for the Colossian audience themselves (2:1), precisely because of Paul's great struggle in proclaiming Christ, the "hidden" (ἀποκεκρυμμένον) mystery now manifested to all God's holy ones (1:26).[34]

In sum, the reasons for Paul's great struggle in proclaiming Christ are, first of all, that the believers in Laodicea, those who have not seen Paul, and the Colossian audience themselves might have their hearts encouraged by God, as they are held together within the realm of being loved by God, by fellow holy ones, and by Paul (2:1-2a). And, secondly, Paul's great struggle is "for" (εἰς) all richness of the full assurance of understanding on the part of all of those to whom he proclaims Christ, that is, "for" (εἰς) knowledge of the mystery of God, which is identified as Christ himself, in whom are hidden all the treasures of wisdom and knowledge (2:2b-3), which are now available to all God's holy ones to whom God has now manifested the long hidden mystery (1:26) of God, Christ.

7. Col 2:4-5 (A ́): Though Absent in the Flesh Paul Is Rejoicing over Their Faith

What Paul has been saying about his great struggle in proclaiming Christ (2:1-3) he now applies more directly to the situation of his Colossian audience: "This I speak, that no one may speak contrary to you with persuasive speech. For even if in the flesh I am absent, yet in the Spirit I am with you, rejoicing at seeing your good order and the firmness of your faith in Christ" (2:4-5). With this concluding A ́ element the audience hear a progression from the introductory A element, by way of the chiastic parallels—from Paul's fulfilling the "word" (λόγον) of God in 1:25 to what "I," Paul, "speak" (λέγω) in 2:4, from Paul's filling up what is lacking of the afflictions of the Christ in my "flesh" (τῇ σαρκί) in 1:24b to Paul's

---

συνέσεως ("for all richness of the full assurance of understanding"); the three "p" sounds introducing the words πᾶν, πλοῦτος, and πληροφορίας and the five "s" sounds concluding the words εἰς, πλοῦτος, τῆς, πληροφορίας, and τῆς reach a climax with the triplet of "s" sounds in the final word, συνέσεως.

34. Charles Francis Digby Moule, *The Epistles to the Colossians and Philemon* (CGTC; Cambridge: Cambridge University Press, 1957), 85-86: "The end to which St. Paul's labours are directed is described in terms reminiscent of the noble prayer of i. 9ff.: that these Christians' hearts (i.e. their wills, their spirits) may be encouraged or stiffened to boldness, that they may be welded together in love (συμβιβασθέντες being a nominative *ad sensum*), and in such a way as to attain to the full wealth of conviction which spiritual insight brings—that is, to the perception of God's 'mystery,' which is Christ." O'Brien, *Colossians*, 94-95: "The knowledge of which Paul speaks is personal. Christ himself is God's mystery revealed, the Christ with whom these Colossian readers had become one. There could be no appreciation of divine wisdom apart from this personal knowledge of him."

being absent in the "flesh" (τῇ σαρκί) in 2:5a, and from Paul's "rejoicing" (χαίρω) in the sufferings on behalf of you in 1:24a to Paul's "rejoicing" (χαίρων) at seeing your good order and the firmness of your faith in Christ in 2:5b.

As part of being a minister of the gospel (1:23) and of the church to fulfill for "you" (ὑμᾶς) the word (λόγον) of God (1:25), which "word" involves the proclaiming of Christ "that" (ἵνα) we may present every human being complete in Christ (1:28), and in reference to his wish for "you" (ὑμᾶς) to know how great a struggle he is having on behalf of "you" (ὑμῶν), as well as of those in Laodicea and those who have not seen Paul (2:1), "that" (ἵνα) their hearts may be encouraged (2:2a), Paul now declares, "This I speak (λέγω), that (ἵνα) no one may speak contrary to you with persuasive speech" (2:4). In other words, "this" (τοῦτο) that Paul is "speaking" refers to the "word" of God (1:25), the mystery of God, which is Christ (1:26-27; 2:2), in whom are all the treasures of wisdom and knowledge that are hidden (2:3) now revealed to all believers so that "you," the Colossian audience, as among those Paul is trying to present as complete in Christ (1:28), and as among those for whom Paul is struggling so that their hearts may be encouraged (2:1-2), need not be persuaded by any speech that speaks to them contrary to what Paul is "speaking," namely the "word" of God, the mystery of God, which is Christ himself.[35]

This is reinforced for the audience by the word play involving the Greek root λογ or λεγ in reference to speech or speaking. The audience hear a progression from the beneficial "speech" or "word" (λόγον) of God (1:27), the mystery, which is Christ (1:26-27; 2:2), that which Paul "is speaking" (λέγω), to the pejorative παρα-λογ-ίζηται—literally, "may speak beside, against, or contrary to,"—and πιθανο-λογ-ίᾳ—"persuasive speech" (2:4). Thus, Paul "is speaking" the "word" of God, "so that" no one may "speak contrary to" the Colossian audience so as to deceive or delude them with "persuasive speech," since Paul is struggling in proclaiming this word "so that" the hearts of all those for whom he is struggling may be encouraged (2:1-2), and "so that" he may present every human being, including his Colossian audience, complete in Christ (1:28).[36]

Paul's statement, "For even if in the flesh (σαρκί) I am absent" (2:5a), not only reconfirms that there are still those who have not seen Paul's face in the "flesh"

---

35. According to Harris (*Colossians*, 86), the most probable meaning of the grammar here is that "ἵνα is telic and τοῦτο retrospective: 'I am telling you this so that no one may delude you.' λέγω refers to the present written communication and the antecedent of τοῦτο is either vv. 1-3 in general, or v. 3 in particular (viz. the all-sufficiency and finality of Christ as God's disclosed mystery)." See also O'Brien, *Colossians*, 97.

36. Dunn, *Colossians*, 133: "For the first time it becomes clear that Paul and Timothy had some concerns regarding the Colossians. These concerns can hardly have been serious; otherwise they would have come to the fore much more quickly (as in 1 Cor. 1:10; Gal. 1:6; 1 Thess. 2:1). Given the evident lack of urgency, we have been hesitant to identify too many echoes of a clear-cut 'false teaching.' But here there is a clear warning against the possibility of being 'deceived' or 'deluded'—παραλογίζηται.... Clearly implied is the claim that there is a power of conviction in the gospel of Paul which specious arguments of popular rhetoricians and religious philosophers in the marketplace cannot match."

(σαρκί) (2:1), but also means that he is not present with his Colossian audience in his "flesh" (σαρκί) in which he is filling up what is lacking of the afflictions of the Christ on behalf of his body, which is the church (1:24). Nevertheless, as Paul goes on to say, "but in the Spirit I am with you" (2:5b).

That Paul is with them in the "Spirit" (πνεύματι, 2:5b) closely bonds Paul with his Colossian audience, who have love for Paul and Timothy, as among all the holy ones (1:4), in the realm of being in the "Spirit" (πνεύματι) (1:8). Since letters were substitutes for personal presence (cf. 1 Cor 5:3–5), it is as his audience are listening to this letter being read to them that Paul is made present with them in the Spirit.[37] This means that the "Spiritual" (πνευματικῇ) understanding, that is, the "understanding" (συνέσει) that comes from the Spirit in the realm of which Paul is with them and in which they may be filled with the "knowledge" (ἐπίγνωσιν) of God's will in all "wisdom" (σοφίᾳ) (1:9) is available to them in what Paul is telling them in the letter, namely that in Christ they now have all the richness of the full assurance of "understanding" (συνέσεως), the "knowledge" (ἐπίγνωσιν) of the mystery of God, and all the treasures of "wisdom" (σοφίας) and "knowledge" (γνώσεως) (2:2–3).

It is in the realm of the Spirit that Paul is with "you" (ὑμῖν, 2:5b), the Colossian audience, as they listen to the letter in which Paul is informing them of his great struggle in proclaiming Christ on behalf of "you" (ὑμῶν) (2:1). It is by listening to the letter in which Paul is with "you" (ὑμῖν) in the Spirit that the audience learn of the mystery, which is Christ among "you" (ὑμῖν) (1:27). And it is through the letter that the audience hear of Paul rejoicing in the sufferings on behalf of "you" (ὑμῶν) (1:24a).

The audience thus hear a progression from Paul's puzzling, paradoxical "rejoicing" (χαίρω) in the sufferings on behalf of "you" (ὑμῶν) (1:24a) to his congratulatory "rejoicing" (χαίρων) at seeing "your" (ὑμῶν) good order and the firmness of "your" (ὑμῶν) faith in Christ (2:5c). Although there are those who have not "seen" (ἑόρακαν) Paul's face in the flesh (2:1), Paul, absent in the flesh but present in the Spirit (2:5ab), "sees" (βλέπων) the good order and firmness of his Colossian audience's faith in Christ.[38] Paul's acknowledgment of the firmness of their "faith" (πίστεως) in Christ (2:5c; and see 1:4) congratulates them for persevering in the "faith" (πίστει), their firmness indicating, as Paul had urged, that they

---

37. According to O'Brien (*Colossians*, 98), Paul is present at Colossae "since the Spirit of God has united both him and the Colossians to Christ."

38. O'Brien, *Colossians*, 99: "Obviously because of Paul's physical absence βλέπω is used figuratively meaning 'perceive,' 'note.'" According to Dunn (*Colossians*, 134), it is "intended more as an expression of what he would hope to see were it possible." Wright, *Colossians*, 96: "'Orderly' and 'firm' are most probably military metaphors: the church is drawn up in proper battle array with a solid wall of defence, namely, its faith in Christ. Paul is there in spirit, like a general inspecting the troops before a battle." Against the idea that these are military metaphors here, see O'Brien, *Colossians*, 99. Wilson, *Colossians*, 189: "The main point in any case is our author's confidence in the firmness and solidity of his readers' faith."

are indeed "established and steadfast and not shifting from the hope of the gospel which you heard" (1:23).[39]

Paul thus adds to his strategy of motivating his audience by praying that they be filled with the knowledge of God's will in all wisdom and Spiritual understanding (1:9) a strategy of motivating them by congratulating them for their firm faith in Christ (2:5c). This places upon the audience a certain pressure to indeed make sure that they have and maintain the faith in Christ that Paul affirms they have. In this final A′ element then the audience are to realize that it is through their firm faith that places them within the realm of being in union with Christ, that is, being in the Christ who is among them (1:27), that they are in a position, as they listen to the letter by which Paul is with them in the Spirit (2:5), of having all the richness of the full assurance of understanding and all the treasures of wisdom and knowledge (2:2–3). With such a deep and extensive understanding, wisdom, and knowledge available to them in Christ they should not be persuaded by any speech contrary to what Paul is speaking in proclaiming Christ to them (2:4).

B. Summary on Colossians 1:24–2:5

1. It is by his sufferings on behalf of his audience that Paul, the minister of the gospel and of the church, fills up what is lacking of the afflictions of the Christ in his flesh on behalf of the body of Christ, which is the church (1:24), in order to make effective and bring to completion the word of God, the gospel, for his audience, enabling them to become members of the body of Christ, the church, of which Christ is the "head" (1:18a) and Paul the preeminent minister (1:25).

2. The audience are to realize that the mystery long hidden by God from past ages and past generations of human beings God has now manifested to them as among the holy ones, all believers (1:26). To them God wished to make known the lavish richness of the glory of this mystery that is among the Gentiles, which is Christ himself, who is among not only the Gentiles but the Colossian audience and who represents for them the assured hope of their participation in the glory of God in the heavens (1:27). In their extensive proclamation of Christ Paul and his co-workers admonish every human being and teach every human being "in all wisdom," that they might present every human being, and thus including the audience, as totally complete and mature persons within the realm of their being "in Christ;" their having been taught "in all wisdom," then, the wisdom that is part of the proclamation of Christ, results in their being presented as perfect "in Christ" (1:28).

3. Paul is not only "laboring," with its connotation of an exhausting and wea-

---

39. Dunn, *Colossians*, 135: "This final recall to faith forms an inclusio with 1:4 and thus brackets the whole of the intervening thanksgiving and personal statement as an expression of that faith."

risome exertion, but in this strenuous labor of proclaiming Christ he is also "struggling," with its connotation of engaging in a fight, battle, or athletic contest (1:29a).

4. It is the working or energy generated by Christ that Paul is relying upon as he struggles in his labor of proclaiming Christ (1:29b).

5. The audience are thus to realize that it is because the energy generated by Christ is working in Paul "in power" (1:29c) that he is empowered interiorly, as he struggles in the work he shares with others of proclaiming Christ, to teach every human being "in all wisdom" that Paul and his co-workers may present every human being complete "in Christ" (1:28).

6. Paul wants his Colossian audience to know that the great struggle he is undergoing in proclaiming Christ is especially on their behalf, but not only on their behalf but on behalf of their fellow believers in Laodicea as well as on behalf of all those other human beings (1:28) who have become believers but who have not yet seen Paul in the "flesh" (2:1), and thus have not yet witnessed and benefited from Paul's afflictions of the Christ in his "flesh" for the sake of the body of Christ, the church (1:24).

7. The reasons for Paul's great struggle in proclaiming Christ are, first of all, that the believers in Laodicea, those who have not seen Paul, and the Colossian audience themselves might have their hearts encouraged by God, as they are held together within the realm of being loved by God, by fellow holy ones, and by Paul (2:1–2a). And, secondly, Paul's great struggle is *for* all richness of the full assurance of understanding on the part of all of those to whom he proclaims Christ, that is, *for* knowledge of the mystery of God, which is identified as Christ himself, in whom are *hidden* all the treasures of wisdom and knowledge (2:2b–3), which are now available to all God's holy ones to whom God has now manifested the long *hidden* mystery (1:26) of God, Christ.

8. The audience are to realize that it is through their firm faith that places them within the realm of being in union with Christ, that is, being in the Christ who is among them (1:27), that they are in a position, as they listen to the letter by which Paul is with them in the Spirit (2:5), of having all the richness of the full assurance of understanding and all the treasures of wisdom and knowledge (2:2–3). With such a deep and extensive understanding, wisdom, and knowledge available to them in Christ they should not be persuaded by any speech contrary to what Paul is speaking in proclaiming Christ to them (2:4).

7
COLOSSIANS 2:6–23

Walk and Live in Christ with Whom You Have Died and Been Raised (E)

Why let yourselves be subjected to decrees as if living in the world?
A: ⁶ *As* then you received the Christ, Jesus the Lord, in him go on walking, ⁷ having been rooted and being built up in him and being confirmed in the faith as you were taught, abounding in thanksgiving. ⁸ See to it that there will not be anyone who is captivating you through the *philosophy* which is empty deceit, *according to the tradition of human beings*, according to *the elemental forces of the world*, and not according to Christ.

    B: ⁹ For in him dwells all the fullness of the deity *bodily*, ¹⁰ and you are in him having been and being filled, who is the *head* of every *principality* and *authority*.

        C: ¹¹ In whom indeed you were circumcised with a circumcision *not made with hands* in the removal of the body of the *flesh*, in the circumcision of the Christ, ¹² having been *buried with* him in the baptism, in whom indeed you were *raised with* him through faith in the working of the God who raised him from the *dead*.

        C′: ¹³ And you, being *dead* in transgressions and in the uncircumcision of your *flesh*, he brought you to *life along with* him, having forgiven us all our transgressions, ¹⁴ having obliterated the *handwritten charge* against us with its decrees, which was opposed to us, and this he has taken from our midst, having nailed it to the cross,

    B′: ¹⁵ having removed the *principalities* and the *authorities*, he exposed them in public, leading them away in triumph in him. ¹⁶ Let then no one judge you in food and in drink or in regard to a festival or new moon or sabbaths, ¹⁷ which things are a shadow of the things that were to come, but the *body* belongs to the Christ. ¹⁸ Let no one condemn you, delighting in humility and worship of the angels, going into detail about what things he had seen, vainly being made arrogant by the mind of his flesh, ¹⁹ not holding to the *head*, from whom the whole *body*, supported and held together through ligaments and bonds, grows with the growth that is from God.

A′: [20] If you died with Christ from *the elemental forces of the world*, why let yourselves be subjected to decrees *as* if living in the *world*? [21] "Do not touch, do not taste, do not handle"— [22] which things are all destined for destruction in being consumed—*according to the commandments and teachings of human beings*; [23] such (decrees) have indeed a reputation of *wisdom* in self-chosen worship and humility and severe treatment of the body, not of value to anyone against self-indulgence of the flesh.[1]

A. Audience Response to Colossians 2:6-23

1. Col 2:6–8 (A): As You Received Christ Not through a Philosophy according to the Tradition of Human Beings or the Elemental Forces of the World

Having joyously affirmed the good order and firmness of his Colossian audience's faith in Christ (2:5), Paul, by repeating "Christ" and "faith" as his catchwords, further challenges his audience: "As then you received the Christ, Jesus the Lord, in him go on walking, having been rooted and being built up in him and being confirmed in the faith as you were taught, abounding in thanksgiving" (2:6-7).[2] When the audience hear the word "Christ" in the reminder that "as then you received the Christ," they hear the transitional word that links this unit (2:6-23) to the previous one (1:24-2:5), which concluded with an occurrence of "Christ" in the phrase "the firmness of your faith in Christ" (2:5).

Paul and Timothy informed the audience that they do not cease praying that God may fill them with the knowledge of God's will in all the wisdom and understanding that comes from the Spirit, to "walk" (περιπατῆσαι), that is, to conduct their lives and behave, as worthy of the Lord (κυρίου) for every desire to please, in every good work bearing fruit and growing with regard to the knowledge of God (1:9-10). Now Paul exhorts his audience that, as they have received the Christ, Jesus the Lord (κύριον),[3] in him, that is within the realm of being in union with

---

1. For the establishment of 2:6-23 as a chiasm, see ch. 2. For a treatment of 2:6-23 according to the ancient rhetorical technique of taking up an interlocutor's language, see Garuti, "L' eresia di Colossi," 303-26. For a treatment of 2:16-3:17 as a "discourse analysis" in a chiastic framework, see Christopher, "Discourse Analysis," 205-20.

2. Wright, *Colossians*, 98: "These two verses sum up neatly the message of the entire letter. In them Paul draws together the awesome Christology of the introduction and the practical teaching that is to be based on it."

3. According to Wright (*Colossians*, 99), "by 'receiving Christ Jesus as Lord' Paul here refers to the Colossian Christians' acceptance of the proclamation of Jesus the Lord, to their consequent confession of faith, and to their new status as members of Christ's body." According to Harris (*Colossians*, 88), "you received" (παρελάβετε) in 2:6 "denotes not simply passive receipt of Christian tradition but active acceptance of the person who was the essence of that tradition." According to O'Brien (*Colossians*, 105-6), "when Paul says that his readers have 'received' (παρελάβετε) Christ Jesus as their Lord he is not simply reflecting on their personal commitment to Christ (though this is no doubt included), but

him,[4] they are to "go on walking" (περιπατεῖτε), as those who have been rooted and are being built up in him. The agricultural image of "bearing fruit and growing" in 1:10 (cf. 1:6) thus receives its basis in the combined agricultural and architectural image of "having been rooted and being built up" in him in 2:7.[5]

Paul reminded the audience of their need to persevere with regard to the "faith" (πίστει), "having been established and steadfast and not shifting" from the hope of the gospel which they heard (1:23). And now they are to "go on walking" (the present active imperative περιπατεῖτε) in the Lord, as those who "have been rooted and are being built up in him and are being confirmed" with regard to the "faith" (πίστει) as they were taught (2:6-7).[6] The triplet of "having been established and steadfast and not shifting" is thus complemented by the triplet of "having been rooted and being built up in him and being confirmed" to reinforce the audience's need to be not only absolutely resolute and solidly stable, that is, "rooted" (the perfect passive participle ἐρριζωμένοι) by God (divine passive) in the realm of being in Christ, but also to be currently and continually "built up" (the present passive participle ἐποικοδομούμενοι) by God (divine passive) in Christ, and so, conse-

---

he uses the semitechnical term specifically employed to denote the receiving of something delivered by tradition.... Certainly the definite article 'the' (τὸν) before 'Lord' (κύριον) makes this term emphatic and probably... gathers up all that Paul has previously said about Christ in Colossians. The one whom the Colossians received as their tradition is the center of God's mystery (1:27, 2:2), and the Lord in both creation and reconciliation (1:15-20)." According to Dunn (*Colossians*, 139), "the thought is not of the reception of Christ's Lordship in baptism, far less the thought of receiving Christ into their lives (cf. 1:27), for which παραλαμβάνω is never used by Paul and for which (προς)δέχομαι (as, e.g., in Gal. 4:14 and Rom. 16:2) would have been more suitable. Rather, Paul refers his readers back to their experience of hearing and receiving the gospel (aorist tense), as he had in responding to the equivalent situation in Galatia (Gal. 3:1-5). As in Galatians, this first decisive experience provides a norm and a starting point for what should follow: their ongoing life of faith should be in accord with the faith with which it began.... As both the Wisdom and 'mystery' spoken of earlier could be simply identified with 'Christ' (1:15-18; 1:27; 2:2), so here the preaching/teaching received could be summed up as focused in Christ."

4. Harris, *Colossians*, 89: "Given the pervasive influence of Paul's ἐν Χριστῷ formula, ἐν here is less probably instr[umental]. ('by him" = 'by his power') than locat[ive]., either 'in union with him,' 'as incorporated in him,' or indicating Christ as the sphere circumscribing the entire life of the believer." Fee, *Pauline Christology*, 326-27: "[T]hey are to 'walk' *in* him, meaning 'in the sphere of his lordship.' ... where the emphasis is on the Colossians' recognition of the lordship of the Christ whom they have 'received.' That is, in their becoming believers they not only believed in Christ Jesus but also revered him as their Lord, via-à-vis all other 'lords' in both the religious cults and the empire."

5. According to Harris (*Colossians*, 90), the alteration of the tense from the perfect to the present in the first two participles in 2:7 is significant: "A previous rooting is implied and the present rootage is stressed in the pf. ptc. ἐρριζωμένοι, whereas the ongoing process of edification is emphasized by the pres. ptc. ἐποικοδομούμενοι."

6. O'Brien (*Colossians*, 108) maintains that it is best "to understand 'faith' (πίστει) as that which is the object of belief, the content of the teaching which Epaphras had faithfully passed on to them. It was this *faith* they were to continue in (at 1:23 note the active voice), for it was only by this *faith* that they would be consolidated (the corresponding passive referring to God's activity; cf. 1 Cor 1:8)" (O'Brien's emphasis).

quently, to be currently and continually "confirmed" (the present passive participle βεβαιούμενοι) by God (divine passive) with regard to their faith in Christ.[7]

In 2:6b–7a the audience hear the following mini-chiasm:

a) in him (ἐν αὐτῷ)
    b) go on walking (περιπατεῖτε)
        b´) having been rooted and being built up (ἐρριζωμένοι καὶ ἐποικοδομούμενοι)
a´) in him (ἐν αὐτῷ)

In the initial "a" sub-element of the mini-chiasm the audience are reminded that they are in the realm of being "in him" (2:6b), that is, of being in union with Christ Jesus the Lord whom they have received (2:6a). In the "b" sub-element the audience are told that they are "to go on walking"—conduct their lives and thus behave—within this realm of being "in him" (2:6b). From the "b" (2:6b) to the "b´" (2:7a) sub-element the audience hear the pivotal transition from the present active command of "go on walking" to the basis for that "walking" in their having been and still being "rooted" (perfect passive participle) so that they are currently being "built up" (present passive participle) by God (divine passives). With the "a´" sub-element (2:7a) the audience hear the repetition of "in him," giving them the realization that they are able to "go on walking *in him*," because they have already been and still are "rooted" and being "built up" continually "*in him*."

The reminder that this was the faith in Christ that the audience were "taught" (ἐδιδάχθητε, 2:7) not only recalls their having learned the gospel from Epaphras (1:7), but also places them squarely within the domain of the Pauline proclamation of Christ, which includes admonishing every human being and "teaching" (διδάσκοντες) every human being in all wisdom for the purpose of presenting every human being complete in Christ (1:28). And that the audience are to be abounding within the realm of "thanksgiving" (εὐχαριστίᾳ, 2:7) reinforces how they are with joy to be "thanking" (εὐχαριστοῦντες) the Father who has made them fit for the share of the inheritance of the holy ones in the light (1:12).[8] They are thus

---

7. According to Harris (*Colossians*, 89), these first three participles in 2:7 are passive, "implying that divine action is essential in Christian growth." O'Brien, *Colossians*, 107: "Having spoken of a path on which one is to walk (v 6) Paul moves to the language of horticulture ('rooted'), then to an architectural metaphor ('built up') and finally on to an image of the law-court ('established,' 'confirmed'). Each of these participles is in the passive voice probably pointing to the divine activity. Whatever responsibilities to Christ the readers had, and these were many, they were not to lose sight of the fact that God had been at work in their midst. It was he who had rooted them in Christ and was presently building them up in him, thereby consolidating them in the faith."

8. O'Brien, *Colossians*, 106–7: "At chapter 1:10, in Paul's intercessory prayer for the Colossians, four participles ('bearing fruit,' 'increasing,' v 10; 'being strengthened,' v 11; and 'giving thanks,' v 12) directly followed the verb 'to walk' (περιπατῆσαι) and defined more precisely what was involved in walking 'worthily of the Lord.' Here also a series of four participles, 'rooted' (ἐρριζωμένοι), 'built up' (ἐποικοδομούμενοι), 'established' (βεβαιούμενοι) and 'abounding in thanksgiving' (περισσεύοντες ἐν

to follow the lead of Paul and Timothy, who are "thanking" (εὐχαριστοῦμεν) God the Father of our Lord Jesus Christ always when praying for their Colossian audience (1:3).[9]

Developing his previous hint of a potential problem facing his Colossian audience, "that no one may speak contrary to you (ὑμᾶς) with persuasive speech" (2:4), Paul warns: "See to it that there will not be anyone who is captivating you (ὑμᾶς) through the philosophy which is empty deceit, according to the tradition of human beings, according to the elemental forces of the world, and not according to Christ" (2:8).[10] Paul's rejoicing at "seeing" (βλέπων) the good order and the firmness of his audience's faith in Christ (2:5) progresses to his command for them to "see" (βλέπετε) to it that there will not be anyone who is captivating them away from that good order and firmness of faith in Christ.[11] That there should be no one

---

εὐχαριστίᾳ) indicate what is meant by walking (the same verb περιπατεῖτε is used) in him. Perhaps it is not coincidental that in both passages the imagery of a tree is employed (at 1:10 the notion of bearing the fruit of good works is in view, while here the idea of being firmly rooted is to the fore), as well as the theme of thanksgiving which appears as the last of the series in each section."

9. Harris, *Colossians*, 91: "'Ἐν εὐχαριστίᾳ defines the sphere in which the overflow was evident ('abounding in thanksgiving')." Dunn, *Colossians*, 143: "[T]he implication is that a characteristic and fundamental feature of their relation with Jesus as Christ and Lord should be gratitude for what God has done in and through him. As rootedness and foundation depends on the faith called forth by the gospel, so growing from the root and building up on the foundation can be successful only in an atmosphere of thankfulness to God." Deterding, *Colossians*, 91: "In contrast to the other participles in this verse, περισσεύοντες, 'abounding,' is not passive but active. While the passive participles point to God's Word as the agent and basis for being in Christ through faith, this phrase describes abundant thanksgiving as a way in which that faith is to express itself in the believer's life."

10. O'Brien, *Colossians*, 109: "By means of a strong warning the congregation is alerted to the dangers touched upon in verse 4. They are to be on guard *lest* anyone carry them off as booty or spoil (O'Brien's emphasis).... The verb συλαγωγέω is a rare word—appearing nowhere else in the NT—probably meaning 'carry off as booty' or 'as a captive' rather than 'rob' or 'despoil.' Accordingly the word is used figuratively of carrying someone away from the truth into the slavery of error. The term is a vivid one and shows how seriously Paul regarded the evil designs of those trying to influence the congregation." Dunn, *Colossians*, 146-47: "[H]ere the singular (τις) followed by the future tense (ἔσται), suggests ... that a possibility is being envisaged rather than a current state of affairs described.... This suggests in turn that the participle συλαγωγῶν should be taken as a conative present, 'who tries to ..., who wants to'... the thought is of some popular rhetorician (2:4) or philosopher captivating some in his audience by the power of his rhetoric or the impressiveness of his claims. The visual metaphor is of such a marketplace preacher gathering together those impressed by his discourse and taking them off for a fuller exposition and induction. If indeed, then, the challenge to the Colossian believers stemmed primarily from the synagogue, as appears to be the case, this allusion confirms the likelihood that the Colossian Jews included some effective apologists and rhetoricians in their number, well able to hold their own in learned debate." Smith, *Heavenly Perspective*, 77: "If, as we intend to argue, there was a movement of Jewish mysticism which was affecting the Colossian church, it seems most likely that the threat was real and present from a group of Jewish Christians within the Colossian church. Paul does not name these errorists as he does not personally know them. This, however, does not negate the present reality of the threat."

11. If the main source of the pejorative "persuasive speech" (2:4) and the "philosophy" (2:8) is the Jewish synagogue or synagogues at Colossae or in the area, then the audience are to hear in the present participle "captivating" a cleverly penetrating wordplay. Paul is warning them not to allow the

captivating the audience through the "philosophy" (φιλο-σοφίας)—literally the "love of wisdom"—which is empty deceit creates a clash in the ears of the audience with all the "wisdom" (σοφία) that comes from the Spirit and in which they are to be filled (1:9), with all the "wisdom" (σοφία) in which Paul is teaching every human being in his proclamation of Christ (1:28), and with all the treasures of "wisdom" (σοφίας) which are hidden in Christ (2:3).[12]

The audience are to make sure that there will not be anyone who is captivating them through the philosophy which is empty deceit, according to the tradition of "human beings" (ἀνθρώπων, 2:8), because that would not accord with what Paul and his cohorts are trying to do for human beings by proclaiming Christ—admonishing every "human being" (ἄνθρωπον) and teaching every "human being" (ἄνθρωπον), that they may present every "human being" (ἄνθρωπον) complete in Christ (1:28). "According to the tradition of human beings" is further described as "according to the elemental forces of the world (κόσμου)" (2:8) to remind the audience that the philosophy which is empty deceit and that could captivate them contradicts the word of the truth of the gospel that has come to them, as indeed in all the world (κόσμῳ) it is bearing fruit and growing, so also among them, from the day they heard and came to know the grace of God in truth (1:5-6).

In 2:8 the audience hear a triplet of phrases each introduced by the preposition "according to." After first hearing that the philosophy which is empty deceit and that could captivate them is "according to" (κατά) the tradition of (mere) human beings,[13] and thus "according to" (κατά) the elemental forces of the world, they

---

"synagogue" (συναγωγή) to be "captivating" (συλαγωγῶν) them. Wright, *Colossians*, 100: "I suggest that Paul uses it ['captivating' (συλαγωγῶν)] because it makes a contemptuous pun with the word *synagogue*: see to it that no-one snatches you as a prey from the flock of Christ, to lock you up instead within Judaism."

12. Carson and Moo, *Introduction*, 33: "In the ancient world philosophy meant something like what we mean by 'worldview.' Various teachers taught competing worldviews." O'Brien, *Colossians*, 109-10: "The term 'philosophy' (φιλοσοφία) which occurs only here in the NT, carried a wide range of meanings describing all sorts of groups, tendencies and viewpoints within the Greek and Jewish worlds, from the Greek pursuit of knowledge and wisdom to the sects of Hellenistic Judaism which sought to present themselves as 'philosophies.'... As 'deceitful' it stands opposed to the gospel, 'the word of *truth*' (1:5), and to 'wisdom and knowledge' (2:3), while the designation of it as 'empty' (κενή) sets this philosophy in sharp contrast to the mystery and its 'glorious *riches*' (τὸ πλοῦτος τῆς δόξης, 1:27), and Christ in whom all the *treasures* (θησαυροί) of wisdom and knowledge are hidden (2:3)" (O'Brien's emphases). Dunn, *Colossians*, 148: " 'Empty deceit' (κενῆς ἀπάτης) is doubly condemnatory. Κενός signifies 'without content, without any basis, without truth, without power,' and ἀπάτη 'deception or deceitfulness'... The language, of course, is pejorative and expresses the contempt which Paul, confident in the rootedness and firmness of his own gospel, evidently felt for the teachings masquerading as philosophies which competed for the ear of his own audiences when he spoke in the open." Deterding, *Colossians*, 92: "The term 'deceit' need not imply the deliberate intention of leading astray; it may designate that which is offered sincerely but which fails to be or to do what is claimed. Such failure is indicated by the term's modification by 'empty.' It is vacuous, powerless, and pernicious. The apostle, therefore, does not intend to accuse the false teachers of insincerity but of deadly error."

13. Harris, *Colossians*, 92-93: "Κατά sets forth the basis or source of the 'philosophy,' viz. 'the tradition of humans.'... ('emanating from humans,' 'man-made'; 'handed down by humans')." O'Brien,

hear the climactic and emphatic denunciation of it as not "according to" (κατά) Christ.[14] That the philosophy which is empty deceit is not according to "Christ" (Χριστόν) impresses upon the audience that this potentially captivating false teaching is thus not in accord with the "Christ" (Χριστόν), Jesus the Lord, whom the audience have received, and in whom they are to "go on walking," as those who have been rooted and are being built up in Christ and being confirmed with regard to the faith as they were taught (2:6-7).

Colossians, 110: "[T]he manner in which the words are introduced here does suggest that the false teachers had set forth their 'philosophy' as 'tradition' (παράδοσις), thereby pointing to its antiquity, dignity and revelational character. Paul, however, rejects any suggestion of divine origin. This was a human fabrication standing over against the apostolic tradition which centered on 'Christ Jesus as Lord.'" Dunn, *Colossians*, 148: "The use of παράδοσις ('tradition') no doubt glances back to the tradition received (παραλαμβανειν) according to 2:6. The tradition on which the Colossian church was founded was divinely authenticated (Jesus the Christ was also the divine Wisdom and mystery); in contrast, any 'philosophy' that discounted that tradition could only be of human origin.... Paul the Pharisee would be bound to think of the importance of 'traditions' in the 'philosophy' of the Pharisees, as he recalled his own devotion to them (Gal. 1:14). Most striking is the fact that the very same phrase, 'the traditions of human beings' (τὴν παράδοσιν τῶν ἀνθρώπων), occurs in Mark's account of Jesus' denunciation of such pharisaic traditions (Mark 7:8; Mark 7:3-13/Matt. 15:2-9). This adds strength to the likelihood that the sort of 'philosophy' in mind here was essentially a form of Jewish thought being presented as a 'philosophy' by Jewish apologists."

14. The combination τὰ στοιχεῖα τοῦ κόσμου has to do with the four physical elements (fire, water, earth, air) of the universe according to Dietrich Rusam, "Neue Belege zu den στοιχεῖα τοῦ κόσμου (Gal 4,3.9; Kol 2,8.20)," *ZNW* 83 (1992): 119-25. But according to Bevere, *Sharing*, 91: "[T]he view of the majority of scholars in the twentieth century was that the στοιχεῖα ['elements'] are spiritual beings who control the world and the universe.... These cosmic powers were associated with heavenly bodies and exercised control over human beings directing the course of the stars and thus the order of the calendar." According to Eckhard Plümacher, "στοιχεῖον," *EDNT* 3.278: "[T]he mention of the *elemental spirits* in Col 2:8, 20 undoubtedly does make use of the terminology of the false teachers in Colossae, in whose mystery-oriented (?—cf. v. 18) φιλοσοφία such spirits might have played a significant role. This philosophy amplified the traditional Christian message with its own παράδοσις (v. 8) and regarded these spirits as powers capable of preventing a person from attaining the fullness of salvation (cf. v. 9), if that person did not submit to them by following certain religious practices." But there is the possibility "that τὰ στοιχεῖα τοῦ κόσμου is a polemical phrase coined by our author, which *caricatures* the 'heresy' as enslavement to phyiscal or cosmological 'elements' (e.g. in rules concerning things which may not be touched or eaten), but hardly reflects its own view of the matter, let alone its precise terminology," according to John M. G. Barclay, *Colossians and Philemon* (Sheffield: Sheffield Academic Press, 1997), 51. Dunn, *Colossians*, 149-50: "[T]here is a clear implication that the στοιχεῖα were closely associated with heavenly beings ... The allusion, in other words, is to the belief that was no doubt then common (as still among not a few today) that human beings had to live their lives under the influence or sway of primal and cosmic forces, however precisely conceptualized." O'Brien, *Colossians*, 110: "[T]he phrase ['the elements of the world'] denotes the 'elemental spirits of the universe,' the principalities and powers which sought to tyrannize over the lives of men (cf. 2:10, 15).... The apostle sets a stark contrast: whatever is in accordance with these demonic, personal powers stands over against Christ, the one at the center of the apostolic tradition, and the person who embodies God's mystery." See also BDAG, 946; Smith, *Heavenly Perspective*, 80-87, esp. 87: "It can therefore be concluded that any understanding of στοιχεῖα needs to take into account personalized angelic powers."

2. Col 2:9-10 (B): In Him Who Is the Head of Every Principality and Authority

The audience then hear more about the significance of the Christ with whom the "philosophy" of empty deceit does not accord (2:8), but whom they have received (2:6): "For in him dwells all the fullness of the deity bodily" (2:9). With this third occurrence of the prepositional phrase, "in him," in this unit, the audience learn that they are to go on "walking"—conducting their lives—"in him" (ἐν αὐτῷ), that is, in the Christ they received (2:6), as those who are being built up by God (divine passive) "in him" (ἐν αὐτῷ) (2:7), because "in him" (ἐν αὐτῷ), with this phrase in emphatic position before the verb, dwells all the fullness of the deity bodily.[15] Echoing the previous hymnic assertion in 1:19, "for in him all the fullness was pleased to dwell," the assertion in 2:9 explicitly develops its implications regarding "all the fullness":

1:19 ὅτι ἐν αὐτῷ εὐδόκησεν πᾶν τὸ πλήρωμα κατοικῆσαι
2:9 ὅτι ἐν αὐτῷ κατοικεῖ πᾶν τὸ πλήρωμα τῆς θεότητος σωματικῶς

The implication in 1:19 that "all the fullness" (πᾶν τὸ πλήρωμα) refers to all the fullness of God that was pleased "to dwell" (κατοικῆσαι) "in him" (ἐν αὐτῷ), that is, in Christ, the image of the invisible "God" (θεοῦ, 1:15), becomes fully and richly explicit in 2:9 as the audience hear that "in him" (ἐν αὐτῷ) is presently "dwelling" (κατοικεῖ) "all the fullness" (πᾶν τὸ πλήρωμα) that is further explained as all the fullness of the "deity" (θεότητος), that is, of the very nature of God.[16] For the audience, who have heard that Christ alone is the head of the "body" (σώματος), which is the church (1:18, 24), and that God has now reconciled them in the "body" (σώματι) of Christ's flesh through his death (1:22), that all the fullness of the deity is now dwelling in Christ "bodily" (σωματικῶς), that is, by the manner and way of a body,[17] means that the absolute fullness of God now dwells not only by the man-

---

15. Harris, *Colossians*, 99: "Since πᾶν is pleonastic with πλήρωμα and ἐν αὐτῷ is emphatic by position, the whole statement is probably polemical: it is in Christ, and Christ alone, that the sum total of the fullness of the Godhead, no part or aspect excepted, permanently resides in bodily form." Dunn, *Colossians*, 151: "The force of κατὰ Χριστόν is explained (ὅτι) by a sequence of 'in him' clauses (2:9-12) which build into a powerful exposition of the cross."

16. Harris, *Colossians*, 98: "Κατοικεῖ is a timeless pres., 'permanently dwells,' 'continues to live.'" Gerhard Schneider, "θεότης," *EDNT* 2.143: "The abstract noun θεότης, derived from θεός, appears in the NT only in Col 2:9 ... θεότης means (in contrast to θειότης, 'divinity, divine quality') 'deity, the rank of God.' ... In light of 1:19 ... the gen. τῆς θεότητος appears to be epexegetical: In Christ the entire fullness, i.e., *the deity*, lives bodily/actually. The actualizing extension of 1:19 gives additional explanation of the term πλήρωμα with respect to its essential content" (Schneider's emphasis). See also Suzanne Watts Henderson, "God's Fullness in Bodily Form: Christ and Church in Colossians," *ExpTim* 118 (2007): 169-73.

17. Dübbers, *Christologie*, 214: "Welcher Art dieses Einwohnens ist, bestimmt der Verfasser des Kolosserbriefes durch das angehängte Adverb σωματικῶς näher, das sich von dem im Kolosserbrief häufig gebrauchten Nomen σῶμα ableitet: Gott wohnt 'auf die Art und Weise eines σῶμα' in Christus." Smith, *Heavenly Perspective*, 92: "Paul's use of the adverb σωματικῶς is also polemical as he seeks to

ner and way of the body of Christ as an individual person—the Christ, Jesus the Lord, whom they received (2:6),[18] but also by the manner and way of the corporate body of Christ that is the church of which they are members and of which Christ is the head.[19]

That all the fullness of the deity dwells not only in the individual body of Christ but also in the corporate body of Christ (2:9), which is the church, is confirmed and developed as next the audience hear that "you are in him having been and being filled, who is the head of every principality and authority" (2:10). That "you," the Colossian audience, are "in him" (ἐν αὐτῷ) having been and being filled, with its fourth occurrence in this unit of the prepositional phrase "in him," which is here in an emphatic position in the middle of the periphrastic construction formed by "you are" and "having been and being filled" (perfect passive participle), pointedly underscores that it is as the audience are "in him" (ἐν αὐτῷ), that is, in the Christ in whom dwells all the fullness of the deity bodily (2:9), that they have been and are still being filled.

That the audience are "in him" means that they are in the realm of being in union with Christ, of being incorporated into the body of Christ, which is the church. That the audience are "in him," that is, in him as members of the body of Christ, "having been and being filled" (πεπληρωμένοι) by God (divine passive) (2:10) means that God has already filled and still is filling them with all the "fullness" (πλήρωμα) of

---

counter a movement that focused on heavenly ascent and 'out of body' experiences attained through asceticism."

18. On all the fullness of God dwelling in Christ as an individual, Wright (*Colossians*, 103) states: "The man Jesus Christ, now exalted, is not one of a hierarchy of intermediary beings, angelic or (in some sense) 'divine'. He is, uniquely, 'God's presence and his very self'. Second, Paul is anxious to show that all the advantages of monotheism (which attracted many Gentiles by its contrast to the confused and unedifying pagan pantheon) accrue to Christianity. Christ is not a second, different Deity: he is the embodiment and full expression of the one God of Abraham, Isaac and Jacob." Harris, *Colossians*, 99–100: "Σωματικῶς describes the permanent *post-incarnational state* of Christ, viz. 'having bodily form,' and does not point directly to the act of incarnation (Harris's emphasis) ... The separation of κατοικεῖ from σωματικῶς suggests that two distinct affirmations are being made: that the total plenitude of the Godhead dwells in Christ eternally and that this fullness now permanently resides in the incarnate Christ in bodily form. It is true that before the incarnation the πλήρωμα did not reside in Christ σωματικῶς; it is not true that before the incarnation the πλήρωμα did not reside in him at all. Thus, Paul implies both the eternal deity and the permanent humanity of Christ. Moreover, κατοικεῖ ... σωματικῶς implies that both before and after his resurrection Christ 'possessed' a σῶμα (cf. 1:22; 1 Cor. 15:44; Phil. 3:21)." Dunn, *Colossians*, 152: "The latter addition, σωματικῶς, reinforces the encounterable reality of the indwelling: as the human σῶμα is what enables a person to be in relationship with other persons, so the somatic character of this indwelling means that God could be encountered directly in and through this particular human being, Christ. Here, as in 1:19, σωματικῶς underscores the accessibility of the divine epiphany ... In all this a common concern for access to the ultimate of reality is presupposed; to be a Christian is to recognize Christ as the point and means of that access."

19. With regard to the meaning of "bodily" (σωματικῶς) in 2:9, Eduard Schweizer ("σωματικῶς," *EDNT* 3.325) states: "The discussion in Colossians emphasizes the corporeality and concreteness of God's presence in Christ and then also in his σῶμα, the Church." See also Pierre Benoit, "Corps, tête et plérôme dans les épîtres de la captivité," *RB* 63 (1956): 5–44.

the deity that is dwelling "in him" bodily (2:9), that is, in the Christ who is head of the body, which is the church (1:18, 24).²⁰ All the fullness of the deity that dwells in Christ bodily as an individual, as the head of the body, also dwells in Christ corporately, in those who are "in him" bodily—as his body—having been and being filled with all the fullness of the deity. The previous prayer that the audience "may be filled" (πληρωθῆτε) by God (divine passive) with the knowledge of God's will in all wisdom and Spiritual understanding (1:9) has thus progressed to the assertion that the audience "have been and presently are being filled" (πεπληρωμένοι) by God (2:10) with all the fullness of the deity (2:9).²¹ In ironic contrast to the philosophy that offers only "empty" deceit (2:8), in Christ the audience have been and are being "filled" with all the "fullness" of the deity (2:9-10).

The Christ in whom the audience have been and are being filled with all the fullness of the deity is "the head of every principality and authority" (2:10). That Christ is the "head" (κεφαλή) of every principality and authority develops Christ's being the "head" (κεφαλή) of the body, the church (1:18). Christ is not only head of the earthly, visible body, which is the church, but also, as the head of *every* "principality and authority" (ἀρχῆς καὶ ἐξουσίας), is the head of all the heavenly, invisible "principalities or authorities" (ἀρχαὶ εἴτε ἐξουσίαι) that were created in him (1:16). As part of the body of Christ, which is the church, the audience have been and are being filled with "all" (πᾶν) the fullness of the deity that dwells in Christ (2:9) in their union with the Christ who is not only the head of the body but the head of "all" or "every" (πάσης) principality and authority in creation (2:10), so that there is nothing in the cosmos outside of his authority, his "headship." The audience are thus to infer that with Christ as their head they have an absolute, divine fullness and cosmic authority that is vastly superior to all of the "elemental forces of the world" which stand behind the potentially captivating philosophy of empty deceit (2:8).²²

---

20. Harris, *Colossians*, 100: "[T]he verbal link with v. 9 is clear: 'you have been made full (πεπληρωμένοι) in him, in whom all the fullness (πλήρωμα) of deity resides.'" O'Brien, *Colossians*, 113: "There is clearly a play on the word 'fullness' here (v 9 πλήρωμα, v 10 πεπληρωμένοι), though the tense of the verb (a perfect) points to a continuing state as the result of some prior action, and the passive voice suggests the readers have been filled *by God* (O'Brien's emphasis). The language and word order again draw attention to the motif of incorporation—it is in union with Christ alone that they possess this fullness already." Garland, *Colossians*, 146: "Since Christ is the fullness of God and believers are in him, they have all the fullness humans can ever possess."

21. In Eph 1:23 the "body" (σῶμα) of Christ is further described as the "fullness" (πλήρωμα) of the one (Christ) who "is filling" (πληρουμένου) all things in all ways. And in Eph 3:19 is the prayer that the audience "may be filled" (πληρωθῆτε) by God (divine passive) to "all the fullness of God" (πᾶν τὸ πλήρωμα τοῦ θεοῦ).

22. Wright, *Colossians*, 104: "It is probable that 'every power and authority' here, and in verse 15, refers primarily to the same entities as the στοιχεῖα of verse 8 (and perhaps the list of 'powers' in 1:16). They, at least, are the powers and authorities which are relevant to Paul's argument at this point." O'Brien, *Colossians*, 114: "These words hark back to the language of the hymn where Christ is said to be creator of all powers and authorities (1:16) as well as their sustainer (1:17). He is 'head' over the principalities and powers for God has divested them of all authority in him (2:15). Although they

3. Col 2:11–12 (C): With a Circumcision Not Made with Hands in the Removal of the Flesh, Buried with and Raised with Christ from the Dead

The Colossian audience continue to hear what has happened to them now that they have received the Christ, Jesus the Lord (2:6), so that they are "in him," that is, within the sphere of being in union with Christ: "In whom indeed you were circumcised with a circumcision not made with hands in the removal of the body of the flesh, in the circumcision of the Christ, having been buried with him in the baptism, in whom indeed you were raised with him through faith in the working of the God who raised him from the dead" (2:11–12). The audience hear these two verses as a tightly knit parallel set of a-b-a patterns, in which explicit references to Christ and/or union with Christ in the "a" sub-elements frame the "b" sub-elements, which contain only indirect or implicit references to Christ:

a¹: in whom indeed (ἐν ᾧ καί) you were circumcised with a circumcision (περιτομῇ) not made with hands
b¹: in (ἐν) the removal of the body of the flesh,
a²: in (ἐν) the circumcision (περιτομῇ) of the Christ,
a³: having been buried with (συνταφέντες) him (αὐτῷ)
b²: in (ἐν) the baptism,
a⁴: in whom indeed (ἐν ᾧ καί) you were raised with (συνηγέρθητε) him through faith in the working of the God who raised him (αὐτὸν) from the dead.

In the a-b-a pattern in 2:11 references to "circumcision" and to Christ ("in whom" and "of the Christ") in phrases introduced by the preposition "in" (ἐν) in the "a" sub-elements frame the "b" sub-element, which is introduced by the same preposition but without an explicit reference to Christ. In the parallel a-b-a pattern in 2:12 the verbal expressions "having been buried with" and "you were raised with" as well as occurrences of the third person singular pronoun "him" in reference to Christ—"with him" and "raised him"—in the "a" sub-elements frame the

---

continue to exist, inimical to man and his interests their final defeat is inevitable." Dunn, *Colossians*, 153: "[T]he reaffirmation of Christ's headship over the cosmos (1:18a), including the heavenly powers mentioned in the hymn (1:16), is explicitly stated with regard to 'every rule and authority,' not as a matter of idle cosmic speculation, but as a matter of vital interest to an understanding of the way heavenly forces determined earthly conduct. For these 'rule(r)s and authorities' were presumably another way of speaking about the 'elemental forces' (2:8), also understood as exercising rule and authority over and within the world of humanity. To know that Christ was above the addressees and was their head was therefore important, partly for the confidence with which other claims to access to such heavenly powers could be confronted and partly for the 'full assurance of understanding' out of which they sought to live their own daily lives." Smith, *Heavenly Perspective*, 94: "The fullness that the Colossian Christians can experience is due to Christ's headship (κεφαλή) over the cosmos. This headship has ramifications for everyday life, in that the forces mentioned in 2.8 (στοιχεῖα τοῦ κόσμου) no longer control human destiny. The Colossians have emancipation from the world of these elemental spirits, who are here expressed as πάσης ἀρχῆς καὶ ἐξουσίας."

"b" sub-element, which contains no explicit reference to Christ. This parallel pattern thus creates for the audience a parallelism between the two "b" sub-elements, each introduced with "in" (ἐν) and without an explicit reference to Christ—"in the removal of the body of the flesh" (2:11) and "in the baptism" (2:12). And, in turn, the first two "a" sub-elements with their references to Christ and circumcision (2:11) are paralleled by the final two "a" sub-elements with their references to Christ and having been buried and raised with him (2:12). Finally, both a-b-a patterns are unified by and enveloped within the inclusion formed by "in whom indeed" at the beginning of the first and last "a" sub-elements.

How "in him," in Christ, the audience have been filled by God (2:10) begins to be elaborated by the statement "in whom indeed you were circumcised with a circumcision not made with hands" (2:11a).[23] With its use of both the verb and its cognate noun, the statement that the audience "were circumcised with a circumcision" emphatically underlines the reality of their being "circumcised."[24] But the qualification that this circumcision is "not made with hands" (ἀχειροποιήτῳ), that is, not performed by human hands, together with the divine passive, "were circumcised," as

---

23. Dübbers, *Christologie*, 225-26: "Das adverbiale καί stellt den Bezug zwischen dem Aorist περιετμήθητε und der resultativen Wendung ἐστὲ πεπληρωμένοι (2,10a) her, mit der der Verfasser des Kolosserbriefes die in Gottes Handeln gründende, gegenwärtige Heilswirklichkeit der Adressaten umschreibt. Dabei dürfte—vor allem im Zusammenhang des Kolosserbriefes, der nur *ein* Heilshandeln Gottes in Wort und Tat kennt—evident sein, daß mit dem περιετμήθητε kein zu dem πληροῦσθαι hinzukommenden Handeln Gottes im Blick steht. Vielmehr bezieht sich der Aorist περιετμήθητε (wie auch die folgenden Ausdrücke συνταφέντες und συνηγέρθητε) auf eben jene vergangene Heilstat, die dem gegenwärtigen Erfülltsein der Gemeinde zugrunde liegt. So macht der Verfasser des Kolosserbriefes durch das adverbiale καί kenntlich, daß die triadische Entfaltung in 2,11 f. als *Explikation* des die erfüllte heilswirklichkeit konstituierenden Handelns Gottes durch Christus zu verstehen ist" (Dübbers's emphasis). On "you were circumcised" (περιετμήθητε) here, O'Brien (*Colossians*, 115) notes: "The verb περιτέμνω meaning to 'cut (off) around' occurred frequently in the LXX as a ritual technical term to denote physical circumcision, an outward sign of the covenant between Yahweh and his people."

24. The cognate noun for circumcision precedes the future tense of the verb in LXX Gen 17:13: "The one born in your house and the one bought with money shall be surely circumcised (περιτομῇ περιτμηθήσεται)." John William Wevers, *Notes on the Greek Text of Genesis* (SBLSCS 35; Atlanta: Scholars Press, 1993), 235: "The verb is preceded by a cognate noun in the dative which like the cognate free infinitive which it represents serves to intensify the verbal idea: 'shall really be circumcized.'" Wright, *Colossians*, 104: "Paul emphasizes that the Colossians have *already* been 'circumcised,' and therefore do not need to undergo the operation again in a physical sense, as would be required if they were to become proselytes to Judaism. The emphatic position of this statement in Paul's argument is one of the strongest reasons for seeing Judaism as his main target in the present chapter" (Wright's emphasis). Dunn, *Colossians*, 154: "[C]ircumcision had always been central to Israel's self-understanding as the people of God (at least from the formulation of Gen. 17:9-14). And the Maccabean crisis had made it a crucial mark of national and religious identity and loyalty, the mark which most clearly distinguished Judaism from Hellenism (1 Macc. 1:15, 48, 60-61; 2:46; 2 Macc. 6:9-10; Josephus, *Antiquities* 12:241)." Garland, *Colossians*, 147: "For most Jews in the first century, circumcision had become the fundamental identity badge for membership in God's people.... Paul himself uses the terms *circumcision* and *uncircumcison* as shorthand for the distinction between Jew and Gentile (Rom. 2:25-27; 3:30; 4:9-12; Gal. 2:7-8)" (Garland's emphases).

a further specification of the divine passive, "having been and being filled" (2:10), indicate that this "circumcision" was not a literal or physical circumcision but a metaphorical or spiritual circumcision accomplished not by human beings but by God.[25]

Whereas literal or physical circumcision takes place in the removal of the flesh of the foreskin, the metaphorical or spiritual "circumcision" with which the audience were "circumcised" happened "in the removal of the body (σώματος) of the flesh (σαρκός)" (2:11b), recalling for the audience that God has now reconciled them in the "body" (σώματι) of the "flesh" (σαρκός) of Christ through his sacrificial death (1:22a). The audience are to infer that by this reconciliation that God accomplished for them through the body of the flesh of Christ in his sacrificial death they have had their own body of the flesh metaphorically or spiritually "removed," so that they are now part of the "body" (σώματος), which is the church (1:18, 24), and of which Christ is the head (1:18).[26] This is confirmed for the audience as "in the removal of the body of the flesh" (2:11b) is further explained as "in the circumcision of the Christ" (2:11c). This metaphorical or spiritual "circumcision" not made with hands, taking place in the "removal" of the body of the flesh, is the "circumcision" God accomplished for the audience in and through the sacrificial death of the Christ, whom the audience have received (2:6), but with whom the philosophy of empty deceit is not in accord (2:8).[27]

---

25. Bruce, *Colossians*, 103 n. 62: "The negative ἀχειραποίητος was almost a technical term of primitive Christianity to denote the realities of the new order, used not only of the new circumcision (as here) but of the new temple (Mark 14:58) and the resurrection body (2 Cor 5:1)." Harris, *Colossians*, 101: "This περιτομὴ ἀχειροποίητος is to be equated with the περιτομὴ τοῦ Χριστοῦ of v. 11c."

26. Wright, *Colossians*, 106: "As a result of their baptism into Christ, the Colossians now belong first and foremost to the family of God, and not, therefore, to the human families (and their local 'rulers') to which they formerly belonged. 'Body' can, in fact, easily carry the connotation of a group of people, needing further redefinition to make it clear which group is envisaged (as in 'body of Christ'). In that context 'flesh' can easily provide the further requisite definition, since it can carry not only the meanings of 'sinful human nature' but also, simultaneously, the meanings of *family* solidarity. The phrase can thus easily mean 'in the stripping off of the old human solidarities.'" Dunn, *Colossians*, 158: "It is because they share in a body which transmutes, as it were, from cosmic body ('head over all rule and authority,' 2:10), through body of flesh done to death, to his body the church, that their conversion has cosmic and eschatological implications."

27. Harris, *Colossians*, 103: "v. 11 presents spiritual circumcision, not baptism, as the Christian counterpart to physical circumcision. A contrast is implied between circumcision as an external, physical act performed by human hands on a portion of the flesh eight days after birth and circumcision as an inward, spiritual act carried out by divine agency on the whole fleshly nature at the time of regeneration. Although the OT knew of such a 'circumcision of the heart' (Deut. 10:16, 30:6; Jer. 4:4; Ezek. 44:7), Paul speaks of this divestiture of the old man as distinctively 'Christ's circumcision,' a circumcision that characterizes the followers of Christ." Maisch, *Gemeinde in Kolossä*, 166: "Die Beschneidung Christi wird nicht körperlich vollzogen; sie ist ein geistlicher Vorgang" (Maisch's emphasis). Smith, *Heavenly Perspective*, 96: "It is therefore more helpful to look at the reference to circumcision as not primarily concerned with an initiation rite, but as a metaphor for death as seen through the expression τῇ ἀπεκδύσει. The emphatic double prefix ἀπεκ- denotes a complete putting off and laying aside as the whole body is cast aside in death. This putting aside of the flesh in death is not only repeated in 2.15 with ἀπεκδυσάμενος, but also appears in 2 Cor. 5.2–4. Christians have already received the true cir-

The audience then hear their metaphorical or spiritual "circumcision" (2:11) further delineated as their "having been buried with" Christ (2:12a) metaphorically or spiritually "in the baptism" (2:12b), that is, in their immersion or washing in water as the initiation ritual they underwent when they became Christians.[28] In accord with the parallelism between 2:11 and 2:12, the audience's circumcision "in (ἐν) the removal of the body of the flesh" (2:11b), that is, "in (ἐν) the circumcision of the Christ" (2:11c), has progressed to their having been buried with Christ "in (ἐν) the baptism" (2:12b). It is in and through their baptism then that the audience have experienced the "removal" of the body of the flesh, and thus the "circumcision" of the Christ, by which they became part of the body of Christ, the church. Their having been "buried with" Christ in their baptism is thus part of their having received the Christ (2:6) and appropriated the reconciliation God accomplished for them in the body of the flesh of Christ through his sacrificial death (1:22a), with the implication of that death including a burial which the audience have undergone metaphorically, spiritually, and ritually with Christ in their baptism.[29]

Not only have the audience been "buried with" Christ in their baptism, but "in him indeed you were raised with him through faith in the working of the God who raised him from the dead" (2:12c).[30] What has happened to the audience in their union with Christ, "in whom indeed" (ἐν ᾧ καί) they were "circumcised" with a "circumcision" not made with hands, that is, in the "circumcision" of the Christ (2:11), *with* whom they were "buried" (συνταφέντες) in their baptism (2:12ab) is elaborated by the parallel assertion that "in whom indeed" (ἐν ᾧ καί) "you were raised *with*" (συνηγέρθητε) Christ.[31]

The audience are to realize that everything that has happened to them in their union with the Christ whom they have received (2:6), in whom they have been

---

cumcision in the putting off of the body of flesh in the circumcision of Christ. No further ascetic practice, as a means of putting off fleshly desires, can enhance this. There is therefore a further reminder here of the sufficiency of Christ."

28. Dunn, *Colossians*, 145 n. 2: "The less usual Christian word for baptism, βαπτισμός ('washing'; cf. Mark 7:4; Heb. 6:2; 9:10) is probably original, having been altered by many in transmission to the more usual word βάπτισμα." See also Harris, *Colossians*, 103–4.

29. Dunn, *Colossians*, 159: "The imagery is forceful, of sinking below the waters of baptism as a kind of burial. Baptism, presumably by immersion, represented mimetically the commitment to enter the tomb with Jesus after he has been taken down from the cross. Since burial was understood as the conclusion of the event of dying, this commitment meant the enacted willingness to identify oneself with the complete event of Jesus' death. The passive tense indicates also the yielding of those being baptized to the baptizer as indicative of their surrender to God."

30. On "you were raised with" Christ here, Harris (*Colossians*, 104) notes: "The ref. is to a past, spiritual resurrection to 'newness of life' (Rom. 6:4), not a future, somatic resurrection to immortality, although the former both precedes and guarantees the latter. For Paul the resurrection of believers is a two-stage event—a resurrection with Christ in baptism (cf. Eph. 2:5-6), and a resurrection to become like Christ at the End (Rom. 8:29; Phil. 3:20-21)."

31. Smith, *Heavenly Perspective*, 96: "[I]n vv. 9–12 there are four occurrences of ἐν αὐτῷ/ἐν ᾧ, each of which refers to Christ. Therefore in v. 12 ἐν ᾧ refers to Christ, and in particular his death and Resurrection, and not to its direct antecedent, baptism." See also Dübbers, *Christologie*, 238.

and are being filled with all the fullness of God (2:9–10), has happened through their faith, indeed, "through faith in the working of the God who raised him from the dead" (2:12c). The audience's "faith" (πίστιν) in Christ Jesus (1:4), their "faith" (πίστει) in which they are to persevere (1:23), their "faith" (πίστεως) in Christ that is firm (2:5), and their "faith" (πίστει) in which they are being confirmed (2:7) is here more precisely identified as "faith" (πίστεως) in the working of the God who raised Christ from the dead. The "working" (ἐνεργείας) of God in raising Christ from the dead is the same "working" (ἐνέργειαν) of God that is "working" (ἐνεργουμένην) in Paul in power, enabling him to labor and struggle in the proclamation of the gospel of the Christ (1:29). The audience may infer that this same "working" of God is at work in them who have been raised with Christ.[32] They have been raised with Christ through faith in the working of God who raised him from the "dead" (νεκρῶν) because they are part of the body of Christ, the church, whose head is Christ, the firstborn from the "dead" (νεκρῶν) (1:18).[33]

In sum, in this C element of the chiasm the audience have heard that they have been metaphorically or spiritually "circumcised" with a "circumcision" not made with human hands but accomplished by God in the metaphorical or spiritual "removal" of the body of their flesh, in the "circumcision" of Christ (2:11), by which they became part of the body of Christ, which is the church. As part of the body in union with Christ as their head, the audience have been metaphorically or spiritually "buried" with Christ in their baptism, and in their union with Christ they have also been raised by God with him through their faith in the working of the God who raised Christ from the realm of the dead (2:12).

4. *Col 2:13–14 (C´): Being Dead in Your Flesh, He Brought You to Life with Christ, Obliterating the Handwritten Charge*

The Colossian audience hear yet more elaboration of what has happened to them now that they have received the Christ, Jesus the Lord (2:6), so that they are in union with him: "And you, being dead in transgressions and in the uncircumcision of your flesh, he brought you to life along with him, having forgiven us all our transgressions, having obliterated the handwritten charge against us with its decrees, which was opposed to us, and this he has taken from our midst, having nailed it to the cross" (2:13–14). Having now been presented with the central, pivotal elements of the chiasm in 2:6–23, the audience hear a pivot in parallels from "the circumcision not made with hands (ἀχειροποιήτῳ)" (2:11a), "the body of the flesh (σαρκός)" (2:11b), "having been buried with (συνταφέντες) him"

---

32. Wilson, *Colossians*, 206: "[T]he power of God that was at work in Paul's labours for the Church was also effective in the conversion and renewal of life for his readers."

33. Smith, *Heavenly Perspective*, 97: "Paul therefore shows how religious rituals, whether circumcision or baptism, point to the death and Resurrection of Christ. They point to a new life that is lived in the fullness of Christ and imply release from the bondage of the στοιχεῖα τοῦ κόσμου. This focus is a corrective for those involved with the religious rituals of the Colossain philosophy, in that it disarms any desire to boast of super-spirituality based on human achievement."

(2:12a), "you were raised with (συνηγέρθητε) him" (2:12c), and "from the dead (νεκρῶν)" (2:12c) in the C element (2:11–12) to "being dead (νεκρούς)" (2:13a), "in the uncircumcision of your flesh (σαρκός)" (2:13b), "he brought you to life (συνεζωοποίησεν) along with (σύν) him" (2:13c), and "the handwritten charge (χειρόγραφον)" (2:14a) in the C′ element (2:13–14).

After hearing that God raised Christ from the realm of those literally and physically "dead" (νεκρῶν) (2:12c), the audience are immediately reminded that they were metaphorically or spiritually "dead" (νεκρούς) in and through their transgressions (2:13a; cf. 1:21),[34] which thus placed them in a situation of being "dead" analogous to that of Christ before God raised him. That the audience were "dead" in and through their transgressions is further explicated as their being "dead" in and through the uncircumcision of their "flesh" (σαρκός) (2:13b), that is, in their situation of being physically uncircumcised as Gentiles.[35] This reminds the audience of their situation before they were metaphorically or spiritually "circumcised with a circumcision not made with hands in the removal of the body of the flesh (σαρκός), in the circumcision of Christ" (2:11), that is, their situation before they were part of the body of Christ.

But now that the audience are part of the body, which is the church, in union with Christ as their head, God has "brought you to life along with him" (συνεζωοποίησεν ὑμᾶς σὺν αὐτῷ), along with Christ (2:13c). The redundant double use of the preposition "with" (σύν), first as the prefix of the verb, "brought to life with (συν)," and then again in the phrase "with (σύν) him," not only emphatically underlines that it is in their union *with* Christ that God brought them to life, but emphatically reinforces that it is in their union *with* Christ that they, "having been buried *with* (συνταφέντες) him in the baptism" (2:12ab), were also raised by God *with* him—"in whom indeed you were raised *with* (συνηγέρθητε) him" (2:12c).[36]

---

34. Harris, *Colossians*, 105: "Although in v. 12 νεκροί refers to those physically dead, here it is used of persons spiritually dead (cf. Rom. 7:9) rather than of those liable to physical or eternal death." See also Dübbers, *Christologie*, 249. Dunn, *Colossians*, 163: "Their 'being dead' refers to their status outside the covenant made by God with Israel. That is to say, their 'transgressions' (παραπτώματα, usually violations of God's commands) would be those referred to already in a similar passage (1:21), the transgressions of the law that from a Jewish perspective were typical of lawless Gentiles." Deterding, *Colossians*, 95: "The present participle (ὄντας) . . . indicates that this was the readers' ongoing condition."

35. Dunn, *Colossians*, 155: "The disparaging note of 2:13—'the uncircumcision of your flesh'— should not be taken as 'the uncircumcision which is your flesh,' with 'flesh' understood as a moral category. Rather, it echoes the classic description of circumcision as marking God's covenant with Israel . . . 'The uncircumcision of your flesh' means simply 'your status as Gentiles,' primarily an ethnic distinction." O'Brien, *Colossians*, 122–23: "Physical 'uncircumcision' was a *symbol* of their spiritual alienation from God and his covenant of grace; they were both heathen and godless" (O'Brien's emphasis).

36. O'Brien, *Colossians*, 123: "Only here and in Ephesians 2:5 is the compound συζωοποιέω ('make alive together with') to be found, though the additional phrase 'with him' (σὺν αὐτῷ) indicates that the prefix here is important. The Colossians have come to life with Christ, who was dead and rose again; their new life, then, is a sharing in the new life which he received when he rose from the dead. It

The audience are to realize that God brought them to life along with Christ (2:13c) because God forgave all the transgressions not only of "you," the Colossian audience as the "you" (ὑμᾶς) God brought to life with Christ, but "us" (ἡμῖν), that is, all of us believers, whether Jews circumcised with human hands (the implication of 2:11a) or Gentiles, who, like the Colossian audience, were in the uncircumcision of their flesh (2:13b) before the "removal of the body of the flesh" (2:11b).[37] God's forgiveness of all of the transgressions of us believers reinforces the previous assertion that in union with Christ "we have redemption, the forgiveness of sins" (1:14). That God has forgiven us all of our "transgressions" (παραπτώματα) thus means that the audience are no longer "dead" in and through their "transgressions" (παραπτώμασιν) (2:13a). Indeed, they have now been brought to life by God together with Christ (2:13a).

God's having forgiven us all of our transgressions (2:13d) is more fully explained in a metaphorical way as God's "having obliterated the handwritten charge against us with its decrees, which was opposed to us" (2:14a). The audience are to appreciate that in forgiving all of the transgressions of us believers God obliterated the "handwritten charge" (χειρόγραφον), that is, what was written by mere human hands and thus stands in contrast to the circumcision "not made with human hands" (ἀχειροποιήτῳ) that God himself accomplished for the audience (2:11a).[38]

While not simply identified with the Jewish law in its totality, this "handwritten charge," with its connotation of metaphorically "charging" us with a "debt" to be paid, portrays that aspect of the law that increases our transgressions against God, thus increasing the "debt" to be paid.[39] That this "handwritten charge" with

---

is only in union with him that death is vanquished and new life, an integral part of God's new creation, is received."

37. Wright, *Colossians*, 110: "Paul has altered his pronouns here: he has now shifted from 'you' to 'we'. Jews were not 'dead in physical uncircumcision', but they, just as much as pagans, needed forgiveness of sins. The Colossians have joined Paul in the people of God; Paul joins them to the category of forgiven sinners." O'Brien, *Colossians*, 124: "The change of person from 'you' to 'us' (ἡμῖν) indicates that Paul, along with other Jewish Christians, as well as the readers who were Gentile believers, alike had been 'forgiven.'"

38. Smith, *Heavenly Perspective*, 97–99: "Χειρόγραφον means a document written by a responsible person, therefore a 'receipt' (which is its use in the LXX: Tob. 5.3; 9.5). . . . In this context it is a metaphor drawn from the legal world. . . . The essential concept of χειρόγραφον is an autograph, something that one has written by one's own hand."

39. In Rom 5:20a Paul states that "law (νόμος) entered in so that transgression (παράπτωμα) might increase." Joram Luttenberger, "Der gekreuzigte Schuldschein: Ein Aspekt der Deutung des Todes Jesu im Kolosserbrief," *NTS* 51 (2005): 93, 94–95: "Kol 2.14 identifiziert den außer Kraft gesetzen Schuldschein mit dem gekreuzigten Christus. Gott hat die Schulden beglichen und in Christus den persönlichen Schuldschein eines jeden durch den Tod Jesu am Kreuz getötet. Das Kreuz ist der Beweis dafür, dass unsere Schuld bezahlt werden ist. . . . Der sicher nicht zufällig gewählte Begriff χειρόγραφον legt den Akzent auf das Persönliche, Unmittelbare in dem zur Sprache gebrachten Vorgang zwischen dem Schuldner und seinem Gläubiger. Daraus ergibt sich, χειρόγραφον als *Schuldbrief (je-)des Einzelnen* zu verstehen. Ähnlich den Aussagen Jesu werden persönliche Schuld bzw. Verfehlungen des Menschen (παραπτώματα Kol 2.13; vgl. Mt 6.14–15) mittels finanzieller Schulden veranschaulicht"

its "decrees" (δόγμασιν), that is, its various commandments that charge us with transgressions,[40] was completely "against us" (καθ' ἡμῶν) is intensely underscored not only by the emphatic position of this phrase inserted after the article "the" (τό) and immediately before the term "handwritten charge," but also by the additional relative clause describing the "handwritten charge" as that "which was opposed to us" (ὃ ἦν ὑπεναντίον ἡμῖν).[41]

But this "handwritten charge" that was completely opposed to us (2:14a) God completely "obliterated," "erased," or "wiped out" (ἐξαλείψας), as "he took it from our midst, having nailed it to the cross" (2:14b).[42] This graphic figurative language

---

(Luttenberger's emphasis). For the various other past interpretations, see Roy Yates, "Colossians 2,14: Metaphor of Forgiveness," *Bib* 71 (1990): 248-59; Smith, *Heavenly Perspective*, 98-102.

40. Nikolaus Walter, "δόγμα," *EDNT* 1.340: "The general expression δόγματα may have been deliberately chosen in order to include the commandments of the Mosaic law." See also Eph 2:15a, where Paul speaks of "abolishing the law of the commandments in decrees (δόγμασιν)." Wright, *Colossians*, 112: "It would be in keeping with the ironic tone we find at various points in this chapter that Paul should refer to the Mosaic Law as a mere IOU note, or perhaps as a book which does nothing but keep a tally of one's sins (see, e.g., Rom. 4:15; 5:20; and Gal. 3:19-20, where the law, given by angels, has the purpose and effect of shutting people up in their sins). τοῖς δόγμασιν is then an almost equally ironic explanatory phrase, referring to the detailed commandments of the Law as that in which the 'handwritten note' consisted." Harris, *Colossians*, 107-8: "Suggested identifications of this IOU or bond are numerous, the most probable being the Mosaic law itself (cf. Eph. 2:15), regarded as a bill of debt.... Not only was the χειρόγραφον an accusation of guilt; it also constituted a threat of penalty because of human inability to discharge the debt." O'Brien, *Colossians*, 125: "[I]n Hellenistic Judaism the commandments of God were called δόγματα: 3 Macc 1:3; 4 Macc 10:2." Dunn, *Colossians*, 165: "[I]n the context the δόγματα must be formal 'decrees or ordinances or regulations'. They presumably, therefore, refer to that which constituted the record of transgression as condemnatory ('against us,' 'hostile to us').... Thus, although τὸ καθ' ἡμῶν χειρόγραφον itself cannot be identified with the law as such, behind it lie the decrees of the law giving the χειρόγραφον its condemnatory force."

41. Wright, *Colossians*, 112-13: "The difference between 'against us' and 'opposed to us' is slight but not altogether insignificant. The first indicates active opposition or enmity; the second, a barrier which stands in one's way. The word-order in Greek is 'having blotted out the against-us handwriting, with its regulations, which was opposed to us'. This may indicate that Paul added the last phrase to emphasize the effect of the detailed regulations, because of which the 'handwriting'—i.e. the Law—kept both Jews and Gentiles locked up in sin. The Mosaic Torah did not, we should note, stand over against Jews and Gentiles in the same way. In Paul's view, it shut *up* the Jews under sin and shut *out* the Gentiles from the hope and promise of membership in God's people" (Wright's emphasis). Bruce, *Colossians*, 109 n. 91: "[I]t is this bond, representing the power which the law has over us, rather than the law itself, which Paul views as cancelled by Christ." Harris, *Colossians*, 108: "If καθ' ἡμῶν highlights the brute fact of indebtedness, the rel. clause ὃ ἦν ὑπεναντίον ἡμῖν emphasizes the direct and active opposition of the ... indebtedness: 'which was directly hostile to us.'" According to O'Brien (*Colossians*, 125), "with decrees" (τοῖς δόγμασιν) is probably causal, "indicating why the bond or certificate of indebtedness has a case against us." Smith, *Heavenly Perspective*, 102: "[T]he likely meaning of χειρόγραφον is a signed acknowledgment of culpability before God. The Jews were culpable because of their agreement to obey the law (Deut. 27.14-26; 30:15-20); the Gentiles were guilty for disobedience to their moral law (Rom. 2.14, 15). As neither group had discharged its responsibilities, the bond continued καθ' ἡμῶν (against us)."

42. In LXX Isa 43:25 God declares: "I am, I am the one who obliterates (ἐξαλείφων) your lawless deeds and I will not remember them." According to O'Brien (*Colossians*, 126) the expression "he took

with its implication of God taking the "handwritten charge" with his own hands out of our midst and nailing it with his own hands to the cross of Christ appropriately counters this charge written with mere human hands with the dramatic image of God totally eliminating it with his own hands by attaching it to the cross of Christ's death. That God brought the audience to life with Christ from their situation of "death" in their transgressions—"and you, being dead (καὶ ὑμᾶς νεκροὺς ὄντας) in transgressions" (2:13)—by obliterating the handwritten charge against us, having nailed it to the cross of Christ's sacrificial death (2:14), thus reinforces and develops God's reconciliation of the audience from their alienation—"and you, once being alienated (καὶ ὑμᾶς ποτε ὄντας ἀπηλλοτριωμένους) and enemies in mind in works that are evil" (1:21)—through the sacrificial death of Christ (1:22).[43]

In sum, in this C' element the audience have heard that they, being metaphorically or spiritually "dead" in their transgressions and in the "uncircumcision" of their flesh as Gentiles, God has brought to life with Christ, having forgiven the transgressions not only of the audience but of all of us (2:13). God's forgiveness of these transgressions which rendered us "dead" is emphatically underlined for the audience with the dramatic image of God himself totally obliterating the "charge"

---

it from our midst" (ἦρκεν ἐκ τοῦ μέσου) "signifies the decisive removal of the 'certificate of indebtedness' (the change from the aorist tense to the perfect points to the permanence of the removal).... God has canceled the bond by nailing it to the cross—this is a vivid way of saying that because Christ was nailed to the cross our debt has been completely forgiven." Dunn, *Colossians*, 166 n. 40: "ἐκ τοῦ μέσου, 'from the midst,' simply strengthens the verb ('removed out of the way completely')." Smith, *Heavenly Perspective*, 104–5: "The image that is given in v. 14 is the practice within the Roman Empire of attaching the indictment of a crucified man to his cross (Mark 15.26). Through the crucifixion, justice is wrought and atonement procured and thereby the indictment is destroyed. Note also the use of the perfect tense for ἦρκεν ἐκ τοῦ μέσου, which points to the permanent and ongoing nature of the effects of the removal. The indictment that was pinned to the cross of Christ was the χειρόγραφον: a signed acknowledgment of culpability of both Jews and Gentiles before God. This indictment had made the Colossians enslaved to the powers of darkness (1.12–14). With the removal of the indictment there was also liberation from the powers of darkness, the στοιχεῖα τοῦ κόσμου. It is not that the law *per se* was erased, but its 'hostility' to us. Therefore ἐξαλείφω denotes the erasure of an entry on the indictment rather than the laws themselves."

43. Dübbers, *Christologie*, 249 n. 224: "Daß sich der Verfasser hier auf die gottlose Vergangenheit der Adressaten bezieht, wird besonders auch durch der Vergleich mit der analogen Satzkonstruktion in 1,21 f. deutlich, wo das temporale Verhältnis durch die Opposition ποτέ und νυνί explizit gemacht wird. Dem Sinn nach ist diese Gegenüberstellung von 'Einst' und 'Jetzt' auf 2,13 zu übertragen." Dunn, *Colossians*, 166: "The thought is rather of the indictment itself being destroyed by means of crucifixion, as though it was the indictment which was itself nailed to the cross in execution. The play, then, is rather with the thought of Christ as himself the condemnatory bond and his death as its destruction. The metaphor is convoluted, but presumably reflects again the idea of Christ's death as a sin offering and thus of Christ as embodying the sins of the offerer and destroying them in his death." Garland, *Colossians*, 152: "The note was not simply torn up and thrown away, however. The full penalty was exacted in Christ's death.... the guilty parties were not nailed to the cross with it, only Christ. Christ stood in our place, taking our sin upon himself and taking away our guilt." Smith, *Heavenly Perspective*, 104: "That which was nailed to the cross was not the regulations broken but the offence committed; the χειρόγραφον is a list of indictments rather than a list of regulations."

for our transgressions with its decrees written by human hands, which was totally against us, by taking it out of our midst with his own hands and nailing it with his own hands upon the cross of Christ's sacrificial death (2:14).

5. Col 2:15–19 (B´): The Whole Body Grows from the Head with the Growth That Comes from God Who Exposed the Principalities and Authorities

The audience continue to hear what God in the death and resurrection of Christ has done for them and all believers in their union with Christ: "having removed the principalities and the authorities, he exposed them in public,[44] leading them away in triumph in him" (2:15). God's removal of the "principalities" (ἀρχάς) and the "authorities" (ἐξουσίας) in this B´ element (2:15–19) develops for the audience,[45] by way of the chiastic parallelism, the previous statement in the B element (2:9–10) that Christ is the head of every "principality" (ἀρχῆς) and "authority" (ἐξουσίας) (2:10).

God's having "removed" (ἀπεκδυσάμενος) the principalities and the authorities (2:15a) develops what he has done for the audience in his "removal" (ἀπεκδύσει) of their body of the flesh (2:11b), so that they are now part of the body, the church, of which Christ is the head (1:18, 24).[46] The audience are to realize and appreciate that God's having removed "the principalities and the authorities," representative of "the elemental forces of the world" (2:8), means that these cosmic powers no longer have any rule or authority either to hinder or help their lives.[47] The sole rule and authority, as well as source of salvific power, in their lives is now Christ as the "head" not only of the body, the church, to which they belong but of "*every* principality and authority" (2:10b).

In having removed the cosmic principalities and authorities, God is portrayed with imagery suggesting an exuberant celebration of a victorious destruction and despoiling of enemies by a conqueror who "exposed them in public,[48] leading

---

44. Dunn, *Colossians*, 168: "The addition of ἐν παρρησίᾳ, 'openly, in public,' simply reinforces the note of public shame, though the phrase could also mean 'boldly.'"

45. Harris, *Colossians*, 111: "After the two fem. nouns ἀρχάς and ἐξουσίας, one would expect αὐτας, not αὐτούς. This is a case of 'construction according to sense,' showing that the powers and authorities are not abstract entities but personal beings."

46. With regard to the significance of the middle voice of the participle "having removed" (ἀπεκδυσάμενος), Harris (*Colossians*, 110) states: "ἀπεκδύομαι connotes the complete (ἀπ[ο]-) stripping of oneself or another person, in one's own interest." On the active sense of the middle voice of this participle, see BDF §316.

47. On the imagery of "removing" here, Dunn (*Colossians*, 168) suggests that we have "the powerful imagery of old and wasted garments being discarded . . . the spiritual powers, including the elemental forces (2:8), should be counted as of no greater value and significance than a bunch of old rags."

48. With regard to the meaning of the verb "exposed" (ἐδειγμάτισεν) here, O'Brien (*Colossians*, 128) explains that "δειγματίζω occurs on only one other occasion in the Greek Bible, at Matthew 1:19, where it is found with reference to Joseph not wishing to cite Mary publicly and thus expose her. Here the term means not to 'make an example' of them (which would be παραδειγματίζω), but to 'show them in their true character.' By putting on public display God exposed the principalities and powers to ridicule. This open manifestation of their being divested of dignity and authority only serves to

them away in triumph in him (ἐν αὐτῷ)" (2:15b), that is, in Christ, in the death and resurrection of Christ.[49] It is in union with this same Christ, that is, "in him" (ἐν αὐτῷ), that the audience are to go on walking (2:6), living their lives, having been rooted and being built up "in him" (ἐν αὐτῷ) (2:7a). For "in him" (ἐν αὐτῷ) dwells all the fullness of the deity in a bodily manner (2:9), so that the audience, as part of the body of which Christ is the head, have been and are being likewise filled with all the fullness of the deity "in him" (ἐν αὐτῷ), who is the absolutely authoritative head of every principality and authority in the cosmos (2:10). Indeed, it is in Christ "in whom" (ἐν ᾧ) the audience were "circumcised" with a "circumcision" not made with hands in the removal of their body of the flesh (2:11ab), so that they are now part of the body of Christ, the church, having been buried with Christ in the baptism, "in whom" (ἐν ᾧ) indeed the audience were raised with Christ from the dead (2:12).

The audience then hear what they are not to do, in reference to the potentially

---

demonstrate more clearly the infinite superiority of Christ." That God exposed the true character of the principalities and authorities means that he exposed them as mere creatures created in Christ, as indicated in Col 1:16. Dübbers, *Christologie*, 162: "Am Kreuz nämlich machte Gott offenbar, wer Christus von Anfang an ist: der Präexistente, in dem allein alles Sein und Neusein seinen Grund hat. Und damit wird zugleich klar, wer ἀρχαὶ καὶ ἐξουσίαι sind: nichts als Geschöpfe—ohne jede Heilsmacht. *Dies* ist der soteriologische Triumph, den Gott durch Christus über die Engel der Philosophen feiert und an dem die Adressaten teilhaben" (Dübbers's emphasis).

49. Regarding the meaning of the participle "triumphing over" (θριαμβεύσας) here, O'Brien (*Colossians*, 128-29) explains: "The word Θριαμβεύω occurs only here and at 2 Corinthians 2:14 in the NT. The image behind this verb is that of a tumultuous procession through the streets of Rome to celebrate a military victory. The term ought to be translated . . . to 'lead as a conquered enemy in a victory parade,' when followed by a direct personal object (as at 2 Cor 2:14 and Col 2:15). . . . In the Colossians reference, however, the victims are true enemies. . . . God parades these powerless 'powers' and 'principalities' to make plain to all the magnitude of the victory. Their period of rule is finished . . . They have been pacified (1:20), overcome and reconciled, yet not finally destroyed or appeased. They continue to exist, opposed to man and his interests. But they cannot finally harm the person who is in Christ, and their ultimate overthrow, although in the future, is sure and certain." See also Edgar Krentz, "De Caesare et Christo," *CurTM* 28 (2001): 341-45. Dunn (*Colossians*, 169) points out that "the object of Θριαμβεύω would most naturally refer to those over whom the triumph was celebrated. The flow of the discussion has been: (1) talk of 'deliverance from the authority of darkness' (1:13), (2) the implication of a state of cosmic warfare which the cross brought to reconciliation (1:20), (3) the implication that the στοιχεῖα are a force opposed to Christ (2:8), from which believers need to escape (2:10), and (4) the sustained impression in the immediate context of a fatally disadvantaged, condemned status from which the cross has provided deliverance (2:11-15). . . . The final ἐν αὐτῷ (the fifteenth 'in him' in the letter and the fifth since 2:9) . . . is simply Paul's attempt to retain the focus on what has been done 'in Christ' on the cross." Dunn's interpretation thus counters the idea that the principalities and authorities here are not portrayed as conquered enemies, as proposed by Roy Yates, "Colossians 2.15: Christ Triumphant," *NTS* 37 (1991): 573-91. Smith, *Heavenly Perspective*, 109: It is important to realize that Θριαμβεύω does not refer to the actual triumph over the vanquished foes; the triumph is presupposed. . . . Θριαμβεύω followed by a direct object means 'to lead as a conquered enemy in a victory parade.' " See also L. Williamson, "Led in Triumph: Paul's Use of THRIAMBEUO," *Int* 22 (1968): 317-22; Andreas Hock, "Christ Is the Parade: A Comparative Study of the Triumphal Procession in 2 Cor 2,14 and Col 2,15," *Bib* 88 (2007): 110-19.

captivating philosophy of empty deceit that is not according to Christ (2:8), as a consequence of what God has done for them as part of the body of Christ: "Let then no one judge you in food and in drink or in regard to a festival or new moon or sabbaths, which things are a shadow of the things that were to come, but the body belongs to the Christ. Let no one condemn you, delighting in humility and worship of the angels, going into detail about what things he had seen, vainly being made arrogant by the mind of his flesh, not holding to the head, from whom the whole body, supported and held together through ligaments and bonds, grows with the growth that is from God" (2:16–19). That the "body" (σῶμα) belongs to the Christ (2:17) and not holding to the "head" (κεφαλήν), from whom the whole "body" (σῶμα) grows with the growth that is from God (2:19) in the B´ element (2:15–19) recalls for the audience, by way of the chiastic parallelism, that all the fullness of the deity dwells "bodily" (σωματικῶς) in Christ, who is the "head" (κεφαλή) of every principality and authority in the B element (2:9–10).

Resuming the address of his audience as "you" (ὑμᾶς), echoing that God brought "you" (ὑμᾶς) to life with Christ (2:13b), after the triple reference to "us" (ἡμῖν-ἡμῶν-ἡμῖν, 2:13c–14), and recalling his previous warning, "See to it that there will not be anyone (μή τις) who is captivating you (ὑμᾶς) through the philosophy which is empty deceit" (2:8a), Paul here elaborates upon it: "Let then no one (μὴ οὖν τις) judge you (ὑμᾶς) in food and in drink or in regard to a festival or new moon or sabbaths" (2:16). The audience must take heed lest any advocate of the "philosophy of empty deceit" with its association to the teachings and practices of the Jewish synagogue "judge" (κρινέτω), that is, criticize, find fault with, or even condemn them for not adhering to the Jewish regulations regarding what not to eat and drink, or for not observing the annual Jewish festivals, or monthly (new moon) celebrations, or weekly periods of rest and worship in the synagogue on the sabbath.[50]

---

50. The Colossian Christians already participated in these religious events according to Troy W. Martin, "Pagan and Judeo-Christian Time-Keeping Schemes in Gal 4.10 and Col 2.16," *NTS* 42 (1996): 105–19. But the practices in 2:16 are those not of the Colossian Christians but rather of their critics according to H. R. Cole, "The Christian and Time-Keeping in Colossians 2:16 and Galatians 4:10," *AUSS* 39 (2001): 273–82. See also T. C. G. Thornton, "Jewish New Moon Festivals, Galatians 4:3–11 and Colossians 2:16," *JTS* 40 (1989): 97–100; F. B. Holbrook, "Did the Apostle Paul Abolish the Sabbath? Colossians 2:14–17 Revisited," *Journal of the Adventist Theological Society* 13 (2002): 64–72. There is a list of what takes place on the "festivals" (ἑορταῖς), the "new moons" (νουμηνίαις), and "sabbaths" (σαββάτοις) in LXX Ezek 45:17, references to "sabbath" (σαββάτοις) and "new moons" (νουμηνίαις) in LXX Ezek 46:3, and references to "festivals" (ἑορτάς), "new moons" (νουμηνίας), and "sabbaths" (σάββατα) in LXX Hos 2:13. Bevere, *Sharing*, 90: "Colossians 2:16 is best seen as a reference to Jewish dietary regulations. Indeed, the character of the verse is strongly Jewish. The authors' comments concerning food and drink come in the context of circumcision, the keeping of special days, and Sabbath, which, as I have argued, are also best understood as Jewish in nature." Bruce, *Colossians*, 115: "[T]he sabbath was peculiarly Jewish. It is therefore probable that the festivals in question are those of the Jewish year, and that the reference to the new moon is to the Jewish celebration of the first of the month (Num. 10:10; 28:11–15). . . . the Colossians are now told that the observance of these occasions as obligatory is an acknowledgment of the continuing authority of the powers through which such regula-

While these Jewish practices and observances are a "shadow" (σκιά), that is, a forerunner or anticipation, of the things that were to come, the "body" (σῶμα) belongs to the Christ (2:17).[51] For the audience the phrase "the body belongs to the Christ" carries a double meaning. That the "body" belongs to the Christ means that the substance or reality of the things to come, which the previously mentioned Jewish practices and observances only anticipate or foreshadow, have already become a reality in Christ.[52] At the same time, that the "body" belongs to the Christ means that the audience, as part of the "body" which is the church, belongs to the Christ as the head who both rules over and sustains the body (1:18, 24).[53] The audience are to realize, then, that as part of the "body" they have been and are being filled with all the fullness of the deity in their union with Christ, the head, in whom all the fullness of the deity dwells in a "bodily" manner (2:9–10), so that they have already begun to enjoy the reality (the "body") of "the things that were to come," to which these Jewish practices, as a "shadow," are still looking forward. They therefore need not observe them.[54]

That the audience are to "let then no one judge you (μὴ οὖν τις ὑμᾶς κρινέτω)" (2:16a) progresses to the further exhortation, "let no one condemn you (μηδεὶς

---

tions were mediated—the powers that were decisively subjugated by Christ. It would be preposterous indeed for those who had reaped the benefit of Christ's victory to put themselves voluntarily under the control of the powers which he had conquered." Dunn, *Colossians*, 175: "We must conclude, therefore, that all the elements of this verse bear a characteristically and distinctively Jewish color, that those who cherished them so critically must have been the (or some) Jews of Colossae, and that their criticism arose from Jewish suspicion of Gentiles making what they would regard as unacceptable claims to the distinctive Jewish heritage without taking on all that was most distinctive of that heritage."

51. O'Brien, *Colossians*, 140: "'[S]hadow' is used not so much in the Platonic sense of a copy of the heavenly and eternal 'idea' as in the sense of a foreshadowing of what is to come.... the expression is to be interpreted from the period when the legal restrictions of verse 16 were enjoined; it is future from the standpoint of the OT." Garland, *Colossians*, 174: "The shadow/reality contrast as used by Paul applies to promise and fulfillment. Since Paul would never describe pagan rituals as a shadow or outline of what was to come in Christ, the promise/fulfillment motif is more fitting as an evaluation of Judaism." As Deterding (*Colossians*, 113) points out, "the things that were to come" is a participial phrase that "is almost a technical term for the messianic age and kingdom that arrived with Christ at his first advent and that will be consummated at his return." See also W. C. Vergeer, "Σκία and Σῶμα: The Strategy of Contextualisation in Colossians 2:17: A Contribution to the Quest for a Legitimate Contextual Theology Today," *Neot* 28 (1994): 379–93; Sang-Won Son, "τὸ σῶμα τοῦ Χριστοῦ In Colossians 2:17," in *History and Exegesis: New Testament Essays in Honor of Dr. E. Earle Ellis for His 80th Birthday* (ed. Sang-Won Son; London: Clark, 2006), 222–38.

52. On the meaning of "substantive reality" for σῶμα, see BDAG, 984.

53. Wright, *Colossians*, 121: "[T]he proximity, within the same argument, of verse 19, where the 'head' and the 'body' are introduced quite casually, may suggest that Paul is aware of, and wishes to exploit, a *double entendre* here. He manages to refer at the same time to the substantiality of the new people of God, as opposed to the shadowy nature of the old, and to the fact that this new people is the 'body of Christ.'" MacDonald (*Colossians*, 111) translates: "but the reality is the body of Christ."

54. Bruce, *Colossians*, 117: "[I]t is as members of the body of Christ that his people now possess the substance, so that they may cheerfully let the shadow go." For a different interpretation of Col 2:17, see Troy W. Martin, "But Let Everyone Discern the Body of Christ (Col 2:17)," *JBL* 114 (1995): 249–55.

ὑμᾶς καταβραβευέτω)" (2:18a). But now the one who would condemn is characterized and caricatured as one "delighting in humility and worship of the angels, going into detail about what things he had seen, vainly being made arrogant by the mind of his flesh" (2:18). This description serves as a polemical parody of the kind of conduct practiced by one proudly engaging in the experience of a type of Jewish mystical or ecstatic visions of heavenly worship. For one "delighting in humility" (θέλων ἐν ταπεινοφροσύνῃ, 2:18b) to condemn ironically contradicts the very nature of humility as something one would not proudly delight in nor use to condemn others.[55] Furthermore, "delighting in humility" may connote an inappropriate or incongruous taking of pleasure in the humble submission to the kind of Jewish regulations involved in judging the audience (2:16). But more to the point, "delighting in humility" parodies the taking of pleasure in the kind of humility that involves fasting as an inducement to ecstatic, mystical, visionary experiences.[56]

That the one who would condemn the audience delights also "in worship of the angels" (θρησκείᾳ τῶν ἀγγέλων, 2:18c) further parodies these visions of heavenly worship. Although one delighting in this kind of visionary worship stimulated by the "humility" of fasting may highly esteem it as a participation in the angelic worship of God in heaven, the audience are to devalue it as an obsessive and idolatrous worship of merely the angels themselves rather than authentic worship of God.[57] Such a person would be in danger of worshiping the angels as a

---

55. Heinz Giesen, "ταπεινοφροσύνη," *EDNT* 3.334: "Humility is doubtless perverted whenever heretics take pleasure in it."

56. Wilson, *Colossians* 220-21: "The verb θέλω normally means to wish, will or desire, as in 2.1 above, but the sense required here is rather to take pleasure in. Its use here is commonly regarded as a Semitism translating the Hebrew ב חפץ." Dunn, *Colossians*, 178-79: "Ταπεινοφροσύνη usually means 'humility,' but most follow the observation that the LXX uses the repeated phrase 'to humble (ταπεινόω) one's soul' in the sense of 'to mortify oneself' (Lev. 16:29, 31; 23:27, 29, 32) or more specifically 'to fast' (Ps. 35:13; Isa. 58:3, 5; Jdt. 4:9) . . . This suggests a fair degree of ascetic practice as part of the Colossian 'philosophy.'" O'Brien, *Colossians*, 142: "These ascetic practices in Jewish mystical-pietistic literature were effectual for receiving visions of the heavenly mysteries. . . . the apostle is stating that the advocates of the Colossian 'philosophy' delighted in ascetic practices as a prelude to the reception of heavenly visions." See also Garland, *Colossians*, 177. Smith, *Heavenly Perspective*, 121: "What is referred to, therefore, is not the Galatian situation where one group is compelling the whole congregation to follow legalistic practices. Rather, there was a group which was delighting in its higher spirituality. The members of this group saw Christians outside their group as defective or even disqualified because they did not share the same experiences. These experiences, we will see, were reflective of first-century Jewish mysticism."

57. According to Dunn (*Colossians*, 180-81), there "is the evidence of a desire particularly within apocalyptic and mystical circles of first-century Judaism to join in with the worship of angels in heaven. . . . It is quite possible, therefore, to envisage a Jewish (or Christian Jewish) synagogue in Colossae which was influenced by such ideas and which delighted in their worship sabbath by sabbath as a participation in the worship of the angels in heaven. In this case the 'humility' associated with this worship could very well denote the spiritual discipline and mortification regarded as essential to maintain the holiness required to participate with the holy ones and the holy angels." Dübbers, *Christologie*, 271-72: "Vielmehr wird man die scharfe Polemik des Kontextes zu berücksichtigen haben, mit

general category of spiritual beings which would include "the principalities and the authorities" God has exposed in the death and resurrection of Christ (2:15) as mere creatures created in Christ (1:16), who is superior to them as their authoritative "head" (2:10).[58]

"Going into detail about what he has seen" (ἃ ἑόρακεν ἐμβατεύων, 2:18d) seems to confirm that this sort of "worship" involves visionary experiences—indeed, visions of heavenly worship that one proudly delights in delineating to others in detail.[59] But the audience are to consider such a person who would condemn

---

der der Verfasser des Kolosserbriefes auf die philosophische Propaganda reagiert; diese spricht gerade nicht dafür, daß der Verfasser seinen Kontrahenten die Partizipation am himmlischen Gottesdienst zugesteht. Wahrscheinlicher ist dagegen die Annahme, daß er ihnen mit dieser Wendung vorwirft, sie würden *lediglich* Engeln dienen—Geschöpfen also (1,16) und daher soteriologischen Nichtsen (2,10. 15)—, um die Absurdität ihres Handelns bloßzustellen" (Dübbers's emphasis). Bevere, *Sharing*, 114: "I suggested that more emphasis should be placed on θρησκεία τῶν ἀγγέλων as an accusatory phrase from the authors of the letter, and not a phrase the Colossian philosophers would have embraced to describe the nature of their particular practice.... Thus the accusatory phrase θρησκεία τῶν ἀγγέλων most likely refers to a mystical Judaism in which the philosophers are seeking the experience of participating with the hosts of heaven in the worship of God. This does not exclude the possibility that there may indeed have been some angel veneration taking place as well." Garland, *Colossians*, 179: "In the polemical context that expresses Paul's contempt for the arrogance of the 'philosophy,' the reference to 'the worship of angels' may well be a biased description of its practices. If the errorists were actually and actively worshiping angels, we would expect Paul to spew forth a far more passionate denunciation of such idolatry. We may infer from his relative calm on the issue that they are not actually offering worship to angelic beings or invoking them. Thus, Paul may only be disdainfully caricaturing the 'philosophy's' ritual concerns and attention to New Moons as the worship of angels." See also Smith, *Heavenly Perspective*, 122–27.

58. Dübbers, *Christologie*, 272 n. 329: "Der Zusammenhang der Argumentation wider die Philosophie legt die Annahme nahe, daß die hier erwähnten ἄγγελοι für den Verfasser des Kolosserbriefes mit den ἀρχαὶ καὶ ἐξουσίαι aus 2,10. 15 identische sind: Zumindest scheint er davon auszugehen, daß den ἀρχαὶ καὶ ἐξουσίαι von den Philosophen eine soteriologische Bedeutung zugemessen wurde. Ansonsten wäre es wenig sinnvoll, die Engelmächte Christus, dem exklusiven Heilsmittler Gottes, gegenüberzustellen. Diese soteriologische Funktion der ἀρχαὶ καὶ ἐξουσίαι korrespondiert wiederum mit der den Philosophen zugeschriebenen Engelverehrung in 2,18."

59. Dübbers, *Christologie*, 273: "Man wird das ἃ ἑόρακεν ἐμβατεύων daher am ehesten in dem Sinn zu verstehen haben, daß die Gegner (fortlaufend) in das, was sie gesehen haben, eindringen. Doch auch hier bleibt immer noch die Frage offen, ob damit die gegnerische Praxis—wie in der Regel vorausgesetzt wird—korrekt beschrieben ist oder ob man nicht eher davon ausgehen muß, daß der Verfasser des Kolosserbriefes den gegnerischen Ansatz auch hier polemisch destruiert.... Der Verfasser hält den Gegnern vor, daß sie *nur* in das, was sie gesehen haben, (intellektuell) eindringen. Sie nehmen *bloß* das für sich an, was vor Augen liegt, und halten dies bereits für göttlichen Erkenntnis. Gott, den ἀόρατος und den transzendenten (1,15), erfassen sie damit jedoch gerade nicht" (Dübbers's emphasis). Barth and Blanke, *Colossians*, 349: "It as much as says that the 'opponents' of Paul are preoccupied with their own religious experiences." Garland, *Colossians*, 181: "Paul does not need to give the Colossians an objective description of the opponents' beliefs and practices and only wants to deflate their false boasts by subverting them with sarcasm. Their exaggerated visions are all smoke and mirrors, much ado about nothing. Their nervy conceit is all folly." For a different interpretation, see Fred O. Francis, "The Background of EMBATEUEIN (Col 2:18) in Legal Papyri and Oralce Inscriptions," in *Conflict at Colossae: A Problem in the Interpretation of Early Christianity Illustrated by Selected Modern*

them for not engaging in this kind of visionary worship as "vainly being made arrogant by the mind of his flesh" (εἰκῇ φυσιούμενος ὑπὸ τοῦ νοὸς τῆς σαρκὸς αὐτοῦ, 2:18e). Such worship cannot be seen as involving true humility or amounting to anything significant, since it ironically leads to "vainly being made arrogant." And the visions involved in such worship, alleged to be seen in heaven, actually take place nowhere but in "the mind of his flesh."[60] The audience are thus to shun such "worship" that leads to one being made arrogant in his "flesh" (σαρκός), since they, who were once spiritually "dead" in the "uncircumcision" of their "flesh" (σαρκός) (2:13), have had the body of their "flesh" (σαρκός) removed by God in the "circumcision" of the Christ (2:11), so that they are now part of the body, the church, of which Christ is the head (1:18, 24).

Unlike the audience, such a condemnatory, proud, and vainly arrogant person preoccupied with a merely fleshly way of thinking amounting to a very individualistic kind of "worship" is consequently "not holding to the head, from whom the whole body, supported and held together through ligaments and bonds, grows with the growth that is from God" (2:19). The audience are to realize and appreciate that they, who have received the Christ (2:6), are thus holding to the Christ who is the "head" (κεφαλήν), the authoritative "head" (κεφαλή) superior to every angelic principality and authority (2:10), so that they need not engage in any type of individualistic, visionary "worship" of the angels. Instead, the audience are to hold to the Christ as the "head" from whom the whole "body" (σῶμα), the "body" (σῶμα) that is the church of which Christ is the "head" (κεφαλή) (1:18), the "body" (σῶμα) that belongs to Christ (2:17), is supported and held together through its individual members, metaphorically described as its "ligaments and bonds," so that it grows, not individualistically but corporately, with the growth that is authentically from God.[61]

Studies: Revised Edition (ed. Fred O. Francis and Wayne A. Meeks; Sources for Biblical Study 4; Missoula, Mont.: Society of Biblical Literature, 1975), 197–207; Smith, *Heavenly Perspective*, 127–30. See also Christopher Rowland, "Apocalyptic Visions and the Exaltation of Christ in the Letter to the Colossians," *JSNT* 19 (1983): 73–83.

60. Alexander Sand, "νοῦς," *EDNT* 2.479: "In Col 2:18 νοῦς τῆς σαρκός designates literally the *mind* or *habits* of the flesh, which is negatively defined as a false disposition determined by the world. The expression describes the person whose *spirit* is determined only by fleshly existence" (Sand's emphasis). Dunn, *Colossians*, 185: "To speak of 'the mind of flesh' was therefore in effect to deny that this Colossian worshiper with angels could ever have 'lifted off' from earth: even his mind was 'flesh,' fast bound to earth." Garland, *Colossians*, 181: "For Paul, the mind of the flesh is something set over against God and lacks any true spiritual enlightenment." Smith, *Heavenly Perspective*, 131: "The irony of this passage shows that boasting of 'heavenly' visions was, in fact, worldly."

61. Bruce, *Colossians*, 123 n. 139: "Paul may be developing a conception of the interlinking of bodily joints and ligaments which had already begun to take shape in his mind as a figure of the mutual dependence and harmonious cooperation of believers as members of the body of Christ." O'Brien, *Colossians*, 147: "The physiological language is metaphorical; the joints and ligaments are not to be understood ... of ministers, who are distinct from ordinary church members." Dunn, *Colossians*, 186: "The emphasis seems to be more on the interconnectedness of the members of the body than on the joints and ligaments as actually channels of nurture." Wilson, *Colossians*, 225: "κεφαλή in the light of 1.18 and 2.10 naturally refers to Christ ... ἐξ οὗ is then a natural *constructio ad sensum*, our author

That the whole body of the church is "held together" (συμβιβαζόμενον) through its "ligaments and bonds" (2:19), that is, through its believing members, recalls how the believers in Laodicea, those who have not yet seen Paul, and the Colossian audience (2:1) are "held together" (συμβιβασθέντες) in love (2:2), that is, in their mutual love for one another as members of the body of Christ. The implication for the audience is that they are to remain firmly united to Christ as the "head" from whom the whole "body" is supported and held together through its individual members in their mutual love for one another, rather than to engage in any kind of visionary "worship" of the angels (2:18), which would result in their being separated both from their "head," Christ, and his "body," the church.

That the whole body of the church "grows" (αὔξει) with the "growth" (αὔξησιν) that is from God (θεοῦ) (2:19) further develops how the Colossian audience, who have learned the gospel that is "growing" (αὐξανόμενον) among them (1:6), are themselves "growing" (αὐξανόμενοι) with regard to their experiential knowledge of God (θεοῦ) (1:10). That the whole body of the church grows with the growth that is from God reminds the audience that it is as part of the body in union with Christ, its head, that they have been raised with Christ through their faith in the working of the God (θεοῦ) who raised him from the dead (2:12). The audience are thus to grasp that, as those "rooted" (2:7) in the body of Christ, which is growing with the growth that comes from God himself, they have no need of any visionary "worship" of the angels (2:18), which is directed neither by nor to God himself. Indeed, the audience have been and are being filled by God with all the fullness of the very deity (θεότητος) itself in a "bodily" (σωματικῶς) manner (2:9–10), that is, as part of the whole "body" (σῶμα) holding firmly to Christ, the "head" from whom the whole body is growing with the growth that comes from God himself (2:19).[62]

In sum, in this B´ element (2:15–19) the audience have heard that in the

---

thinking not of the grammatical antecedent but of Christ who is implied. The head is the organ which controls all that happens in the body, and it is from it, from Christ, that the body which is the Church derives its growth." Smith, *Heavenly Perspective*, 132: "Paul is therefore appealing to the sufficiency of Christ who is the source of nourishment for the body. This growth of the church is dependent on a correct understanding of the person of Christ, not on ecstatic heavenly ascents. The individual Christian is to be more concerned for the unity of the body than for boasting in heavenly experiences."

62. Harris, *Colossians*, 124: "Since all three verbal forms in v. 19b are pres. tense Paul is affirming that the Body's receipt of vitality and the preservation of its integrity are ongoing processes related to its overall growth, which is simultaneously dependent on Christ and stimulated by God." Smith, *Heavenly Perspective*, 132–33: "The Colossian Christians were very aware of the reality of the heavenly realm and its interaction with the earthly realm. It was because the spiritual realm had been subjugated by the victory of Christ on the cross that they were able to participate in the worship of heaven. What Paul is attacking, however, is not their world view, but the ironic practical result of this heavenly worship. Humility was resulting in boasting. Ascetic practices were resulting in pride. Heavenly worship was little more than the worship of self. The defeat of the elemental spirits, that should have produced unity in the worship of God, was actually producing pride and division. Indeed, the Colossian philosophy was empty deceit, as it was giving the principalities and powers a means of enslaving the Colossian Christians again through asceticism and rituals. The proclamation of the victory of the cross was undermined."

death and resurrection of Christ God has exposed the angelic principalities and authorities (2:15) as mere creatures created in Christ, their head. Consequently, as part of the "body" that belongs to Christ (2:17), they are not to allow anyone to judge them for not observing various Jewish regulations (2:16). Nor are they to allow anyone to condemn them for not engaging in a Jewish mystical and visionary "worship" of the angels that is not from God (2:18), since, as those holding to Christ as the "head" from whom the whole "body," supported and held together through the mutual love of its members, they are growing with the growth that comes from God himself (2:19).

6. *Col 2:20–23 (A´): Having Died with Christ from the Elemental Forces of the World, Do Not Live in the World according to the Commandments and Teachings of Human Beings, Which Are Not Wisdom*

The audience hear yet more reasons why they should not allow anyone to captivate them through the "philosophy" of empty deceit (2:8): "If you died with Christ from the elemental forces of the world, why let yourselves be subjected to decrees as if living in the world? 'Do not touch, do not taste, do not handle'—which things are all destined for destruction in being consumed—according to the commandments and teachings of human beings; such (decrees) indeed have a reputation of wisdom in self-chosen worship and humility and severe treatment of the body, not of value to anyone against self-indulgence of the flesh" (2:20–23).

That the audience have died with Christ from the "elemental forces of the world" (στοιχείων τοῦ κόσμου) and "as living in the world (κόσμῳ" (2:20) in this A´ element (2:20–23) recalls for the audience, by way of the chiastic parallelism, that the "philosophy" of empty deceit was according to the "elemental forces of the world" (στοιχεῖα τοῦ κόσμου, 2:8) in the A element (2:6–8). "As if (ὡς) living in the world" (2:20) in the A´ element recalls "as (ὡς) then you received the Christ" (2:6) in the A element. The decrees that are "according to the commandments and teachings of human beings" (κατὰ τὰ ἐντάλματα καὶ διδασκαλίας τῶν ἀνθρώπων, 2:22) in the A´ element recall that the "philosophy" of empty deceit is "according to the tradition of human beings" (κατὰ τὴν παράδοσιν τῶν ἀνθρώπων, 2:8) in the A element. And that these decrees have only a reputation of "wisdom" (σοφίας, 2:23) in the A´ element recalls the so-called "philosophy"—the "love of wisdom" (φιλο-σοφίας, 2:8) in the A element.

Complementing that the audience, "having been buried with" (συνταφέντες) Christ in the baptism, "were raised with" (συνηγέρθητε) Christ from the dead (2:12), they now hear that they "died with" (ἀπεθάνετε σὺν) Christ, so that, now in the realm of being in union with the death of Christ, they have "died" and thus been separated from (ἀπό) the realm ruled by the elemental forces of the world (2:20a) with which the "philosophy" of empty deceit is in accord (2:8).[63] If the

---

63. Harris, *Colossians*, 127: "Ἀπό repeats the pref. in ἀπεθάνετε and points not simply to the separation effected by death but also to the freedom that follows severance: 'from the control of.'" Smith,

audience have thus "died" with Christ from the elemental forces of the world, they are not to submit to decrees as if they are still "living" within the realm governed by the world rather than within the realm determined by the death and resurrection of Christ (2:20b). For the audience thus to "let yourselves be subjected to decrees" (δογματίζεσθε) would involve them in the contradiction of submitting to the "decrees" (δόγμασιν) of the handwritten charge against us, which was opposed to us, but which God obliterated and has taken from our midst, having nailed it to the cross (2:14).[64] "As" (ὡς) then the audience have received the Christ, Jesus the Lord, so that they are to "walk," that is, to behave and "live," in union with him (2:6), they are not to behave "as if" (ὡς) still "living" in the world.[65]

The audience then hear a quotation of pertinent examples of such decrees, which is addressed to them as individuals (the imperative verbs are in the second person singular), but to which they are not to submit themselves: "'Do not touch, do not taste, do not handle'—which things are all destined for destruction in being consumed—according to the commandments and teachings of human beings; such (decrees) indeed have a reputation of wisdom in self-chosen worship and humility and severe treatment of the body, not of value to anyone against self-indulgence of the flesh" (2:21–23).[66] This sarcastic quotation of decrees not to touch, eat, or handle foods whose consumption only results in their destruction (2:21–22a) further caricatures the foolish "humility" of fasting from these foods

---

Heavenly Perspective, 135: "Liberation from the powers of evil also means liberation from ascetic practices that are grounded in a dualistic world view that is associated with these elemental forces. There is therefore an association between elemental spirits and regulations." See also Thomas H. Olbricht, "The Stoicheia and the Rhetoric of Colossians: Then and Now," in *Rhetoric, Scripture and Theology: Essays from the 1994 Pretoria Conference* (ed. Stanley E. Porter and Thomas H. Olbricht; JSNTSup 131; Sheffield: Sheffield, 1996), 308–28.

64. Wright, *Colossians*, 125: "In the light of the whole passage, it would be better to translate the verb as passive, not middle, seeing the sentence not as a rebuke for a lapse but as a warning of danger ('why should you allow yourselves to be subjected to its rules?')." Dunn, *Colossians*, 188, 190: "[T]he clause is still a warning against a possibility rather than an accusation in reference to already adopted practices.... There can be no doubt that a reference back to the 'regulations' (δόγμασιν) of 2:14 is intended (the passive used of persons is attested only here, so we are dealing with a special formation). The decrees are thus those of 'the rulers and authorities' (2:15), that is, of 'the elemental forces.'" See also Garland, *Colossians*, 182 n. 36. With regard to the present tense of δογματίζεσθε, Smith (*Heavenly Perspective*, 135) points out: "It is important to note that the use of the present tense suggests a real and current situation."

65. Dübbers, *Christologie*, 276 n. 150: "Die Wendung ζῶντες ἐν κόσμῳ ist hier selbstverständlich nicht räumlich gemeint, sondern bezeichnet ein Leben unter der Bestimmung bzw. nach Maßgabe der Welt und daher als Gegenausdruck zu dem ἐν αὐτῷ περιπατεῖτε aus 2,6 zu verstehen." Harris, *Colossians*, 128: "Paul is not denying his readers' earthly existence, only the worldly orientation of their lives." Garland, *Colossians*, 183: "The Colossians still live in the world, but they do not need to live as if the powers had any control over them, and they do not need to give any regard to their rules." Smith, *Heavenly Perspective*, 135: "[T]he mention of κόσμος reminds Paul's readers that τὰ στοιχεῖα are τοῦ κόσμου."

66. Garland, *Colossians*, 183: "The succession of what are clearly Jewish issues in this section (circumcision, New Moons, Sabbath) ... points to a critique of Jewish food laws."

in order to induce heavenly visions (2:18).⁶⁷ That they are not really according to God but only "according to the commandments and teachings of human beings" (κατὰ τὰ ἐντάλματα καὶ διδασκαλίας τῶν ἀνθρώπων, 2:22b)⁶⁸ further impresses upon the audience how the potentially captivating "philosophy" of empty deceit is not from God but only "according to the tradition of human beings" (κατὰ τὴν παράδοσιν τῶν ἀνθρώπων, 2:8).⁶⁹

The audience are assured that while such decrees of the deceitful "philosophy"—"love of wisdom" (φιλο-σοφίας, 2:8)—may have a certain reputation for "wisdom" (σοφίας),⁷⁰ it is a "wisdom" that resides merely in a humanly "self-chosen worship" (ἐθελοθρησκία), another sarcastic reference to "worship" (θρησκείᾳ) of the angels (2:18), rather than in an authentic worship of God.⁷¹ Furthermore, it is a "wisdom" that involves an ultimately foolish "humility" (ταπεινοφροσύνῃ), another sarcastic reference to the "humility" (ταπεινοφροσύνη) of fasting associated with the idolatrous "worship" of the angels (2:18). As such, it is thus a "wisdom"

---

67. For a similar juxtaposition of the verbs for "touching" and "eating" in a command against eating something, see LXX Gen 3:3. In this context the three commands function as a rhetorical triplet to reinforce the prohibition against the eating of certain foods.

68. There seems to be an allusion to LXX Isa 29:13b here: "in vain do they worship me, teaching the commandments and teachings of human beings (ἐντάλματα ἀνθρώπων καὶ διδασκαλίας)." Dunn, *Colossians*, 193–94: "Almost certainly, then, Paul and Timothy here were deliberately alluding to the rebuke of Isaiah. This at once provides a further confirmation of the essentially Jewish character of the threat to the Colossian Christians: the allusion to a rebuke to Israel would only be effective if it came as a rebuke to those who understood themselves as the people of Israel. These regulations of which the Colossian (Christian?) Jews made so much were the very commandments and teachings which Isaiah had long ago warned against."

69. Dübbers, *Christologie*, 278: "Die Prohibitive der Philosophen hätten dann in der Befürchtung ihren Grund, daß der Verbrauch bestimmte Dinge zur Vergänglichkeit führt bzw. den Menschen an die Vergänglichkeit (der Welt) bindet und ihn somit von der Unvergänglichkeit des göttlichen Heils trennt. Dies aber, so wendet der Verfasser des Kolosserbriefes ein, beruht allein auf menschlichen Geboten und menschlicher Lehre (vgl. 2,8) und hat mit göttlicher Erkenntnis nicht das Geringste zu tun." Dunn, *Colossians*, 192: "The likelihood, then, once again, is that the Colossian regulations in view in 2:21 are those of Colossian Jews who are anxious to maintain the purity they regard as necessary both to maintain their status as God's people, set apart by such purity rules from other nations, and for entry into the heavenly temple in their worship. The implication is not so much that these Colossian Jews were trying to enforce such regulations on all the Christians, simply that they were effective and forceful in explaining the theological rationale of their own lifestyle and worship. The overlap between the two groups was evidently such that several Gentile Christians were being enticed by these explanations to copy or join with the Colossian Jews in their ritual purity rules with a view to sharing their access to heaven."

70. Dübbers, *Christologie*, 279 n. 367: "Der Ausdruck σοφία bezeichnet im Kolosserbrief auch sonst die Gottgemäßheit, vgl. 1,9. 28, 2,3, 3,16, 4,5. Vermutlich haben sich jedoch die Philosophen auch einer besonderen σοφία gerühmt (vgl. schon die Bezeichnung der Lehre als φιλο-σοφία)."

71. Dübbers, *Christologie*, 278 n. 364: "Mit diesem Kompositum [ἐθελοθρησκία] nimmt der Verfasser die Wendung θέλων ἐν θρησκείᾳ τῶν ἀγγέλων aus 2,18 wieder auf und dürfte den Willensakt betonen, der zur Ausübung des Dienstes motiviert." Dunn, *Colossians*, 195: "[T]he word [ἐθελοθρησκία] could be a play on the θέλων . . . ἐν θρησκείᾳ of 2:18, denoting 'delighted-in worship,' or it could be intended to convey the sense 'wished-for worship,' implying that participation in angel worship was a figment of an overimaginative desire." See also Wilson, *Colossians*, 230.

that involves a severe treatment of the "body" (σώματος) that is ultimately foolish, since it is of no value to anyone against the gratification or self-indulgence of the "flesh" (σαρκός) (2:23).

In other words, ironically, it is a "wisdom" that results not in a separation from or elevation above the "body" of the "flesh," but only in a foolish obsession with subduing the "body" of the "flesh."[72] This stands in contrast to the situation of the audience whom God has totally removed from the "body" (σώματος) of the "flesh" (σαρκός) in the "circumcision" of the Christ (2:11), so that they are now part of the "body" of the church whose "head" is Christ (1:18, 24; 2:17, 19). Whereas the severe treatment of the "body" (σώματος) is of no value against the "gratification" or "filling up" (πλησμονήν) of the flesh (2:23), the audience have been and are being "filled" (πεπληρωμένοι) with all the "fullness" (πλήρωμα) of the deity "bodily" (σωματικῶς), that is, as part of the "body" of Christ (2:9–10). The audience, then, need not be concerned with the so-called "wisdom" (σοφίας) of the deceitful "philosophy," since as part of the "body" of Christ, which is the church, they are in union with the Christ in whom are all the treasures of authentic, divine "wisdom" (σοφίας) and knowledge hidden (2:3).

In sum, in this A' element (2:20–23) the audience, who have "died with" Christ, so that they are now "living" in union with Christ and no longer within a world dominated by the elemental forces of the world, are exhorted not to submit themselves to decrees (2:20) concerned with abstaining from certain foods which are destroyed in being consumed (2:21–22a). Such decrees are not from God but only according to the commandments and teachings of human beings (2:22b). Although such decrees of the deceitful "philosophy"—"love of wisdom"—have a reputation for "wisdom," they result in the foolishness of a self-chosen, rather than God-given, "worship" of the angels associated with a "humility" of fasting and severe treatment of the body that only involve one in an obsession with matters of the flesh (2:23). But God has removed the audience from the body of the flesh (2:11), so that they are now part of the body of Christ in union with whom they have all the treasures of divine wisdom (2:3).

---

72. Wright, *Colossians*, 128: "The value these practices do *not* have is precisely the one which might make them worth while, and which their supporters claim for them: that they restrain fleshly indulgence" (Wright's emphasis). O'Brien, *Colossians*, 155: "These man-made regulations actually pandered to the flesh." Dunn, *Colossians*, 197–98: "'Gratification of the flesh' should possibly, therefore, be taken as referring to satisfaction felt by the Colossian Jews in their ethnic (fleshly, κατὰ σάρκα) identification as Jews, the people chosen by the one God to be his own elect. And in view of our repeated findings that the most clearly discernible features of the Colossian 'philosophy' are Jewish in character, the likelihood becomes still stronger that what is being critiqued here is an assumption on the part of (many of) the Colossian Jews that rules for living and worship practices were ways of expressing (maintaining and marking out) their distinctiveness as Jews.... such a concern for Jewish identity and Jewish privilege as Jewish is at the end of the day just another form of self-indulgence or national indulgence."

B. Summary on Colossians 2:6–23

1. That the philosophy which is empty deceit is according to the tradition of human beings, and thus according to the elemental forces of the world, but not according to "Christ" (2:8) impresses upon the audience that this potentially captivating false teaching is thus not in accord with the "Christ," Jesus the Lord, whom the audience have received, and in whom they are to "go on walking," as those who have been rooted and are being built up in Christ and being confirmed with regard to the faith as they were taught (2:6-7).

2. As part of the body of Christ, which is the church, the audience have been and are being filled with "all" the fullness of the deity that dwells in Christ (2:9) in their union with the Christ who is not only the head of the body but the head of "all" or "every" principality and authority in creation (2:10), so that there is nothing in the cosmos outside of his authority, his "headship." The audience are thus to infer that with Christ as their head they have an absolute, divine fullness and cosmic authority that is vastly superior to all of the "elemental forces of the world" which stand behind the potentially captivating philosophy of empty deceit (2:8).

3. The audience have heard that they have been metaphorically or spiritually "circumcised" with a "circumcision" not made with human hands but accomplished by God in the metaphorical or spiritual "removal" of the body of their flesh, in the "circumcision" of Christ (2:11), by which they became part of the body of Christ, which is the church. As part of the body in union with Christ as their head, the audience have been metaphorically or spiritually "buried" with Christ in their baptism, and in their union with Christ they have also been raised by God with him through their faith in the working of the God who raised Christ from the realm of the dead (2:12).

4. After being metaphorically or spiritually "dead" in their transgressions and in the "uncircumcision" of their flesh as Gentiles, the audience have heard that God has brought them to life with Christ, having forgiven the transgressions not only of the audience but of all of us (2:13). God's forgiveness of these transgressions which rendered us "dead" is emphatically underlined for the audience with the dramatic image of God himself totally obliterating the "charge" for our transgressions with its decrees written by human hands, which was totally against us, by taking it out of our midst with his own hands and nailing it with his own hands upon the cross of Christ's sacrificial death (2:14).

5. The audience have heard that in the death and resurrection of Christ God has exposed the angelic principalities and authorities (2:15) as mere creatures created in Christ, their head. Consequently, as part of the "body" that belongs to Christ (2:17), they are not to allow anyone to judge them for not observing vari-

ous Jewish regulations (2:16). Nor are they to allow anyone to condemn them for not engaging in a Jewish mystical and visionary "worship" of the angels that is not from God (2:18), since, as those holding to Christ as the "head" from whom the whole "body," supported and held together through the mutual love of its members, they are growing with the growth that comes from God himself (2:19).

6. The audience, who have "died with" Christ, so that they are now "living" in union with Christ and no longer within a world dominated by the elemental forces of the world, are exhorted not to submit themselves to decrees (2:20) concerned with abstaining from certain foods which are destroyed in being consumed (2:21–22a). Such decrees are not from God but only according to the commandments and teachings of human beings (2:22b). Although such decrees of the deceitful "philosophy"—"love of wisdom"—have a reputation for "wisdom," they result in the foolishness of a self-chosen, rather than God-given, "worship" of the angels associated with a "humility" of fasting and severe treatment of the body that only involve one in an obsession with matters of the flesh (2:23). But God has removed the audience from the body of the flesh (2:11), so that they are now part of the body of Christ in union with whom they have all the treasures of divine wisdom (2:3).

8

Colossians 3:1–7

You Died and Were Raised with Christ from Living as You Once Walked (E′)

Put to death then the parts that are upon the earth

A: ³:¹ If *then* you were raised with the Christ, *seek* the things above, where the Christ *is*, seated at the right hand of *God*. ² Think of the things above, not *the things upon the earth*,

    B: ³ for you died and *your life* has been hidden *with the Christ* in God.

    B′: ⁴ Whenever *the Christ, your life*, is manifested, then you also *with* him will be manifested in glory.

A′: ⁵ Put to death *then* the parts *that are upon the earth*: unlawful sex, impurity, passion, evil desire, and the covetousness, which *is* idolatry, ⁶ on account of which things the wrath of *God* is coming upon the sons of disobedience, ⁷ among whom you also walked once, when you *lived* in these.[1]

A. Chiastic Development from Colossians 2:6–23 (E) to 3:1–7 (E′)

With Col 3:1–7, the E′ unit within the macrochiastic structure embracing the entire letter, the audience hear resonances, by way of the chiastic parallelism, of 2:6–23, the corresponding E unit in the overall chiasm. That "you were raised with (συνηγέρθητε) the Christ" (3:1) in the E′ unit reverberates with "you were raised with (συνηγέρθητε) him" (2:12) in the E unit. The assertion, "For you died (ἀπεθάνετε) and your life has been hidden in the Christ with God" (3:3), in the E′ unit reiterates and develops the assertion, "if then you have died (ἀπεθάνετε) with Christ" (2:20), in the E unit. The assertion, "Your life has been hidden with

---

1. For the establishment of 3:1–7 as a chiasm, see ch. 2. On the apocalyptic dimension and background of 3:1–6, see John R. Levison, "2 *Apoc. Bar* 48:42–52:7 and the Apocalyptic Dimension of Colossians 3:1–6," *JBL* 108 (1989): 93–108. For a nuanced French translation of the Greek text of 3:1–4, see É. Delebecque, "Sur un problème de temps chez Saint Paul (Col 3,1–4)," *Bib* 70 (1989): 389–95. On the close relation of the paraenetic material that begins in 3:1 with the first part of the letter, see Roy Yates, "The Christian Way of Life: The Paraenetic Material in Colossians 3:1–4:6," *EvQ* 63 (1991): 241–51.

the Christ (σὺν τῷ Χριστῷ)" (3:3), in the E′ unit explicitly develops the assertion, "he brought you to life along with him (σὺν αὐτῷ)" (2:13), in the E unit. The remembrance, "among whom (the sons of disobedience) you also walked (περιεπατήσατέ) once" (3:7), in the E′ unit provides a resonating reason for the exhortation, "in him (the Christ, Jesus the Lord) go on walking (περιπατεῖτε)" (2:6), in the E unit. And "when you lived (ἐζῆτε) in these (earthly things)" (3:7) in the E′ unit resonates with "as if living (ζῶντες) in the world" (2:20) in the E unit.

B. Audience Response to Colossians 3:1–7

1. Col 3:1–2 (A): If Then You Were Raised with the Christ, Seek and Think Not the Things upon the Earth

The audience, who have heard the assertions that "you were raised with him (Christ)" (2:12) and that "if you died with Christ" (2:20), now begin to hear the consequences of those assertions for the proper perspective they are to maintain in their lives: "If then you were raised with the Christ, seek the things above, where the Christ is, seated at the right hand of God. Think of the things above, not the things upon the earth" (3:1–2).[2] When the audience hear the words, "if then you were raised with the Christ" (εἰ οὖν συνηγέρθητε τῷ Χριστῷ), they hear the transitional words that link this unit (3:1–7) with the previous one (2:6–23), whose conclusion began with the words, "if you died with Christ" (εἰ ἀπεθάνετε σὺν Χριστῷ) (2:20).

Rather than being concerned with "the things which are" (ἅ ἐστιν) only a shadow of the things that were to come (2:17),[3] "the things which are" (ἅ ἐστιν) all destined for destruction in being consumed (2:22), and "such things which are" (ἅτινά ἐστιν) indeed (only) having a reputation of wisdom (2:23), the audience are to seek "the things" (τά) which are above,[4] where the Christ "is" (ἐστιν) (3:1) and think of "the things" (τά) which are above, not "the things" (τά) which are upon

---

2. O'Brien, *Colossians*, 159: "With the assertion, 'since, therefore, you were raised with Christ,' the apostle consciously sets forth the positive counterpart to chapter 2:20, 'since you died with Christ' (the εἰ οὖν is resumptive of εἰ in 2:20, while the εἰ [= 'since'] no more suggests doubt here than it did in the earlier reference." Harris, *Colossians*, 137: "As in 2:20, εἰ introduces an assumed fact, 'if, as is true,' 'since.'"

3. Smith, *Heavenly Perspective*, 176: "The world-view of the things above in 3.1 (τὰ ἄνω) is the same as the things to come expressed in 2.17 (τῶν μελλόντων)."

4. Dunn, *Colossians*, 205: "Ζητεῖτε (present tense) probably has the force not so much of 'try to obtain, desire to possess' as of 'keep looking for' that which is of Christ or from heaven in the situations of daily living. What is in view is a complete reorientation of existence." Deterding, *Colossians*, 135: "The present tense of the imperative (ζητεῖτε) denotes what the readers are to do regularly ('be seeking') as an ongoing characteristic of their existence. The word itself denotes diligent seeking and so finding." Smith, *Heavenly Perspective*, 178: "[T]he force of this imperative was to counter the activity of the false teachers who sought the things above through visionary experiences."

the earth (3:2).[5] The audience are to seek and think about the things above where the Christ is, seated at the right of God (cf. Ps 110:1) in the heavens,[6] rather than "the things upon the earth" (τὰ ἐπὶ τῆς γῆς), because in Christ all "the things" (τά) not only "upon the earth" (ἐπὶ τῆς γῆς) but in the heavens were created (1:16), and because through Christ and for Christ God reconciled not only "the things upon the earth" (τὰ ἐπὶ τῆς γῆς) but the things in the heavens (1:20). Now that the audience have been raised with the Christ, they are in union with the Christ who is seated in a heavenly position of power and authority above the things upon the earth. This gives the audience a heavenly rather than an earthly perspective on the heavenly realities above.[7]

To sum up this A element of the chiasm, the audience need not be concerned with human, earthly decrees (2:23) regulating food, drink, and festal observances on earth aimed at raising their minds to visionary experiences involving the worship of angels in the heavens (2:16-18, 21-22). For the audience have already been raised with the Christ (2:12; 3:1a), so that their life's pursuit and perspective can already, even while they are still on earth, be directly focused on the heavenly things that are above, where the Christ is, seated in a position of power and authority at

---

5. Harris, *Colossians*, 138: "If ζητεῖτε (3:1) focuses on the practical pursuit of heavenly or spiritual goals, φρονεῖτε emphasizes the inner attitude necessary in that pursuit." Dunn, *Colossians*, 205: "Φρονέω means not merely to think but to have a settled way of understanding, to hold an opinion, to maintain an attitude.... what is commended is not an apocalyptic or mystical preoccupation with the furniture of heaven, as 3:1 could be taken to imply, but a cast of mind, a settled way of looking at things, a sustained devotion to and enactment of a life cause." Fee, *Pauline Christology*, 328: "Their minds are set on 'earthly [below] things,' and thus they are enamored with the powers and the law, and their 'ethics' are earthbound, having to do with 'handle, touch, taste' (2:21). They need to have their minds retooled so as to focus on Christ seated at the right hand of God."

6. Harris, *Colossians*, 138: "'God's right hand' is the place of unrivalled prestige and unparalleled authority." Dunn, *Colossians*, 204: "The exalted Christ sat on God's immediate right. The image is one of power. The right (hand) of God was a way of expressing strength, powerful protection, and favor." Smith, *Heavenly Perspective*, 179: "Christ's session at the right hand of God means that the angelic realm, whether heavenly or demonic, has been subjected to him.... the motivation for seeking the things above is to be Christologically driven, rather than motivated by a concern for angelic beings."

7. O'Brien, *Colossians*, 161: "Paul is thus employing spatial categories in a qualitative manner to describe two spheres which correspond to the eschatological schema of the two ages. Here τὰ ἄνω stands for the heavenly world and the new aeon.... The Colossian Christians have already participated in the world to come, the powers of the new age have broken in upon them, they already participate in the resurrection of Christ. Thus their aims, ambitions, indeed their whole orientation is to be directed to this sphere." Smith, *Heavenly Perspective*, 177, 181: "In the light of the Jewish mystical background to the Colossian philosophy, however, it is appropriate that Paul also uses spatial eschatology to argue for the need of a present heavenly-mindedness.... The things that are above (τὰ ἄνω) within the context of Colossians clearly denote an apocalyptic perspective. This is the only place in Pauline literature where ἄνω is used substantively, a periphrasis for the noun οὐρανός which has already been used in 1.5, 16, 20, 23.... Paul wanted to refute a wrong sort of heavenly-mindedness, as practised by the Colossian errorists and that resulted in boasting and division, for a correct sort of heavenly-mindedness that resulted in wisdom, humility and unity.... The goal of heavenly-mindedness is focused on Christ, not angels; the basis of this heavenly perspective is union with the resurrected Christ rather than union with angelic worship."

the right hand of God in the heavens (3:1b). The audience need not regulate the use of earthly things to attain the access to the heavenly things above that they already have in their union with the Christ (3:2).

2. Col 3:3 (B): *Your Life Has Been Hidden with the Christ*

The audience then hear a further reason why they are to seek and think of the things above rather than the things upon the earth (3:1-2): "For you died and your life has been hidden with the Christ in God" (3:3). The audience have already been asked to ponder the question that "if you died (ἀπεθάνετε) with Christ (σὺν Χριστῷ) from the elemental forces of the world, why let yourselves be subjected to decrees as if living (ζῶντες) in the world?" (2:20).[8] The implication is that they already have a life from God and with Christ that is not in this world, since God "brought you to life along with" (συνεζωοποίησεν) Christ (σὺν αὐτῷ), when they were "dead" in transgressions (2:13). And so the audience, who have been "buried with" Christ in their baptism and "raised with" him through faith in the working of God (θεοῦ) who raised him from the dead (2:12), now hear a reinforcement and development of their baptismal "death" and "life" with Christ: "You died" (ἀπεθάνετε) and your "life" (ζωή) has been hidden "with the Christ" (σὺν τῷ Χριστῷ) in God (θεῷ).[9]

That "your life" has been and still remains "hidden" (κέκρυπται in the perfect tense) with the Christ (3:3) reminds the audience of the mystery that has been "hidden" (ἀποκεκρυμμένον) from the ages and from the generations, but that has now been manifested by God to the audience as God's "holy ones" (1:26). This mystery of God is Christ himself (1:27; 2:2), in whom are all the treasures of wisdom and knowledge "hidden" (ἀπόκρυφοι) (2:3). That God has already manifested the hidden mystery arouses an expectation in the audience that God will also manifest

---

8. O'Brien, *Colossians*, 165: "This death with Christ involves a dying to the elemental spirits and by implication to what has been designated τὰ ἐπὶ τῆς γῆς ('the things on earth'), the content of which is spelled out, in part at least, in chapter 2:16–23 with its reference to ascetic regulations, visionary experiences and the like." With regard to the aorist tense of "you died" (ἀπεθάνετε) in 2:20 and 3:3, Dunn (*Colossians*, 206) points out: "The rhetorical character of the bare aorist formulation here . . . needs to be recognized. Its object is to ensure that the change of perspective marked by conversion-initiation is final and fixed."

9. Harris, *Colossians*, 139: "Σὺν Χριστῷ does not simply mean 'along with [the life of] Christ.' Rather, σύν shows that the resurrection lives of believers are intimately connected—in symbiosis—with the risen, heavenly life of Christ. Also it is implied that in a spiritual, real sense believers are already living 'in the company of Christ' in the heavenly realm, all this being hidden from human gaze." Dübbers, *Christologie*, 281: Mit der ζωή ist hier das (wahre) Leben als das von Gott geschaffene, eschatologische Heil schlechtin gemeint, von der her die Gegenwart der Adressaten durch die Sündenvergebung (2,13) und durch den Glauben (2,12b) bereits grundlegend neu bestimmt ist." O'Brien, *Colossians*, 166: "The phrase 'in God' modifies both 'life' (ζωή) and the immediately preceding words 'with Christ' (σὺν τῷ Χριστῷ): our life is hidden with Christ because we died with him and have been raised with him to new life; 'in God' because Christ himself has his being in God and those who belong to Christ have their being there too. Centered in God means that the hidden life is secure, unable to be touched by anyone."

their life that is still hidden with the Christ in God. But for now the audience, who have "died" with the Christ through their baptism, can be completely assured that they possess a "life" that transcends "the things upon the earth" (3:2), a life that has been and still is definitively hidden with the Christ in God (3:3), a life that is their hope of the glory laid up for them in the heavens (1:5, 27) above, where the Christ is, seated at the right hand of God (3:1).[10]

3. Col 3:4 (B ́): You Will Be Manifested with the Christ, Your Life

The focus of the audience is then shifted to the future: "Whenever the Christ, your life, is manifested, then you also with him will be manifested in glory" (3:4).[11] With this B ́ element the audience experience the pivot at the center of the chiasm. They hear the assertion that "your life" (ἡ ζωὴ ὑμῶν) has been hidden "with the Christ" (σὺν τῷ Χριστῷ) in the B element (3:3) progress, by way of the chiastic parallels, to the assertion that whenever "the Christ" (ὁ Χριστός), "your life" (ἡ ζωὴ ὑμῶν), is manifested, then you also "with" (σύν) him will be manifested in glory in the B ́ element (3:4).

The audience thus hear a progression from their "life" described as hidden with the Christ (3:3) to their "life" described as synonymous with the Christ himself (3:4),[12] the Christ who is above, seated at the right hand of God (3:1b),

---

10. Harris, *Colossians*, 139: "[T]he true life of believers 'now lies hidden' or 'remains concealed' until the final revelation (v. 4). Security as well as concealment is implied." Dunn, *Colossians*, 207: "The 'hiddenness' in mind here is therefore probably the hiddenness of the divine mystery (1:26) and of 'all the treasures of wisdom and knowledge' (2:3). That is to say, it refers to a hidden reality, what is not perceived by those who have not yet been let into the secret and so is meaningless or folly to them, but the reality that is actually determining the outworkings of history and is the true source of wisdom and knowledge." Bevere, *Sharing*, 180: "The hidden/revealed motif once again emphasizes the μυστήριον hidden, but now revealed in Christ. It also touches upon the notion of divine wisdom revealed in the present age, while acknowledging there is more yet to be disclosed at the final denouement of history." Smith, *Heavenly Perspective*, 182: "This idea of being hidden and being revealed would have been of special interest to Jewish mystics whose goal was to enter the 'hiddenness' of heaven. Central to apocalyptic was the view that certain events had been hidden in God's eternal purposes but were now revealed to the seer.... Paul declares that the knowledge of such things is not just the property of members of an elite group who claim special knowledge due to an ascent to heaven, but of *all* who are in Christ. Paul is making the point that, since the believer is incorporated with Christ and hidden with Christ in God, the believer's life is already a heavenly life. Such incorporation and hiddenness is historical and not mystical" (Smith's emphasis).

11. A different interpretation of 3:4 as an exhortation rather than eschatological vision with the paraphrase, "If you let it become visible that Christ is your life, then to his glory it will also become manifest that you have been raised to a new life with him," is proposed by G. J. Swart, "Eschatological Vision or Exhortation to Visible Christian Conduct? Notes on the Interpretation of Colossians 3:4," *Neot* 33 (1999): 169–77. But this innovative interpretation strays rather far from the way this verse is normally understood and seems to strain the grammatical structure.

12. Harris, *Colossians*, 140: "The life of Christians *is* Christ, as well as being 'hidden *with* Christ' (v. 3). It 'is' Christ, not in the sense that Christ's risen life in heaven can be equated with believers' spiritual life on earth or that the Church is the resurrection body of Christ, but in the sense that Christ is the source, center, and goal of the individual and corporate lives of believers" (Harris's emphasis).

the Christ with whom the audience were raised (3:1a).[13] They are assured that their new presently hidden "life" will be fully manifested in a divinely glorious way in the future. The mystery of God, which is Christ (2:2) and which has been hidden from the ages and from the generations, has now been "manifested" (ἐφανερώθη) by God (divine passive) to God's holy ones (1:26). Similarly, whenever the Christ, "your life," is fully "manifested" (φανερωθῇ) by God, then you also with him "will be manifested" (φανερωθήσεσθε) by God in a future glory (3:4).[14]

The might of God's "glory" (δόξης) is what can empower the audience in all power for all the endurance and patience they need in their present life (1:11). The audience are among the holy ones (1:26) to whom God wished to make known what is the richness of the "glory" (δόξης) of this mystery among the Gentiles, which is Christ among them, their hope of the future "glory" (δόξης) of God (1:27). And so now the audience may be completely confident that in the future, whenever God fully manifests the Christ, God will also fully manifest them together with the Christ, their "life," in that future "glory" (δόξῃ) of God (3:4) for which they hope. Whereas the "life" of the audience is presently hidden with the Christ "in God" (ἐν τῷ θεῷ)—in the divine realm (3:3), in the future, their "life," the Christ, as well as they themselves with him will be manifested "in glory" (ἐν δόξῃ)—in the realm of divine glory.[15]

---

13. Harris, *Colossians*, 139–40: It is remarkable that although the NT epistles usually omit the art. with Χριστός when it is a proper name, 3:1–4 contains four uses of the art. Χριστός in ref. to Christ." Smith, *Heavenly Perspective*, 183: "All depends on Christ, which is emphasized by the use of ὁ Χριστός in 3.4, the fourth mention of Χριστός in as many verses, when the personal pronoun would have been more natural. Paul's desire is to emphasize that true Christian existence is found 'with Christ' alone."

14. Smith, *Heavenly Perspective*, 183: "It would appear that φανερόω is used in 3.4 as the antithesis of κρύπτω in 3.3 thereby emphasizing the contrast is between present hiddenness 'with Christ' and future revelation. The fullness of life in Christ will be neither seen mystically nor metaphysically revealed, but is displayed historically at the crucifixion, Resurrection and the Parousia."

15. Wilson, *Colossians*, 240: "[T]he word δόξα, which has already been used three times in this letter ... only now appears in its full significance." Dunn, *Colossians*, 209: "This is the confidence which the Colossian believers can cherish despite the 'hiddenness' of their present lives: that the work of glorification already begun in them has already been completed in Christ as a guarantee of its completion also in them." Smith, *Heavenly Perspective*, 183: "The manifestation of this glory is not something that can be gained by human effort as shown by the divine passives φανερωθῇ and φανερωθήσεσθε. This future expectation of 'glory' could be seen as countering the visionaries' desire for a present revelation of glory. This future manifestation will be shown ἐν δόξῃ, a particular goal of heavenly voyagers (note the final position for emphasis). The desire of the Colossian errorists to observe angelic worship shows their failure to recognize that the revelation of such glory is the work of God and centred on the work of Christ. Their elitism shows that they do not appreciate that all believers will be included in this manifestation."

4. Col 3:5–7 (A ́): Put to Death Then the Parts That Are upon the Earth and in Which You Once Lived

The audience then hear a transition from the indicative mood of assured assertion—with the Christ with whom they were raised (3:1) they will be manifested in divine, heavenly glory (3:4)—to the consequent imperative mood of ethical exhortation: "Put to death then the parts that are upon the earth: unlawful sex, impurity, passion, evil desire, and the greed, which is idolatry, on account of which things the wrath of God is coming upon the sons of disobedience, among whom you also walked once, when you lived in these" (3:5–7). "Put to death then (οὖν)" in 3:5 of this A ́ element of the chiasm recalls for the audience "if then (οὖν) you were raised" in 3:1 of the A element. The parts "that are upon earth" (τὰ ἐπὶ τῆς γῆς) in 3:5 of the A ́ element recalls "the things upon the earth" (τὰ ἐπὶ τῆς γῆς) in 3:2 of the A element. The greed, which "is" (ἐστίν) idolatry, in 3:5 of the A ́ element recalls where the Christ "is" (ἐστίν) in 3:1 of the A element. The wrath of "God" (θεοῦ) in 3:6 of the A ́ element recalls the right hand of "God" (θεοῦ) in 3:1 of the A element. And, when you "lived" (ἐζῆτε) in 3:7 of the A ́ element recalls the alliterative "seek" (ζητεῖτε) the things above in 3:1 of the A element.

The audience, once being "dead" (νεκρούς) in transgressions, but who "died" with Christ (2:20; 3:3) and were raised with him, so that "then" (οὖν) (3:1) they are not to think about "the things upon the earth" (τὰ ἐπὶ τῆς γῆς, 3:2), are to "put to death" (νεκρώσατε) "then" (οὖν) the parts of them "that are upon the earth" (τὰ ἐπὶ τῆς γῆς, 3:5a).[16] The audience are then reminded how the parts of their bodies can be involved in "the things upon the earth" with a list of examples of "earthly" behavior concerned with the kind of sexual immorality that Jews often attributed to Gentiles:[17] unlawful sex,[18]

---

16. The "parts" (μέλη) that are upon the earth refers to the bodily parts or limbs of the audience. As Harris (*Colossians*, 146) explains, "Paul is not advocating ascetic suppression or rejection of bodily desires and functions; he is rather calling for termination of the immoral and self-centered use of physical limbs or organs. Not 'those parts of your nature that are earthly,' 'what is earthly in you'; but, 'your limbs as used for earthly purposes.'" Dunn, *Colossians*, 212: "But the metaphor should be allowed its force: the person's interaction with the wider world as through organs and limbs is what is in view. It was precisely the interaction which had characterized the Colossians' old way of life which is now targeted."

17. Bevere, *Sharing*, 199: "Lest the Colossians take the writers' affirmation that they are God's chosen as Gentiles to mean they can live as Gentiles, as Judaism tended to characterize Gentile immorality and idolatry, Paul and Timothy employ a typical Jewish polemic against Gentile immorality to remind the Colossians, that as God's chosen in Christ, their walk, their way of life in Christ rules out Gentile standards of life." Smith, *Heavenly Perspective*, 197: "It is significant to note that all the vices in v. 5 relate to sexual sin. The Colossian errorists' harsh ascetic treatment of the body would mean they would have concurred with this list." Dunn, *Colossians*, 214: "Paul did not want his readers to follow the Colossian Jews in their ritual and worship, but their ethical standards were to be Jewish through and through."

18. Bevere, *Sharing*, 200: "Πορνεία did refer to a wide range of extra-marital activity including incest, marriages between relatives prohibited by rabbinic law and other sorts of 'unnatural' sexual relations.... To commit πορνεία is to live as the Gentiles."

impurity,[19] passion,[20] and evil desire,[21] climaxed by the covetousness that is further characterized as idolatry (3:5b).[22] On account of these kinds of "earthly" conduct eschatological condemnation, characterized as "the wrath of God (θεοῦ) is coming from heaven,[23] where Christ is seated at the right hand of God (θεοῦ, 3:1), upon "the sons of disobedience" (3:6), those who disobey God by such "earthly" sinfulness.[24]

Among such "sons of disobedience" the audience once "walked" or conducted themselves, when they lived in the realm of these kinds of "earthly" behaviors (3:7). The audience hear this verse as a mini-chiasm:

a) among whom (ἐν οἷς)
b) you also walked (περιεπατήσατε)

---

19. Dunn, *Colossians*, 214: "[Ἀ]καθαρσία had by now almost entirely lost its earlier cultic connotation and bears a clear moral sense, especially in reference to sexual immorality." Bevere, *Sharing*, 201: "Ἀκαθαρσία elaborates upon πορνεία. It refers to religious and moral impurity.... While religious and moral purity are concerns often directed to the Israelites, a definite connection is made in Judaism between impurity and Gentile idolatry, particularly when the term is used with πορνεία.... For the Jew, it was a proud thing to contrast his purity with the impurity of the Gentiles."

20. "Passion" (πάθος) refers to the kind of passion that leads to sexual excesses according to Bevere, *Sharing*, 201. Dunn, *Colossians*, 215: "[I]ts two other New Testament occurrences (Rom. 1:26; 1 Thess. 4:5) indicate that it was for Paul a natural associate with the two preceding items, thus giving further emphasis to this primary concern over the danger of unrestrained sexual appetite."

21. Bevere, *Sharing*, 202: "While ἐπιθυμία was not always employed in negative fashion, the use of the adjective κακήν in 3.5 along with πάθος and the other vices clearly makes it, in this context, a negative term. In Numbers 11 and Genesis 30 ἐπιθυμία is the longing for sexual satisfaction outside of marriage and is referred to as sin. In the Synoptic tradition and in the Pauline corpus the word often refers to sexual desire (Mt. 5.28; Rom. 1.24; 1 Thess 4.15). In Judaism such desire is prohibited. It is an offense against God who demands complete devotion from his people."

22. O'Brien, *Colossians*, 183: "The danger of covetousness is stressed emphatically because it is so closely related to idolatry: rather surprisingly the former is equated with the latter. The two sins stood together in Jewish exhortations and were condemned as part of the horrors of paganism." Bevere, *Sharing*, 203: "Πλεονεξία puts the focus of life upon humanity and not God. The distinction between creator and creature is blurred, and idolatry is the result. Covetousness lacks the knowledge of God. While πλεονεξία can have broader connotations than sexual immorality, it can have sexual undertones." According to Dunn (*Colossians*, 215) "covetousness" here "sums up what is primarily a list of sexual sins: the ruthless insatiableness evident when the sexual appetite is unrestrained in a man with power to gratify it." See also Brian S. Rosner, *Greed as Idolatry: The Origin and Meaning of a Pauline Metaphor* (Grand Rapids: Eerdmans, 2007).

23. Harris, *Colossians*, 147-48: "It seems far more likely, considering that God is the personal sustainer as well as author of the moral law and that sinners are his 'enemies,' that ὀργή is an *affectus* ('feeling,' 'emotion'), God's eternal opposition to sin and sinners, than an *effectus* ('action,' 'activity'), an impersonal principle of retribution or law of cause and effect in a moral universe. The latter view tends to evacuate the personal gen. of any significance." O'Brien, *Colossians*, 184: "The expression 'the wrath of God' turns up in both Old and New Testaments to describe God's holy anger against sin and the judgment that results."

24. Dunn, *Colossians*, 217: "[T]he description 'sons of disobedience' is a Semitism (= disobedient persons)."

c) once (ποτε)
c´) when (ὅτε)
b´) you lived (ἐζῆτε)
a´) in these (ἐν τούτοις)

At the center of this mini-chiasm the audience hear a pivotal parallel progression from the temporal "once" (c) to its elaboration in the temporal "when" (c´). That "you lived" (b´) provides the audience with a synonymous parallel clarifying the metaphorical "you also walked" (b). And the audience hear a chiastic parallel progression from "among whom" (the sons of disobedience) (a) to an emphatic "in these" (earthly things) (a´).

That they once "walked" (περιεπατήσατέ) in these immoral ways (3:7) stands in contrast to the exhortation that they are to "go on walking" (περιπατεῖτε) in the Christ, Jesus the Lord, whom they received (2:6) and to the exhortation that they are "to walk" (περιπατῆσαι) worthy of the Lord for every desire to please (1:10), rather then disobey. That once "you lived" (ἐζῆτε) "in" (ἐν) the realm of these "earthly" things contradicts "your life" (ἡ ζωὴ ὑμῶν) which is the Christ with whom you will be manifested "in" (ἐν) glory (3:4), "your life" (ἡ ζωὴ ὑμῶν) with the Christ "in" (ἐν) God (3:3). And, that once "you lived" (ἐζῆτε) in these "earthly" things contradicts the exhortation to "seek" (ζητεῖτε) and think about the things above rather than the things upon the earth (3:1-2).[25]

In sum, in this A´ element (3:5-7) of the chiasm, the audience are to put to death the parts of their bodies involved in the things upon the earth "in" which they once "lived." Such earthly behavior leads to the final condemnation of the wrath of God, whereas the "life" of the audience is now hidden with Christ "in" God, so that they are destined to be manifested with Christ "in" divine, heavenly glory.

C. Summary on Colossians 3:1-7

1. The audience need not be concerned with human, earthly decrees (2:23) regulating food, drink, and festal observances on earth aimed at raising their minds to visionary experiences involving the worship of angels in the heavens (2:16-18, 21-22). For the audience have already been raised with the Christ (2:12; 3:1a), so that their life's pursuit and perspective can already, even while they are still on earth, be directly focused on the heavenly things that are above, where the Christ is, seated in a position of power and authority at the right hand of God in the heavens (3:1b). The audience need not regulate the use of earthly things to at-

---

25. O'Brien, *Colossians*, 186: "[T]he imperfect tense of the verb ζάω, 'live,' draws attention to a continuing state with its fixed attitudes, while ἐν τούτοις, 'in them,' is more emphatic and condemnatory than the expected ἐν αὐτοῖς."

tain the access to the heavenly things above that they already have in their union with the Christ (3:2).

2. The audience, who have "died" with the Christ through their baptism, can be completely assured that they possess a "life" that transcends "the things upon the earth" (3:2), a life that has been and still is definitively hidden with the Christ in God (3:3), a life that is their hope of the glory laid up for them in the heavens (1:5, 27) above, where the Christ is, seated at the right hand of God (3:1).

3. The audience may be completely confident that in the future, whenever God fully manifests the Christ, God will also fully manifest them together with the Christ, their "life," in that future "glory" of God (3:4) for which they hope. Whereas the "life" of the audience is presently hidden with the Christ "in God"—in the divine realm (3:3), in the future their "life," the Christ, as well as they themselves with him will be manifested "in glory"—in the realm of divine glory.

4. The audience are to put to death the parts of their bodies involved in the things upon the earth "in" which they once "lived." Such earthly behavior leads to the final condemnation of the wrath of God, whereas the "life" of the audience is now hidden with Christ "in" God, so that they are destined to be manifested with Christ "in" divine, heavenly glory.

9

COLOSSIANS 3:8–16

In All Wisdom Teaching and Admonishing One Another (D´)

Let the peace of Christ rule in your hearts
A: ⁸ But now *you also* must put them all away: anger, rage, malice, slander, obscene talk from *your* mouth. ⁹ Do not lie to *one another*, having removed the old human being with its practices
    B: ¹⁰ and having *put on* the new which is being renewed for knowledge according to the image of the one who created it,
        C: ¹¹ wherein there is not Greek and Jew, circumcision and uncircumcision, barbarian, Scythian, slave, free, but Christ is all and in all.
    B´: ¹² *Put on* then, as God's chosen ones, holy and beloved, heartfelt compassion, kindness, humility, gentleness, patience,
A´: ¹³ bearing with *one another* and forgiving each other if anyone has a complaint against someone; just as the Lord forgave you, so must *you also*. ¹⁴ And over all these love, that is the bond of completeness. ¹⁵ And let the peace of Christ rule in *your* hearts, to which indeed you were called in one body. And be thankful. ¹⁶ Let the word of Christ dwell in you richly, in all wisdom teaching and admonishing each other with psalms, hymns, and Spiritual songs, in grace singing in *your* hearts to God.[1]

A. CHIASTIC DEVELOPMENT FROM COLOSSIANS 1:24–2:5 (D) TO 3:8–16 (D´)

With Col 3:8–16, the D´ unit within the macrochiastic structure embracing the entire letter, the audience hear resonances of 1:24–2:5, the corresponding D unit in the overall chiasm. That the audience have "removed the old human being (ἄνθρωπον) with its practices" (3:9) in the D´ unit is a consequence of "admonishing every human being (ἄνθρωπον) and teaching every human being (ἄνθρωπον) in all wisdom, that we may present every human being (ἄνθρωπον) complete in Christ" (1:28) in the D unit, the only other occurrences of the term "human being"

---

1. For the establishment of 3:8–16 as a chiasm, see ch. 2.

in the letter. That the audience have "put on the new which is being renewed for knowledge (εἰς ἐπίγνωσιν) according to the image of the one who created it" (3:10) in the D′ unit recalls "for knowledge (εἰς ἐπίγνωσιν) of the mystery of God, Christ" (2:2) in the D unit, the only other occurrence of the prepositional phrase "for knowledge" in the letter.[2] The address of the audience as "holy ones" (ἅγιοι, 3:12) in the D′ unit recalls that the mystery has now been manifested to God's "holy ones" (ἁγίοις, 1:26) in the D unit, these representing the final two occurrences of the term "holy ones" in the letter.[3]

The "love (ἀγάπην), which is the bond of completeness" (3:14), in the D′ unit reminds the audience of those who "are held together in love (ἀγάπῃ)" (2:2) in the D unit, these representing the final two occurrences of the term "love" in the letter.[4] The "bond of completeness (τελειότητος)" (3:14) in the D′ unit recalls presenting "every human being complete (τέλειον) in Christ" (1:28) in the D unit. That the audience were called to the peace of Christ "in one body (σώματι)" (3:15) in the D′ unit recalls Paul's "filling up what is lacking of the afflictions of the Christ in my flesh on behalf of his body (σώματος), which is the church" (1:24), in the D unit. The exhortation to the audience, "let the word (λόγος) of Christ dwell in you richly" (3:16), in the D′ unit follows from and is part of Paul's aim "to fulfill for you the word (λόγον) of God" (1:25) in the D unit, these representing the only occurrences of the term "word" modified by either "God" or "Christ" in the letter.[5]

The final chiastic connection between the D and D′ units is most noteworthy. The exhortation to the audience in 3:16 in the D′ unit recalls, in a precise mini-chiastic order, the description of the authors' ministry to everyone in 1:28 in the D unit:

a) admonishing (νουθετοῦντες) every human being
   b) and teaching (διδάσκοντες) every human being
      c) in all wisdom (ἐν πάσῃ σοφίᾳ) (1:28)
      c′) in all wisdom (ἐν πάσῃ σοφίᾳ)
   b′) teaching (διδάσκοντες)
a′) and admonishing (νουθετοῦντες) each other (3:16)

A further indication of the importance of this particular chiastic connection between the D and D′ units is that these are the only occurrences of the verb "admonishing" and of the participial form of the verb "teaching" in the letter.[6] The only other occurrence of the phrase "in all wisdom" is in 1:9, the first appearance

---

2. The term "knowledge" (ἐπίγνωσις) occurs twice in 1:9–10, but not as the object of a preposition.
3. The term "holy ones" (ἅγιοι) occurred previously in 1:2, 4, 12, 22.
4. The term "love" (ἀγάπη) occurred previously in 1:4, 8, 13.
5. The term "word" (λόγος) occurs also in 1:5; 2:23; 3:17; 4:3, 6.
6. There is a non-participial form of the verb "teach" (διδάσκω) in 2:7.

of the key term "wisdom" in the letter, whereas "in wisdom" occurs in 4:5, the final, climactic appearance of "wisdom" in this letter.

B. Audience Response to Colossians 3:8-16

1. Col 3:8-9 (A): You Also Must Put Away Obscene Talk from Your Mouth and Not Lie to One Another

Having been reminded of how they "once" conducted themselves (3:7), the audience begin to hear how they are to conduct themselves "now":[7] "But now you also must put them all away: anger, rage, malice, slander, obscene talk from your mouth. Do not lie to one another, having removed the old human being with its practices" (3:8-9).[8] When the audience hear the words "you also" (καὶ ὑμεῖς) in Paul's address to them here, they hear the transitional words that link this unit (3:8-16) to the previous one (3:1-7), which concluded with the same words in the reminder that "among whom you also (καὶ ὑμεῖς) walked once" (3:7).

The audience were previously directed to "put to death" the parts of them that are upon the earth, exemplified by a list of five vices involving primarily immoral sexual conduct—unlawful sex, impurity, passion, evil desire, and the covetousness, which is idolatry (3:5). Similarly, they are now directed to "put away" all the things exemplified by another list of five vices, but this one involving primarily immoral interpersonal communication—anger,[9] rage,[10] malice,[11] slander,[12] obscene

---

7. Dunn, *Colossians*, 218: "'But now... ' Νυνὶ δέ echoes the decisive νυνὶ δέ in 1:22: a fundamental shift in ethical norms and character of conduct has taken place, the equivalent in personal time and outworking of the epochal act of reconciliation on the cross."

8. Harris, *Colossians*, 149: "Νυνὶ δέ, 'but now,' complements the ποτὲ ὅτε of v. 7. Καί may emphasize ὑμεῖς, 'you yourselves, in spite of your past, must in fact lay aside...'" O'Brien, *Colossians*, 186: "καὶ ὑμεῖς underscores the contrast with what they once were." For a suggestion that the present subjunctive (μὴ ψεύδησθε, "may you not lie") reading rather than the imperative (μὴ ψεύδεσθε, "do not lie") may be original in 3:9, see Stanley E. Porter, "P. Oxy. 744.4 and Colossians 3,9," *Bib* 73 (1992): 565-67.

9. Dunn, *Colossians*, 218-19: "Ὀργή is now human 'wrath' (in contrast to 3:6), with the implication that what is in view is such a powerful emotion that only God can be trusted to exercise it fairly."

10. O'Brien, *Colossians*, 187: "ὀργή ('wrath') and θυμός ('anger') go together and although Stoic thinkers distinguished the two, the one denoting a more or less settled feeling of hatred, the other a tumultuous outburst of passion, there appears to be little difference between them here: as outbursts of temper they are destructive of harmony in human relationships."

11. O'Brien, *Colossians*, 187: "Along with these 'malice' (κακία) is to be removed since it is an evil force that destroys fellowship." Dübbers, *Christologie*, 295: "Dieser Bezug auf 3,5-7 spiegelt sich auch in der Terminologie: Wer dem Nächsten im Zorn (ὀργή) begegnet und ihm schaden will, obgleich er selbst nicht mehr unter dem Zorn (ὀργή) Gottes steht, handelt seiner neuen Heilswirklichkeit (wie auch der des Nächsten) zuwider. Und wer sich leidenschaftlich über den anderen erregt (θυμός) und Bosheiten gegen ihm losläßt (κακία), der vergißt offensichtlich, daß ihn seine üble Leidenschaft (ἐπιθυμία κακή) einst von der heilvollen Gottesnähe trennte."

12. "Slander" (βλασφημία) "covers any type of vilifying of man, either by lies or gossip," according to O'Brien, *Colossians*, 188.

talk from your mouth (3:8).¹³ Just as the first list of five vices climaxed with a more elaborate expression focusing upon the listed vices as offenses against God — the covetousness, which is idolatry, so also this one climaxes with a more elaborate expression focusing upon the listed vices as offenses in communicating with other human beings — obscene talk from your mouth, which is immediately followed by the command not to lie to one another (3:9a).¹⁴

The audience are to put away these communicative vices and not lie to one another (3:8-9a), because they "have removed" (ἀπεκδυσάμενοι) like old clothing the old human being with its practices (3:9b),¹⁵ as God "removed" (ἀπεκδυσάμενος) the principalities and the authorities in the crucifixion of Christ (2:15). This "removal" on the part of the audience is a consequence of the fact that they were "circumcised" with a "circumcision" not made with hands in the "removal" (ἀπεκδύσει) of the body of the flesh — now described as the "old human being" with its practices — in the "circumcision" of the Christ (2:11).¹⁶ This happened when they were "buried" with Christ in baptism and "raised" with him through faith in the working of the God who raised him from the dead (2:12).¹⁷

---

13. O'Brien, *Colossians*, 188: "αἰσχρολογία occurs only here in the NT but outside the Bible covers the ideas of obscene speech or abusive language." Dübbers, *Christologie*, 295 n. 34: "Es geht in 3,8 vornehmlich um 'Mundsünden.'"

14. Bruce, *Colossians*, 146 n. 76: "The present imperative (μὴ ψεύδεσθε) implies 'Don't go on telling lies.'" For the view that the present tense emphasizes the relationship between the activity and the person, whereas the aorist tense emphasizes the act itself, see James W. Voelz, "Present and Aorist Verbal Aspect: A New Proposal," *Neot* 27 (1993): 153-64. O'Brien, *Colossians*, 188: "The last of the five vices, αἰσχρολογία ('foul talk') like its counterpart in the previous list ('covetousness,' v 5), is especially emphasized this time by the additional words 'out of your mouth.'" Dübbers, *Christologie*, 294: "Hier nämlich geht es nicht mehr um die vergangenen Verfehlungen *wider Gott*, sondern um das zwischenmenschliche Fehlverhalten — und dieses kommt trotz der neuen Heilswirklichkeit auch jetzt noch in der Gemeinde vor.... Das wider den Nächsten gerichtete Fehlverhalten ist für den Verfasser des Kolosserbriefes im Grunde von derselben Qualität wie die Verfehlungen wider Gott und ist daher der neuen Heilswirklichkeit in keiner Weise angemessen" (Dübbers's emphases).

15. O'Brien, *Colossians*, 186: "[T]hey are to discard their old repulsive habits like a set of worn-out clothes... For the representation of behavior or character as a garment see Job 29:14; Psalm 35:26; 109:29; 132:9; Isaiah 11:5; 59:17; 61:10; Romans 13:12, 14; and 1 Thessalonians 5:8."

16. On the term "old human being" here Dunn (*Colossians*, 220) states: "The figure is clearly a way of indicating a whole way of life, a way of life prior to and without Christ and characterized by the sort of vices listed in 3:5 and 8, here referred to as 'its practices.'" Dübbers, *Christologie*, 296: "Mit ἀπεκδύομαι meint der Verfasser dabei entsprechend zu 2,11 (ἀπεκδύσις τοῦ σώματος τῆς σαρκός) die radikale Trennung von der alten Sündenwirklichkeit und damit die Beseitigung der alten, gottlosen Existenz. Dabei macht die Rede von dem παλαιὸς ἄνθρωπος σὺν ταῖς πράξεσιν αὐτοῦ einsdrucksvoll deutlich, daß Gott durch die Sündenvergebung den *ganzen* alten Menschen samt seiner Taten — und nicht etwa nur einen Teil von ihm — vernichtet hat" (Dübbers's emphasis).

17. Wilson, *Colossians*, 250: "Baptism by immersion lent itself to the development of an imagery of 'garment symbolism': the candidate left his garments behind as he entered the water, and put on a fresh set of clothing when he emerged." Smith, *Heavenly Perspective*, 197: "The list in 3.8, 9 is concerned with inter-personal relationships, in particular sins that involve the tongue (wrath, malice, slander, abusive language, lying), a list that most probably relates to the practices of the errorists. It would appear, therefore, that this is where the apostle's emphasis lay. The Colossians needed to appropriate the

According to this A element of the chiasm, then, the audience are to "put away" like old clothing vices of interpersonal communication and not lie to one another, because they have already "removed" like old clothing the "old human being," the earthly body of the flesh (2:11), with its earthly, immoral practices (3:8-9).

2. Col 3:10 (B): You Have Put On the New Human Being

The audience's removal of the old human being with its practices (3:9b) is followed by its counterpart: "and having put on the new which is being renewed for knowledge according to the image of the one who created it" (3:10). The audience have "put on" like a new set of clothing the "new human being" which is constantly being renewed (present participle) by God (divine passive) "for knowledge" (εἰς ἐπίγνωσιν).[18] Although the object of this knowledge is unexpressed, the audience have heard a progression in the objects of previous occurrences of "knowledge," all involving God. The audience heard of Paul's prayer that they may be filled with the "knowledge" (ἐπίγνωσιν) of God's will in all wisdom and Spiritual understanding, to walk worthy of the Lord for every desire to please, in every good work bearing fruit and growing with regard to the "knowledge" (ἐπιγνώσει) of God (1:9-10). And then, most recently, the audience heard of Paul's concern that those who are held together in love might have all the richness of the full assurance of understanding "for knowledge" (εἰς ἐπίγνωσιν) of the mystery of God, Christ (2:2). Hence, God and/or Christ is the implied object of this "knowledge."

Recalling that God created the first human being "according to the image" (κατ' εἰκόνα) of God (LXX Gen 1:26-27), this "new human being" that the audience are to "put on" is being renewed for knowledge "according to the image" (κατ' εἰκόνα) of the one, that is, God, who created (κτίσαντος) it (3:10).[19] That means that this "new human being" with which the audience are to clothe themselves

---

realities of Christ's death and Resurrection not just in the area of sexual sin and ascetic practices *but also* in the area of inter-personal relationships. The need for such an exhortation is consistent with our thesis of the errorists boasting of superior spirituality" (Smith's emphasis).

18. Harris, *Colossians*, 152: "Because ἐνδύομαι has Χριστόν as its obj. in Rom. 13:14 and Gal. 3:27, it is tempting to identify the 'new person/humanity' as Christ himself. But this view destroys the 'old person/humanity—new person/humanity' parallel (Christians do not 'put off' Adam) and ignores the fact that the 'new person' is being 'renewed' and that this renewal promotes conformity to Christ as the image of God.... Ἐπίγνωσις here may merely be equivalent to γνῶσις, but if it forms a goal or outcome of the constant remolding, it means 'ever-increasing knowledge,' 'true knowledge,' or 'full knowledge.'" Dunn, *Colossians*, 222: "For knowledge was at the heart of humanity's primal failure (Gen. 2:17; 3:5, 7)."

19. The "it" (αὐτόν) that God created "refers to 'the new person' or the new Humanity, not mankind in itself or Christ as the new Man, for (i) the only explicit antecedent to αὐτόν is τὸν νέον [ἄνθρωπον]; (ii) 'the old person/humanity' can neither be equated with the first person nor be considered a divine creation; and (iii) in no sense would Paul say that God 'created' Christ (cf. 1:16-17)," according to Harris, *Colossians*, 153. Fee (*Pauline Christology*, 303-4) argues that Christ is the subject of the verb "created" here. But as Harris (*Colossians*, 153) points out: "Τοῦ κτίσαντος refers to God, not Christ, for in the Pauline corpus the expressed or implied subj. of κτίζω is always God." See also O'Brien, *Colossians*, 191; Dunn, *Colossians*, 222.

is continuously being renewed for knowledge according to Christ, since, as the audience have heard, Christ is the "image" (εἰκών) of the invisible God, the one in whom all things "were created" (ἐκτίσθη), and through whom, and to whom all things "have been created" (ἔκτισται) by God (1:15-16).[20]

3. Col 3:11 (C): Christ Is All Things and in All Things

The audience then hear this "new human being" which is being constantly renewed by God for knowledge according to the image of the one who created it (3:10) further described: "wherein there is not Greek and Jew,[21] circumcision and uncircumcision,[22] barbarian, Scythian, slave, free, but Christ is all and in all" (3:11). Within this new situation characterized as the "new human being" previous dichotomies of an ethnic-religious and socio-cultural nature have been eliminated. The audience hear these dichotomies listed as a pair of mini-chiasms based on parallel categories of people:

(a) Greek and (b) Jew, (b´) circumcision and (a´) uncircumcision,
(c) barbarian, (d) Scythian, (d´) slave, (c´) free.

The series begins with "Greek and Jew," referring to a totality of all ethnic-religious differences. This is followed by "circumcision and uncircumcision," in

---

20. Harris, *Colossians*, 153: "Paul is affirming that God created 'the new person/humanity' and is now renewing it after the pattern of Christ, who is God's image. The Creator's aim in this re-creation is not exactly the restoration in the creature of the pristine divine image, now tarnished by sin, but rather the construction of a new image, that of Christ. This ongoing process continues until a full knowledge of God is acquired and Christians finally bear 'the image of the heavenly man' (1 Cor. 15:49; cf. Rom. 8:29) as the result of a resurrection transformation." Dunn, *Colossians*, 222: " '[I]mage is a dynamic concept, as its use in reference to . . . Christ (1:15) confirms. Consequently it does not imply a static status but a relationship, one in which the 'image,' to remain 'fresh' (νέος, 'new'), must continue in contact with the one whose image it is." Bevere, *Sharing*, 174: " 'Being clothed with the new man' is a notion that likely comes from the catechetical traditions which had as their source Gen. 1.26-27. Here we have a communal reference to new humanity in Christ, betraying the theme of Christ as the second Adam. This theme is always employed by Paul in reference to Christ as risen and exalted (1 Cor. 15.21-22; 15.45). The resurrection marks the beginning of this new humanity. This new humanity in Christ is the renewal of creation, marred by sin, into what God intended for creation to be all along. Since the Colossians participate in Christ's resurrection, they are to live as that renewed humanity." Dübbers, *Christologie*, 297: "Der neue Mensch wird in tiefer Entsprechung zu Christus neu gebildet (vgl. 2,11ff.), so daß er 'Erkenntnis' hat, wobei mit dieser ἐπίγνωσις hier nichts anderes als eben der auf Christus gerichtete Glaube der Adressaten gemeint sein dürfte."

21. O'Brien, *Colossians*, 192: "Normally the Jews appear first as an expression of their privileged place in salvation history. Here the order is reversed, probably because the majority of the readers were Gentile Christians."

22. Dunn, *Colossians*, 225: "[T]he third otherwise gratuitous reference to the theme of circumcision versus uncircumcision in the letter (2:11, 13; 3:11; also 4:11) must surely indicate, first, that the primary challenge to the Colossian believers was posed by local Jews and, second, that it presupposed a valuation of circumcision which called the Christians' standing as beneficiaries of Jewish heritage into question."

which "circumcision" chiastically parallels "Jew" and "uncircumcision" chiastically parallels "Greek," as a further expression of the ethnic-religious differences separating people.[23] The elements of these first two dichotomies are linked by "and (καί)," distinguishing them from the second set of dichotomies which are listed without conjunctions.[24] Whereas "barbarian" refers to one who does not speak Greek or participate in Greek culture, "Scythian" refers to one who does not speak Greek or participate in Greek culture as a slave from north of the Black Sea to express a socio-cultural dichotomy.[25] "Slave" chiastically parallels "Scythian" and "free" chiastically parallels "barbarian" as a further expression of the socio-cultural differences separating people.[26]

But within the situation of this "new human being" with which the audience have "clothed" themselves (3:10), all ethnic-religious and socio-cultural differences (3:11a) are transcended by Christ—"but Christ is all and in all" (3:11b). Not only is Christ "all," that is, comprises absolutely all things that matter for the salvation of all, but also Christ is "in all," that is, in all people who believe.[27]

---

23. M. Thekkekara, "Colossians 3:11a: The Abolition of Barriers," *Indian Theological Studies* 36 (1999): 105-25; idem, "Colossians 3,11," *Biblebhashyam* 25 (1999): 266-84.

24. Douglas A. Campbell, "Unravelling Colossians 3.11b," *NTS* 42 (1996): 128 n. 26: "The author's systematic use of asyndeton in the second set of four terms also encourages us both to distinguish it from the first set, which uses καί, and to read it as a self-sufficient semantic unit that, like the first, addresses one basic opposition. Such a variation could also be conceived as good rhetorical form—a minute variation to avoid banal reproduction within repeated figures."

25. Campbell, "Unravelling," 129-32; see also D. Goldenberg, "Scythian-Barbarian: The Permutations of a Classical Topos in Jewish and Christian Texts of Late Antiquity," *JJS* 49 (1998): 87-102; Garland, *Colossians*, 208-9.

26. Campbell, "Unravelling," 131 32: "Hence, it seems likely that the series 'barbarian, Scythian, slave, free' in Col 3.11b proclaims the overcoming, not of a (rather stylistically messy) set of general literary stereotypes and antitheses comprising Jews, Greeks, barbarians, and even more extreme cases of savagery, but the more straight-forward abolition of the *social* antithesis between slaves and owners; a differential entwined with an *ethnic* antithesis between barbarians of diverse geographical and cultural background, in this case, slaves procured from north of the Black Sea and owners originating from Asia itself. Significantly, these were social differentials as potentially troublesome to the early church as the well-known dichotomy NT scholars are accustomed to deploring between Jew and Greek, or that Classicists explore between Greek and barbarian" (Campbell's emphases). A Scythian perspective along with a Cynic reading of the pairing "barbarian/Scythian" that allows it to be interpreted along with the other pairs listed in 3:11 as mutually exclusive categories has been proposed by Troy W. Martin, "The Scythian Perspective in Col 3:11," *NovT* 38 (1995): 249-61. But interpreting "barbarian/Scythian" as an antithesis from a Scythian viewpoint and Cynic reading has been shown to be implausible by Douglas A. Campbell, "The Scythian Perspective in Col. 3:11: A Response to Troy Martin," *NovT* 39 (1997): 81-84; see also Bevere, *Sharing*, 119. The interpretation employed here concurs with that of Campbell despite the rejoinder by Troy W. Martin, "Scythian Perspective or Elusive Chiasm: A Reply to Douglas A. Campbell," *NovT* 41 (1999): 256-64. See also E. Yamauchi, "The Scythians—Who Were They? And Why Did Paul Include Them in Colossians 3.11?" *Priscilla Papers* 21 (2007): 13-18.

27. Harris, *Colossians*, 155: "Christ amounts to everything and indwells all—without distinction—who belong to his new people." O'Brien, *Colossians*, 193: "The first half states in an emphatic way that Christ is 'absolutely everything,' or 'all that matters,' while the words he is 'in all' (ἐν πᾶσιν), which in the light of the preceding statement of verse 11a should probably be regarded as masculine

4. Col 3:12 (B´): Put On a New Way of Behaving toward One Another

Having heard how Christ transcends all the differences separating people in the central C element of the chiasm with its climactic assertion—"Christ is all and in all" (3:11b), the audience then experience the pivot from the B to the B´ element of the chiasm: "Put on then, as God's chosen ones, holy and beloved, heartfelt compassion, kindness, humility, gentleness, patience" (3:12). Corresponding to the fact that in the B element they have "put on" (ἐνδυσάμενοι) the new human being that is being renewed by God for knowledge of God according to the image of the God who created it (3:10), in the B´ element, by way of the chiastic parallelism, the audience are commanded to "put on" (ἐνδύσασθε), as God's chosen ones who are holy and beloved by God, a new way of behaving toward one another (3:12).[28]

That the audience are addressed as God's chosen ones who are also "holy ones" (ἅγιοι) reminds them that this new moral behavior they are enjoined to "put on" (3:12) is appropriate to their status among God's "holy ones" (ἁγίοις) to whom the mystery of God, Christ (2:2), has been manifested (1:26). It correlates to their status as those whom God reconciled through the death of Christ to present them as "holy ones" (ἁγίους) without any moral blemish or blame before Christ (1:22). And it coheres with their status as those God made fit for the share of the inheritance of the "holy ones" (ἁγίων) in the light (1:12). Indeed, as God's holy ones who are also "beloved" (ἠγαπημένοι) by God (3:12),[29] the audience are to put on a new moral behavior as recipients of the love of God just as Christ himself is the Son of the "love" (ἀγάπης) of God (1:13).[30]

(rather than neuter), mean that he permeates and indwells all members of the new man, regardless of race, class or background." Bevere, *Sharing*, 120: "Salvation defined in nationalistic terms cannot do anything but divide humanity. Christ unites humanity in rendering these nationalistic distinctions unimportant." Dübbers, *Christologie*, 298–99: "Aus der irdischen Abstammung der Adressaten lassen sich keine differenzierenden Kriterien mehr ableiten, weder im soteriologischen noch im zwischenmenschlichen Bereich.... Der neue Mensch ist durch nichts bestimmt als durch Christus allein." Smith, *Heavenly Perspective*, 199: "The reconciliation of all Christians is given clearly in 3.11. People of diverse origins are gathered together because of their common identification with Christ. This identification removes all ethnic, cultural and socio-economic barriers ... The purpose of Col. 3.11 is not to abolish social distinctions but to establish unity. This plea for unity would underscore the fact that the actions of the Colossian errorists were divisive."

28. Harris, *Colossians*, 160: "A further reason for the injunction 'put on' is introduced by causal ὡς: 'inasmuch as you are God's chosen people.'... Paul is enjoining the Colossians to wear those moral garments that are appropriate to their calling and status."

29. Harris, *Colossians*, 161: "God is the implied agent; thus, 'loved by God,' 'his beloved,' or 'those on whom God has set his love' (a paraphrase that brings out the sense of the pf. tense)."

30. Dübbers, *Christologie*, 199 n. 51: "*Gott* ist derjenige, der die Adressaten erwählt und geliebt hat; beides ist dem Menschen nicht verfügbar und kann daher nicht erworben werden" (Dübbers's emphasis). Smith, *Heavenly Perspective*, 200: "Paul applies to them three terms that are strongly reminiscent of Israel: ἐκλεκτοὶ τοῦ θεοῦ ['God's chosen ones'], ἅγιοι ['holy'], and ἠγαπημένοι ['beloved']. Therefore, whether Gentile or Jew, Christians were invited to consider themselves as full participants of God's covenant blessings and Israel's heritage. They are not disqualified because of their lack of Jew-

As the audience were commanded to "put to death" (νεκρώσατε) the parts that are upon the earth (3:5) and to "put away" (ἀπόθεσθε) their old immoral behavior toward one another, exemplified by a list of five vices—anger, rage, malice, slander, obscene talk from your mouth (3:8), so, correlatively, they are commanded to "put on" (ἐνδύσασθε) a new moral behavior toward one another,[31] exemplified by a list of five virtues—heartfelt compassion,[32] kindness,[33] humility,[34] gentleness,[35] patience (3:12).[36] This list of virtues exemplifies the new type of moral "clothing" the audience are to "put on" in relating to one another regardless of

---

ish mystical practice." Dunn, *Colossians*, 228: "[T]he particular exhortations which follow assume and expect the Colossians to presuppose that they stood before God as Israel stood before God. It is very likely that this assumption on the part of uncircumcised Gentiles (2:13) was a bone of contention with or provocation to the more traditional Jewish synagogues in Colossae."

31. O'Brien, *Colossians*, 197: "The imperative ἐνδύσασθε ('put on'), like its counterpart in verses 5 (νεκρώσατε, 'put to death') and 8 (ἀπόθεσθε, 'put off') is an aorist tense signifying a decisive initial act which introduces a settled attitude."

32. O'Brien, *Colossians*, 198–99: "σπλάγχνα οἰκτιρμοῦ means 'heartfelt compassion'... οἰκτιρμός in the LXX is predicated first and foremost of God who is described as 'compassionate': he has acted graciously and compassionately on behalf of his people.... σπλάγχνον (almost always in the plural, meaning literally 'inward parts') comes to be used figuratively of the seat of the emotions, i.e. the 'heart.' In fact, like other anthropological terms the word is found in Paul for the whole man, expressing strongly and forcefully what concerns the personality at the deepest level, especially in his capacity of loving.... In this context of Colossians the joint expression means 'a compassionate heart' or 'merciful compassion.'" Wilson, *Colossians*, 258: "[T]he linking of the two words makes the emotional content even stronger: 'heartfelt compassion.'"

33. O'Brien, *Colossians*, 199–200: "χρηστότης ('goodness,' 'kindness,' 'generosity') is a quality which God himself demonstrates in concrete actions. Both noun and cognate adjective are favorite words in the LXX for expressing the abundance of his goodness which he displays to his covenant people—indeed to all men as his creatures.... As a response to God's merciful kindness the person who has put on the new man ... is to show kindness to others." Bevere, *Sharing*, 205: "Χρηστότης in Colossians is a direct outworking of ἀγάπη. As God has acted graciously in Christ toward sinners so Christians must act graciously toward others."

34. O'Brien, *Colossians*, 200: "ταπεινοφροσύνη ... signifies the grace of 'lowliness,' 'humility.' ... Particularly significant are those references to the Lord's acting in history to bring down the proud and arrogant and to exalt the lowly." Bevere, *Sharing*, 208: "ταπεινοφροσύνη is not to be understood as weakness, as in a Greek context but as consideration of others and the surrender of one's privileges."

35. O'Brien, *Colossians*, 201: "πραΰτης ('gentleness,' 'humility,' 'meekness') ... is not to be confused with weakness, but contains the elements of (a) a consideration for others, and (b) a willingness to waive one's rights." Deterding, *Colossians*, 145: "'Gentleness' is the strength to deal gently so as to be of help instead of offending another."

36. O'Brien, *Colossians*, 201: "μακροθυμία ... denotes 'longsuffering' which endures wrong and puts up with the exasperating conduct of others rather than flying into a rage or desiring vengeance." Bevere, *Sharing*, 209: "In the LXX μακροθυμία is found only in the wisdom literature and often marks an attribute of God who restrains himself when it comes to the judgment of his people.... God is patient with his people. They must, therefore, be patient with others ... As with the other virtues already discussed μακροθυμία has a divine origin." Wright, *Colossians*, 143: "[G]entleness is the effect of meek humility on one's *approach* to other people, whereas *patience* is the effect of that humble kindness on one's *reaction* to other people. The first forswears rudeness or arrogance the second, resentment and anger" (Wright's emphases).

their ethnic-religious or socio-cultural status (3:11) now that they have "removed" (ἀπεκδυσάμενοι) the "old human being" (3:9) and "put on" (ἐνδυσάμενοι) the "new human being" (3:10).

In contrast to the false "humility" of the deceitful philosophy (2:8) which delights in "humility" (ταπεινοφροσύνῃ) and worship of angels (2:18) and which has a reputation of wisdom in self-chosen worship and "humility" (ταπεινοφροσύνῃ) and severe treatment of the body, but is not of any value to anyone (2:23), the audience are to "put on" an authentic "humility" (ταπεινοφροσύνην), the central term in the fivefold list of virtues (3:12).[37] That the audience are to "put on" the virtue of "patience" (μακροθυμίαν) as the final, climactic virtue in the fivefold list (3:12) reminds them of the authors' prayer that they be empowered by God for all endurance and "patience" (μακροθυμίαν, 1:11) to "walk," that is, conduct themselves and behave, as worthy of the Lord (1:10).[38]

In sum, in this B´ element the audience, in accord with their being God's chosen ones who are holy and beloved by God, as a consequence of Christ's transcendence over all of the differences that separate people (3:11), and in correspondence to their having "put on" the new human being (3:10) and having "removed" the old human being (3:9), are to "put on" a new, moral way of relating to one another, including an authentic humility and patience (3:12) in replacement of the old, immoral ways of relating to one another that they are to "put away" (3:8).

5. Col 3:13–16 (A´): You Also Must Bear with One Another in Your Hearts

The audience then hear the new virtuous "clothing" they are to "put on" (3:12) illustrated more specifically: "bearing with one another and forgiving each other if anyone has a complaint against someone; just as the Lord forgave you, so must you also. And over all these love, that is the bond of completeness" (3:13–14). In the A element of the chiasm the audience were enjoined not to lie to "one another" (ἀλλήλους, 3:9). Now, in the A´ element, by way of the chiastic parallelism, they are to bear with "one another" (ἀλλήλων, 3:14) as the positive counterpart to that negative command. Addressed with the phrase "you also" (καὶ ὑμεῖς, 3:8),

---

37. Smith, *Heavenly Perspective*, 200: "The list of virtues in 3.12 complements the vices of 3.8 as they are all concerned with human relationships. These virtues clearly relate to the Colossian error as is seen in the use of ταπεινοφροσύνη, a key term in the description of the error in 2.18. . . . in the New Testament it is normally used in a positive sense of 'lowliness of heart.' The only time it is used in a negative sense is in Col. 2:18, 23. As this is the only occurrence of ταπεινοφροσύνη in a New Testament list of ethics, 'it would seem reasonable to suppose that it has been placed here by the author to counter the kind of self-abasement involved as a necessary prelude to receiving heavenly visions' [quote from Yates, "Christian Way of Life," 245]. It would appear, therefore, that Paul is using this term in the list of virtues to show its meaning for Christians. Rather than a means to attain a heavenly ascent, and thereby to cause division by boasting of superior spirituality, the Colossians were to understand ταπεινοφροσύνη as a reflection of the character of Christ (3.13). As the centre in Paul's list of five virtues (3.12), it appears that this is where his emphasis lies."

38. Wright, *Colossians*, 142: "Paul earlier (1:11) prayed that this sort of character would appear in the Colossians; he now urges them to make his prayer come true."

the audience were enjoined with the negative command to put away all the vices associated with the "old human being" (3:9) in the A element. Now, in the A´ element, by way of the chiastic parallelism, they are, as a more positive command, to forgive one another just as the Lord forgave them, addressed once again with the phrase "you also" (καὶ ὑμεῖς, 3:13).

Previously the audience heard that God brought them, being "dead" in transgressions and in the uncircumcision of their flesh, to "life" along with Christ, having "forgiven" (χαρισάμενος) us all our transgressions (2:13). Now the audience hear that forgiveness attributed to "the Lord" (3:13), referring to Christ Jesus himself, as it recalls that they are to go on "walking" in the Christ they have received, the Christ emphatically designated as Jesus "the Lord" (2:6), "the Lord" of whom they are to "walk" worthy for every desire to please (1:10), our "Lord" Jesus Christ, the Son of God the Father (1:3).[39] They are to be "forgiving" (χαριζόμενοι) each other if anyone has a complaint against someone; just as "the Lord" Jesus Christ "forgave" (ἐχαρίσατο) "you" (ὑμῖν), intensified with an additional "so you also (καὶ ὑμεῖς)" in an emphatic final position (3:13), underscoring the audience's responsibility to forgive just as they have been forgiven.[40]

In contrast to "these" (τούτοις) vices—unlawful sex, impurity, passion, evil desire, and the covetousness, which is idolatry (3:5)—in which the audience once lived (3:7), they are to "put on" over all "these" (τούτοις) virtues—heartfelt compassion, kindness, humility, gentleness, patience (3:12b)—"love" (ἀγάπην) as the outer garment or finishing touch to their moral wardrobe (3:14a).[41] Thus, the audience are to "put on" love as the appropriate response to their being God's "beloved" (ἠγαπημένοι) ones (3:12a).[42] This recalls for the audience how it is in "love"

---

39. Dunn, *Colossians*, 231: "[I]n the Paulines, apart from Old Testament quotations, κύριος always denotes Christ." Dübbers, *Christologie*, 300 n. 39: "Daß Christus (ὁ κύριος) hier als Subjekt der Vergebung erscheint, ist im Kolosserbrief wie auch sonst im Neuen Testament singulär. Man wird diese Beobachtung jedoch nicht überbewerten dürfen: Denn Christus steht im Kolosserbrief ganz auf der Seite Gottes. Das Handeln Gottes (durch Christus) und das Handeln Christi sind also nicht scharf voneinander zu trennen."

40. O'Brien, *Colossians*, 202: "χαρίζομαι ('give freely or graciously as a favor,' 'give' = 'remit,' 'forgive,' 'pardon') is not the common word for remission or forgiveness (which is ἀφίημι, 'cancel,' 'remit,' or 'pardon'), but one of richer content emphasizing the gracious nature of the pardon." Dübbers, *Christologie*, 301: "Hier wird nun das Analogieprinzip als der paränetischen Leitgedanke des Kolosserbriefs besonders deutlich: Das Handeln der Adressaten soll der an Christus gebundenen Heilsstat und somit ihrem neuen Sein entsprechen (καθώς-οὕτως). Dies und nichts anderes meint der Verfasser, wenn er die kolossischen Christen auf dem Hintergrund ihrer Heilswirklichkeit dazu anhält, ἀξίως τοῦ κυρίου (1,10) bzw. ἐν αὐτῷ zu leben (2,6)."

41. Harris, *Colossians*, 163: "The art. with ἀγάπην suggests that concrete expressions of love, love dramatized, is in mind." Bevere, *Sharing*, 220: "Love is the supreme Christian virtue of grace as suggested in the phrase ἐπὶ πᾶσιν δὲ τούτοις, that may refer to the outer garment, which holds all the other garments in place."

42. Wilson, *Colossians*, 262: "This love is not something that can be conjured up at will by human beings; it is primarily a response to and inspired by the love of God revealed in Christ." Dübbers, *Christologie*, 301: "Die Liebe ist für den Verfasser die christliche 'Kardinaltugend' im Blick auf das Handeln

(ἀγάπῃ) that believers are brought together and unified (2:2). The "love" (ἀγάπην) in the Spirit that the audience already have (1:8), the "love" (ἀγάπην) they have for all the holy ones (1:4), they are now to "put on" and wear in their dealings with one another, as it is the bond of completeness (3:14b) which unites them with their fellow believers.[43]

The audience are to realize, then, that as the "bond" (σύνδεσμος) of completeness (3:14b), love not only binds and holds together the other virtues the audience are to "put on" like clothing,[44] but is preeminent among the ligaments and "bonds" (συνδέσμων) through which the whole body of Christ is supported and held together, as it holds to Christ, the head, from whom the whole body grows with the growth that is from God (2:19). That love is the bond of "completeness" (τελειότητος), that is, the "maturity" which is the goal of the growth of "all" (πᾶν) the body, reminds the audience that Paul and Timothy are admonishing "every" (πάντα) human being and teaching "every" (πάντα) human being in all wisdom that they may present "every" (πάντα) human being "complete" (τέλειον) or "mature" in the body of Christ (1:28).[45] Thus, the love, the ardent care and concern for each other, that the audience are to "put on" and wear as they relate to one another is the bond that unites them together within the body of Christ as all within the body grow together to their "completeness" or "maturity" as human beings in Christ.[46]

The audience then hear what is to take place within their hearts: "And let the peace of Christ rule in your hearts, to which indeed you were called in one body. And be thankful. Let the word of Christ dwell in you richly, in all wisdom teaching

---

gegenüber dem Nächsten, denn sie entspricht in höchstem Maße dem Handeln Gottes am Menschen: Aus Liebe hat sich Gott dem Menschen zugewandt und ihn heilig gemacht (3,12)."

43. On the clause "that is (ὅ ἐστιν) the bond of completeness" here Deterding (*Colossians*, 145) points out: "Paul employs the neuter relative pronoun (ὅ) in apposition to the feminine noun 'love' (ἀγάπη). As he regularly uses the correct gender of the relative pronoun elsewhere in this letter, his departure from the usual rules of syntax here points to the relative clause being less an identification and more an interpretation."

44. Bruce, *Colossians*, 156 n. 137: "Simplicius (*Epictetus* 208a) says that the Pythagoreans regarded friendship (φιλία) as the σύνδεσμος πασῶν τῶν ἀρετῶν, 'the bond of all the virtues.'"

45. Dunn, *Colossians*, 232-33: "If τελειότης does not have a specific reference (to clothes perfectly fitted and worn), it simply denotes the 'completeness' and 'maturity' of the community where ἀγάπη is 'on top of all.'"

46. O'Brien, *Colossians*, 204: "Love binds together the members of the congregation into unity in the body of Christ so producing perfection. Paul is concerned with the readers' corporate life and the perfection he sets before them is not something narrowly individual. It is attained only as Christians, in fellowship, show love to one another. It is by this love, one of the graces of Christ, that his body is built up." Dübbers, *Christologie*, 301-2: "Der Ausdruck σύνδεσμος ist auf dem Hintergrund von 2,19 als physiologische (und nicht als kosmische) Metapher zu verstehen. Wie die Bänder eines Körpers den Zusammenhalt der verschiedenen Glieder gewähren, so wirkt auch die Liebe den Zusammenhalt—und damit die Einheit—der Gemeinde (vgl. 3,15). Denn die Liebe verhindert gemeinschaftszerstörendes Verhalten wie Zorn, Bosheit und Lüge (3,8) und schafft somit die Vollkommenheit der christlichen Gemeinschaft, die der soteriologischen Vollkommenheit der Christen entspricht (1,28; 4,12)."

and admonishing each other with psalms, hymns, and Spiritual songs, in grace singing in your hearts to God" (3:15–16).[47] In the A element of the chiasm the audience were directed to put away obscene talk "from your (ὑμῶν) mouth" (3:8). And now, by way of the chiastic parallelism, the focus shifts from their mouth to their hearts, as they are exhorted to let the peace of Christ rule "in your (ὑμῶν) hearts" (3:15) and to sing "in your (ὑμῶν) hearts" to God (3:16) in the A′ element.

At the beginning of the letter the audience heard the authors' prayer-wish for them, "grace to you and peace (εἰρήνη) from God our Father" (1:2). And now, in the next occurrence of the term "peace" in the letter, they hear the progression from the peace that comes from God to the peace of Christ, as they are exhorted to "let the peace (εἰρήνη) of Christ rule in your hearts" (3:15a). Just as it can be said that both God (2:13) and Christ (3:13b) have forgiven the audience, so it can be said that peace comes from both God and Christ. As the audience have heard, through Christ God reconciled all things to Christ, "making peace" (εἰρηνοποιήσας) through the blood of the cross of Christ, that is, through Christ himself, whether the things of the earth or the things in heavens (1:20).[48] The "peace of Christ" is based on the assertion that "Christ is all and in all," transcending the various differences that separate and cause enmity between human beings, and thus making it possible for them to live in peace with one another (3:11).[49]

The peace of Christ which is to "rule," that is, be the decisive factor,[50] "in your hearts (καρδίαις, 3:15a)," that is, in the center of their beings, provides the interior motivation for the audience's external actions of the "love" (ἀγάπην) they are to "put on" in bearing with one another and forgiving each other as the Lord Christ forgave them (3:13), and thus made it possible for them to live in peace with God. The peace of Christ which is to rule interiorly "in your hearts" (ἐν ταῖς καρδίαις ὑμῶν, 3:15a), then, provides the motivation for the audience to "put away" the obscene talk that comes exteriorly "out of your mouth" (ἐκ τοῦ στόματος ὑμῶν, 3:8), so that they may live in peace with one another. Paul's wish that the "hearts"

---

47. For this construal and punctuation of 3:16 in which a comma is placed after rather than before "psalms, hymns, and Spiritual songs", see Fee, *God's Empowering Presence*, 653, who adds that this "view results in a (typically Pauline) nicely balanced set of ideas, each of which expresses the twin dimensions of Christian worship—horizontal and vertical—with the various kinds of songs as the 'swing component' that conceptually ties the two parts together."

48. Dunn, *Colossians*, 233: "The thought here, however, should not be reduced to a merely spiritualized or individualized sensation, for no doubt what was in mind was the state of peace achieved by Christ already spoken of in 1:20." Dübbers, *Christologie*, 302: "Dabei nimmt der Ausdruck εἰρήνη τοῦ Χριστοῦ im Kontext des Briefes auf die grundlegende Heilswirklichkeit der Adressaten Bezug, die durch die Versöhnungstat Gottes am Kreuz Jesu Christi konstituiert wurde (1,20): Gott schuf durch Christus Frieden, indem er die Feindschaft des alten Menschen brach und die alte Sündenexistenz vernichtete (1,21 f.). Weil also die Adressaten—die einst Feinde waren, jetzt aber als Heilige vor Gott stehen—durch die εἰρήνη τοῦ Χριστοῦ ganz bestimmt sind, soll der Friede in ihren Herzen regieren."

49. Wilson, *Colossians*, 263: "[U]ltimately it is God's peace, the gift of the God of peace, but it is mediated through Christ and may therefore be described as his peace."

50. BDAG, 183.

(καρδίαι) of believers may be encouraged interiorly as they are held together in the "love" (ἀγάπῃ) they exhibit externally (2:2) is now complemented by his exhortation for the peace of Christ to rule interiorly in the "hearts" of the audience as the inspiration for the "love" they are to display externally. Thus, whereas external love can bring about interior encouragement in "hearts," the peace of Christ which is to rule interiorly in "hearts" can bring about external love.[51]

As "chosen ones" (ἐκλεκτοί) of God (3:12), the audience were indeed "called" (ἐκλήθητε) by God (divine passive) to that peace of Christ which is to rule interiorly "in" (ἐν) their hearts (3:15a) and be manifested exteriorly "in" (ἐν) one body (3:15b).[52] The audience are to display the peace of Christ by their love for one another in the one "body" (σώματι), that is, the "body" (σώματος), which is the church (1:18, 24), of which Christ is the "head," from whom the whole "body" (σῶμα), supported and held together through ligaments and bonds so that it is unified as "one" body, grows with the growth that is from God (2:19).

As an appropriate response to being called by God in one body (3:15b) to the peace of Christ which is to rule in their hearts (3:15a), so that they may be at peace with God and one another in that one body, the audience are enjoined to be "thankful" (εὐχάριστοι) to God (3:15c). This recalls and reinforces how they are to be abounding in "thanksgiving" (εὐχαριστίᾳ) to God who "rooted" and "built" them up in Christ and confirmed them in the faith (2:7). It also recalls and reinforces how they are to be "thanking" (εὐχαριστοῦντες) the Father who has made them fit for the share of the inheritance of the holy ones in the light (1:12). And it more closely associates them with the authors, Paul and Timothy, who "thank"

---

51. Bruce, *Colossians*, 156 n. 140: "βραβεύω (here only in the NT) is the simple verb from which is derived the compound καταβραβεύω, used in Col. 2:18." Smith, *Heavenly Perspective*, 201: "Of particular interest is the use of βραβευέτω in 3.15. . . . βραβεύω is drawn from the context of the arena, meaning to award prizes. Therefore the meaning within the context of the Colossian error is to allow the peace of Christ to qualify them (ἡ εἰρήνη τοῦ Χριστοῦ βραβευέτω) . . . 3.15) rather than the Colossian errorists to disqualify them (cf. καταβραβευέτω 2.18)." Harris, *Colossians*, 165: "Here καρδία may signify the mind or the thinking process or, by synecdoche, the whole person. Tr.: 'let the peace that Christ gives act as arbitrator in your hearts.' That is, 'in making your decisions, in choosing between alternatives, in settling conflicts of will, a concern to preserve the inward and communal peace that Christ gave and gives should be your controlling principle.'" O'Brien, *Colossians*, 204-5: "'[H]eart' is being employed in its customary OT sense to denote the center of one's personality as the source of will, emotion, thoughts and affections. The peace of Christ is to hold sway over the whole of the readers' lives as they relate to one another." Dunn, *Colossians*, 234: "Here is the true arbiter ('peace'), not the Colossian Jews referred to in 2:18. To be noted is the fact that the subject is 'the peace of Christ,' not 'you'; this is something the Colossians have not to accomplish but to let happen—to let go any attempt to control and manipulate and to let the peace of Christ be the determiner—just as in the following clause peace is a call to which they can only respond."

52. Dunn, *Colossians*, 234: "The thought is also entirely Jewish and closely related to the theme of a chosen people (3:12), as we see particularly in deutero-Isaiah (Isa. 41:8-9; 42:6; 43:3-4; 48:12; 49:1; 51:2). The continued use of such themes close to the heart of Israel's self-understanding is significant and reinforces the view that what Paul and Timothy were trying to do was to mark out more carefully both the Jewish character of the Christian message and the Christian focus of the Jewish heritage."

(εὐχαριστοῦμεν) the God and Father of our Lord Jesus Christ always when praying for the audience (1:3).

Correlative to the exhortation for the audience to let the peace of Christ rule "in (ἐν) your hearts" (3:15a) is the exhortation that they are to let the "word" of Christ dwell "in (ἐν) you," that is, both within them and in their midst, richly (3:16a).[53] This "word" (λόγος) of Christ recalls the synonymous "word" (λόγῳ) of the truth of the gospel (1:5) and the "word" (λόγον) of God (1:25), which is the mystery of Christ (1:26; 2:2). That the word of Christ is to dwell in them "richly" (πλουσίως) recalls that God wished to make known to the audience, as holy ones, what is the "richness" (πλοῦτος) of the glory of this mystery among the Gentiles, which is Christ among them, the hope of the glory (1:27). It also recalls how the hearts of believers may be encouraged as they are held together in love for all "richness" (πλοῦτος) of the full assurance of understanding, for knowledge of the mystery of God, Christ (2:2), in whom are all the treasures of wisdom and knowledge hidden (2:3). That the audience are to let the word of Christ dwell in them richly, then, means they are to appropriate within them all the richness of understanding, knowledge, and wisdom associated with the mystery of Christ.[54]

The audience have already been informed of the authors' continual praying that they may be filled with the knowledge of God's will "in all wisdom" (ἐν πάσῃ σοφίᾳ) and Spiritual understanding (1:9). As they proclaim Christ, the authors are "admonishing" (νουθετοῦντες) every human being and "teaching" (διδάσκοντες) every human being "in all wisdom" (ἐν πάσῃ σοφίᾳ), that they may present every human being complete in Christ (1:28). And now the Colossian audience are to be part of this ministry. As a result of their allowing the word of Christ to dwell in them richly (3:16a), appropriating all the richness of understanding, knowledge, and wisdom which comes from the mystery of Christ, they are enabled "in all wisdom" (ἐν πάσῃ σοφίᾳ) to be "teaching" (διδάσκοντες) and "admonishing" (νουθετοῦντες) each other with psalms, hymns, and Spiritual songs (3:16b).[55] The audience, then, are not merely to forgive "each other" (ἑαυτοῖς, 3:13), but to teach and admonish "each other" (ἑαυτούς, 3:16b) with all the wisdom they have in

---

53. O'Brien, *Colossians*, 205: "[T]he phrase 'in your hearts' is picked up in v 16 with the words 'in you' . . . Christ himself is to be present and ruling in their midst."

54. O'Brien, *Colossians*, 207: "If the double reference of ἐν ὑμῖν ('within you' and 'among you') is in view then this rich indwelling would occur when they came together, listened to the Word of Christ as it was preached and expounded to them and bowed to its authority. By this means Christ's rule would be exercised in their lives." Dunn, *Colossians*, 236–37: "In this context the ἐν ὑμῖν may also signify 'among you,' indicating an element of preaching/teaching in the communal gatherings of the Colossian Christians for worship and instruction. Πλουσίως ('richly') picks up the same theme of divine richness already announced in 1:27 and 2:2. There is a richness in 'the word of Christ' which makes it an inexhaustible source of spiritual resource, intellectual stimulus, and personal and corporate challenge; but without the participants' positive response its 'indwelling' might be feeble rather than rich."

55. Thus, "singing can be both 'to God' and a means of 'teaching one another,'" as pointed out by Fee, *God's Empowering Presence*, 652, 656: "Such songs are at the same time creedal, full of theological grist and give evidence of what the early Christians most truly believed about God and his Christ."

Christ, in whom are hidden all the treasures of "wisdom" (σοφίας) and knowledge (2:3), a wisdom vastly superior to the mere reputation of "wisdom" (σοφίας, 2:23) associated with the "philosophy" (φιλο-σοφίας) which is empty deceit (2:8).

The audience may actualize their being thankful to God (3:15c) in their corporate worship in the one body (3:15b) by gratefully singing "in grace" (χάριτι, 3:16c), that is, within the realm of the "grace" (χάρις) of God the authors have wished for them (1:2), the "grace" (χάριν) of God in truth they came to know (1:6), as they learned the gospel from Epaphras (1:7).[56] In this grace they are to be singing with psalms, hymns, and Spiritual songs (3:16c)—a rhetorical triplet of synonymous terms climaxing with a more elaborate third term, "Spiritual" (πνευματικαῖς) songs, that is, songs appropriate to their being within the realm of the divine "Spirit" (πνεύματι, 1:8; cf. 2:5) of God, echoing the "Spiritual" (πνευματικῇ) understanding with which they are to be filled by God (1:9).[57] They are to be singing these songs not only externally with their mouths but internally "in your hearts" (ἐν ταῖς καρδίαις ὑμῶν) to God (3:16c),[58] just as they are to let the peace of Christ dwell internally "in your hearts" (ἐν ταῖς καρδίαις ὑμῶν, 3:15a). They are thus to be singing in their hearts to "God" (θεῷ) as an appropriate response to their being chosen ones of "God" (θεοῦ, 3:12).[59]

In sum, in this A´ element of the chiasm, instead of lying to one another (3:9), the audience are to bear with one another and forgive each other as the Lord has forgiven them (3:13). The love that the audience are to "put on" and wear as they relate to one another is the bond that unites them together within the body of Christ as all within the body grow together to their maturity as human beings in Christ (3:14). As an appropriate response to being called by God in one body to

---

56. With reference to the meaning of the attitude of being "in grace" in 3:16, Fee (*God's Empowering Presence*, 655) states that "the focus is not so much on *our* attitude toward God as we sing, but on our awareness of *his* toward us that prompts such singing in the first place" (Fee's emphases). Dunn, *Colossians*, 239: "[T]he response of praise depends as much on God's grace as their initial reception of the gospel."

57. Fee, *God's Empowering Presence*, 653–54: "We are dealing with songs that are inspired by the Spirit.... Therefore, even though πνευματικός could well modify all three nouns—the psalms and hymns would also be 'of the Spirit'—it is more likely that it is intended to modify 'songs' only, referring especially to this one kind of Spirit-inspired singing. This word, after all, is the one which the recipients of the letter would least likely associate with worship, since it covers the whole range of 'songs' in the Greek world, whereas the other two are usually sung to a deity."

58. O'Brien, *Colossians*, 210: "As in verse 15 καρδία ('heart') is employed to refer to the whole of one's being." The sense is " 'singing with your whole heart,' " according to Fee, *God's Empowering Presence*, 655. Dunn, *Colossians*, 239–40: "As in 3:15 the addition of 'in (or with) your hearts' underlines the importance of a worship rooted in the depths of personal experience and springing up from that source—heart worship and not merely lip worship."

59. Smith, *Heavenly Perspective*, 201: "It is thus consistent that Paul should conclude this issue of reconciliation by referring to worship in 3.16–17. This has direct relevance to the Colossian error, where the adherents of the philosophy were belittling the worship of the Colossian Christians by claiming a higher heavenly worship with the angels (2.18). In this context, Paul implies that the worship of the Colossian Christians should be sufficient."

the peace of Christ which is to rule in their hearts, so that they may be at peace with God and one another, the audience are enjoined to be thankful to God (3:15). As a result of their allowing the word of Christ to dwell in them richly, appropriating all the richness of understanding, knowledge, and wisdom which comes from the mystery of Christ, they are enabled in all wisdom to be teaching and admonishing each other. They may actualize their being thankful to God in their corporate worship by gratefully singing, within the realm of the grace of God, with psalms, hymns, and Spiritual songs, appropriate to their being in the realm of the Spirit of God, not only externally with their mouths but internally in their hearts to the God who has chosen them (3:16).

C. Summary on Colossians 3:8–16

1. The audience are to "put away" like old clothing vices of interpersonal communication and not lie to one another, because they have already "removed" like old clothing the "old human being," the earthly body of the flesh (2:11), with its earthly, immoral practices (3:8-9).

2. Recalling that God created the first human being "according to the image" of God (LXX Gen 1:26-27), this "new human being" that the audience are to "put on" is being renewed for knowledge "according to the image" of the one, that is, God, who created it (3:10). That means that this "new human being" with which the audience are to clothe themselves is continuously being renewed for knowledge according to Christ, since, as the audience have heard, Christ is the "image" of the invisible God, the one in whom all things "were created," and through whom, and to whom all things "have been created" by God (1:15-16).

3. Within the situation of this "new human being" with which the audience have "clothed" themselves (3:10), all ethnic-religious and socio-cultural differences (3:11a) are transcended by Christ—"but Christ is all and in all" (3:11b). Not only is Christ "all," that is, comprises absolutely all things that matter for the salvation of all, but also Christ is "in all," that is, in all people who believe.

4. The audience, in accord with their being God's chosen ones who are holy and beloved by God, as a consequence of Christ's transcendence over all of the differences that separate people (3:11), and in correspondence to their having "put on" the new human being (3:10) and having "removed" the old human being (3:9), are to "put on" a new, moral way of relating to one another, including an authentic humility and patience (3:12) in replacement of the old, immoral ways of relating to one another that they are to "put away" (3:8).

5. Instead of lying to one another (3:9), the audience are to bear with one another and forgive each other as the Lord has forgiven them (3:13). The love that

the audience are to "put on" and wear as they relate to one another is the bond that unites them together within the body of Christ as all within the body grow together to their maturity as human beings in Christ (3:14). As an appropriate response to being called by God in one body to the peace of Christ which is to rule in their hearts, so that they may be at peace with God and one another, the audience are enjoined to be thankful to God (3:15). As a result of their allowing the word of Christ to dwell in them richly, appropriating all the richness of understanding, knowledge, and wisdom which comes from the mystery of Christ, they are enabled in all wisdom to be teaching and admonishing each other. They may actualize their being thankful to God in their corporate worship by gratefully singing, within the realm of the grace of God, with psalms, hymns, and Spiritual songs, appropriate to their being in the realm of the Spirit of God, not only externally with their mouths but internally in their hearts to the God who has chosen them (3:16).

10

Colossians 3:17–4:1

You Have a Master in Heaven (C′)

Work as for the Lord and not human beings
A: ¹⁷ And all, *whatever you do* in word or in *work*, do all things in the name of the Lord Jesus, thanking God the Father through him.
    B: ¹⁸ Wives, submit to your husbands as is fitting in the Lord. ¹⁹ Husbands, love your wives and do not become bitter toward them. ²⁰ Children, *obey* your parents *in all things*, for this is pleasing in the Lord. ²¹ Fathers, do not provoke your children, so that they do not become discouraged.
    B′: ²² Slaves, *obey in all things* those who are your masters according to the flesh, not with eye service as human-pleasers, but with sincerity of heart, fearing the Lord.
A′: ²³ *Whatever you do*, from your soul *work* as for the Lord and not human beings, ²⁴ knowing that from the Lord you will receive the reward of the inheritance; to the Lord Christ be slaves. ²⁵ For the wrongdoer will be paid back for the wrong he has done, and there is no partiality. ⁴:¹ Masters, what is just and fair grant to the slaves, knowing that you also have a Master in heaven.[1]

A. Chiastic Development from Colossians 1:15–23 (C) to 3:17–4:1 (C′)

With Col 3:17–4:1, the C′ unit within the macrochiastic structure embracing the entire letter, the audience hear resonances, by way of the chiastic parallelism, with 1:15–23, the corresponding C unit in the overall chiasm. The exhortation, "whatever you do in word or in work (ἔργῳ), do all things in the name of the Lord Jesus" (3:17), in the C′ unit counters the audience's past behavior regarding their "works"—"and you, once being alienated and enemies in mind in works (ἔργοις) that are evil" (1:21), in the C unit.[2] "Thanking God the Father through him (δι' αὐτοῦ)" (3:17) in the C′ unit complements both "all things through him

---

1. For the establishment of 3:17–4:1 as a chiasm, see ch. 2.
2. These are the last two of the three occurrences of the word "work" in the letter, the first being in 1:10.

(δι' αὐτοῦ) and to him have been created" (1:16) and "through him (δι' αὐτοῦ) to reconcile all things to him, making peace through the blood of the cross, through him (δι' αὐτοῦ)" (1:20) in the C unit.

"Those who are your masters according to the flesh (σάρκα, 3:22)" in the C′ unit, the last occurrence of the word "flesh" in the letter, recalls that "he (God) has now reconciled (you) in the body of his (Christ's) flesh (σαρκός, 1:22)" in the C unit, the first of the nine occurrences of the word "flesh" in the letter. And "knowing that you also have a Master in heaven (οὐρανῷ, 4:1)" in the C′ unit resonates with "(the gospel) which was proclaimed in all creation that is under heaven (οὐρανόν, 1:23)," God's making of peace among all things in the cosmos— "whether the things on the earth or the things in the heavens (οὐρανοῖς, 1:20)," and God's creation in Christ of "all things in the heavens (οὐρανοῖς) and on the earth" (1:16) in the C unit.[3]

B. Audience Response to Colossians 3:17–4:1

1. Col 3:17 (A): Whatever You Do in Word or in Work

The audience then hear a generalizing summary of the previous exhortatory directives given to them (3:12–16): "And all, whatever you do in word or in work, do all things in the name of the Lord Jesus,[4] thanking God the Father through him" (3:17).[5] In all that the audience speaks in "word" (λόγῳ) to one another, as they in all wisdom teach and admonish one another, inspired by the "word" (λόγος) of Christ they are to allow to dwell among and within them (3:16), and in all that they do in "work" (ἔργῳ), in contrast to their former "works" (ἔργοις) that were evil (1:21), and in answer to the authors' prayer that they in every good "work" (ἔργῳ) bear fruit and grow with regard to the knowledge of God (1:10), they are to do all things in the name of the Lord Jesus (3:17a),[6] that is, as believers under the dominion of the lordship of Jesus, the Christ, whom they have received and in whom they are to go on "walking" (2:6).[7]

---

3. These are the last three of the four occurrences of the word "heaven" in the letter, the first being in 1:5.

4. O'Brien, *Colossians*, 211: "The verb in this principal clause has to be supplied, but it is clear from the context that it should be the imperative ποιεῖτε, 'Do.'"

5. Deterding, *Colossians*, 147: "In several ways Paul emphasizes that the Christian is to do *everything* in thanksgiving to God. In addition to the repetition of πᾶς ('everything,' 'all things'), he employs the indefinite relative pronoun (ὅ τι), then heightens its indefiniteness by the addition of ἐάν. In colloquial English, 'everything, whatever *ever* you may do' perhaps captures the flavor of the expression."

6. Dunn, *Colossians*, 240: "The fact that the Lord is here 'the Lord Jesus' is a further indication of the significance of κύριος as attributed to Jesus. Not that Jesus is thought to have taken over, far less usurped, the role of Yahweh; rather, that God has shared his sovereign role with Christ."

7. Wright, *Colossians*, 145: "Acting 'in someone's name' means both representing him and being empowered to do so. Paul's exhortation is therefore a salutary check on behaviour and an encouragement to persevere with difficult tasks undertaken for him, knowing that necessary strength will be provided." Harris, *Colossians*, 171: "'In the name of' could mean 'as representatives of' or 'while calling

Having just been told to be "thankful" (εὐχάριστοι, 3:15), the audience are now directed that in all that they say and do in the name of the Lord Jesus (3:17a) they are to be "thanking" (εὐχαριστοῦντες) God the Father through that Lord Jesus (3:17b).[8] This reinforces the previous directive that the audience are to be "thanking" (εὐχαριστοῦντες) the Father who has made them fit for the share of the inheritance of the holy ones in the light (1:12), and further associates them with the authors of the letter, who "thank" (εὐχαριστοῦμεν) God the Father of our Lord Jesus Christ always when praying for the audience (1:3).[9] When the audience hear the word "God" (τῷ θεῷ) in the directive that they are to be "thanking God the Father," they hear the transitional word that links this unit (3:17–4:1) with the previous one (3:8–16), which concluded with a reference to "God" in the directive that the audience are to be "singing in your heart to God (τῷ θεῷ)" (3:16).

In this A element of the chiasm, then, in every word that the audience speaks and in every work that they do, they are to do everything in the name of their Lord Jesus, gratefully thanking God the Father through that same Lord, the Christ whom they have received and in union with whom they are to conduct all aspects of their lives (3:17; 2:6).

2. Col 3:18–21 (B): Wives Are to Submit to Husbands and Children Are to Obey Parents in Everything

Having been directed in very general terms that they are to do everything in the name of the Lord Jesus (3:17), the audience are given more specific instructions regarding their behavior in correspondence to their various relationships and roles

---

on the name of,' i.e., in prayer. This universal exhortation of v. 17a sums up the more specific preceding injunctions (vv. 12–16). Not only Christian worship (v. 16) but the Christian's entire life should be conducted in Christ's name." O'Brien, *Colossians*, 211–12: "[T]he point is strongly driven home that the Christian's whole life must be lived in obedience to the Lord Jesus. . . . In becoming a Christian the believer calls upon Jesus as Lord (Rom 10:9, 10) and comes under the authority of Christ. He belongs wholly to him; thus everything he says or does ought to be in the light of the fact that Jesus is his Lord. His behavior should be entirely consistent with Jesus' character and this will occur as the word of Christ richly indwells him and other members of the congregation (v 16)." Garland, *Colossians*, 213: "The final admonition in this section, 'Whatever you do . . . do it all in the name of the Lord Jesus' (3:17), recalls the beginning in 2:6, 'So then, just as you received Christ Jesus as Lord, continue to live in him.' It prepares the reader for the next set of instructions in 3:18–4:1, which mentions 'the Lord' seven times." Dunn, *Colossians*, 241: "[T]he thought is of those who have put themselves under the name of Jesus as Lord and who seek to do everything in consciousness of his commissioning and enabling. In this way an effective *inclusio* with the thematic of 2:6–7 is achieved: to walk in Christ Jesus as Lord is to do everything in the name of the Lord Jesus. This is what should mark out the Colossian Christians, in life as in worship, not a hankering for worship with often unnamed angels (2:18)."

8. O'Brien, *Colossians*, 212: "'[T]hrough him' (δι' αὐτοῦ) signifies that Christ is the mediator of the thanksgiving."

9. Harris, *Colossians*, 171: "The expression of thanks to God should be the concomitant of all Christian behavior." See also Ben Witherington, "Do Everything in the Name of God: Ethics and Ethos in Colossians," in *Identity, Ethics, and Ethos in the New Testament* (ed. Jan G. van der Watt; BZNW 141; Berlin: De Gruyter, 2006), 303–33.

within their respective households.¹⁰ The audience as a whole are thus presented with a "household code" beginning with the wife-husband relationship:¹¹ "Wives, submit to your husbands as is fitting in the Lord. Husbands, love your wives and do not become bitter toward them" (3:18-19). As a development and further specification of the audience's doing everything in the name of the "Lord" (κυρίου) Jesus (3:17), the wives among the audience are to submit, subordinate, or subject themselves to, thus recognizing and accepting their God-given and societal role in relation to, their husbands as is fitting in the "Lord" (κυρίω, 3:18).¹² This is fitting or proper behavior "in the Lord," that is, in their union with the Lord Jesus as believers and in the sphere or realm established by the lordship of the Christ, Jesus

---

10. Smith, *Heavenly Perspective*, 201-2: "The household code addresses six different groups of persons, who form three reciprocal relationships (wives-husbands in 3.18-19; children-parents in 3.20-21; slaves-masters in 3.22-4.1). Within each pair, the weaker party is addressed first. The exhortations within the household code are an extension of the virtues already enjoined upon the Colossians in this chapter. All members of the Colossian church were to be controlled by an attitude of humility and gratitude to God, regardless of social standing." See also Carolyn Osiek and David L. Balch, *Families in the New Testament World: Households and House Churches* (Louisville: Westminster John Knox, 1997); S. Wronka, "La proveniensa e il contesto del codice domestico di Col 3,18-4,1," *Analecta Cracoviensia* 36 (2004): 365-80.

11. For recent research on various issues and aspects of the household code in Col 3:18-4:1, see Pierre Jordaan, "The Function of the Household Code in Colossians 3:18-4:1," *Ekklesiastikos Pharos* 80 (1998): 39-46; Andrew T. Lincoln, "The Household Code and Wisdom Mode of Colossians," *JSNT* 74 (1999): 93-112; Angela Standhartinger, "The Origin and Intention of the Household Code in the Letter to the Colossians," *JSNT* 79 (2000): 117-30; John M. G. Barclay, "Ordinary but Different: Colossians and Hidden Moral Identity," *ABR* 49 (2001): 34-52; Suzanne Watts Henderson, "Taking Liberties with the Text: The Colossians Household Code as Hermeneutical Paradigm," *Int* 60 (2006): 420-32; Margaret Y. MacDonald, "Slavery, Sexuality and House Churches: A Reassessment of Colossians 3.18-4.1 in Light of New Research on the Roman Family," *NTS* 53 (2007): 94-113.

12. Harris, *Colossians*, 178: "This apostolic injunction does not imply the inferiority of the wife ... It is a case of voluntary submission in recognition of the God-appointed leadership of the husband and the divinely ordained hierarchical order in creation." O'Brien, *Colossians*, 222: "[T]he admonition is an appeal to free and responsible agents that can only be heeded voluntarily, never by the elimination or breaking of the human will, much less by means of a servile submissiveness.... Paul is not suggesting here that the woman is naturally or spiritually inferior to the man, or the wife to the husband. But he does mention elsewhere that there is a divinely instituted hierarchy in the order of creation, and in this order the wife follows that of her husband (1 Cor 11:3, 7-9)." Dunn, *Colossians*, 247: "The teaching simply reflects the legal state of affairs, under Roman law at least, whereby the *paterfamilias* had absolute power over the other members of the family. And while there were variations in Greek and Jewish law, the basic fact held true throughout the Mediterranean world that the household was essentially a patriarchal institution, with other members of the household subject to the authority of its male head." Henderson, "Taking Liberties," 423: "If a contemporary reader bristles at any injunction to 'be subject,' she must also recognize the chasm that separates her own outlook from that of the letter's original addressees. A secondary assumption that consistently undergirds secular writings on this topic is the notion that orderly management of the household ensures an orderly society, and moreover, that accepting one's place in that order constitutes a noble goal.... In the Colossians' world, the connection between household order and social order was a close one."

the "Lord" (κύριον), whom the audience received as believers and in whom they are to go on "walking," that is, conducting their lives (2:6).[13]

The submission or subordination of the wives in the audience to their husbands (3:18) allows the husbands to play their reciprocal role of loving their wives and not becoming bitter toward them (3:19).[14] The submission or subordination is thus for the purpose of enabling wives to receive love from their husbands. They are to allow and enable their husbands to love them.[15] That husbands are to "love" (ἀγαπᾶτε) their wives actualizes for the marital relationship the "love" (ἀγάπην, 3:14) the audience are to "put on" as the bond of completeness over all the other virtues comprising their moral "clothing" or behavior (3:12–14).[16] Husbands are thus to extend to their wives the love that all believers have received from God as God's chosen ones, who are holy and "beloved" (ἠγαπημένοι) by God (3:12; cf. 1:13).[17] And husbands are to extend to their wives the "love" (ἀγάπην) that the

---

13. Bruce, *Colossians*, 164 n. 178: "The phrase ἐν κυρίῳ occurs four times in Colossians (cf. v. 20; 4:7, 17); it appears some forty times in the Pauline corpus. For its application to domestic relationships cf. 1 Cor. 7:22, 39; Eph. 6:1; Philem. 16. It sums up the relationship existing among fellow-members of Christ—a relationship which does not supersede earthly relationships but subsumes them and lifts them on to a higher plane." Dunn, *Colossians*, 248: "But 'in the Lord' implies . . . that life should be lived in accordance with the traditions received regarding Jesus as Christ and Lord (2:6–7)." Henderson, "Taking Liberties," 424: "Whereas the term 'Christ' appears some twenty-five times in the letter, 'Lord' appears only sixteen times, nine of which are found in the passage under consideration [3:18–4:1]. Particularly in matters that deal with social relationships, the writer asserts that all 'subjugation' occurs within the framework of Christ's lordship. Moreover, the verse that precedes the Code establishes that lordship is the thematic hinge linking the previous passage to the household instruction: 'And whatever you do, in word or deed, do everything in the name of the Lord Jesus . . .' (Col 3:17). While this charge aptly summarizes the paranesis that spans Col 3:1–16, it provides the overarching logic of Christ's lordship that lends coherence to the Household Code as well. The dense concentration of lordship language, together with the concept of lordship as a rhetorical launching point, provide a conceptual foundation for this Code that distinguishes it from the Greco-Roman writings that parallel it. Without challenging hierarchy per se, the writer does introduce a new echelon of authority, another 'lord' strategically positioned above the entire household structure."

14. Garland, *Colossians*, 245: "Paul recognizes that if bitterness is allowed to taint the relationship between husband and wife, the whole household will suffer."

15. Garland, *Colossians*, 244: "The command therefore promotes a demeanor that was believed to help elicit kindness from the husband."

16. Garland, *Colossians*, 244: "Most in the ancient world did not expect a marriage to be grounded in love. It was considered to be an accord, albeit an unequal one, between a man and a woman to produce legitimate heirs." Henderson, "Taking Liberties," 425: "[W]hen the household instruction does address the superior parties, it calls not for the assertion of their control but for the tempering of it. Thus, husbands are urged to love their wives, applying the earlier exhortation to 'clothe yourselves in love' (3:14) to the marriage relationship. . . . the Code subverts authoritarian power by setting ethical standards of love, compassion, and humility for those in the dominant social position."

17. Garland, *Colossians*, 245: "In a Christian marriage, the husband knows himself to be dearly loved by God (3:12) and is commanded to love his wife in the same way. . . . he never thinks in terms of rights and is always willing to forego them."

audience have for all the holy ones (1:4; cf. 1:8), as well as the "love" (ἀγάπη) in which believers are held together (2:2).[18]

The "household code" with which the audience are presented continues with an address of the child-parent relationship: "Children, obey your parents in all things, for this is pleasing in the Lord.[19] Fathers, do not provoke your children, so that they do not become discouraged" (3:20–21). That children are to obey their parents in "all things" (πάντα), for this is pleasing in the "Lord" (κυρίῳ) (3:20) adapts for the child-parent relationship the injunction given to the entire audience that "all" (πᾶν), whatever they do in word or in work, they are to do "all things" (πάντα) in the name of the "Lord" (κυρίου) Jesus (3:17). Just as wives are to submit to their husbands as is fitting "in the Lord" (ἐν κυρίῳ, 3:18), so children are to obey their parents in all things, for this is pleasing "in the Lord" (ἐν κυρίῳ, 3:20), thus continuing and reinforcing the focus on the proper household conduct that is appropriate within the realm or sphere of being in union with the Lord Jesus Christ.[20] Just as there is a reciprocal duty of the husbands to love their wives and not become bitter toward them (3:19), so there is a reciprocal duty of fathers, the paternal, authoritative parents within patriarchal households, not to provoke their children, so that they do not become discouraged (3:21).[21]

---

18. O'Brien, *Colossians*, 223: "Paul has already made reference to 'love' in this letter (2:2; 3:14) and the first recipients would have heard these household rules read publicly at the conclusion of that section in which they were exhorted to put on 'love' as one of the graces of the new man. The injunction to husbands to love their wives is to be understood, in part at least, in the light of that preceding admonition."

19. O'Brien (*Colossians*, 224) points out that children here "are addressed as responsible persons within the congregation and this is noteworthy. The injunction to children, like that to slaves, is put rather more strongly than the one to wives. While the latter was expressed in the middle voice, suggesting voluntary submission, the admonitions to children and slaves are in the active imperative denoting absolute obedience. The absoluteness of the command is strengthened by the phrase 'in all things' (κατὰ πάντα, cf. v 22). Also the verb ὑπακούω (to 'obey') is employed rather than ὑποτάσσομαι ('be subordinate') which may only sometimes imply obedience." Dunn, *Colossians*, 250: "[C]hildren who were presumably still minors are directly addressed; evidently they are thought of as both present in the Christian meeting where the letter would be read out and as responsible agents despite their youth."

20. O'Brien, *Colossians*, 225: "[O]bedience to parents is fit and proper in that sphere in which the Christian now lives, that is, in the new fellowship of those who own Christ as Lord (on this showing the parallel with v 18 is maintained)." Garland, *Colossians*, 246: "Children are told here to 'obey your parents in everything,' a variation of the command to honor one's mother and father (Ex. 20:12).... But the children's duty to obey their parents is transformed into obedience 'in the Lord.' Paul emphasizes a child's pleasing the Lord, not just the parents. He or she owes obedience above all to the Lord. The child's independent relationship with the Lord surpasses the relationship with parents."

21. O'Brien, *Colossians*, 225: "[T]he relationship ἐν κυρίῳ ('in the Lord') was new, and in this household table fathers are told nothing about their power of disposal over their children; instead their duties are spelled out—they are not to provoke or irritate them." Deterding, *Colossians*, 166: "πατέρες here likely singles out fathers for special mention. This does not mean that the injunction is inapplicable to mothers, but it emphasizes that fathers are to take the lead in the nurture of their children." Dunn, *Colossians*, 251: "Corresponding to his responsibility to love his wife, the father has a responsibility not to 'provoke,' that is, 'irritate' or 'embitter' his children.... It is striking, however, that the stress once

In this B element of the chiasm, then, the audience hear of the reciprocal conduct that is fitting and pleasing for wives and husbands as well as for children and parents as believers within the realm of being "in the Lord," within the sphere in which they are united with one another under the lordship of Jesus Christ: Wives are to submit to their husbands as is fitting in the Lord, in order to receive love and not bitterness from their husbands (3:18-19), and children are to obey their parents in all things as is pleasing in the Lord, while fathers are not to provoke or discourage their children (3:20-21).

3. Col 3:22 (B´): Slaves Are to Obey Their Masters in Everything, Fearing the Lord

The "household code" with which the audience are presented continues as the slave-master relationship begins to be addressed: "Slaves, obey in all things those who are your masters according to the flesh,[22] not with eye service as human-pleasers,[23] but with sincerity of heart, fearing the Lord" (3:22).[24] With this injunction to slaves the audience experience the pivot of the chiasm from the B (3:18-21) to the B´ (3:22) element. That slaves are to "obey" (ὑπακούετε) "in all things" (κατὰ πάντα) those who are their masters according to the flesh in the B´ element (3:22a) echoes and recalls, by way of the chiastic parallelism, that children are to "obey" (ὑπακούετε) their parents "in all things" (κατὰ πάντα) in the B element (3:20a).

Previously the audience heard a negative aspect in the injunctions to the authoritatively superior members of the reciprocal household relationships, to the heads of the households in their roles as husbands and fathers. As husbands, they were directed "not" (μή) to become bitter toward their wives (3:19b), and, as fathers, "not" (μή) to provoke their children, so that they do "not" (μή) become

---

again is not on the father's discipline or authority but on his duties." Garland, *Colossians*, 248: "[O]verly stern and heavy-handed parents might drive their children away from the faith."

22. O'Brien, *Colossians*, 226-27: "The expression κατὰ σάρκα κύριοι ('your masters according to the flesh') is not to be understood negatively or disparagingly, but rather shows that they are only lords within an earthly realm, within the sphere of human relations, in contrast to the Lord who is in heaven (cf. 4:1)."

23. On "eye service" (ὀφθαλμοδουλία) here, Harris (*Colossians*, 182) points out: "This word, probably a Pauline coinage, describes (i) service that is concerned only with what the eye can see (i.e., external appearances), (ii) service that is rendered only under the master's eye (i.e, only when he is watching), or (iii) 'service that is performed only to attract attention.'" Dunn, *Colossians*, 254: "Ὀφθαλμοδουλία occurs in Greek only here and in the parallel Eph. 6:6, but it is an effective construct and its meaning is fairly obvious as denoting service performed only to attract attention, lacking in sincerity, going through the visible movements of work without any personal commitment to it."

24. Garland, *Colossians*, 248: "Paul addresses slaves as responsible human beings when most regarded slaves as little more than animated machines.... By assigning them moral duties, Paul treats them as morally responsible individuals.... By issuing them commands, he gives them a measure of respect.... Since Paul begins with commands to slaves and then addresses masters, he has no interest in how to help masters run their slaves more efficiently. He is concerned to enhance the mutual solidarity between slaves and masters."

discouraged (3:21). Now, for the first time, the audience hear a negative aspect in the injunction to the subordinate members of a household relationship, as slaves are directed to obey their human masters "not" (μή) with eye service as human-pleasers, but with sincerity of heart (3:22b).[25]

The audience heard previously that the subordinate members of household relationships are to relate to their superiors out of a Christian motivation. They heard that wives are to submit to their husbands as is fitting in the "Lord" (κυρίῳ, 3:18), and that children are to obey their parents, for this is pleasing in the "Lord" (κυρίῳ, 3:20). And now the audience hear the continuation of this pattern in the motivation for the injunctions to the subordinate members of household relationships, as slaves are to obey their human masters as slaves who fear the "Lord" (κύριον, 3:22c) Jesus Christ (cf. 2:6-7).[26]

In sum, in the B´ element the audience hear that slaves are to obey in all things their human masters not from a motivation of merely trying to please them on an external level, but with an interior sincerity of heart, as part of their reverence for the Lord (3:22).

4. Col 3:23–4:1 (A´): Whatever You Do, Work as for the Lord in Heaven

The audience then hear the continuation of the address to the slaves within the "household code": "Whatever you do, from your soul work as for the Lord and not human beings, knowing that from the Lord you will receive the reward of the inheritance; to the Lord Christ be slaves. For the wrongdoer will be paid back for the wrong he has done, and there is no partiality" (3:23-25). With this A´ element of the chiasm (3:23-4:1) the audience hear a progression, by way of the chiastic parallelism, of the A element (3:17). The command to the entire audience in the A element—"And all, whatever you do (ὅ τι ἐὰν ποιῆτε) in word or in work (ἔργῳ), do all things in the name of the Lord Jesus" (3:17a)—is now developed and applied more specifically in the A´ element to slaves within the household —"Whatever

---

25. Harris, *Colossians*, 182: "The neg. particle οὐ normally negates individual words or phrases; perhaps μή is used here because it negates two phrases—ἐν ὀφθαλμοδουλίᾳ and ὡς ἀνθρωπάρεσκοι."

26. Harris, *Colossians*, 183: "The motive for the slave's wholehearted, obedient service is not to be cringing servility before an earthly master but reverential fear before the heavenly Lord." On "fearing" (φοβούμενοι) the Lord here, O'Brien (*Colossians*, 227-28) notes: "Within the NT φόβος and its cognates are used in the sense of fear, awe and reverence before God or Christ. Such reverence provides both the motive and manner of Christian conduct, not only in a general or basic sense but also in specific life situations within the structures of authority. Thus, the motive of fear turns up some seven times in the household tables (Col 3:22; Eph 6:5; 1 Pet 2:17, 18; 3:2, 6; cf. Eph 5:33). Christian slaves are above all else servants of Christ and they are to work first and foremost so as to please him. Not fear of an earthly master, but reverence for the Lord Christ should be their primary motive." Dunn, *Colossians*, 255: "The further fact that now for the Christians 'the Lord' is Christ confirms not only the thematic role of 2:6-7 but also that the affirmation of Christ as Lord constituted for the first Christians a line of continuity and not breach with their Jewish heritage. Here again the subtext is not only a policy of social quietism in order to avoid attracting hostile attention from the civil authorities, but also a theology of continuity with historic Jewish principles which should help counter the attractiveness of the Colossian synagogue."

you do (ὃ ἐὰν ποιῆτε), from your soul work (ἐργάζεσθε) as for the Lord and not human beings" (3:23).²⁷ Thus, although they are subordinate members according to their social status within households, slaves are nevertheless placed on par with all the other members of the audience when it comes to their behavior as believers.

The command for slaves to obey their masters not "as" (ὡς) "human-pleasers" (ἀνθρωπάρεσκοι) but with sincerity of heart, fearing "the Lord" (τὸν κύριον) (3:22) is reinforced with the further elaboration that they are to work from their soul "as" (ὡς) to "the Lord" (τῷ κυρίῳ) and not "human beings" (ἀνθρώποις) (3:23).²⁸ The motivation for the obedience of slaves continues to be focused on their relationship to the Lord, as they are addressed as those knowing that from the "Lord" (κυρίου) they will receive the reward of the inheritance (3:24a). That slaves will receive from the Lord the reward of the "inheritance" (κληρονομίας) recalls that God the Father has made the entire Colossian audience fit to share in the "inheritance" (κλήρου) of the holy ones—all believers—in the light (1:12). This makes not only the slaves but the audience as a whole realize that, despite their inferior social status, slaves have a share in the "inheritance" to which all believers are destined, thus reinforcing the assertion that in the new situation brought about by Christ there is not "barbarian, Scythian, slave, free, but Christ is all and in all" (3:11).²⁹

The emphatic reminder that the "slaves" (δοῦλοι, 3:22) "are to be slaves" (δουλεύετε) to the Lord Christ (3:24b) reinforces the concerted concentration of the motivation for the slaves' obedience on their relationship to the Lord Jesus

---

27. O'Brien, *Colossians*, 228: "It is just possible that ἐργάζεσθε ('do the work') is an advance upon ποιῆτε ('do'), because the things done are ἔργα ('works')."
28. O'Brien, *Colossians*, 228: "As they engage in whole-hearted work for their masters so in that very action they are serving their heavenly Lord."
29. Wright, *Colossians*, 150: "One should properly read '*the* inheritance'; the reference is clearly to the life of the age to come. This is ironic, since in earthly terms slaves could not inherit property" (Wright's emphasis). O'Brien, *Colossians*, 229: "Retribution might be what the slave would normally expect from his earthly lord. This Lord is different giving as his reward an eternal inheritance of life in the age to come." Dunn, *Colossians*, 257: "The paradox of slaves becoming heirs of God's kingdom would not be lost on the Colossians. Under Roman law slaves could not inherit anything; so it was only by being integrated into this distinctively Jewish heritage that their legal disability as slaves could be surmounted. This persistent Jewish character of the gospel preached to the Colossians would help explain both the further attraction to the Gentile Christians of the more elaborate Jewish worship practiced in Colossae and the degree of antipathy shown to the new movement by (some of) the Colossian Jews." MacDonald, "Slavery," 108: "[W]hat is striking in Colossians is that this inheritance is not merely metaphorically promised to the whole community, but explicitly so to the group of real slaves who otherwise stand outside the domain of real inheritance. However difficult it is to determine how it was being lived . . . something has changed for slaves in house church communities. Col 3.11 suggests that this change was experienced in baptism and reaffirmed in worship through mutual admonition and the giving of thanks to a new patron, God the Father (Col 3.15–17)."

Christ.³⁰ They are to obey their masters as slaves fearing the "Lord" (κύριον, 3:22), as slaves working as for the "Lord" (κυρίῳ, 3:23), as slaves knowing the inheritance they will receive from the "Lord" (κυρίου, 3:24a), since, as slaves, they are to be slaves above all to the "Lord" (κυρίῳ) Christ.³¹ That they are to be slaves to the "Lord Christ" (κυρίῳ Χριστῷ) reminds them that since they, like the whole Colossian audience, have received the "Christ" (Χριστόν), Jesus the "Lord" (κύριον), in him they are to go on "walking" (2:6), that is, conducting their lives as obedient slaves within the household. As a final boost to the motivation for the slaves' obedience, they are solemnly warned that the wrongdoer will be paid back by God (divine passive) for the wrong he has done, and there is no partiality when it comes to God's judgment (3:25).³²

The "household code" directed to the audience reaches its climactic conclusion with the address to the masters of the slaves: "Masters, what is just and fair grant to the slaves, knowing that you also have a Master in heaven" (4:1). Just as the motivation for the obedience of the slaves to their human "masters" (κυρίοις, 3:22) was grounded in what they know about their "Lord"—"knowing that" (εἰδότες ὅτι) from their "Lord" (κυρίου) they will receive the reward of the inheritance (3:24a), so the motivation for the just and fair treatment of the slaves by their masters is grounded in what they, as "masters" (κύριοι), know about their "Lord"—"knowing that" (εἰδότες ὅτι) they have a "Lord" (κύριον), who is indeed their "Master," in heaven (4:1).³³ Following upon the emphatic reminder that it is to the "Lord" (κυρίῳ) Christ that the slaves are to be slaves (3:24b), the address to the masters makes not only the masters and slaves of the households but the audience as a whole realize that there is a profound sense in which they and all believers are indeed "slaves" who have a "Master/Lord" (κύριον) in heaven. This thus climactically

---

30. Wright, *Colossians*, 150: "The force of this unusual phrase could be brought out by a paraphrase: 'so work for the true Master—Christ!'" Wilson, *Colossians*, 285: "[T]he words τῷ κυρίῳ Χριστῷ ['to Lord Christ'] are brought forward into an emphatic position at the beginning." For the reasons for construing δουλεύετε as an imperative rather than an indicative, see Harris, *Colossians*, 186; O'Brien, *Colossians*, 229.

31. Dunn, *Colossians*, 257: "The triple repetition suggests that slaves would need to keep reminding themselves that their loyalty to Christ transcended their loyalty to their masters, thus making it easier to bear the harsher features of their enslavement."

32. O'Brien, *Colossians*, 231: "Righteous behavior is required of slaves and masters alike." Dunn, *Colossians*, 258: "The force of this warning or reassurance is twofold: it encouraged harshly treated slaves that their masters could not escape the judgment, in the final judgment if not in this life, and it warned the slaves themselves to maintain their own high standards of integrity so far as possible."

33. O'Brien, *Colossians*, 233: "The relationship between masters and slaves has undergone a basic change. Both owe obedience to the one Lord and therefore both have the true standard for their conduct toward one another." MacDonald, "Slavery," 112: "Taken together with the directives concerning sexual propriety in Colossians, there seems good reason to believe that the sexual violation of slaves and the break-up of slave families—so closely associated with the lack of honour attributed to slaves generally—was something to be avoided by masters in the *ekklesia* who sought to treat their slaves 'justly and fairly.'"

reinforces the assertion that in and through the heavenly Lordship of Christ the societal distinction between slave and free has been transcended (3:11).

The audience heard how the motivation for the behavior of the subordinates to the heads of households is to be determined by the Lordship of Christ. Wives are to submit to their husbands, who are the heads of households, as is fitting in the *Lord* (3:18). Children are to obey their parents in all things, for this is pleasing to the *Lord* (3:20). Slaves are to obey their human masters in all things, fearing the *Lord* (3:22), knowing that from the *Lord* they will receive the reward of the inheritance (3:24a), for it is above all to the *Lord* Christ that they are to be slaves (3:24b). That the Lordship of Christ is to be the motivation for the reciprocal behavior of husbands (3:19) and fathers (3:21), as heads of households, is surely implicit. But only now, as the climactic conclusion of the "household code," do the audience explicitly and emphatically hear how the motivation for the behavior of the superiors, the heads of households, is likewise to be determined by the heavenly Lordship of Christ:[34] Masters are to grant what is just and fair to the slaves, knowing that they also have a Master, the *Lord* Christ, in heaven (4:1).[35]

The assertion at the conclusion of this C′ chiasm (3:17–4:1) that masters, as indeed all believers, have a Master/Lord, namely the Lord Christ, in "heaven" (οὐρανῷ) thus recalls and develops for the audience the conclusion of the C chiasm (1:15–23). There Paul asserted that he became a minister of the gospel that was proclaimed in all creation that is under "heaven" (οὐρανόν, 1:23), that is, as now becomes clear, under the heavenly lordship of Jesus Christ. The audience are to realize then that Christ is the heavenly Lord not only of the different household relationships, but of all creation, for in him were created all things in the "heavens" (οὐρανοῖς) and on the earth (1:16a). He is also the heavenly Lord of the reconciliation and peaceful existence of all things within creation, since through Christ God reconciled and brought to peace all things, whether the things on the earth

---

34. Dunn, *Colossians*, 259: "[T]he *paterfamilias* is now addressed for the third time—the first as husband, then as father, now as master. The greater his authority, the greater his responsibility."

35. Dunn, *Colossians*, 259: "The Christian master will grant his slaves what is 'just,' in contrast to the injustice envisaged in 3:25." Garland, *Colossians*, 251: "[M]asters are not free to set their own standards on how to treat their slaves; rather, it must match what any would regard as 'right and fair.'" Wilson, *Colossians*, 286–87: "[M]asters were concerned to get the best out of their slaves, and in any consideration for their welfare the primary thought was likely to be maintaining their fitness for work rather than the well-being of the slaves themselves. A slave who did not meet the required standard would soon be got rid of. Here again we have to remember the circumstances in which these early Christians lived: it simply was not possible for them to advocate far-reaching measures of social-reform." Smith, *Heavenly Perspective*, 202–3: "What relevance, if any, does the household code have to the Colossian error? The adoption of social conventions may be seen as a reaction to the asceticism of the philosophy whose adherents wanted to keep themselves pure from the simple duties of family life. However, the life that is focused on the things above where Christ is (3.2), is indeed a life of everyday marriage, parenthood and work. The fact that Paul is referring to heavenly-mindedness in all this can be seen in how he motivates masters to deal fairly with their slaves. The masters' relationship with their slaves is determined by their own relationship with their Master in heaven, as expressed in 4.1."

or the things in the "heavens" (οὐρανοῖς) (1:20). Because of the reconciliation and peace of all things through the heavenly Lord Christ, "there is not Greek and Jew, circumcision and uncircumcision, barbarian, Scythian, slave, free, but Christ is all and in all" (3:11).[36] The heavenly Lordship of the Christ is thus to be the dominating motivation for how household members relate to one another.[37]

In sum, in this A′ element (3:23–4:1), following upon the emphatic reminder that it is to the "Lord" Christ that the slaves are to be slaves (3:24b), the address to the masters makes not only the masters (4:1) and slaves (3:23-25) of the households but the audience as a whole realize that there is a profound sense in which they and all believers are indeed "slaves" who have a "Master/Lord" in heaven. This thus climactically reinforces the assertion that in and through the heavenly Lordship of Christ the societal distinction between slave and free has been transcended (3:11). The heavenly Lordship of Christ (1:23) in whom were created all things in the "heavens" (1:16a) and through whom God brought reconciliation and peace to all things, whether on the earth or in the "heavens" (1:20), is thus to be the dominating motivation for how believing household members relate to one another.

C. Summary on Colossians 3:17–4:1

1. In every word that the audience speaks and in every work that they do, they are to do everything in the name of their Lord Jesus, gratefully thanking God the Father through that same Lord, the Christ whom they have received and in union with whom they are to conduct all aspects of their lives (3:17; 2:6).

2. The audience hear of the reciprocal conduct that is fitting and pleasing for wives and husbands as well as for children and parents as believers within the realm of being "in the Lord," within the sphere in which they are united with one another under the lordship of Jesus Christ: Wives are to submit to their husbands as is fit-

---

36. Smith, *Heavenly Perspective*, 203: "The Colossian errorists were focused on the cosmic realm. Paul shows that true heavenly-mindedness is to be lived out in earthly existence as a reflection of cosmic reconciliation. For those who are 'in Christ' this reconciliation is borne out in everyday relationships within church, family and work that bring unity despite social, ethnic and class barriers. Such an understanding of heavenly-minded reconciliation is the opposite to the practices of the errorists, whose focus on the things of heaven led to division and elitism."

37. Bevere, *Sharing*, 253–54: "The house-code is one more example of how the Colossians are to live ἐν κυρίῳ, as persons who no longer live in the shadow of what was to come, but in the fullness of what has come in Christ.... the house-code could be a response to an accusation from the synagogue that the Colossian Christians, who were not playing by the rules of Judaism, were also not playing by the rules of what ordered a good household.... Thus the *Haustafel* was another way of reminding the Colossians they could be faithful 'in the Lord' as Gentile believers without taking on Jewish identity, even in the household." Smith, *Heavenly Perspective*, 203: "In a congregation that was overly concerned with asceticism, visions and angelic worship, all of which led to inflated pride, the household code is used to recall the simple duties of family life and to correct social behaviour as a demonstration of what it means to set one's mind on things above (3.2)."

ting in the Lord, in order to receive love and not bitterness from their husbands (3:18–19), and children are to obey their parents in all things as is pleasing in the Lord, while fathers are not to provoke or discourage their children (3:20–21).

3. The audience hear that slaves are to obey in all things their human masters not from a motivation of merely trying to please them on an external level, but with an interior sincerity of heart, as part of their reverence for the Lord (3:22).

4. Following upon the emphatic reminder that it is to the "Lord" Christ that the slaves are to be slaves (3:24b), the address to the masters makes not only the masters (4:1) and slaves (3:23–25) of the households but the audience as a whole realize that there is a profound sense in which they and all believers are indeed "slaves" who have a "Master/Lord" in heaven. This thus climactically reinforces the assertion that in and through the heavenly Lordship of Christ the societal distinction between slave and free has been transcended (3:11). The heavenly Lordship of Christ (1:23) in whom were created all things in the "heavens" (1:16a) and through whom God brought reconciliation and peace to all things, whether on the earth or in the "heavens" (1:20), is thus to be the dominating motivation for how believing household members relate to one another.

11

Colossians 4:2–6

Pray for Us in Thanksgiving and Walk in Wisdom (B′)

That God may open for us a door for the word about the mystery of Christ
A: ² In prayer persevere, being watchful in it in thanksgiving, ³ᵃ praying at the same time also for us, that God may open to us a door for the *word*
　B: ³ᶜ to *speak* the mystery of the Christ,
　　C: ³ᵈ on account of which indeed I have been bound,
　B′: ⁴ that I may manifest it as it is necessary for me to *speak*.
A′: ⁵ In wisdom walk toward those outside, making the most of the opportunity. ⁶ Let your *word* always be in grace, seasoned with salt, to know how it is necessary for you to answer each one.[1]

A. Chiastic Development from Colossians 1:3–14 (B) to 4:2–6 (B′)

With Col 4:2–6, the B′ unit within the letter's macrochiastic structure, the audience hear echoes of 1:3–14, the corresponding B unit in the overall chiasm. The directives regarding the audience's praying for Paul and Timothy in the B′ unit—"in prayer (προσευχῇ) persevere" (4:2a) and "praying (προσευχόμενοι) at the same time also for us" (4:3a)—recall the repeated reports of Paul and Timothy's reciprocal praying for the audience in the B unit—"always when praying (προσευχόμενοι) for you" (1:3b) and "we do not cease praying (προσευχόμενοι) on behalf of you" (1:9a). And likewise, the audience's "being watchful in it (prayer) in thanksgiving (εὐχαριστίᾳ)" (4:2b) in the B′ unit recalls and reciprocates Paul and Timothy's "thanking (εὐχαριστοῦμεν) God the Father of our Lord Jesus Christ" (1:3a) and "thanking (εὐχαριστοῦντες) the Father" (1:12a) in the B unit.

The prayer, "that God may open for us a door for the word (λόγου)" (4:3b), and the exhortation, "let your word (λόγος) always be in grace" (4:6a), in the B′ unit recall that the audience have heard before of the hope laid up for them in the heavens "in the word (λόγῳ) of the truth of the gospel" (1:5b) in the B unit. And the exhortation to the audience, "in wisdom (σοφίᾳ) walk (περιπατεῖτε) toward

---

1. For the establishment of 4:2–6 as a chiasm, see ch. 2.

those outside" (4:5a), in the B´ unit recalls the prayer for the audience "in all wisdom (σοφίᾳ) and Spiritual understanding, to walk (περιπατῆσαι) worthy of the Lord" (1:9b-10a) in the B unit.

B. Audience Response to Colossians 4:2–6

1. Col 4:2–3a (A): That God May Open to Us a Door for the Word

The audience hear more exhortatory directives, this time regarding their relationship with the authors of the letter: "In prayer persevere, being watchful in it in thanksgiving, praying at the same time also for us, that God may open to us a door for the word" (4:2-3b). When the audience hear the words "also for us" (καὶ περὶ ἡμῶν), they hear the transitional words that link this unit (4:2-6) with the previous one (3:17-4:1), which concluded with the resonant reciprocal words "you also" in the statement that "you also (καὶ ὑμεῖς) have a master in heaven" (4:1).

At the beginning of the letter the audience heard how the praying of the authors for them was closely combined with their thanksgiving to God: "We thank (εὐχαριστοῦμεν) God the Father of our Lord Jesus Christ always when praying (προσευχόμενοι) for you (περὶ ὑμῶν)" (1:3). The audience were assured of the authors' perseverance in this regard, as they repeat: "We do not cease praying (προσευχόμενοι) on behalf of you (ὑπὲρ ὑμῶν)" (1:9). The audience are likewise to be "thanking (εὐχαριστοῦντες) the Father" (1:12), "abounding in thanksgiving (εὐχαριστίᾳ)" (2:7), "be thankful (εὐχάριστοι)" (3:15), and "thanking (εὐχαριστοῦντες) God the Father through him (Christ)" (3:17). And now, just as the authors do not cease in praying for the audience when they thank God, so the audience are to "persevere in prayer (προσευχῇ), being watchful in it in thanksgiving (εὐχαριστίᾳ)" (4:2).[2] They are to be "praying" (προσευχόμενοι) not only for themselves but at the same time, in reciprocation of the authors' praying for them, "for us" (περὶ ἡμῶν)—Paul and Timothy (4:3a; cf. 1:1-2).[3]

But the audience's praying for the authors is to contain a very specific petition: "that God may open to us a door for the word" (4:3b). It was "in the word (λόγῳ) of the truth of the gospel" that the audience heard before of the hope laid up for them in the heavens (1:5). Indeed, this "word" is bearing fruit and growing in all the world (1:6). To Paul, who became a minister of the word of the gospel, which was proclaimed in all creation that is under heaven (1:23), it was given according

---

2. Harris, *Colossians*, 193: "Paul is encouraging mental and spiritual alertness in prayer, perhaps even watchfulness against temptation or for the Advent." Dunn, *Colossians*, 262: "The other accompanying exhortation is once again that their prayers should be made in a spirit of thanksgiving (ἐν εὐχαριστίᾳ). This repeated emphasis in Colossians makes it one of the most 'thankful' documents in the New Testament (1:3, 12; 2:7; 3:17; 4:2). Here it provides an important balance to the call for watchfulness: they are to keep alert, not in a spirit of fear or anxiety, but with the confidence and assurance that their resources (in Christ) are more than equal to the potential challenges."

3. Harris, *Colossians*, 193: "Περί here does not mean 'concerning,' but 'for' = 'on behalf of'; it is equivalent to ὑπέρ and introduces the person in whose interest the petition is being made."

to the plan of God to fulfill for the Colossian audience the "word" (λόγον) of God (1:25). This "word" stands in contrast to the "word" (λόγον) or "reputation" of wisdom (2:23) claimed by the "philosophy" of empty deceit that threatens to captivate the audience (2:8). The audience are to let the "word" (λόγος) of Christ dwell in them richly so that in all wisdom they may teach and admonish each other (3:16), as Paul and Timothy admonish and teach every human being in all wisdom (1:28). And so now the audience are to pray that God may open a door to Paul and Timothy for the "word" (λόγου) of the gospel about Christ to be proclaimed by them, so that it may be heard and received elsewhere in all the world as it was heard and received by the audience at Colossae (4:3b).[4]

In this A element (4:2-3b), then, the audience are told to persevere in prayer in thanksgiving, praying for the authors as they have not ceased to pray for the audience, and praying specifically that God may open for Paul and Timothy a door for the word of the gospel about Christ, that it may be heard and received by others as it was by the Colossian believers.

2. Col 4:3c (B): To Speak the Mystery of the Christ

The purpose of the audience's intercessory prayer that God may open for Paul and Timothy a door for the word is then elaborated: "to speak the mystery of the Christ" (4:3c). As the audience have already heard, the "word" of the truth of the gospel about the hope laid up for them in the heavens (1:5), the "word" of God (1:25), has been further described as the "mystery" (μυστήριον), hidden from the ages and from the generations, but now manifested to God's holy ones to make known what is the richness of the glory of this "mystery" (μυστηρίου) among the Gentiles, which is Christ among you, the hope of the glory (1:26-27). The audience have also heard of Paul's great personal struggle to extend to those who have not seen him the knowledge of the "mystery" (μυστηρίου) of God, Christ, in whom are all the treasures of wisdom and knowledge hidden (2:1-3). And so now, in this B element, the audience are exhorted to play their role in Paul's ministry by praying that God may open a door to Paul and Timothy for the "word," so that they may speak the "mystery" (μυστήριον) of the Christ (4:3c) for other Gentiles to know, as do the believers at Colossae, of the hope of the glory laid up for them in the heavens (1:26-27; 2:1-3).[5]

---

4. Wright, *Colossians*, 152: "Paul refers to the 'door' that allows the word of God into the hearts, minds and lives of individuals and communities." Harris, *Colossians*, 193: "'that God may open up for us a door' = '... may afford us opportunities' or '... may provide us with an opening.'" O'Brien, *Colossians*, 239: "Within the New Testament this picture of an open door, which is used in missionary contexts, denotes the provision of opportunity. God opens a door for the missionary by giving him a field in which to work (1 Cor 16:9; 2 Cor 2:12) and he opens a door of faith to Gentiles so that they might believe (Acts 14:27)."

5. O'Brien, *Colossians*, 239: "Once again in Colossians the word 'mystery' is used to denote God's plan of salvation centered in Christ and which has special reference to Gentiles... it is in the effective preaching and teaching of the gospel that the mystery is made known." Dunn, *Colossians*, 263: "The content here of his speaking is the 'mystery of [the] Christ,' that is, the mystery which is Christ and

3. Col 4:3d (C): On Account of Which Indeed I Have Been Bound

The audience then hear a focus on Paul's personal relationship to the mystery of the Christ (4:3c) with regard to his current situation of imprisonment, which only now, for the first time in the letter, receives explicit and emphatic expression: "on account of which indeed I have been bound" (4:3d).[6] In Paul's disclosure that "I have been (and still am) bound" (δέδεμαι, perfect tense) the audience are to hear an artful double meaning.[7] On the one hand, that Paul is "bound" on account of the mystery of the Christ expresses the reason why he finds himself physically bound in chains at the hands of Roman authorities. But on the other hand, that Paul is "bound" on account of the mystery of the Christ expresses his metaphorical or spiritual "binding" by God as a minister of the gospel (1:23) and of the church (1:24), who is "bound," necessitated, and completely devoted to proclaiming this mystery. The audience have already heard that Paul became a minister *according to the plan of God* that was given to him, or that "bound" him, to proclaim the mystery of the Christ to every human being (1:25-28). Indeed, Paul has been physically bound in chains precisely because he has been spiritually bound by God's plan.

The artful double meaning of the expression that Paul has been "bound" on account of the mystery of the Christ in this central C element (4:3d), then, assures the audience that Paul's current physical "binding" in chains by human beings is subsumed within his spiritual "binding" by God to be a minister of the gospel and of the church, a minister who is "bound" to proclaim that mystery to every human being (1:23-28).[8]

---

which Christ has unveiled. This was certainly a primary theme of the letter itself (1:26-27; 2:2), so the request at this point is a way of reinforcing the emphasis of the letter."

6. Harris, *Colossians*, 195: "Καί may be emphatic ('because of which I am, *in fact*, in prison') or else strengthens the rel[ative pronoun]. and either remains untranslated or has the sense, 'because of this *very* mystery.'" Wilson, *Colossians*, 291: "On the traditional view of Col., taking it as a 'captivity' epistle, one naturally thinks of the Jewish hostility to Paul's gospel for the Gentiles, which led to his arrest in the Temple and subsequent imprisonment."

7. That no agent is expressed for the passive "I have been bound" facilitates the double meaning. It allows for the understanding that Paul has been bound by both human authorities and by God. O'Brien, *Colossians*, 240: "This is the only place in which Paul uses this verb in a literal sense, though he employs δεσμοί of his 'bonds' or 'fetters' at Philippians 1:7, 13, 14, 17; Colossians 4:18 and Philemon 10, 13 (cf. 2 Tim 1:8)."

8. Wright, *Colossians*, 152: "Paul's sufferings and present imprisonment were therefore, as he indicated in 1:24, part and parcel of his apostolic vocation, which itself was bound up with the mystery of Christ." Dunn, *Colossians*, 263-64: "This, of course, does not refer to the formal charge on which Paul had been imprisoned, but indicates rather the Pauline perspective: since preaching this mystery was his primary raison d'être, this was also the reason for his imprisonment. It was this preaching which had incited the opposition to him and resulted in his imprisonment; but he also believed that the imprisonment was itself part of God's eschatological purpose to unfold the mystery." Cassidy, *Paul in Chains*, 90: "Paul's status as a chained prisoner has resulted from his faithfulness on Christ's behalf. The Christians at Colossae are not to think that Paul has been involved in any form of wrongdoing. Rather, it is because of his efforts 'to declare the mystery of Christ' that Paul now finds himself in Roman custody. There is a note of nobility and idealism proclaimed here. Paul has been zealous as regards God's saving purpose

4. Col 4:4 (B ′): That I May Manifest It as It Is Necessary for Me to Speak

Paul then discloses the more specific and personal reason the audience are to pray that God may open a door for him to speak the mystery of the Christ, on account of which he is bound (4:2–3): "That I may manifest it as it is necessary for me to speak" (4:4).[9] After the transition to a verb in the first person singular, "I have been bound," in the central C element (4:3d) of the chiasm, the audience hear a pivotal development, by way of the chiastic parallelism, from the general purpose "to speak" (λαλῆσαι) the "mystery of the Christ" in the B element (4:3c) to an individual focus on Paul himself "to speak" (λαλῆσαι) it in the B′ element (4:4).[10]

With the expression, "that I may manifest (φανερώσω) it" (4:4a), the audience are to hear Paul's desire to play his role in God's plan that the mystery of the Christ, which "has been manifested" (ἐφανερώθη) by God to God's holy ones (1:26), may also be "manifested"—ultimately by God but through Paul—to others as well, indeed, to every human being (1:27–28). Then, as "you," the audience, "will be manifested" (φανερωθήσεσθε) with Christ in glory, whenever the Christ is finally "manifested" (φανερωθῇ) by God (3:4), then those who are still to hear and receive the mystery through its "manifestation" by Paul will likewise participate in the final manifestation of Christ in glory.[11]

With the expression, "as it is necessary for me to speak" (4:4bc), the audience hear the completion of a mini-chiasm concerning the "binding/necessity" of Paul to speak the mystery of the Christ in 4:3c–4:

a) to speak (λαλῆσαι) the mystery of the Christ (4:3c)
   b) on account of which indeed I have been bound (δέδεμαι) (4:3d)
   b′) that I may manifest it as it is necessary (δει) for me (4:4ab)
a′) to speak (λαλῆσαι) (4:4c)[12]

The "a" sub-element of this mini-chiasm expresses the more general reason the audience are to pray for God to open a door for the word (4:3b)—for "us,"

---

in Christ for Jews and Gentiles alike. And it is because of his unswerving commitment to this high mission that he presently suffers confinement and constraint."

9. O'Brien, *Colossians*, 240: "[T]he ἵνα clause, 'that . . . ,' of v 4 is dependent on the preceding ἵνα ὁ θεὸς ἀνοίξῃ, 'that God may open . . . ,' of v 3."

10. O'Brien, *Colossians*, 240: "The transition to the singular was natural since he moved from what was common to himself and others to what was peculiar to himself."

11. O'Brien, *Colossians*, 240: "[W]hen Paul's activity is described as making known the mystery its unique significance of being the proclamation of divine revelation is emphasized. What is elsewhere called the work of God is here said to be Paul's activity, no doubt because of his key role in the plan of God that includes Gentiles. His ministry has salvation historical significance. Yet it is no less the revelation of God for all that, since it is God who is asked to open a door for the Word and it is he alone who can enable the apostle to publish the mystery openly and in a manner that Paul ought to."

12. This chiastic substructure has been suggested by Bockmuehl, *Revelation*, 192. For a discussion of a variant reading in 4:3, see also Markus N. A. Bockmuehl, "A Note on the Text of Colossians 4:3," *JTS* 39 (1988): 489–94; Wilson, *Colossians*, 292.

presumably Paul and Timothy but perhaps others as well, "to speak" the mystery of the Christ (4:3c). The "b" sub-element assures the audience that it is on account of this mystery that Paul has been "bound" both by human beings and by God (4:3d). In the "b'" sub-element the audience hear the chiastic pivot to an emphasis on the divine necessity or "binding" for Paul's personal responsibility as a minister to manifest the mystery—"it is necessary for me" (δεῖ με), that is, Paul is necessitated or "bound" by God's plan to manifest this mystery (4:4ab).[13] With the "a'" sub-element the audience hear the transition from the general purpose "to speak" the mystery of the Christ to the more specific and personal responsibility of Paul in particular "to speak" this mystery (4:4c).[14]

The B' element, "that I may manifest it as it is necessary for me to speak" (4:4), impresses upon the audience their need to pray for the divine assistance Paul in particular needs to complete his ministry to manifest the mystery of the Christ to every human being, as he is divinely "bound" and necessitated to speak it (4:2-3).[15]

5. Col 4:5–6 (A'): Let Your Word Always Be in Grace

The audience then hear how they are to behave toward and communicate with outsiders: "In wisdom walk toward those outside, making the most of the opportunity. Let your word always be in grace, seasoned with salt, to know how it is necessary for you to answer each one" (4:5-6). In the A element (4:2-3b) the audience were exhorted to pray that God may open for us a door for the "word" (λόγου, 4:3b). And now, by way of the chiastic parallelism, the audience are exhorted to let their own "word" (λόγος, 4:6) toward outsiders always be in grace in the A' element (4:5-6). Thus, the audience hear a progression from a focus on the extension to others of the "word" of the gospel about Christ in the A element to a focus on their own "word" in communicating with others in the A' element.

The authors of the letter, Paul and Timothy, do not cease praying that the au-

---

13. The parallelism between the two forms of the verb "bind" (δέω) is enhanced by the alliterative word play between them—"I have been bound" (δέ-δε-μαι) and "it is necessary for me" or "I am bound" (δεῖ με). O'Brien, *Colossians*, 240: "[T]he final clause ὡς δεῖ με λαλῆσαι could refer to the necessity of the preaching (so keeping strictly to the meaning of δεῖ) and be rendered 'since I am bound to speak it' (see 1 Cor 9:16; Acts 23:11)." Bockmuehl, *Revelation*, 192: "Paul's chains may in this passage be seen as illustrative, indeed as symbolic of his ministry: he is *bound* to speak" (Bockmuehl's emphasis). Garland, *Colossians*, 273: "A better translation might be, 'as I am bound to do.' Paul is bound more by his commission to preach the gospel (1 Cor. 9:16-23) than by his chains." Dunn, *Colossians*, 264: "The verse underlines Paul's own conviction that he has been given the primary privilege, as apostle to the Gentiles, to disclose the secret of God's overarching design in creation and salvation. This sense here is reinforced by δεῖ, indicating a predestined destiny and unavoidable compulsion."

14. This text asserts "not simply that Paul is bound for the sake of the mystery of Christ, but that in fact his preaching and his very bonds together constitute his manifestation of the mystery," according to Bockmuehl, "Note," 493.

15. There are four characteristics of prayer present in 4:2-4—persistence, vigilance, thankfulness, and mission-mindedness—according to J. P. Sweeney, "The Priority of Prayer in Colossians 4:2-4," *BSac* 159 (2002): 318-33.

dience may be filled with the knowledge of God's will in all "wisdom" (σοφίᾳ) and Spiritual understanding (1:9). They proclaim Christ, admonishing every human being and teaching every human being in all "wisdom" (σοφίᾳ), that they may present every human being complete in Christ (1:28), in whom are all the treasures of "wisdom" (σοφίας) and knowledge hidden (2:3). This wisdom is in contrast to the "philosophy" of empty deceit (2:8), which has a reputation for "wisdom" (σοφίας) but is without value (2:23). Imitating Paul and Timothy, the audience are in all "wisdom" (σοφίᾳ) to be teaching and admonishing each other (3:16). And now, the audience hear how it is in this "wisdom" (σοφίᾳ) that comes from Christ that they are to "walk" or conduct themselves toward those outside the community of believers (4:5).[16]

Being filled with this wisdom that comes from Christ (1:9) enables the audience to "walk" (περιπατῆσαι), that is, behave or conduct themselves, worthy of the Lord for every desire to please, in every good work bearing fruit and growing with regard to the knowledge of God (1:10). The audience were exhorted that as believers "you are to go on walking" (περιπατεῖτε)" in the Christ whom they received (2:6) rather than be captivated through the philosophy of empty deceit (2:8), which is devoid of authentic wisdom (2:23). They are to behave in contrast to the way "you walked" (περιεπατήσατέ) once as non-believers in Christ (3:7). And now, within the sphere of the wisdom hidden in Christ in which they find themselves as believers, the audience are directed to "walk" (περιπατεῖτε) or conduct themselves toward those outside who are not yet believers, making the most of the opportunity (4:5).[17]

The audience came to know the "grace" (χάριν) of God in truth (1:6), the "grace" (χάρις) Paul wishes to continue to come to them from God as faithful brothers in Christ (1:2), when they heard of the hope laid up for them in the heavens in the "word" (λόγῳ) of the truth of the gospel (1:5), the "word" (λόγον) of God that Paul is to fulfill for them (1:25). They were exhorted to let this "word" (λόγος) of Christ dwell in them richly, so that in all the wisdom that comes from this word they may be able to teach and admonish each other with psalms, hymns, and Spiritual songs, singing in their hearts to God "in grace" (ἐν χάριτι), within the new situation in which they find themselves as grateful recipients of redemption, the forgiveness of sins (1:14), and the reconciliation God has graciously granted them (1:21-22). And now, the audience, in addition to praying that God may open

---

16. "Those outside" (τοὺς ἔξω) "were the proper targets for evangelistic activity, but they would be put off rather than encouraged to come inside by unworthy conduct on the part of Christians," according to Bruce, *Colossians*, 174 n. 16.

17. On "making the most (ἐξαγοραζόμενοι) of the opportunity," O'Brien (*Colossians*, 241) notes: "The verb ἐξαγοράζω ('buy,' 'buy up,' 'redeem') is drawn from the commercial language of the market place (ἀγορά), and its prefix, the preposition ἐκ, denotes an intensive activity, a buying which exhausts the possibilities available." Harris, *Colossians*, 196: "As well as referring to 'time' in general, καιρός often denotes critical or unique time, a moment of destiny, a fitting season. Here it refers to each opportunity or all the opportunities afforded by time."

a door for the "word" (λόγου) about Christ (4:3b), that Paul may proclaim and manifest it to others (4:3c-4), are to let their own "word" (λόγος) spoken to non-believing outsiders always be "in grace" (ἐν χάριτι), "seasoned with salt" (4:6a),[18] inspired and imbued with the "word" of the truth of the gospel in which the grace of God for every human being is made known (1:26-28).[19]

How the audience are to play a part in Paul's ministry to proclaim and manifest to others the "word" about the mystery of Christ is further indicated and reinforced as they are told the reason they are to let their own "word" always be within the realm of grace—so that they "know how it is necessary for you to answer each one" (4:6b). Just as "it is necessary" (δεῖ) for Paul to speak to others the "word" about the mystery of the Christ (4:3-4), so "it is necessary" (δεῖ) for the audience to know how to answer each outsider who is not yet a believer from their own "word" that is to be spoken "in grace" (4:6).[20]

In this A′ element, then, the audience are exhorted to become part of Paul's ministry of speaking the word about the mystery of the Christ to others by conducting themselves toward non-believing outsiders in the wisdom that comes from Christ, allowing their own word to be always spoken from within their situation as grateful recipients of the grace God has graciously granted them in Christ, so that they may know how "it is necessary" for them to answer each non-believer (4:5-6), just as "it is necessary" for Paul to speak and manifest to every human being the mystery of Christ (4:3-4).[21]

---

18. Dunn, *Colossians*, 266-67: "This slightly unexpected sense of agreeable speech is enhanced by the addition, ἅλατι ἠρτυμένος ['seasoned with salt']. The image is clear: salt that seasons, that is, makes more interesting what would otherwise be bland to the taste.... The conversation envisaged, then, should be agreeable and 'never insipid,' 'with a flavour of wit.'" Deterding, *Colossians*, 178: "[H]aving one's speech seasoned with salt means having one's speech characterized by those things (such as forthrightness, sincerity, tact, and eloquence) that make one's conversation more readily 'palatable' to the hearer." Garland, *Colossians*, 274: "'Seasoned with salt' was used to refer to witty, amusing, clever, humorous speech. Their saltiness will prevent them from being ignored as irrelevant bores."

19. O'Brien, *Colossians*, 242: "ὁ λόγος ὑμῶν ('your speech') appears to be a deliberate echo of the apostle's preaching of the Word (λόγος) in verse 3 and includes both private conversation and public proclamation." Dunn, *Colossians*, 266: "Here the last term ['in grace'] certainly echoes the normal usage of χάρις in relation to speech, that is, 'graciousness, attractiveness,' that which delights and charms, though no Paulinist would intend such a usage to be independent of the χάρις manifested in Christ and fundamental to the Pauline gospel."

20. Wright, *Colossians*, 153-54: "'Answer' implies that outsiders will ask Christians about their new life, as indeed they will if verse 5 is being obeyed. Many such questions are predictable, but each questioner is an individual and must be respected and loved as such. If the 'answer' is heard or felt as an oracular pronouncement or a rebuke for ignorance, the argument may be won but the person lost." Harris, *Colossians*, 198: "'Ἑνὶ ἑκάστῳ is not simply 'everyone' (= παντί) but 'each separate person,' the emphasis being on perceptive answers that have that delicate blend of pungency and graciousness suited to the varying needs of individuals."

21. Garland, *Colossians*, 273: "The Colossians share the responsibility of evangelizing unbelievers as much as the traveling missionaries. They must blend wisdom with a sense of reckless urgency that exhausts every opportunity to reach unbelievers." For a treatment of the Christian witness in 4:5-6

C. Summary on Colossians 4:2–6

1. The audience are to persevere in prayer in thanksgiving, praying for the authors as they have not ceased to pray for the audience, and praying specifically that God may open for Paul and Timothy a "door" for the word of the gospel about Christ, that it may be heard and received by others as it was by the Colossian believers (4:2–3b).

2. The audience are exhorted to play their role in Paul's ministry by praying that God may open a door to Paul and Timothy for the "word" (4:3ab) so that they may speak the "mystery" of the Christ (4:3c) for other Gentiles to know, as do the believers at Colossae, of the hope of the glory laid up for them in the heavens (1:26–27; 2:1–3).

3. The artful double meaning of the expression that Paul has been "bound" on account of the mystery of the Christ (4:3d) assures the audience that Paul's current physical "binding" in chains by human beings is subsumed within his spiritual "binding" by God to be a minister of the gospel and of the church, a minister who is "bound" to proclaim that mystery to every human being (1:23–28).

4. "That I may manifest it as it is necessary for me to speak" (4:4) impresses upon the audience their need to pray for the divine assistance Paul in particular needs to complete his ministry to manifest the mystery of the Christ to every human being, as he is divinely "bound" and necessitated to speak it (4:2–3).

5. The audience are exhorted to become part of Paul's ministry of speaking the word about the mystery of Christ to others by conducting themselves toward non-believing outsiders in the wisdom that comes from Christ, allowing their own word to be always spoken from within their situation as grateful recipients of the grace God has graciously granted them in Christ, so that they know how "it is necessary" for them to answer each non-believer (4:5–6), just as "it is necessary" for Paul to speak and manifest to every human being the mystery of Christ (4:3–4).

---

with respect to both behavioral and verbal witness, see J. P. Sweeney, "Guidelines on Christian Witness in Colossians 4:5–6," *BSac* 159 (2002): 449–61.

12

COLOSSIANS 4:7–18

Assurance in All the Will of God and Grace from Paul (A′)

Greet the brothers and fulfill the ministry in the Lord
A: ⁷ All the things regarding me Tychicus, the beloved *brother* and faithful *minister* and fellow slave *in the Lord*, will make known to you, ⁸ whom I am sending to you for this very purpose, that you may know the things concerning us and that he may encourage your hearts, ⁹ with Onesimus, the faithful and beloved *brother*, who is one of you. They will make known to you all the things that are happening here.
    B: ¹⁰ Aristarchus, my fellow prisoner, *greets you*, also Mark, the cousin of Barnabas (concerning whom you have received instructions; if he comes to you, receive him), ¹¹ also Jesus who is called Justus, who are the only ones of the circumcision who are fellow workers for the kingdom of God, who have become to me a comfort. ¹²ᵃ Epaphras, who is one of you, a slave of Christ Jesus, *greets you*,
        C: ¹²ᵇ always struggling *on behalf of you* in the prayers,
            D: ¹²ᶜ that you may stand complete and fully assured in all the will of God.
        C′: ¹³ For I testify for him that he is having much labor *on behalf of you* and those in Laodicea and those in Hierapolis.
    B′: ¹⁴ Luke, the beloved physician, *greets you*, and Demas.
A′: ¹⁵ Greet the *brothers* in Laodicea also Nympha and the church at her house. ¹⁶ And when the letter has been read among you, make sure that it is read also in the church of the Laodiceans, and that you also read the one from Laodicea. ¹⁷ And say to Archippus, "Look to the *ministry* which you received *in the Lord*, that you fulfill it." ¹⁸ The greeting in my own hand, of Paul: Keep on remembering my chains. Grace be with you.[1]

---

1. For the establishment of 4:7–18 as a chiasm, see ch. 2.

A. Chiastic Development from Colossians 1:1–2 (A) to 4:7–18 (A′)

With Col 4:7–18, the closing A′ unit within the letter's macrochiastic structure, the audience hear resonances of 1:1–2, the corresponding A unit that opens the letter. The description of Tychicus as the beloved "brother" (ἀδελφός) and "faithful" (πιστός) minister" (4:7), the description of Onesimus as the "faithful" (πιστῷ) and beloved "brother" (ἀδελφῷ) (4:9), and the directive to greet the "brothers" (ἀδελφοὺς) in Laodicea (4:15) in the A′ unit recall for the audience the description of Timothy as the "brother" (ἀδελφός) (1:1) and the description of the audience themselves as "faithful" (πιστοῖς) "brothers" (ἀδελφοῖς) in Christ (1:2) in the A unit. That the audience "may stand complete and fully assured in all the will of God (θελήματι τοῦ θεοῦ)" (4:12) in the A′ unit echoes that Paul is an "apostle of Christ Jesus through the will of God (θελήματος θεοῦ)" (1:1) in the A unit. And the letter's closing greeting in the hand of "Paul" (Παύλου), "grace (χάρις) be with you" (4:18), in the A′ unit resonates with its opening greeting from "Paul" (Παῦλος) and Timothy (1:1), "grace (χάρις) to you and peace from God our Father" (1:2) in the A unit.

B. Audience Response to Colossians 4:7–18

1. Col 4:7–9 (A): Two Beloved Brothers in the Lord

For the first part of the letter the audience were addressed by both authors—Paul and Timothy (cf. 1:1–2). But eventually they heard an emphatic focus on Paul himself as a minister of the gospel, with its world-wide target, emerge: "if indeed you persevere in the faith, having been established and steadfast and not shifting from the hope of the gospel which you heard, which was proclaimed in all creation that is under heaven, of which I became, I, Paul, a minister" (1:23). The use of the first person singular verb "I became" (ἐγενόμην), intensified by the first person singular pronoun "I" (ἐγώ) together with the proper name "Paul" accentuates this focus on Paul himself.

The focus on Paul himself continued as the audience heard of the relationship of Paul's ministry specifically with regard to them, with more employment of first person singular verbs together with first person singular pronouns. They were informed that "I," Paul, "am rejoicing" in the sufferings "on behalf of you" and that "I am filling up" what is lacking of the afflictions of the Christ in "my" (μου) flesh on behalf of his body, which is the church, of which "I became" (ἐγενόμην), "I" (ἐγώ), a minister according to the plan of God given to "me" (μοι) to fulfill "for you" the word of God (1:24–25). The audience were made aware of Paul's deep personal involvement in his continuing struggles for them and others in this ministry of his: For this "I also labor," struggling according to his working that is working in "me" (ἐμοί) in power. For "I wish" you to know how great a struggle "I am having on behalf of you" and those in Laodicea and as many as have not seen "my" (μου) face in the flesh (1:29–2:1). And the audience were assured that this "I speak," that no one may speak contrary to "you" with persuasive speech. For even if in the flesh "I am absent," yet in the Spirit "I am with you," rejoicing at seeing "your" good order and the firmness of "your" faith in Christ (2:4-5).

And then, with more focus upon Paul himself, the audience were drawn into his ministry as they were exhorted to pray that God may open for Paul and Timothy a "door" for the word to speak the mystery of the Christ, on account of which indeed "I have been bound," that "I may manifest" it as it is necessary for "me" (με) to speak, and as it is necessary for "you" to answer each one (4:3-6). Having been partially informed throughout the letter, then, of Paul's personal sufferings, struggles, and imprisonment in his ministry for the gospel, the audience are now assured that *all the things* regarding "me" (ἐμέ) Tychicus will make known "to you" (4:7a). When the audience hear the word "you" (ὑμῖν) here, they hear the transitional word that links this unit (4:7-18) with the previous one (4:2-6), which concluded with a reference to "you" in the statement about "how it is necessary for you (ὑμᾶς) to answer each one" (4:6).

The audience were already made aware that to them, as among God's "holy ones" (1:26; 1:2), God wished "to make known" (γνωρίσαι) what is the richness of the glory of this mystery among the Gentiles, which is Christ among you, the hope of the glory (1:27). And now the audience are assured that Tychicus "will make known" (γνωρίσει) to them all the things concerning the imprisoned Paul, the minister through whom God made known to them the mystery of the Christ.[2]

That Tychicus is described as the "beloved" (ἀγαπητός) "brother" (ἀδελφός) and "faithful minister" (πιστὸς διάκονος) and "fellow slave" (σύνδουλος) in the Lord (4:7b) likens him to Epaphras, our "beloved" (ἀγαπητου) "fellow slave" (συνδούλου), who is a "faithful minister" (πιστὸς διάκονος) of Christ on behalf of you, from whom the audience learned (1:7) of the grace of God in truth (1:6) in the word of the truth of the gospel (1:5). As a faithful "minister" (διάκονος), Tychicus is likened as well to Paul himself, a "minister" (διάκονος) of the gospel (1:23) and a "minister" (διάκονος) of the church (1:24b-25). These characteristics of Tychicus, presumably the one carrying and responsible for arranging the public reading of the letter to the audience, foster a favorable, hospitable, and cooperative reception of him and of the letter itself on the part of the audience, who are themselves "faithful brothers" (πιστοῖς ἀδελφοῖς) in Colossae (1:2).[3]

---

2. Dunn, *Colossians*, 271: "Paul's affairs, everything to do with him, was evidently important to the Colossians: they would want to know how things were with him."

3. Wright, *Colossians*, 155: "'Brother' means 'fellow-Christian'; 'minister' (not a semi-technical term as today) refers simply to the fact that Christ works in the church through servants like Tychicus; 'fellow-servant' indicates that, like Paul, Tychicus belongs not to himself but to the Lord." O'Brien, *Colossians*, 247: "In Acts 20:4 Tychicus is mentioned as a native of the province of Asia who was with Paul in Greece and journeyed with him to Troas at the end of the third missionary journey. He accompanied Paul to Jerusalem when the latter took the collection from the gentile churches to their needy Jewish brethren in Jerusalem. According to 2 Timothy 4:12 Paul sent him on some undesignated mission to Ephesus, while later Paul planned to send either him or Artemas to Crete to take Titus' place (Tit 3:12)." Dunn, *Colossians*, 271-72: "[H]e was sent by Paul to Colossae (here) and to Ephesus (Eph. 6:21) . . . If

The focus on Paul alone broadens to include his co-author, Timothy, and perhaps others with them, when the audience hear that Paul is sending Tychicus with the letter for the precise purpose that they may know not only "all the things regarding me" (τὰ κατ' ἐμὲ πάντα, 4:7) but also "the things concerning us" (τὰ περὶ ἡμῶν) and that Tychicus may "encourage" (παρακαλέσῃ) their "hearts" (καρδίας) (4:8).[4] The audience may receive this knowledge and encouragement by listening both to the letter that Tychicus will present and to his additional conversations with them. They are thus now made aware that Paul's desire that the "hearts" (καρδίαι) of those who have not seen his face (2:1) may be "encouraged" (παρακληθῶσιν) (2:2) is also a desire that Tychicus can fulfill for them. This encouragement from Tychicus, then, may facilitate Paul's exhortations for the audience to let the peace of Christ rule in their "hearts" (καρδίαις, 3:15), the word of Christ dwell in them as they sing in their "hearts" (καρδίαις) to God (3:16), and for slaves to obey their masters with sincerity of "heart" (καρδίας, 3:22).[5]

The description of Onesimus (cf. Phlm 10–19), whom Paul is sending with Tychicus, as "the faithful and beloved brother" (τῷ πιστῷ καὶ ἀγαπητῷ ἀδελφῷ, 4:9a), likens him to Tychicus, "the beloved brother and faithful (ὁ ἀγαπητὸς ἀδελφὸς καὶ πιστός) minister and fellow slave in the Lord" (4:7b),[6] to Epaphras, "our beloved (ἀγαπητοῦ) fellow slave, who is a faithful (πιστός) minister of Christ" (1:7), and to the audience themselves, who are "faithful brothers (πιστοῖς ἀδελφοῖς) in Christ" (1:2a). In addition, Onesimus is "one of you" (4:9b), both a fellow believer and a fellow Colossian.[7] That both Tychicus and Onesimus "will make known to you all the things that are happening here" (πάντα ὑμῖν γνωρίσουσιν τὰ ὧδε, 4:9b)

---

number of mentions is significant, this would make Tychicus, along with Silvanus, one of Paul's closest associates after Timothy and Titus." See also Bonnie B. Thurston, "Paul's Associates in Colossians 4:7-17," *ResQ* 41 (1999): 45–53.

4. O'Brien, *Colossians*, 247–48: "ἔπεμψα, with most commentators, is to be understood as an epistolary aorist, that is, it views the action from the standpoint of the recipients as they read the letter, and so should be translated 'I am sending'; the RSV rendering 'I have sent' could be interpreted to mean Tychicus had been dispatched before Paul wrote to the Colossians."

5. O'Brien, *Colossians*, 248: "The letter itself does not mention how Paul is getting on personally and the congregation wants to know how things are with him. But Tychicus will be able to give them all the details. At the same time as Paul's colleague and co-worker he will impress the apostle's teaching on the congregation and so strengthen their hearts."

6. Dunn, *Colossians*, 272: "[T]he 'in the Lord' formulation echoes the prominence of references to the Lord in the preceding parenesis (ten occurrences in 3:13–4:1) and ties in the final sequence of messages to the thematic concern of 2:6-7." Deterding, *Colossians*, 184: "By styling Tychicus a servant and his fellow slave and modifying both terms with the phrase 'in the Lord,' the apostle indicates that Tychicus is more than an errand boy; he also serves in the cause of proclaiming the Gospel."

7. O'Brien, *Colossians*, 248: "By describing him as 'the faithful and beloved brother' Paul gives him the same predicates as Tychicus and Epaphras (though he is not called a διάκονος, 'minister,' or σύνδουλος, 'fellow-slave') and this suggests that Onesimus the slave is to receive the same warm greeting from the Colossian church that would be extended to any visiting Christian. As one who is a native of Colossae he comes armed with a letter of commendation from the apostle to the Gentiles." Dunn, *Colossians*, 273: "Presumably Onesimus does not count as one of Paul's team of fellow workers; he is a Christian ('brother') and well regarded ('faithful and beloved'), but he carries no explicit responsibility

strengthens Paul's promise that Tychicus "will make known to you all the things regarding me" (τὰ κατ' ἐμὲ πάντα γνωρίσει ὑμῖν, 4:7a), as well as his desire that "you may know the things concerning us" (γνῶτε τὰ περὶ ἡμῶν, 4:8a). All of these similarities and reinforcements further enhance the favorable and hospitable reception not only of Tychicus and Onesimus, the bringers of the letter, but of the letter itself on the part of its Colossian audience.

In this A element, then, the audience, as faithful brothers in Christ (1:2), are assured that Tychicus and Onesimus, their fellow beloved and faithful brothers who have brought them the letter from Paul and Timothy, will also personally inform them of all that has been happening with Paul and those with him in his imprisonment, further motivating them to do all that they have heard Paul, the minister suffering and struggling on their behalf, exhort them to do in the letter (4:7–9).

2. Col 4:10–12a (B): Aristarchus, Mark, Justus, and Epaphras Greet the Audience

The audience are greeted in the letter by the Jewish associates of Paul in his current imprisonment: "Aristarchus, my fellow prisoner, greets you, also Mark, the cousin of Barnabas (concerning whom you have received instructions; if he comes to you, receive him), also Jesus who is called Justus, who are the only ones of the circumcision who are fellow workers for the kingdom of God, who have become to me a comfort" (4:10–11). Paul and Timothy's initial greeting of the audience, "grace to you and peace from God our Father" (1:2c), is now supplemented by those associated with Paul in his imprisonment, who "greet (ἀσπάζεται) you."[8] Although Tychicus and Onesimus will further inform the audience of more details regarding Paul's situation (4:7–9), the audience learn more about that situation now in the letter itself, namely that Paul is not alone in his imprisonment but has several associates with him. The concern of these associates of Paul to greet the Colossian audience adds weight to the authority of Paul and thus further motivates the audience to meet the expectations Paul (and Timothy) have of them, as expressed in the letter.

These greetings of individuals with Paul begin with that from Aristarchus whose designation as "my fellow prisoner" (ὁ συναιχμάλωτός μου) not only underscores for the audience that Paul is in prison but that other fellow believers are also imprisoned with him for the cause of the gospel (4:10a).[9] The audience are also

---

in Paul's missionary and pastoral work.... While it is clearly Tychicus who is to be the chief spokesperson, Onesimus, as one of their own, will no doubt have much to tell on his own part."

8. Harris, *Colossians*, 206: "In expressing greetings at the end of a letter, this v[er]b. [ἀσπάζεται] regularly stands first in the sentence, and where more than one person gives greetings, it agrees with the number of the first noun."

9. Aristarchus was a Macedonian from Thessalonica and fellow traveler of Paul (Acts 19:29; 20:4; 27:2). He is mentioned together with Epaphras, Mark, Demas, and Luke also in Phlm 23–24 (cf. Col 4:10, 12–14). Bruce, *Colossians*, 178 n. 40: "In Philem. 23, where Aristarchus and Epaphras are named

greeted by Mark, described as the cousin of Barnabas.[10] They have already received instructions regarding Mark, so that, if he comes to them, they are to "receive," that is, welcome him with full hospitality (4:10b).[11] And the audience are greeted by a certain "Jesus" also known as Justus (4:11a).[12] All three of these greeters are "of the circumcision" (4:11b), meaning they are Jewish. They are the only such Jews who have become fellow workers of Paul for the "kingdom" (βασιλείαν) of God (4:11c), thus sharing in Paul's ministry to proclaim the "kingdom" (βασιλείαν) of the Son of God's love, in whom the audience and all believers have redemption, the forgiveness of sins (1:13–14).[13]

---

together, it is Epaphras who is called συναιχμάλωτός." Dunn, *Colossians*, 276: "[I]t is hard to avoid the conclusion that Paul alludes here to physical captivity." Garland, *Colossians*, 277: "Paul refers to his actual captivity in 4:3, 18, so one assumes that he is referring to the actual imprisonment of his fellow workers. Aristrarchus and Epaphras could have rotated in voluntarily sharing Paul's quarters and hence his captivity, though they were not charged with any crime."

10. Dunn, *Colossians*, 276-77: "The present passage adds significant information given us nowhere else, namely that Mark was Barnabas's 'cousin.' This in itself would be sufficient to explain why Mark was so well known. For Barnabas was evidently an important figure from the very beginnings of the Jerusalem church (Acts 4:36) and an absolutely key figure in ensuring that the breakthrough at Antioch did not itself become a break (11:22-24), in the development in the church at Antioch itself (11:22; 13:1; 15:35), in bringing Saul the convert into the mainstream of the movement (9:27; 11:25-26), in leading the first missionary expedition from Antioch to the east of Colossae (13:2, 7; 14:12), and in the initial defense of the Gentile mission with Paul (15:2, 12, 22, 25; Gal. 2:1, 9)." Wilson, *Colossians*, 300: "ἀνεψιός is another of the hapax legomena in this letter, and means a cousin, although in very late writers it came to be used for a nephew."

11. This Mark is, in all probability, the one referred to as "John Mark" in Acts 12:12, 25: 13:13; 15:37-39; he is mentioned together with Aristarchus, Demas, and Luke in Phlm 24 (cf. Col 4:14), and in 2 Tim 4:11; 1 Pet 5:13. The audience may have some apprehension about receiving Mark, since Paul and Barnabas parted ways over Paul's decision not to take Mark with them on a journey to revisit the cities where thay had together proclaimed the word of the Lord, because Mark had earlier deserted them at Pamphylia (Acts 15:36-40). Hence, the need for Paul to commend Mark to the Colossians as worthy of their hospitable reception. "Receive" (δέξασθε) "is the appropriate word for the hospitable reception of a guest or visitor," according to O'Brien, *Colossians*, 250. Dunn, *Colossians*, 277: "The kinship of Barnabas and Mark could also explain why Barnabas was so sympathetic to Mark (Acts 15:37-39), or why Mark would have sided with Barnabas and the other Christian Jews at Antioch (Gal. 2:13), and so makes more understandable any part Mark played in the breach between Paul and Barnabas." Deterding, *Colossians*, 186: "From Mark's presence with Paul when he wrote Philemon (v 24) and Colossians, we conclude that the two were sooner or later reconciled, as is also seen from the apostle's commendation of Mark in the present passage (Col 4:10) and in 2 Timothy (4:11)." Garland, *Colossians*, 277: "Mark is no longer a cause for dispute (Acts 15:36-41) but has become a source of comfort as a coworker."

12. O'Brien, *Colossians*, 251: " 'Jesus' was his Jewish name (the Greek form of 'Joshua' or 'Jeshua') and this was common among Jews (Acts 13:6) until the second century A.D. when it disappeared as a proper name, no doubt because of the conflict between the synagogue and the Church. . . . this Jesus called himself 'Justus' (a name that was commonly borne by Jews and proselytes; Acts 1:23; 18:7)."

13. On these and other co-workers of Paul, see E. Earle Ellis, "Paul and His Co-Workers," *NTS* 17 (1970–71): 437-52; Ollrog, *Paulus und seiner Mitarbeiter*. Dunn, *Colossians*, 279-80: "The qualification is not very extensive: it refers only to Paul's 'fellow workers,' and since his circle of 'co-workers' at previous and other times certainly included other Jews, the reference here must be to those presently with

That these three greeters are of the "circumcision" (περιτομῆς, 4:11b) reminds the audience that they too have been metaphorically or spiritually "circumcised" by their baptism. In Christ they were "circumcised" (περιετμήθητε) with a "circumcision" (περιτομῇ) not made with hands in the removal of the body of the flesh, in the "circumcision" (περιτομῇ) of the Christ, having been buried with him in the baptism, in whom indeed they were raised with him through faith in the working of the God who raised him from the dead (2:11-12). Furthermore, the audience have "put on" the "new human being" wherein there is not Greek and Jew, "circumcision" (περιτομή) and uncircumcision, barbarian, Scythian, slave, free, but Christ is all and in all (3:11). Thus, that there are Jewish associates who have become for Paul a "comfort" in his imprisonment (4:11d) serves as a subtle, additional prompting for the audience, who have their own "circumcision" in Christ, likewise to become a comfort to Paul, imprisoned, suffering, and struggling on their behalf, by carrying out the exhortations he has extended to them in the letter, especially that they not be captivated by the "philosophy" of empty deceit emanating from the Jewish synagogue (2:8).[14]

The audience are also "greeted" (ἀσπάζεται) by Epaphras (4:12a), the one from whom they learned the word of the truth of the gospel (1:5-7). His greeting of the audience now indicates that he has returned to be with Paul in his imprisonment. That he is "one of you" (4:12b) likens him to Onesimus as a fellow Colossian of the audience (4:9). And his designation as "a slave (δοῦλος) of Christ Jesus" (4:12c) underscores that he is "our beloved fellow slave (συνδούλου)" (1:7), reminding the audience once again that there is a metaphorical or spiritual "slavery" to Christ as a believer that transcends the sociological slavery of their time (3:11, 22; 4:1).[15]

---

him. In fact, the immediate circle does not seem to have been very large (six names in 4:10-14), so that the note of evident sadness ('these only') is all the more striking. . . . Also to be noted is the fact that no tension is even hinted at between the idea of 'God's kingdom' and that of 'the kingdom of his Son.'"

14. "Comfort" is in an emphatic final position in the sentence; see Harris, *Colossians*, 208. Deterding, *Colossians*, 186: "The noun παρηγορία, only here in the NT, means 'a source of encouragement, comfort' (BDAG) and refers to the companionship and emotional solace that the apostle received from his fellow Christians." Dunn, *Colossians*, 278-79: "The reference presumably is intended to assure the Colossians that there were such Jews, or at any rate other Jews apart from himself, who, as Jews, were fully approving of and cooperative in the Gentile mission ('fellow workers'), despite, presumably, the disapproval of most of their compatriots. . . . That the reference is thus made strengthens the likelihood that any threats to the Colossian church's self-understanding came from the Colossian synagogue. . . . Furthermore, that the reference is made without any sign of resentment or hostility to 'the circumcision' (contrast Gal. 2:12 and Tit. 1:10) equally strengthens the suggestion that the threat from the Colossian synagogue was not at all so forceful as earlier in Galatia, nor was it making such an issue of circumcision as there." Garland, *Colossians*, 278: "Paul wants to remind them that some Jews, whom they know or know about, have been willing to throw aside their religious entitlements for the sake of the gospel in which there is no Jew nor Greek, circumcised or uncircumcised."

15. O'Brien, *Colossians*, 252-53: "Epaphras is given this title of honor which speaks of him as an obedient slave of his Lord in the same service as Paul. In fact, the apostle goes out of his way to stress the close correspondence between his own ministry and that of Epaphras. Both are involved in the same struggle for the gospel." Dunn, *Colossians*, 280: "As before, he is described as a 'slave,' here

In this B element, then, the audience are greeted by the only Jews ("those who are of the circumcision," 4:11) who are fellow workers of Paul for the kingdom of God—Aristarchus, a fellow prisoner, Mark, the cousin of Barnabas, and Jesus also known as Justus. That they have become a comfort to Paul prompts the audience, who have their own "circumcision" in Christ (2:11), to likewise comfort Paul in his imprisonment on their behalf by not being captivated by a Jewish "philosophy" of empty deceit (2:8). In addition, their fellow Colossian and "slave" of Christ Jesus, the one from whom they learned the gospel, Epaphras (1:5-7), greets them (4:10-12a).

3. Col 4:12b (C): Always Struggling on Behalf of You in the Prayers

Epaphras is further described as "always struggling on behalf of you in the prayers" (4:12b). That Epaphras is always "struggling" (ἀγωνιζόμενος) "on behalf of you" (ὑπὲρ ὑμῶν), the audience, further likens him to Paul, who is also "struggling" (ἀγωνιζόμενος) for the audience (1:29), indeed, is having a great "struggle" (ἀγῶνα) "on behalf of you" (ὑπὲρ ὑμῶν) in his ministry for the gospel (2:1). That Epaphras is "always" (πάντοτε) struggling "on behalf of you" in the "prayers" (προσευχαῖς) strengthens his similarity to Paul and Timothy, who are "always" (πάντοτε) "praying" (προσευχόμενοι) for the audience (1:3), indeed, who do not cease "praying" (προσευχόμενοι) "on behalf of you" (ὑπὲρ ὑμῶν)(1:9). These similarities in the C element make the audience aware of the continuing concern of Epaphras, from whom they learned the word of the truth of the gospel (1:5-7), as he struggles and prays for them. They add weight to the authority of Paul (and Timothy), further prompting the audience to fulfill the letter's expectations of them.[16]

4. Col 4:12c (D): That You May Stand Complete and Fully Assured in All the Will of God

The audience are then informed of the more specific content of the prayers of Epaphras on their behalf: "that you may stand complete and fully assured in all the will of God" (4:12c). That Epaphras is praying that the audience may stand "complete" (τέλειοι) complements and applies specifically to the audience the goal of the proclamation of the mystery of Christ by Paul and Timothy: "Him we proclaim, admonishing every human being and teaching every human being in all wisdom, that we may present every human being complete (τέλειον) in Christ" (1:28).[17]

---

explicitly of Christ Jesus, one of Paul's favorite self-designations and images of the total commitment involved in his concept of discipleship, all the more potent an image following the household rules given in 3:22-4:1."

16. O'Brien, *Colossians*, 253: "Epaphras was intimately acquainted with the affairs of the congregation. He, perhaps as no other, knew of the destructive nature of the false teaching and responded in regular, urgent intercession."

17. O'Brien, *Colossians*, 253: "The reference to perfection (τέλειος) touches on one of the key issues at Colossae in which members of the congregation were encouraged by the false teachers to

And that Epaphras is praying that the audience may stand "fully assured" (πεπληροφορημένοι) by God (divine passive) in "all" (παντί) the "will of God" (θελήματι τοῦ θεοῦ) (4:12c) reinforces the praying for the audience by Timothy and Paul, an apostle of Christ Jesus through the "will of God" (θελήματος θεοῦ, 1:1), that "you may be filled" (πληρωθῆτε) with the knowledge of his "will" (θελήματος) in "all" (πάσῃ) wisdom and Spiritual understanding (1:9).[18] The praying by Epaphras complements for the audience Paul's prayer-wish that the hearts of those who have not seen him (2:1) may be encouraged as they are held together in love, for all richness of the "full assurance" (πληροφορίας) of understanding, for the knowledge of the mystery of God, Christ (2:2).

In this D element, then, Epaphras's prayer that the audience may stand complete in Christ, in whom are "all" (πάντες) the treasures of wisdom and knowledge hidden (2:3), and that they may be fully assured in "all" (παντί) the will of God (4:12c) bolsters the exhortations for them in "all" (πάσῃ) wisdom to teach and admonish each other (3:16), as Paul and Timothy are admonishing every human being and teaching every human being in "all" (πάσῃ) wisdom, that they may present every human being complete in Christ (1:28).[19]

5. Col 4:13 (C´): Epaphras Is Having Much Labor on Behalf of You and Those in Laodicea and Hierapolis

The audience continue to be informed of the great concern of Epaphras for them as well as the other believers in their region: "For I testify for him that he is having much labor on behalf of you and those in Laodicea and those in Hier-

---

seek maturity or perfection through their philosophy (2:8) with its ascetic practices, visionary experiences and special revelations, rather than through Christ." Deterding, *Colossians*, 187: "Such prayers are closely related to the task of proclamation, for the purpose of the prayers of Epaphras is accomplished through the proclamation of the Word. Epaphras is diligently praying that his people would stand faithful in the status first bestowed on them through the Gospel and that continues to be theirs in the Gospel. In view of the temptations confronting them to abandon that status, his prayers were certainly needed and apropos."

18. Wright, *Colossians*, 138: "God's 'will' is not restricted to the question 'what does God want the Colossian Christians to do?', but is a larger entity ... It refers to God's whole strategy for the salvation of the world. Epaphras is praying (like Paul) that the young church will understand what it is that God is doing and order their lives accordingly, growing into well-grounded Christian (and human) maturity." O'Brien, *Colossians*, 154: "The participle here [πεπληροφορημένοι—'fully assured'] reminds us of the teaching on 'fullness' (πλήρωμα) which runs through the heresy as well as Paul's corrective. Accordingly, the prayer addressed to God recalls the polemic against the 'philosophy.' Christ is the one in whom the whole fullness of the Godhead dwells bodily (2:9). Only in him is fullness to be found. And the readers have been filled in Christ (2:10)."

19. Dunn, *Colossians*, 280–81: "The reuse of these earlier phrases and prayer-hopes presumably carries the same echoes as earlier to the threat envisaged as confronting the Colossian community: in particular, that 'maturity, perfection' is to be attained by standing firm within the Christian group and not by wandering off after other philosophies. Who could make this prayer more knowledgeably and more effectively than their own Epaphras?" Garland, *Colossians*, 279: "Epaphras, like Paul, wants the Colossians to become less tenuous in their understanding of all that God has done in Christ so that they will not become easy marks for false teaching that has an 'appearance of wisdom' (2:23)."

apolis" (4:13). The audience now experience the pivot of the chiasm by way of the parallel that progresses from Epaphras always struggling "on behalf of you" (ὑπὲρ ὑμῶν) in his prayers in the C element (4:12b) to the much labor that Epaphras is having not only "on behalf of you" (ὑπὲρ ὑμῶν) but of those in Laodicea and those in Hierapolis as well in the C´ element.

The audience have already heard of Paul's wish that they know how great a struggle "I am having" (ἔχω) "on behalf of you and those in Laodicea and as many as have not seen my face in the flesh" (2:1). And now they hear how this intense effort on their behalf is reinforced and complemented by that of Epaphras. Paul testifies about him that "he is having" (ἔχει) "much labor on behalf of you and those in Laodicea and those in Hierapolis" (4:13), a city, like Laodicea, located in the same region as Colossae in the Lycus river valley.[20] That Epaphras is having much labor in his prayers and perhaps in additional ways "on behalf of you" continues the various expressions of solicitude on behalf of the Colossian audience by Paul, Timothy, and Epaphras:

1:7: Epaphras our beloved fellow slave, who is a faithful minister of Christ on behalf of you (ὑπὲρ ὑμῶν)

1:9: We (Paul and Timothy) do not cease praying on behalf of you (ὑπὲρ ὑμῶν)

1:24: Now I (Paul) am rejoicing in the sufferings on behalf of you (ὑπὲρ ὑμῶν)

2:1: For I (Paul) wish you to know how great a struggle I am having on behalf of you (ὑπὲρ ὑμῶν)

4:12: Epaphras, who is one of you, a slave of Christ Jesus, greets you, always struggling on behalf of you (ὑπὲρ ὑμῶν)

4:13: He (Epaphras) is having much labor on behalf of you (ὑπὲρ ὑμῶν)

---

20. Wright, *Colossians*, 158: "Though not physically present there, Epaphras has a vision for God's work in the Lycus valley, and is working hard to bring it to reality." Bruce, *Colossians*, 181: "Praying is working; and by such fervent prayer Epaphras toiled effectively on behalf of the churches of Colossae, Laodicea, and Hierapolis." The present tense "he is having" (ἔχει) "implies Epaphras's habit of toiling strenuously in prayer," according to Harris, *Colossians*, 211. O'Brien, *Colossians*, 254–55: "Paul's testimony is high praise indeed for one who had worked so hard. πόνος ('hard labor,' 'toil,' 'pain,' 'distress,' 'affliction') only turns up four times in the NT and three of these are in the Book of Revelation (with the meaning 'pain,' or 'distress,' 16:10, 11; 21:4). The term was a common one for struggle in battle and here, like the ἀγών ('struggle') word-group [cf. 1:29; 2:1; 4:12], is related to Paul and Epaphras' toil for the gospel." Dunn, *Colossians*, 281–82: "Again like Paul, Epaphras had put himself to much effort on behalf of the Colossians and those in Laodicea (cf. 2:1). The main difference is the word used (there ἀγών; here πόνος). Both indicate considerable exertion, but in the case of πόνος what is usually in mind is the hard work of battle or of physical labor, the consequence of the fall from paradise in both Greek and Jewish thought; hence also it has the sense of 'pain'. . . . The present tense refers the 'labor' to Epaphras's continuing prayers, or perhaps also to work done by Epaphras on the Colossians' behalf."

In this C′ element, then, that in his prayers and perhaps in other ways Epaphras is having much labor "on behalf of you" and those in the nearby cities of Laodicea and Hierapolis (4:13), continuing and complementing the letter's previous expressions of solicitude "on behalf of you" (1:7, 9, 24; 2:1; 4:12), serves as additional motivation for the Colossian audience, who have learned of the word of the truth of the gospel from Epaphras (1:5-7), to fulfill the letter's expectations of them, particularly that they not be captivated by the "philosophy" of empty deceit (2:8), devoid of authentic wisdom (2:23).

6. Col 4:14 (B′): Luke, the Beloved Physician, Greets You, and Demas

Next the audience hear of additional greetings from two other individuals with Paul in his imprisonment: "Luke, the beloved physician, greets you, and Demas" (4:14).[21] With the notice in the B′ element that Luke "greets you" (ἀσπάζεται ὑμᾶς), as well as Demas, the audience hear a continuation, by way of the chiastic parallelism, of the notices that Aristarchus "greets you" (ἀσπάζεται ὑμᾶς), as well as Mark and Justus (4:10-11), and that Epaphras "greets you" (ἀσπάζεται ὑμᾶς, 4:12a) in the B element of the chiasm. That Luke is designated as the "beloved" (ἀγαπητός) physician likens him, as a valued associate of Paul, to Onesimus, the "beloved" (ἀγαπητῷ) brother (4:9), to Tychicus, the "beloved" (ἀγαπητός) brother (4:7), and to Epaphras, our "beloved" (ἀγαπητοῦ) fellow slave (1:7).[22] With the B′ element the audience have been made aware of the greetings to them from both explicitly Jewish (Aristarchus, Mark, Justus; 4:10-11) and other (Epaphras, Luke, Demas; 4:12a, 14) associates of Paul in his imprisonment, supplementing Paul's solicitude for them and thus further prompting them to do what Paul is telling them to do in the letter.[23]

7. Col 4:15-18 (A′): Greeting the Brothers and Fulfilling the Ministry in the Lord

Having been greeted by associates of Paul, the audience are directed to greet their fellow believers in Laodicea: "Greet the brothers in Laodicea also Nympha and the church at her house. And when the letter has been read among you, make sure that it is read also in the church of the Laodiceans, and that you also read the one from Laodicea" (4:15-16). The audience now hear a progression, by way of the chiastic parallelism, from a focus in the A element (4:7-9) on two individual "brothers" who are coming to them with more information about Paul's situation—Tychicus, the beloved "brother" (ἀδελφός, 4:7), and Onesimus, the faithful

---

21. Luke and Demas are mentioned, along with other associates of Paul, in Phlm 24 and 2 Tim 4:10-11. Bruce, *Colossians*, 181: "Since the second century at least he [Luke] has been identified in the tradition with the author of the Third Gospel and the Acts of the Apostles."

22. Dunn, *Colossians*, 283: "The note of affection here indicates a closeness of relationship with Paul, a quality of friendship shared with Epaphras, Tychicus, and Onesimus."

23. For a recent discussion of 4:10-14, see Jerome Murphy-O'Connor, "The Greeters in Col 4:10-14 and Phlm 23-24," *RB* 114 (2007): 416-26.

and beloved "brother" (ἀδελφός, 4:9), to a focus in the A′ element (4:15-18) on their visit to a wider group of "brothers," as they are directed to greet the "brothers" (ἀδελφούς) in Laodicea (4:15a). In addition, they hear a progression from greetings extended to them from individual fellow believers—Aristarchus "greets" (ἀσπάζεται) you (4:10), Epaphras "greets" (ἀσπάζεται) you (4:12), and Luke "greets" (ἀσπάζεται) you (4:14)—to greetings they themselves are to extend to a number of fellow believers—"greet" (ἀσπάσασθε) the brothers in Laodicea (4:15a).

The audience have already been made aware of Paul's concern not only for them but for the wider, universal church in general. He told them of his sufferings on behalf of them and that he is filling up what is lacking in the afflictions of the Christ in his flesh on behalf of the "body" which is the entire "church" (ἐκκλησία) (1:24), the "body" of the "church" (ἐκκλησίας) of which Christ is the "head" (1:18). And now Paul draws his Colossian church into his concern not only for the church as a whole but for the individual manifestations of it. He directs them not only to greet Nympha and the "church" (ἐκκλησίαν) at her house (4:15),[24] but also to make sure that after the letter has been read among them, it is also read in the "church" (ἐκκλησίᾳ) of the Laodiceans (4:16ab). And that they are also to read the one from Laodicea makes them aware not only of their interrelatedness to another individual church within the universal church, but that they are not the only local church in danger of being captivated by the "philosophy" of empty deceit (2:8).[25]

The audience then hear a directive regarding an individual among them, followed by the letter's concluding personal greeting from the imprisoned Paul: "And say to Archippus, 'Look to the ministry which you received in the Lord, that you

---

24. Dunn, *Colossians*, 285: "Nympha as the named householder must have been either a widow or unmarried; it would hardly have been referred to as 'her house' otherwise.... She must therefore have been a person of some means and probably was able to maintain a household. At all events, her house was large enough to accommodate a meeting ('church') of (some of) the Laodicean believers." Garland, *Colossians*, 279 n. 28: "Churches did not have separate buildings in the first century, and Christians met in the home, in the courtyard, or on the roof of someone with a large enough house to accommodate the group (see Acts 12:12; 16:40; Rom. 16:3-5, 23; 1 Cor. 16:19; Philem. 2)." Wilson, *Colossians*, 305: "[I]f the wife made her home available while her husband remained pagan, it would be natural to use her name rather than his."

25. Harris, *Colossians*, 213-14: "'The letter from (ἐκ) Laodicea' means 'the letter that will be forwarded to you from Laodicea,' not 'the letter written by the Laodiceans and sent from Laodicea.' In a piece of typical brachylogy, Paul directs that the letter he had written to the Laodiceans should be read by the Colossians after its arrival 'from Laodicea.'" O'Brien, *Colossians*, 257-59: "The Epistles of the NT were from the first intended to be read aloud in the Christian assembly.... Perhaps the Laodicean church required a letter along similar lines to the Epistle to the Colossians; yet the two were sufficiently different for Paul to direct that each letter should be read in the other church. The philosophical ideas which were gaining currency in Colossae were probably very much alive in the Lycus neighborhood so that the exchange of both was important. From this admonition one can understand how Paul's letters would be copied, disseminated and collected at an early date." Garland, *Colossians*, 280: "The greetings assume that the Colossians will go to Laodicea with their letter and will retrieve a copy of the letter sent to them (4:16)." For an interpretation of 4:16 as a "cryptic mandate" to do what the letter says, see A. E. Drake, "The Riddle of Colossians: *Quaerendo Invenietis*," *NTS* 41 (1995): 123-44.

fulfill it.' The greeting in my own hand, of Paul: Keep on remembering my chains. Grace be with you" (4:17-18). In the A element Paul promised the audience that Tychicus, the beloved brother and faithful "minister" (διάκονος) and fellow slave "in the Lord" (ἐν κυρίῳ), will make known to them all of the things regarding Paul (4:7). And now, by way of the chiastic parallelism, in the A' element (4:17) Paul directs the audience to tell one of their members, Archippus, to look to the "ministry" (διακονίαν) he received "in the Lord" (ἐν κυρίῳ), to make sure that he fulfills it. Thus, the ministry that Tychicus, as a faithful minister and fellow slave in the Lord, will fulfill for the audience implicitly serves as an example to be followed by Archippus, so that he fulfills the ministry he received in the Lord.[26]

As the audience, "you" who "received" (παρελάβετε) the Christ, Jesus the "Lord," are to go on walking in him (2:6), so the audience are to tell Archippus to fulfill the ministry "you received" (παρέλαβες) in the "Lord." As Epaphras was a faithful "minister" (διάκονος) of Christ on behalf of the audience (1:7) in teaching them the word of the truth of the gospel (1:5), and as Paul became a "minister" (διάκονος) of the gospel (1:23) as well as a "minister" (διάκονος) of the church, to "fulfill" (πληρῶσαι) for the audience the word of God (1:25), so the audience are to tell Archippus that "you are to fulfill" (πληροῖς) whatever the "ministry" (διακονίαν) is that he received in the Lord (4:17).[27]

At the beginning of the letter the audience were addressed by both "Paul" (Παῦλος) and Timothy (1:1). But eventually they were addressed solely by Paul with great emphasis upon his own person, as they heard him tell them not to shift from the hope of the gospel, of which "I became, I (ἐγώ), Paul (Παῦλος), a minister" (1:23). The audience were then informed, with more emphasis upon the person of Paul, that he is suffering on behalf of them and on behalf of the whole church, of which "I became, I (ἐγώ), a minister" (1:25). And now the audience hear, again with great emphasis upon the person of Paul, of the greeting "in my own (ἐμῇ) hand, of Paul (Παύλου)" (4:18a).[28]

The first part of Paul's greeting, the exhortation to keep on remembering my "chains (δεσμῶν)" (4:18b), reinforces for the audience Paul's assertion that it is on

---

26. This Archippus is, in all probability, the same Archippus who is listed, together with Philemon and Apphia, as a recipient of Paul's letter to Philemon (Phlm 1-2) and who is therein described as "our fellow soldier."

27. Deterding, *Colossians*, 189: "The apostle uses 'sevice/ministry' (διακονία) and its cognate 'servant/minister' (διάκονος) often, although by no means exclusively, for ministry in the Gospel of Christ. This usage, the coupling of the term here with the prepositional phrase 'in the Lord,' and the designation of Archippus as Paul's fellow soldier indicate that the service of Archippus referred to here supported and perhaps included the proclamation of Christ's Gospel."

28. O'Brien, *Colossians*, 259: "Having finished dictating, Paul takes up his pen to add a personal greeting in his own handwriting. The apostle always concluded his letters autobiographically even where there is no explicit acknowledgment of it. His personal signatures occur frequently (1 Cor 16:21; 2 Cor 10:1; Gal 6:11; Col 4:18; 2 Thess 3:17 and Philem 19) and were a common epistolary technique in the first century." Dunn, *Colossians*, 289: "At all events it reinforces the effect of the letter in providing a real substitute for the personal presence of the one absent."

account of the mystery of the Christ that "I have been bound (δέδεμαι)" (4:3d). This "binding" carries a double nuance. Paul is "bound" literally and physically in prison, and Paul is "bound" metaphorically and spiritually, on account of his speaking the mystery of the Christ. Thus, Paul's exhortation to the audience to remember my "chains" not only serves as a final reminder to them of Paul's literal and physical suffering in prison on their behalf and on behalf of the whole church (1:24-25), but reminds them to pray (4:2-3b) that he may manifest the mystery of the Christ as it is necessary, as he is "bound," to speak it (4:3c-4).[29]

The second part of Paul's greeting, which concludes the letter, "grace (χάρις) be with you" (4:18c), brings to a climax the audience's involvement in the grace that comes from God. It reinforces Paul and Timothy's prayerful greeting at the beginning of the letter of "grace" (χάρις) to you and peace from God our Father (1:2c).[30] It prays for a continuation in the "grace" (χάριν) of God in truth that the audience have already come to know (1:6), so that they are not captivated by the false "philosophy" of empty deceit (2:8). It complements the exhortation for the audience to "let the word of Christ dwell in you richly, in all wisdom teaching and admonishing each other with psalms, hymns, and Spiritual songs, in grace (χάριτι) singing in your hearts to God" (3:16). And it complements the exhortation for the

---

29. Harris, *Colossians*, 215-16: "It is possible that Paul is here requesting continued intercession for himself. The sense would then be, 'Keep remembering before God in prayer my imprisonment for the gospel' (cf. 4:3-4)." Deterding, *Colossians*, 190: "In this context, the present imperative μνημονεύετε refers to action that is regular and ongoing. The exhortation to 'keep on remembering my bonds' is clearly a request for the Colossians to pray for the apostle in this time of personal distress. However, since μνημονεύω , 'to remember,' sometimes connotes the act of believing acceptance (Acts 20:31, 35; 2 Tim 2:8), its use here may perhaps be additionally a request to accept the validity of Paul's ministry. 'Do not despise my afflictions,' the apostle seems to be saying, 'but rather be mindful that suffering for Christ is a mark of authentic discipleship and ministry' (see Col 1:24)." Cassidy, *Paul in Chains*, 92-93: "It should be stressed that two aspects serve to place these words regarding Paul's chains in extraordinarily high relief. The first aspect pertains to placement. This entreaty is positioned at the very end of the letter, a positioning that makes Paul in chains the closing image imparted to the Colossians. The second aspect pertains to the rendering of this appeal in Paul's own script. . . . to have his chains remembered is so exigent that he expresses it personally and emphatically in his own hand. . . . the full image communicated is that of Paul actually writing these sentences, perhaps roughly and somewhat clumsily, *with manacled hands* (Cassidy's emphasis)." Dunn, *Colossians*, 290: "Again the brevity and the failure to follow Paul's normal practice of citing the title of Christ with its liturgical resonance strongly suggest that the words here were penned under considerable difficulty, so that only the most basic benediction could be given." Garland, *Colossians*, 282: "The call to remember his chains is not some forlorn plea for pity from a woebegone and disheartened apostle. He does not ask for commiseration. He is glad to suffer for Christ (1:24) and his bonds are the bonds of the gospel (Philem. 13). It is better to regard this call as a note of encouragement for those who may also suffer persecution for their faith as well as another request for their prayer support."

30. O'Brien, *Colossians*, 260: "The final benediction picks up the introductory greeting (1:2) where Paul desires that the Colossians may apprehend more fully the grace of God in which they stand. At the same time the note of confidence is also struck. God's grace will sustain the community, for it is by grace alone that they will stand."

audience to "let your word always be in grace (χάριτι), seasoned with salt, to know how it is necessary for you to answer each one" (4:6).[31]

In sum, in this A´ element the audience are to greet their fellow believers in Laodicea as well as Nympha and the local church at her house (4:15). They are to make sure that the letter is read also in the church of the Laodiceans and that they are also to read the one from Laodicea (4:16) makes them aware not only of their interrelatedness to another individual church within the universal church, but that they are not the only local church in danger of being captivated by the "philosophy" of empty deceit (2:8). The audience, who have received the Christ (2:6), are to tell Archippus to fulfill the ministry he received in the Lord (4:17), as Paul fulfilled for the audience the word of God (1:25). Finally, the audience are greeted in the hand of Paul himself, reminding them of his literal and metaphorical "chains" on account of the mystery of the Christ, and praying again that the grace of God (cf. 1:2), in the realm of which they already live (1:6; 3:16; 4:6), continue to be with them (4:18).

C. Summary on Colossians 4:7–18

1. The audience, as faithful brothers in Christ (1:2), are assured that Tychicus and Onesimus, their fellow beloved and faithful brothers who have brought them the letter from Paul and Timothy, will also personally inform them of all that has been happening with Paul and those with him in his imprisonment, further motivating them to do all that they have heard Paul, the minister suffering and struggling on their behalf, exhort them to do in the letter (4:7–9).

2. The audience are greeted by the only Jews ("those who are of the circumcision," 4:11) who are fellow workers of Paul for the kingdom of God—Aristarchus, a fellow prisoner, Mark, the cousin of Barnabas, and Jesus also known as Justus. That they have become a comfort to Paul prompts the audience, who have their own "circumcision" in Christ (2:11), to likewise comfort Paul in his imprisonment on their behalf by not being captivated by a Jewish "philosophy" of empty deceit (2:8). In addition, their fellow Colossian and "slave" of Christ Jesus, the one from whom they learned the gospel, Epaphras (1:5–7), greets them (4:10–12a).

3. The audience are made aware of the continuing concern of Epaphras, from whom they learned the word of the truth of the gospel (1:5–7), as he struggles

---

31. Wright, *Colossians*, 162: "From one point of view, grace has been the subject of the whole letter. Paul has written in order to emphasize the undeserved love of God in Christ, and all that follows from it. From another point of view, grace has been the *object* of the letter: Paul has written in order to be a *means* of grace, not merely to describe it. The letter closes as it began, in grateful prayer (Wright's emphases)."

and prays for them (4:12b), adding weight to the authority of Paul (and Timothy), and thus further prompting the audience to fulfill the letter's expectations of them.

4. Epaphras's prayer that the audience may stand complete in Christ, in whom are "all" the treasures of wisdom and knowledge hidden (2:3), and that they may be fully assured in "all" the will of God (4:12c) bolsters the exhortations for them in "all" wisdom to teach and admonish each other (3:16), as Paul and Timothy are admonishing every human being and teaching every human being in "all" wisdom, that they may present every human being complete in Christ (1:28).

5. That in his prayers and perhaps in other ways Epaphras is having much labor "on behalf of you" and those in the nearby cities of Laodicea and Hierapolis (4:13), continuing and complementing the letter's previous expressions of solicitude "on behalf of you" (1:7, 9, 24; 2:1; 4:12), serves as additional motivation for the Colossian audience, who have learned of the word of the truth of the gospel from Epaphras (1:5-7), to fulfill the letter's expectations of them, particularly that they not be captivated by the "philosophy" of empty deceit (2:8).

6. The audience have been made aware of the greetings to them from both explicitly Jewish (Aristarchus, Mark, Justus; 4:10-11) and other (Epaphras, Luke, Demas; 4:12a, 14) associates of Paul in his imprisonment, supplementing Paul's solicitude for them and thus further prompting them to do what Paul is telling them to do in the letter (4:14).

7. The audience are to greet their fellow believers in Laodicea as well as Nympha and the local church at her house (4:15). They are to make sure that the letter is read also in the church of the Laodiceans and that they are also to read the one from Laodicea (4:16) makes them aware not only of their interrelatedness to another individual church within the universal church, but that they are not the only local church in danger of being captivated by the "philosophy" of empty deceit (2:8), devoid of wisdom (2:23). The audience, who have received the Christ (2:6), are to tell Archippus to fulfill the ministry he received in the Lord (4:17), as Paul fulfilled for the audience the word of God (1:25). Finally, the audience are greeted in the hand of Paul himself, reminding them of his literal and metaphorical "chains" on account of the mystery of the Christ, and praying again that the grace of God (cf. 1:2), in the realm of which they already live (1:6; 3:16; 4:6), continue to be with them (4:18).

13
Summary and Conclusion

Encouragement To Walk in All Wisdom as Holy Ones in Christ

Having provided detailed summary conclusions for each of the ten chiastic units in the preceding chapters, I offer in this final chapter an overview of how Paul's letter to the Colossians, through the rhetorical dynamics of its intricate and intriguing chiastic structures, encourages its listeners not to be captivated by a "philosophy" of empty deceit having only the appearance of wisdom, but to walk in all wisdom as holy ones in Christ.

In the opening elements of the chiastic A unit (1:1-2) that introduces the letter to the Colossians, Paul indicates that he has not only received God's grace in being designated an authoritative apostle of Christ Jesus through the salvific will of *God* (1:1a), but responds to God's grace by exercising his apostleship in composing and sending, together with Timothy, "the brother" (1:1b), this letter. The central element of the chiasm then identifies the audience of the letter—those located in Colossae (1:2a), a city in the Lycus valley in Asia Minor. The audience then experience a pivot in the chiasm from Timothy, "the *brother*," to themselves as those who have also received God's grace and the empowerment to respond to it not only as "holy ones"—those set apart and consecrated by God for special benefits from and service to God, but also "faithful *brothers* in Christ"—believing fellow Christians now within the realm of being "in Christ" (1:2b) while also in Colossae. The climactic conclusion of the chiasm prepares the audience to further receive and experience, by listening to the letter, the empowerment that comes from the grace and peace Paul and Timothy wish for them as special gifts from *God* as "our Father"—the Father of all brotherly believers (1:2c) (ch. 3).

At the center of the chiastic B unit (1:3-14) the audience hear that Epaphras, from whom they learned the gospel, has informed Paul and Timothy of the audience's *love* in the Spirit (1:7-8). The audience then experience a chiastic parallel progression from the affirmation of *the day they (the audience) heard* and *came to know* the grace of *God* in truth in the word of the truth of the gospel that in *all* the world is *bearing fruit and growing* (1:5-6) to the prayer *from the day we (Paul and Timothy) heard* that they be filled with the *knowledge* of God's will in all wisdom and Spiritual understanding, to "walk," that is, behave and conduct their

203

lives, worthy of the Lord for every desire to please, in *every* good work *bearing fruit and growing* with regard to the *knowledge* of God (1:9-11). In the conclusion of the chiasm the audience experience a parallel progression from Paul and Timothy's *thanking* God the *Father* of our Lord Jesus Christ for the *love* the audience *have* for all the *holy ones* (1:3-4) to the audience's *thanking* the *Father* who made them fit for the share of the inheritance of the *holy ones* in the light and transferred all of us into the kingdom of the Son of his *love*, in whom *we have* redemption, the forgiveness of sins (1:12-14) (ch. 4).

The center of the chiastic C unit (1:15-23) makes the Colossian audience aware of the cosmic peace God has achieved among the things on the earth and the things in the heavens through the blood of the cross of Christ (1:20b). The audience then experience a chiastic parallel progression from Christ alone as the "head" of the *body*, the church, in whom all the divine fullness of God chose to dwell and through whom to *reconcile* all things to Christ (1:18-20a), to the audience now being *reconciled* by God in the *body* of the flesh of Christ through his death to present the audience as holy, that is, "holy ones" (1:2, 12), who are unblemished and blameless before Christ (1:21-22). In the conclusion of the chiasm the audience experience a parallel progression from the hymnic acclamation of Christ being the firstborn of *all creation*, for in him were created all things in the *heavens* and on the earth (1:15-17), to the exhortation for the audience to persevere in the faith, having been established and steadfast and not shifting from the hope of the gospel which they heard, which was proclaimed in *all creation* that is under *heaven*, and of which "I became, I, Paul, a minister" (1:23) (ch. 5).

At the center of the chiastic D unit (1:24-2:5) the audience hear a pivot from the labor involved in proclaiming Christ, for which Paul is *struggling* according to Christ's *working* (1:29ab), to that *working* of Christ in Paul in power, as he wishes the audience to know how great a *struggle* he is having on behalf of them and others (1:29c-2:1). The audience then experience a chiastic parallel progression from the *mystery* that has been *hidden* from the ages but now has been manifested to God's holy ones, to whom God wished to make known what is the *richness* of the glory of this *mystery* among the Gentiles, which is Christ among them, the proclamation of whom is in all *wisdom* (1:26-28), to Paul's wish that hearts may be held together for all *richness* of the full assurance of understanding, for knowledge of the *mystery* of God, Christ, in whom are all the treasures of *wisdom* and knowledge *hidden* (2:2-3). In the conclusion of the chiasm the audience hear a parallel progression from Paul's *rejoicing* in his *flesh* to fulfill for the audience the *word* of God (1:24-25) to his *speaking* (the word) that no one may speak contrary to them with persuasive speech, for even if absent in the *flesh*, he is *rejoicing* at seeing their good order and the firmness of their faith in Christ (2:4-5) (ch. 6).

At the center of the chiastic E unit (2:6-23) the audience hear a pivotal parallel progression from the affirmation that in Christ they were "circumcised" with a "circumcision" *not made with hands* in the removal of the body of the *flesh*, having been *buried with* him in the baptism, in whom indeed they were *raised with* him through faith in the working of the God who raised him from the *dead* (2:11–12), to the affirmation that God brought them, being *dead* in the "uncircumcision" of their *flesh*, to *life along with* Christ, having obliterated the *handwritten charge against us* (2:13–14). The audience then hear a chiastic parallel progression from the assertion that in Christ dwells all the fullness of the deity *bodily*, who is the *head* of every *principality* and *authority* (2:9–10), to the exhortation that, since God has removed the *principalities* and the *authorities*, the audience are not to let anyone judge them in regard to things not related to the *body* which belongs to the Christ, and not to let anyone, not holding to the *head*, from whom the whole *body* grows, condemn them (2:15–19).

In the conclusion of the chiastic E unit (2:6–23) the audience experience a parallel progression from the assertion that, *as* they received the Christ, they are to go on "walking," that is, behaving and conducting their lives, in him, not letting anyone captivate them through the *philosophy* (love of *wisdom*) which is empty deceit, *according to the tradition of human beings*, according to *the elemental forces of the world* (2:6–8), to the exhortation that, if they died with Christ from *the elemental forces of the world*, they should not let themselves be subjected to decrees *as* if living in the *world*, which things are all *according to the commandments and teachings of human beings*, not having *wisdom* (2:20–23) (ch. 7).

With Col 3:1–7, the E′ unit within the macrochiastic structure embracing the entire letter, the audience hear resonances, by way of the chiastic parallelism, with the corresponding E unit (2:6–23), which together with the E′ unit forms the pivotal center within the macrochiasm. That "*you were raised with* the Christ" (3:1) in the E′ unit reverberates with "*you were raised with* him" (2:12) in the E unit. The assertion, "for *you died* and your life has been hidden in the Christ with God" (3:3), in the E′ unit reiterates and develops the assertion, "if then *you have died* with Christ" (2:20), in the E unit. The assertion, "your life has been hidden *with the Christ*" (3:3), in the E′ unit explicitly elaborates on the assertion, "he brought you to life along *with him*" (2:13), in the E unit. The reminder, "among whom (the sons of disobedience) you also *walked* once" (3:7), in the E′ unit provides a resonating reason for the exhortation, "in him (the Christ, Jesus the Lord) *go on walking*" (2:6), in the E unit. And "when you *lived* in these (earthly things)" (3:7) in the E′ unit resonates with "as if *living* in the world" (2:20) in the E unit.

At the center of the chiastic E′ unit (3:1–7) the audience hear a pivotal parallel progression from the assertion, "for you died and *your life* has been hidden *with the Christ* in God" (3:3), to the promise, "whenever *the Christ, your life*, is manifested, then you also *with* him will be manifested in glory" (3:4). In the conclusion of the chiasm the audience hear a parallel progression from the exhortation, "if *then* you were raised with the Christ (3:1a) . . . think of the things above, not *the things upon the earth*" (3:2), to the exhortation, "put to death *then* the parts *that are upon the earth*" (3:5a). The audience also hear distinctive contrasts in parallels from the assertion, "where the Christ *is*, seated at the right hand of *God*" (3:1c), to the assertion about "the covetousness, which *is* idolatry, on account of which things the wrath of *God* is coming upon the sons of disobedience" (3:5c–6); and from the exhortation to "*seek* (ζητεῖτε) the things above" (3:1b) to an alliterative reminder of "when you *lived* (ἐζῆτε) in these (earthly things)" (3:7b) (ch. 8).

With Col 3:8–16, the D′ unit within the macrochiastic structure embracing the entire letter, the audience hear resonances of the corresponding D unit (1:24–2:5) in the overall chiasm. That the audience have "removed the old *human being* with its practices" (3:9) in the D′ unit is a consequence of "admonishing every *human being* and teaching every *human being* in all wisdom, that we may present every *human being* complete in Christ" (1:28) in the D unit. That the audience have "put on the new which is being renewed *for knowledge* according to the image of the one who created it" (3:10) in the D′ unit recalls "*for knowledge* of the mystery of God, Christ" (2:2) in the D unit. The address of the audience as "*holy ones*" (3:12) in the D′ unit recalls that the mystery has now been manifested to God's "*holy ones*" (1:26) in the D unit.

The "*love*, which is the bond of completeness" (3:14), in the D′ unit reminds the audience of those who "are held together in *love*" (2:2) in the D unit. The "bond of *completeness*" (3:14) in the D′ unit recalls the authors' aim to present "every human being *complete* in Christ" (1:28) in the D unit. That the audience were called to the peace of Christ "in one *body*" (3:15) in the D′ unit recalls Paul's "filling up what is lacking of the afflictions of the Christ in my flesh on behalf of his *body*, which is the church" (1:24), in the D unit. The exhortation to the audience, "let the *word* of Christ dwell in you richly" (3:16), in the D′ unit follows from and is part of Paul's aim "to fulfill for you the *word* of God" (1:25) in the D unit. And, finally, the exhortation for the audience to be "(a) *in all wisdom* (b) *teaching* and (c) *admonishing* each other" (3:16) in the D′ unit recalls, in a precise mini-chiastic order, the description of the authors' ministry to everyone, "(c) *admonishing* every human being and (b) *teaching* every human being (a) *in all wisdom*" (1:28) in the D unit.

The center of the chiastic D′ unit (3:8–16) poignantly, emphatically, and climactically affirms for the audience that in Christ "there is not Greek and Jew, circumcision and uncircumcision, barbarian, Scythian, slave, free, but Christ is all and in all" (3:11). The audience then hear a chiastic parallel progression from the assertion that they have "*put on* the new which is being renewed for knowledge according to the image of the one who created it" (3:10) to the consequent exhortation for them to "*put on* then, as God's chosen ones, holy and beloved, heartfelt compassion, kindness, humility, gentleness, patience" (3:12). In the conclusion of the chiasm the audience hear a parallel progression from the exhortation, "but now *you also* must put them all away: anger, rage, malice, slander, obscene talk from *your* mouth. Do not lie to *one another*, having removed the old human being with its practices" (3:8–9), to the exhortations that they are to be "bearing with *one another* . . . just as the Lord forgave you, so must *you also*" (3:13), and that they are to "let the peace of Christ rule in *your* hearts" (3:15) . . . in grace singing in *your* hearts to God" (3:16) (ch. 9).

With Col 3:17–4:1, the C′ unit within the macrochiastic structure embracing the entire letter, the audience hear resonances, by way of the chiastic parallelism, with the corresponding C unit (1:15–23) in the overall chiasm. The exhortation, "whatever you do in word or in *work*, do all things in the name of the Lord Jesus" (3:17), in the C′ unit counters the audience's past behavior regarding their "works"—"and you, once being alienated and enemies in mind in *works* that are evil" (1:21), in the C unit. "Those who are your masters according to the *flesh*" (3:22) in the C′ unit, the last occurrence of the word "flesh" in the letter, recalls that "he (God) has now reconciled (you) in the body of his (Christ's) *flesh*" (1:22) in the C unit, the first of the nine occurrences of the word "flesh" in the letter. And "knowing that you also have a Master in *heaven*" (4:1) in the C′ unit resonates with "(the gospel) which was proclaimed in all creation that is under *heaven*" (1:23), God's making of peace among all things in the cosmos—"whether the things on the earth or the things in the *heavens*" (1:20), and God's creation in Christ of "all things in the *heavens* and on the earth" (1:16) in the C unit.

At the center of the chiastic C′ unit (3:17–4:1) the audience hear a pivotal parallel progression from the exhortation for children to *obey* their parents *in all things* (3:20) to the exhortation for slaves to *obey in all things* those who are their masters according to the flesh (3:22). And in the conclusion of the chiasm the audience experience a parallel progression from the general exhortation to the whole audience, "*whatever you do* in word or in *work*, do all things in the name of the Lord Jesus" (3:17), to the more specific exhortation to the slaves within the audience, "*whatever you do*, from your soul *work* as for the Lord and not human beings" (3:23) (ch. 10).

With Col 4:2–6, the B′ unit within the letter's macrochiastic structure, the audience hear echoes of 1:3–14, the corresponding B unit in the overall chiasm. The directives regarding the audience's praying for Paul and Timothy in the B′ unit—"in *prayer* persevere" (4:2a) and "*praying* at the same time also for us" (4:3a)—recall the repeated reports of Paul and Timothy's reciprocal praying for the audience in the B unit—"always when *praying* for you" (1:3b) and "we do not cease *praying* on behalf of you" (1:9a). And likewise, the audience's "being watchful in it (prayer) in *thanksgiving*" (4:2b) in the B′ unit recalls and reciprocates Paul and Timothy's "*thanking* God the Father of our Lord Jesus Christ" (1:3a) and "*thanking* the Father" (1:12a) in the B unit.

The prayer, "that God may open for us a door for the *word*" (4:3b), and the exhortation, "let your *word* always be in grace" (4:6a), in the B′ unit recall that the audience have heard before of the hope laid up for them in the heavens "in the *word* of the truth of the gospel" (1:5b) in the B unit. And the exhortation to the audience, "in *wisdom walk* toward those outside" (4:5a), in the B′ unit recalls the prayer for the audience "in all *wisdom* and Spiritual understanding, to *walk* worthy of the Lord" (1:9b–10a) in the B unit.

The center of the chiastic B′ unit makes the audience keenly aware that it is on account of the mystery of the Christ that Paul is both physically "bound" in prison and metaphorically or spiritually "bound" to making that mystery known to others (4:3d). The audience then hear a chiastic parallel progression from the task of Paul and others to *speak* the mystery of the Christ (4:3c) to an emphasis on the divine necessity for Paul especially to carry out that task personally—"that I may manifest it as it is necessary for me to *speak*" (4:4). In the conclusion of the chiasm the audience hear a parallel progression from the request for the audience to pray "that God may open to us a door for the *word*" (4:2–3ab) to the exhortation for the audience to "let your *word* always be in grace, seasoned with salt, to know how it is necessary for you to answer each one" (4:6) (ch. 11).

With Col 4:7–18, the closing A′ unit within the letter's macrochiastic structure, the audience hear resonances of the corresponding A unit (1:1–2) that opens the letter. The description of Tychicus as the beloved "*brother*" and "*faithful*" minister" (4:7), the description of Onesimus as the "*faithful*" and beloved "*brother*" (4:9), and the directive to greet the "*brothers*" in Laodicea (4:15) in the A′ unit recall for the audience the description of Timothy as the "*brother*" (1:1) and the description of the audience themselves as "*faithful*" "*brothers*" in Christ (1:2) in the A unit. That the audience "may stand complete and fully assured in all the *will of God*" (4:12) in the A′ unit echoes that Paul is an "apostle of Christ Jesus through the *will of God*" (1:1) in the A unit. And the letter's closing greeting in the hand of Paul, "*grace* be with you" (4:18), in the A′ unit resonates with its opening greeting from *Paul* and Timothy (1:1), "*grace* to you and peace from God our Father" (1:2) in the A unit.

The center of the chiastic A′ unit assures the audience of Epaphras's prayer "that you may stand complete and fully assured in all the will of God" (4:12c). The audience then hear a chiastic parallel progression from the report that Epaphras is "always struggling *on behalf of you* in the prayers" (4:12b) to Paul's personal testifying for him "that he is having much labor *on behalf of you* and those in Laodicea and those in Hierapolis" (4:13). They then hear a chiastic parallel progression from the assurance that "Aristarchus, my fellow prisoner, *greets you*" (4:10a) to the assurance that "Luke, the beloved physician, *greets you*, and Demas" (4:14). In the conclusion of the chiasm the audience experience a parallel progression from the assurance that "Tychicus, the beloved *brother* and faithful *minister* and fellow slave *in the Lord*" (4:7), "with Onesimus, the faithful and beloved *brother*, who is one of you" (4:9a), "will make known to you all the things that are happening here" (4:9b) with regard to the situation of Paul in his imprisonment to a final exhortation for the audience to "greet the *brothers* in Laodicea" (4:15a) and to "say to Archippus, 'Look to the *ministry* which you received *in the Lord*, that you fulfill it'" (4:17) (ch. 12).

In sum, the chiastic structure of Colossians begins by exhorting its audience of "holy ones and faithful brothers in Christ" (1:2) that they, who have love for all the "holy ones" (1:4), are to be thanking the Father who has made them fit for the share of the inheritance of the "holy ones" in the light, as they have been rescued by God from the authority of the darkness and transferred into the kingdom of the

Son of God's love, in whom all of us believers have redemption, the forgiveness of sins (1:12–14). At the pivotal center of the chiastic structure of the letter the audience, who have "died with Christ," are urged not to behave as if living in the world (2:20), captivated by a "philosophy" of empty deceit (2:6), having only a reputation of wisdom (2:23), but rather, as those who were "raised with the Christ" (3:1a), to no longer "walk" or live in accord with the things on the earth (3:5–7), seeking instead the things above, where the Christ is, seated at the right hand of God (3:1b), so that they may be "in all wisdom teaching and admonishing each other" (3:16). Chiastically developing its opening prayer wish from Paul and Timothy of "grace to you" (1:2), the letter climactically concludes with Paul's personal greeting: "Keep on remembering my chains! Grace be with you!" (4:18).

In conclusion, listening to and experiencing the rhetorical dynamics of the intricate and intriguing chiastic patterns of Paul's letter to the Colossians encourages its audience, as "holy ones" in Christ, to "walk," that is, behave and conduct themselves, "in all wisdom," that is, within the dynamic realm of being in all the wisdom that is hidden in Christ (1:9, 28; 2:3; 3:16; 4:5), rather than "walking" in accord with a philosophy of empty deceit (2:6), only having a false reputation of wisdom (2:23). In short, Colossians functions as a concerted encouragement for its audience to walk in all wisdom as holy ones in Christ.

Bibliography

Aasgaard, Reidar. *"My Beloved Brothers and Sisters!" Christian Siblingship in Paul.* JSNTSup 265. London: Clark, 2004.
——. " 'Role Ethics' in Paul: The Significance of the Sibling Role for Paul's Ethical Thinking." *NTS* 48 (2002): 513-30.
Agnew, Francis H. "The Origin of the NT Apostle-Concept: A Review of Research." *JBL* 105 (1986): 75-96.
Aletti, Jean-Noel. *Colossiens 1:15-20: Genre et exégese du texte: Fonction de la thématique sapientielle.* AnBib 91. Rome: Biblical Institute, 1981.
——. *Saint Paul Épitre aux Colossiens: Introduction, traduction et commentaire.* EBib 20. Paris: Gabalda, 1993.
Allan, John A. "The 'In Christ' Formula in Ephesians." *NTS* 5 (1958-59): 54-62.
Arnold Clinton E. "Jesus Christ: 'Head' of the Church (Colossians and Ephesians)." Pp. 346-66 in *Jesus of Nazareth: Lord and Christ. Essays on the Historical Jesus and New Testament Christology.* Ed. Joel B. Green and Max Turner. Grand Rapids: Eerdmans, 1994.
——. *The Colossian Syncretism: The Interface Between Christianity and Folk Belief at Colossae.* WUNT 77. Tübingen: Mohr Siebeck, 1995.
Attridge, Harold W. "Becoming an Angel: Rival Baptismal Theologies at Colossae." Pp. 481-98 in *Religious Propaganda and Missionary Competition in the New Testament World: Essays Honoring Dieter Georgi.* Ed. Lukas Bormann, Kelly Del Tredici, and Angela Standhartinger. NovTSup 74. Leiden: Brill, 1994.
Balz, Horst. "ἅγιος." *EDNT* 1.16-20.
Barclay, John M. G. *Colossians and Philemon.* Sheffield: Sheffield Academic Press, 1997.
——. "Ordinary but Different: Colossians and Hidden Moral Identity." *ABR* 49 (2001): 34-52.
Barnett, Paul W. "Apostle." *DPL*, 45-51.
Barth, Markus, and Helmut Blanke. *Colossians: A New Translation with Introduction and Commentary.* AB 34B. New York: Doubleday, 1994.
Basevi, Claudio. "Col 1,15-20: Las posibles fuentes del 'himno' cristológico y su importancia para la interpretación." *ScrTh* 30 (1998): 779-802.
——. "La doctrina cristológica del 'himno' de Col 1,15-20." *ScrTh* 31 (1999): 317-44.
Baugh, Steven M. "The Poetic Form of Col 1:15-20." *WTJ* 47 (1985): 227-44.
Bedale, Stephen. "The Meaning of Kephale in the Pauline Epistles." *JTS* 5 (1954): 211-15.
Beetham, Christopher A. *Echoes of Scripture in the Letter of Paul to the Colossians.* BIS 96. Leiden: Brill, 2008.
Behr, J. "Colossians 1:13-20: A Chiastic Reading." *SVTQ* 40 (1996): 247-64.
Benoit, Pierre. "Corps, tête et plérôme dans les épîtres de la captivité." *RB* 63 (1956): 5-44.
——. " Ἅγιοι en Colossiens 1.12: hommes our anges?" Pp. 83-101 in *Paul and Paulinism: Essays in Honour of Charles Kingsley Barrett.* Ed. Morna D. Hooker and Stephen G. Wilson. London: SPCK, 1982.

Berger, Klaus. "Apostelbrief und apostolische Rede: Zum Formular frühchristlicher Briefe." *ZNW* 65 (1974): 190–231.
Bergmeier Roland. "περιπατέω." *EDNT* 3.75–76.
Beutler, Johannes. "ἀδελφός." *EDNT* 1.28–30.
Bevere, Allan R. *Sharing in the Inheritance: Identity and the Moral Life in Colossians*. JSNTSup 226. London: Sheffield Academic Press, 2003.
Bing, C. C. "The Warning in Colossians 1:21–23." *BSac* 164 (2007): 74–88.
Blomberg, Craig L. "The Structure of 2 Corinthians 1–7." *CTR* 4 (1989): 3–20.
Bockmuehl, Markus N. A. "A Note on the Text of Colossians 4:3." *JTS* 39 (1988): 489–94.
———. *Revelation and Mystery in Ancient Judaism and Pauline Christianity*. WUNT 2/36. Tübingen: Mohr, 1990.
Borchert, Gerald L. *Worship in the New Testament: Divine Mystery and Human Response*. St. Louis: Chalice, 2008.
Botha, Pieter J. J. "The Verbal Art of the Pauline Letters: Rhetoric, Performance and Presence." Pp. 409–28 in *Rhetoric and the New Testament: Essays from the 1992 Heidelberg Conference*. Ed. Stanley E. Porter and Thomas H. Olbricht. JSNTSup 90. Sheffield: JSOT, 1993.
Bouttier, Michel. *En Christ: Étude d'exégèse et de théologie pauliniennes*. Paris: Presses Universitaires, 1962.
Breck, John. "Biblical Chiasmus: Exploring Structure for Meaning." *BTB* 17 (1987): 70–74.
———. *The Shape of Biblical Language: Chiasmus in the Scriptures and Beyond*. Crestwood, NY: St. Vladimir's Seminary Press, 1994.
Brouwer, Wayne. *The Literary Development of John 13–17: A Chiastic Reading*. SBLDS 182. Atlanta: Society of Biblical Literature, 2000.
Bruce, Frederick Fyvie. *The Epistles to the Colossians, to Philemon, and to the Ephesians*. NICNT. Grand Rapids: Eerdmans, 1984.
Bujard, Walter. *Stilanalytische Untersuchungen zum Kolosserbrief als Beitrag zur Methodik von Sprachvergleichen*. SUNT 11. Göttingen: Vandenhoeck & Ruprecht, 1973.
Büchsel, Friedrich. "'In Christus' bei Paulus." *ZNW* 42 (1949): 141–58.
Bühner, Jan-Adolf. "ἀπόστολος." *EDNT* 1.142–46.
Cahill, Michael. "The Neglected Parallelism in Colossians 1,24–25." *ETL* 68 (1992): 142–47.
Campbell, Douglas A. "Unravelling Colossians 3.11b." *NTS* 42 (1996): 120–32.
———. "The Scythian Perspective in Col. 3:11: A Response to Troy Martin." *NovT* 39 (1997): 81–84.
Cannon, George E. *The Use of Traditional Materials in Colossians*. Macon, Ga.: Mercer University Press, 1983.
Carlos Reyes, Luis. "The Structure and Rhetoric of Colossians 1:15–20." *Filología Neotestamentaria* 12 (1999): 139–54.
Carr, Wesley A. *Angels and Principalities: The Background, Meaning and Development of the Pauline Phrase Hai Archai Kai Hai Exousiai*. SNTSMS 42. Cambridge: Cambridge University Press, 1981.
Carson, D. A., and Douglas J. Moo. *An Introduction to the New Testament*. Grand Rapids: Zondervan, 2005.
Carter, Warren, and John Paul Heil. *Matthew's Parables: Audience-Oriented Perspectives*. CBQMS 30. Washington: Catholic Biblical Association, 1998.
Cassidy, Richard J. *Paul in Chains: Roman Imprisonment and the Letters of St. Paul*. New York: Crossroad, 2001.
Cervin, Richard S. "Does Κεφαλή Mean 'Source' or 'Authority Over' in Greek Literature? A Rebuttal." *TJ* 10 (1989): 85–112.
Christopher, G. T. "A Discourse Analysis of Colossians 2:16–3:17." *Grace Theological Journal* 11 (1990): 205–20.
Clarke, Andrew D. "Equality or Mutuality? Paul's Use of 'Brother' Language." Pp. 151–64 in *The New Testament in Its First Century Setting: Essays on Context and Background in Honour of B. W. Winter on His 65th Birthday*. Ed. P. J. Williams, Andrew D. Clarke, Peter M. Head, and David Instone-Brewer. Grand Rapids: Eerdmans, 2004.

Cole, H. R. "The Christian and Time-Keeping in Colossians 2:16 and Galatians 4:10." *AUSS* 39 (2001): 273–82.
Craddock, Fred B. "'All Things in Him': A Critical Note on Col. i. 15–20." *NTS* 12 (1965): 78–80.
Dautzenberg, Gerhard. "ἀγωνίζομαι," *EDNT* 1.25–27.
Delebecque, É. "Sur un problème de temps chez Saint Paul (Col 3,1–4)." *Bib* 70 (1989): 389–95.
DeMaris, Richard E. *The Colossian Controversy: Wisdom in Dispute at Colossae.* JSNTSup 96. Sheffield: JSOT, 1994.
DeSilva, David A. "X Marks the Spot? A Critique of the Use of Chiasmus in Macro-Structural Analyses of Revelation." *JSNT* 30 (2008): 343–71.
Deterding, Paul E. *Colossians.* Concordia Commentary. St. Louis: Concordia, 2003.
Dewey, Joanna. "Mark as Aural Narrative: Structures as Clues to Understanding." *Sewanee Theological Review* 36 (1992): 45–56.
Drake, A. E. "The Riddle of Colossians: Quaerendo Invenietis." *NTS* 41 (1995): 123–44.
Dübbers, Michael. *Christologie und Existenz im Kolosserbrief: Exegetische und semantische Untersuchungen zur Intention des Kolosserbriefes.* WUNT 2/191. Tübingen: Mohr Siebeck, 2005.
Dunn, James D. G. "The Colossian Philosophy: A Confident Jewish Apologia." *Bib* 76 (1995): 153–81.
———. *The Epistles to the Colossians and to Philemon.* NIGTC. Grand Rapids: Eerdmans, 1996.
———. *The Theology of Paul the Apostle.* Grand Rapids: Eerdmans, 1998.
———. "Colossians, Letter To." Pp. 702–6 in *The New Interpreter's Dictionary of the Bible A-C Volume 1.* Nashville: Abingdon, 2006.
Elliger, Winfried. "ἐν." *EDNT* 1.447–49.
Ellis, E. Earle. "Paul and His Co-Workers." *NTS* 17 (1970–71): 437–52.
———. *History and Interpretation in New Testament Perspective.* BIS 54. Atlanta: Society of Biblical Literature, 2001.
———. *The Making of the New Testament Documents.* Leiden: Brill, 2002.
Evans, Craig A. "The Colossian Mystics." *Bib* 63 (1982): 188–205.
Fatehi, Mehrdad. *The Spirit's Relation to the Risen Lord in Paul: An Examination of Its Christological Implications.* WUNT 128. Tübingen: Mohr Siebeck, 2000.
Fee, Gordon D. *God's Empowering Presence: The Holy Spirit in the Letters of Paul.* Peabody, Mass.: Hendrickson, 1994.
———. "Old Testament Intertextuality in Colossians: Reflections on Pauline Christology and Gentile Inclusion in God's Story." Pp. 201–21 in *History and Exegesis: New Testament Essays in Honor of Dr. E. Earle Ellis for His 80th Birthday.* Ed. Sang-Won Son. London: Clark, 2006.
———. *Pauline Christology: An Exegetical-Theological Study.* Peabody, Mass.: Hendrickson, 2007.
Finlan, Stephen. *The Background and Content of Paul's Cultic Atonement Metaphors.* SBLAbib 19. Atlanta: Society of Biblical Literature, 2004.
———. *The Apostle Paul and the Pauline Tradition.* Collegeville, Minn.: Liturgical Press, 2008.
Fossum, Jarl E. "Colossians 1.15–18a in the Light of Jewish Mysticism and Gnosticism." *NTS* 35 (1989): 183–201.
Francis, Fred O. "Humility and Angelic Worship in Col 2:18." Pp. 163–95 in *Conflict at Colossae: A Problem in the Interpretation of Early Christianity Illustrated by Selected Modern Studies: Revised Edition.* Ed. Fred O. Francis and Wayne A. Meeks. Sources for Biblical Study 4. Missoula, Mont.: Scholars Press, 1975.
———. "The Background of EMBATEUEIN (Col 2:18) in Legal Papyri and Oralce Inscriptions." Pp. 197–207 in *Conflict at Colossae: A Problem in the Interpretation of Early Christianity Illustrated by Selected Modern Studies: Revised Edition.* Ed. Fred O. Francis and Wayne A. Meeks. Sources for Biblical Study 4. Missoula, Mont.: Society of Biblical Literature, 1975.
———. "The Christological Argument of Colossians." Pp. 192–208 in *God's Christ and His People: Studies in Honour of Nils Alstrup Dahl.* Ed. Jacob Jervell and Wayne A. Meeks. Oslo: Universitetsforlaget, 1977.
Garland, David E. *Colossians and Philemon: The NIV Application Commentary.* Grand Rapids: Zondervan, 1998.

Garuti, Paolo. "Il Primogenito, immagine del Dio invisibile: Qualche spunto di cristologia da Col 1,15–20 ed Ef 2,14–18." *DivThom* 28 (2001): 119–37.

———. "L' eresia di Colossi, l'antanaclasi e la storia della redazione: Qualche considerazione a proposito di Col 2,6–23." *Ang* 79 (2002): 303–26.

Gelardini, Gabriella. *"Verhärtet eure Herzen nicht": Der Hebräer, eine Synagogenhomilie zu Tischa be-Aw.* BIS 83. Leiden: Brill, 2007.

Giesen, Heinz. "ταπεινοφροσύνη." *EDNT* 3.333–34.

Gilfillan Upton, Bridget. *Hearing Mark's Endings: Listening to Ancient Popular Texts Through Speech Act Theory.* BIS 79. Leiden: Brill, 2006.

Goldenberg, D. "Scythian-Barbarian: The Permutations of a Classical Topos in Jewish and Christian Texts of Late Antiquity." *JJS* 49 (1998): 87–102.

Gordley, Matthew E. *The Colossian Hymn in Context: An Exegesis in Light of Jewish and Greco-Roman Hymnic and Epistolary Conventions.* WUNT 228. Tübingen: Mohr Siebeck, 2007.

Gorman, Michael J. *Apostle of the Crucified Lord: A Theological Introduction to Paul and His Letters.* Grand Rapids: Eerdmans, 2004.

Goulder, Michael D. "Colossians and Barbelo." *NTS* 41 (1995): 601–19.

Grudem, Wayne A. "Does Kephalē ('Head') Mean 'Source' or 'Authority Over' in Greek Literature? A Survey of 2,336 Examples." *TJ* 6 (1985): 38–59.

———. "The Meaning of Κεφαλή ('Head'): A Response to Recent Studies." *TJ* 11 (1990): 3–72.

Hackenberg, Wolfgang. "ἐπιγινώσκω." *EDNT* 2.24–25.

Harland, Philip A. "Familial Dimensions of Group Identity: 'Brothers' (Ἀδελφοί) in Associations of the Greek East." *JBL* 124 (2005): 491–513.

Harrington, Daniel J. "Christians and Jews in Colossians." Pp. 153–61 in *Diaspora Jews and Judaism: Essays in Honor of, and in Dialogue with, A. Thomas Kraabel.* Ed. J. Andrew Overmann and Robert S. MacLennan. South Florida Studies in the History of Judaism 41. Atlanta: Scholars Press, 1992.

Harris, Murray J. *Colossians & Philemon.* Exegetical Guide to the Greek New Testament. Grand Rapids: Eerdmans, 1991.

———. *The Second Epistle to the Corinthians: A Commentary on the Greek Text.* NIGTC. Grand Rapids: Eerdmans, 2005.

Harrison, James R. *Paul's Language of Grace in Its Graeco-Roman Context.* WUNT 172. Tübingen: Mohr Siebeck, 2003.

Hartman, L. "Universal Reconciliation (Col 1,20)." *Studien Zum Neuen Testament und Seiner Umwelt* 10 (1985): 109–21.

———. "Humble and Confident: On the So-Called Philosophers in Colossae." *ST* 49 (1995): 25–39.

Harvey, John D. *Listening to the Text: Oral Patterning in Paul's Letters.* Grand Rapids: Baker, 1998.

Hay, David M. *Colossians.* ANTC. Nashville: Abingdon, 2000.

Hearon, Holly E. "The Implications of Orality for Studies of the Biblical Text." Pp. 3–20 in *Performing the Gospel: Orality, Memory, and Mark.* Ed. Richard A. Horsley, Jonathan A. Draper, and John Miles Foley. Minneapolis: Fortress, 2006.

Heil, John Paul. *The Meal Scenes in Luke-Acts: An Audience-Oriented Approach.* SBLMS 52. Atlanta: Society of Biblical Literature, 1999.

———. "The Chiastic Structure and Meaning of Paul's Letter to Philemon." *Bib* 82 (2001): 178–206.

———. *The Transfiguration of Jesus: Narrative Meaning and Function of Mark 9:2–8, Matt 17:1–8 and Luke 9:28–36.* AnBib 144. Rome: Editrice Pontificio Istituto Biblico, 2000.

———. *The Rhetorical Role of Scripture in 1 Corinthians.* Studies in Biblical Literature 15. Atlanta: Society of Biblical Literature, 2005.

———. *Ephesians: Empowerment to Walk in Love for the Unity of All in Christ,* Studies in Biblical Literature 13. Atlanta: Society of Biblical Literature, 2007.

Helyer, Larry L. "Cosmic Christology and Col 1:15–20." *JETS* 37 (1994): 235–46.

Helyer, Larry R. "Arius Revisited: The Firstborn Over All Creation (Col 1:15)." *JETS* 31 (1988): 59–67.

———. "Recent Research on Colossians 1:15–20." *Grace Theological Journal* 12 (1991): 51–67.
Henderson, Suzanne Watts. "Taking Liberties with the Text: The Colossians Household Code as Hermeneutical Paradigm." *Int* 60 (2006): 420–32.
———. "God's Fullness in Bodily Form: Christ and Church in Colossians." *ExpTim* 118 (2007): 169–73.
Hock, Andreas. "Christ is the Parade: A Comparative Study of the Triumphal Procession in 2 Cor 2,14 and Col 2,15." *Bib* 88 (2007): 110–19.
Hofius, Otfried. "'Erstgeborener vor aller Schöpfung'—'Erstgeborener aus den Toten': Erwägungen zu Struktur und Aussage des Christushumnus Kol 1, 15–20." Pp. 185–203 in *Auferstehung—Resurrection: The Fourth Durham-Tübingen Research Symposium: Resurrection, Tranfiguration and Exaltation in Old Testament, Ancient Judaism and Early Christianity (Tübingen, September, 1999)*. Ed. Friedrich Avemarie and Hermann Lichtenberger. WUNT 135. Tübingen: Mohr Siebeck, 2001.
Holbrook, F. B. "Did the Apostle Paul Abolish the Sabbath? Colossians 2:14–17 Revisited." *Journal of the Adventist Theological Society* 13 (2002): 64–72.
Holland, Tom. "Firstborn and the Colossian Hymn." *Trinity Theological Journal* 12 (2004): 22–53.
Hooker, Morna D. "Were There False Teachers in Colossae?" Pp. 315–31 in *Christ and Spirit in the New Testament: Essays in Honour of Charles Francis Digby Moule*. Ed. Barnabas Lindars and Stephen S. Smalley. Cambridge: Cambridge University Press, 1973.
Hoppe, Rudolf. *Der Triumph des Kreuzes: Studien zum Verhältnis des Kolosserbriefes zur paulinischen Kreuzestheologie*. SBB 28. Stuttgart: Katholisches Bibelwerk, 1994.
House, H. Wayne. "Doctrinal Issues in Colossians. Part 1 (of 4 Parts): Heresies in the Colossian Church." *BSac* 149 (1992): 45–59.
———. "Doctrinal Issues in Colossians. Part 2 (of 4 Parts): The Doctrine of Christ in Colossians." *BSac* 149 (1992): 180–92.
Jeremias, Joachim. "Chiasmus in den Paulusbriefen." *ZNW* 49 (1958): 145–56.
Johnson, Luke Timothy. *The Writings of the New Testament: An Interpretation: Revised Edition*. Minneapolis: Fortress, 1999.
Jones, P. "L'Évangile pour l'âge du verseau: Colossiens 1:15–20." *RRef* 50 (1999): 13–23.
Jordaan, Pierre. "The Inscriptio Colossians 1:1–2." *Ekklesiastikos Pharos* 79 (1997): 62–69.
———. "The Function of the Household Code in Colossians 3:18–4:1." *Ekklesiastikos Pharos* 80 (1998): 39–46.
Keesmaat, Sylvia C. "In the Face of the Empire: Paul's Use of Scripture in the Shorter Epistles." Pp. 182–212 in *Hearing the Old Testament in the New Testament*. Ed. Stanley E. Porter. McMaster New Testament Studies. Grand Rapids: Eerdmans, 2006.
Kiley, Mark. *Colossians as Pseudepigraphy*. The Biblical Seminar 4. Sheffield: JSOT, 1986.
Kourie, Celia E. T. "In Christ and Related Expressions in Paul." *Theologia Evangelica* 20 (1987): 33–43.
Kremer, Jacob. "πάθημα." *EDNT* 3.1–2.
———. "Was an den Bedrängnissen des Christus mangelt: Versuch einer bibeltheologischen Neuinterpretation von Kol 1,24." *Bib* 82 (2001): 130–46.
Krentz, Edgar. "De Caesare et Christo." *CurTM* 28 (2001): 341–45.
Kuhli, Horst. "εἰκών." *EDNT* 1.388–91.
Lähnemann, Johannes. *Der Kolosserbrief: Komposition, Situation und Argumentation*. SNT 3. Gütersloh: Gerd Mohn, 1971.
Lamp, Jeffrey S. "Wisdom in Col 1:15–20: Contribution and Significance." *JETS* 41 (1998): 45–53.
Langkammer, Hugolinus. "πρωτότοκος." *EDNT* 3.189–191.
Légasse, Simon. "εὐδοκέω." *EDNT* 2.75.
Levison, John R. "2 Apoc. Bar 48:42–52:7 and the Apocalyptic Dimension of Colossians 3:1–6." *JBL* 108 (1989): 93–108.
Lieu, Judith M. "'Grace to You and Peace': The Apostolic Greeting." *BJRL* 68 (1985): 161–78.
Lightfoot, Joseph Barber. *The Epistles of St Paul: Colossians and Philemon*. London: Macmillan, 1875.

Lincoln, Andrew T. "The Household Code and Wisdom Mode of Colossians." *JSNT* 74 (1999): 93-112.
Longenecker, Bruce W. *Rhetoric at the Boundaries: The Art and Theology of the New Testament Chain-Link Transitions*. Waco, Texas: Baylor University Press, 2005.
Luter, A. Boyd, and Michelle V. Lee. "Philippians as Chiasmus: Key to the Structure, Unity and Theme Questions." *NTS* 41 (1995): 89-101.
Luter, A. Boyd. "Grace." *DPL*, 372-74.
Luttenberger, Joram. "Der gekreuzigte Schuldschein: Ein Aspekt der Deutung des Todes Jesu im Kolosserbrief." *NTS* 51 (2005): 80-95.
Luz, Ulrich. "Bild des unsichtbaren Gottes—Christus: Der Kolosserhymnus (Kol 1,15-20)." *BK* 63 (2008): 13-17.
Lyonnet, Stanislas. "Paul's Adversaries in Colossae." Pp. 147-61 in *Conflict at Colossae: A Problem in the Interpretation of Early Christianity Illustrated by Selected Modern Studies: Revised Edition*. Ed. Fred O. Francis and Wayne A. Meeks. Sources for Biblical Study 4. Missoula, Mont.: Society of Biblical Literature, 1975.
MacDonald, Margaret Y. *Colossians and Ephesians*. SP 17. Collegeville, Minn.: Liturgical Press, 2000.
———. "Slavery, Sexuality and House Churches: A Reassessment of Colossians 3.18-4.1 in Light of New Research on the Roman Family." *NTS* 53 (2007): 94-113.
Maier, Harry O. "A Sly Civility: Colossians and Empire." *JSNT* 27 (2005): 323-49.
Maisch, Ingrid. *Der Brief an die Gemeinde in Kolossä*. Theologischer Kommentar Zum Neuen Testament 12. Stuttgart: Kohlhammer, 2003.
Man, Ronald E. "The Value of Chiasm for New Testament Interpretation." *BSac* 141 (1984): 146-57.
Martin, Ralph P. *Colossians and Philemon*. 3d ed. NCB. Grand Rapids: Eerdmans, 1981.
Martin, Troy W. "The Scythian Perspective in Col 3:11." *NovT* 38 (1995): 249-61.
———. "But Let Everyone Discern the Body of Christ (Col 2:17)." *JBL* 114 (1995): 249-55.
———. *By Philosophy and Empty Deceit: Colossians as Response to a Cynic Critique*. JSNTSup 118. Sheffield: Sheffield Academic Press, 1996.
———. "Pagan and Judeo-Christian Time-Keeping Schemes in Gal 4.10 and Col 2.16." *NTS* 42 (1996): 105-19.
———. "Scythian Perspective or Elusive Chiasm: A Reply to Douglas A. Campbell." *NovT* 41 (1999): 256-64.
Matera, Frank J. *New Testament Theology: Exploring Diversity and Unity*. Louisville: Westminster John Knox, 2007.
McCown, Wayne. "The Hymnic Structure of Colossians 1:15-20." *EvQ* 51 (1979): 156-62.
Merkel, Helmut. "ἀποκαταλλάσσω." *EDNT* 2.261-63.
Metzger, Bruce Manning. *A Textual Commentary on the Greek New Testament: Second Edition*. Stuttgart: Deutsche Bibelgesellschaft, 1994.
Michel, Otto. "πατήρ." *EDNT* 3.53-57.
Moo, Douglas J. *The Letters to Colossians and to Philemon*. Pillar New Testament Commentary. Grand Rapids: Eerdmans, 2008.
Moser, Paul K. "Apostle." Pp. 78-79 in *Eerdmans Dictionary of the Bible*. Edited by David Noel Freedman. Grand Rapids: Eerdmans, 2000.
Moule, Charles Francis Digby. *The Epistles to the Colossians and Philemon*. CGTC. Cambridge: Cambridge University Press, 1957.
Mullins, Terrence Y. "The Thanksgivings of Philemon and Colossians." *NTS* 30 (1984): 288-93.
Murphy-O'Connor, Jerome. "Tradition and Redaction in Col 1:15-20." *RB* 102 (1995): 231-41.
———. "The Greeters in Col 4:10-14 and Phlm 23-24." *RB* 114 (2007): 416-26.
Neugebauer, Fritz. "Das Paulinische 'In Christo.'" *NTS* 4 (1957-58): 124-38.
Nobbs, Alanna. "'Beloved Brothers' in the New Testament and Early Christian World." Pp. 143-50 in *The New Testament in Its First Century Setting: Essays on Context and Background in Honour of B. W. Winter on His 65th Birthday*. Ed. P. J. Williams, Andrew D. Clarke, Peter M. Head, and David Instone-Brewer. Grand Rapids: Eerdmans, 2004.
Nolland, John. "Grace as Power." *NovT* 28 (1986): 26-31.

O'Brien, Peter Thomas. *Introductory Thanksgivings in the Letters of Paul*. NovTSup 49. Leiden: Brill, 1977.
———. *Colossians, Philemon*. WBC 44. Waco, Texas: Word, 1982.
Olbricht, Thomas H. "The Stoicheia and the Rhetoric of Colossians: Then and Now." Pp. 308–28 in *Rhetoric, Scripture and Theology: Essays from the 1994 Pretoria Conference*. Ed. Stanley E. Porter and Thomas H. Olbricht. JSNTSup 131. Sheffield: Sheffield, 1996.
Ollrog, Wolf-Henning. *Paulus und seine Mitarbeiter: Untersuchungen zu Theorie und Praxis der paulinischen Mission*. WMANT 50. Neukirchen-Vluyn: Neukirchener Verlag, 1979.
Osiek, Carolyn, and David L. Balch. *Families in the New Testament World: Households and House Churches*. Louisville: Westminster John Knox, 1997.
Otero Lázaro, Tomás. *Col 1,15-20 en el contexto de la carta*. Tesi Gregoriana, Serie Teologia 48. Rome: Editrice Pontificia Università Gregoriana, 1999.
Overfield, P. D. "Pleroma: A Study in Content and Context." *NTS* 25 (1979): 384–96.
Pahl, Michael W. "The 'Gospel' and the 'Word': Exploring Some Early Christian Patterns." *JSNT* 29 (2006): 211–27.
Perriman, Andrew C. "The Pattern of Christ's Sufferings: Colossians 1:24 and Philippians 3:10–11." *TynBul* 42 (1991): 62–79.
Plümacher, Eckhard. "στοιχεῖον." *EDNT* 3.277–78.
Porter, Stanley E., and Jeffrey T. Reed. "Philippians as a Macro-Chiasm and Its Exegetical Significance." *NTS* 44 (1998): 213–31.
Porter, Stanley E. "Holiness, Sanctification." *DPL*, 397–402.
———. "P. Oxy. 744.4 and Colossians 3,9." *Bib* 73 (1992): 565–67.
Reicke, Bo. "The Historical Setting of Colossians." *RevExp* 70 (1973): 429–38.
———. *Re-Examining Paul's Letters: The History of the Pauline Correspondence*. Harrisburg: Trinity, 2001.
Richards, E. Randolph. *The Secretary in the Letters of Paul*. WUNT 42. Tübingen: Mohr Siebeck, 1991.
———. *Paul and First-Century Letter Writing: Secretaries, Composition and Collection*. Downers Grove, Ill.: InterVarsity, 2004.
Roberts, J. H. "Jewish Mystical Experience in the Early Christian Era as Background to Understanding Colossians." *Neot* 32 (1998): 161–89.
———. "Die sintaktiese binding van μετὰ χαρᾶς in Kolossense 1:11: 'n Strukturele motivering." *HvTSt* 57 (2001): 187–209.
Robinson, John A. T. *Redating the New Testament*. London: SCM, 1976.
Romanello, Stefano. "Col 1,15–20: la posta in gioco di una cristologia singolarmente pregnante." *Teol* 30 (2005): 13–48.
Rosner, Brian S. *Greed as Idolatry: The Origin and Meaning of a Pauline Metaphor*. Grand Rapids: Eerdmans, 2007.
Rowland, Christopher. "Apocalyptic Visions and the Exaltation of Christ in the Letter to the Colossians." *JSNT* 19 (1983): 73–83.
Royalty, Robert M. "Dwelling on Visions: On the Nature of the So-Called 'Colossians Heresy.'" *Bib* 83 (2002): 329–57.
Rusam, Dietrich. "Neue Belege zu den στοιχεῖα τοῦ κόσμου (Gal 4,3.9; Kol 2,8.20)." *ZNW* 83 (1992): 119–25.
Sand, Alexander. "νοῦς." *EDNT* 2.478–79.
Sappington, Thomas J. *Revelation and Redemption at Colossae*. JSNTSup 53. Sheffield: JSOT, 1991.
Schneider, Gerhard. "θεότης." *EDNT* 2.143.
Schubert, Paul. *Form and Function of the Pauline Thanksgiving*. BZNW 20. Berlin: Töpelmann, 1939.
Schweizer, Eduard. *The Letter to the Colossians: A Commentary*. Minneapolis: Augsburg, 1982.
———. "σωματικῶς." *EDNT* 3.325.
Seifrid, Mark A. "In Christ." *DPL*, 433–36.
Shiell, William David. *Reading Acts: The Lector and the Early Christian Audience*. BIS 70. Boston: Brill, 2004.

Shiner, Whitney Taylor. *Proclaiming the Gospel: First Century Performance of Mark*. Harrisburg: Trinity, 2003.
Shogren, Gary S. "Presently Entering the Kingdom of Christ: The Background and Purpose of Col 1:12–14." *JETS* 31 (1988): 173–80.
Slater, Thomas B. "Translating ἅγιος in Col 1,2 and Eph 1,1." *Bib* 87 (2006): 52–54.
Smith, Ian K. *Heavenly Perspective: A Study of the Apostle Paul's Response to a Jewish Mystical Movement at Colossae*. LNTS 326. London: Clark, 2006.
Son, Sang-Won. "τὸ σῶμα τοῦ Χριστοῦ In Colossians 2:17." Pp. 222–38 in *History and Exegesis: New Testament Essays in Honor of Dr. E. Earle Ellis for His 80th Birthday*. Ed. Sang-Won Son. London: Clark, 2006.
Spicq, Ceslas. *Theological Lexicon of the New Testament*. Translated and edited by James D. Ernest. 3 vols. Peabody, Mass.: Hendrickson, 1994.
Standhartinger, Angela. "The Origin and Intention of the Household Code in the Letter to the Colossians." *JSNT* 79 (2000): 117–30.
Sterling, Gregory E. "Prepositional Metaphysics in Jewish Wisdom Speculation and Early Christian Liturgical Texts." Pp. 219–38 in *Wisdom and Logos: Studies in Jewish Thought in Honor of David Winston*. Ed. David T. Runia and Gregory E. Sterling. Studia Philonica Annual 9. Atlanta: Scholars Press, 1997.
———. "A Philosophy According to the Elements of the Cosmos: Colossian Christianity and Philo of Alexandria." Pp. 349–73 in *Philon d'Alexandrie et le langage de la philosophie: Actes du colloque international organisé par le Centre d'études sur la philosophie hellénistique et romaine de l'Université de Paris XII-Val de Marne (Créteil, Fontenay, Paris, 26-28 octobre 1995)*. Ed. Carlos Lévy. Turnhout, Belgium: Brepols, 1998.
Stettler, Christian. *Der Kolosserhymnus: Untersuchungen zu Form, traditionsgeschichtlichen Hintergrund und Aussage von Kol 1,15–20*. WUNT 2/131. Tübingen: Mohr Siebeck, 2000.
———. "The Opponents at Colossae." Pp. 169–200 in *Paul and His Opponents*. Ed. Stanley E. Porter. Pauline Studies 2. Leiden: Brill, 2005.
Still, Todd D. "Eschatology in Colossians: How Realized is It?" *NTS* 50 (2004): 125–38.
———. "Colossians." Pp. 265–360 in *The Expositor's Bible Commentary: Revised Edition*, Vol. 12. Ed. Tremper Longman and David E. Garland. Grand Rapids: Zondervan, 2006.
Stirewalt, Luther M. *Paul: The Letter Writer*. Grand Rapids: Eerdmans, 2003.
Stock, Augustine. "Chiastic Awareness and Education in Antiquity." *BTB* 14 (1984): 23–27.
Sumney, Jerry L. "Those Who 'Pass Judgment': The Identity of the Opponents in Colossians." *Bib* 74 (1993): 366–88.
———. "'I Fill Up What Is Lacking in the Afflictions of Christ': Paul's Vicarious Suffering in Colossians." *CBQ* 68 (2006): 664–80.
———. *Colossians: A Commentary*. NTL. Louisville: Westminster John Knox, 2008.
Swart, G. J. "Eschatological Vision or Exhortation to Visible Christian Conduct? Notes on the Interpretation of Colossians 3:4." *Neot* 33 (1999): 169–77.
Sweeney, J. P. "The Priority of Prayer in Colossians 4:2–4." *BSac* 159 (2002): 318–33.
———. "Guidelines on Christian Witness in Colossians 4:5–6." *BSac* 159 (2002): 449–61.
Talbert, Charles H. *Ephesians and Colossians*. Paideia Commentaries on the New Testament. Grand Rapids: Baker, 2007.
Thekkekara, M. "Colossians 3:11a: The Abolition of Barriers." *Indian Theological Studies* 36 (1999): 105–25.
———. "Colossians 3,11." *Biblebhashyam* 25 (1999): 266–84.
Thompson, Marianne Meye. *Colossians & Philemon*. The Two Horizons New Testament Commentary. Grand Rapids: Eerdmans, 2005.
Thomson, Ian H. *Chiasmus in the Pauline Letters*. JSNTSup 111. Sheffield: Sheffield Academic Press, 1995.
Thornton, T. C. G. "Jewish New Moon Festivals, Galatians 4:3–11 and Colossians 2:16." *JTS* 40 (1989): 97–100.

Thurston, Bonnie B. "Paul's Associates in Colossians 4:7-17." *ResQ* 41 (1999): 45-53.
Tolmie, D. Francois. *Persuading the Galatians: A Text-Centered Rhetorical Analysis of a Pauline Letter.* WUNT 190. Tübingen: Mohr Siebeck, 2005.
Trainor, Michael. "The Cosmic Christology of Colossians 1:15-20 in the Light of Contemporary Ecological Issues." *ABR* 53 (2005): 54-69.
Tripp, David. "ΚΑΤΟΙΚΗΣΑΙ, ΚΑΤΟΙΚΕΙ (Colossians 1:19, 2:9): Christology, or Soteriology Also?" *ExpTim* 116 (2004): 78-79.
Van Broekhoven, H. "The Social Profiles in the Colossian Debate." *JSNT* 66 (1997): 73-90.
van Kooten, George H. *Cosmic Christology in Paul and the Pauline School: Colossians and Ephesians in the Context of Graeco-Roman Cosmology, with a New Synopsis of the Greek Texts.* WUNT 2/171. Tübingen: Mohr Siebeck, 2003.
Vergeer, W. C. "Σκία and Σῶμα: The Strategy of Contextualisation in Colossians 2:17: A Contribution to the Quest for a Legitimate Contextual Theology Today." *Neot* 28 (1994): 379-93.
Voelz, James W. "Present and Aorist Verbal Aspect: A New Proposal." *Neot* 27 (1993): 153-64.
Walsh, Brian J., and Sylvia C. Keesmaat. *Colossians Remixed: Subverting the Empire.* Downers Grove, Ill.: InterVarsity, 2004.
Walter, Nikolaus. "δόγμα." *EDNT* 1.339-40.
Wedderburn, Alexander J. M. "Some Observations on Paul's Use of the Phrases 'in Christ' and 'with Christ.'" *JSNT* 25 (1985): 83-97.
———. "The Theology of Colossians." Pp. 3-71 in *The Theology of the Later Pauline Letters.* Ed. James D. G. Dunn. New Testament Theology. Cambridge: Cambridge University Press, 1993.
Welch, John W. "Chiasmus in the New Testament." Pp. 211-49 in *Chiasmus in Antiquity: Structures, Analyses, Exegesis.* Ed. John W. Welch. Hildesheim: Gerstenberg, 1981.
———. "Criteria for Identifying and Evaluating the Presence of Chiasmus." Pp. 157-74 in *Chiasmus Bibliography.* Ed. John W. Welch and Daniel B. McKinlay. Provo, Utah: Research, 1999.
Wendland, Ernst R. "Cohesion in Colossians: A Structural-Thematic Outline." *Notes on Translation* 6 (1992): 28-62.
Wevers, John William. *Notes on the Greek Text of Genesis.* SBLSCS 35. Atlanta: Scholars Press, 1993.
Wilder, Terry L. *Pseudonymity, the New Testament and Deception: An Inquiry Into Intention and Reception.* Lanham, Md.: University Press of America, 2004.
Wiles, Gordon P. *Paul's Intercessory Prayers: The Significance of the Intercessory Prayer Passages in the Letters of St. Paul.* SNTSMS 24. Cambridge: Cambridge University Press, 1974.
Williamson, L. "Led in Triumph: Paul's Use of THRIAMBEUO." *Int* 22 (1968): 317-22.
Wilson, Mark. *The Victor Sayings in the Book of Revelation.* Eugene, Oreg.: Wipf and Stock, 2007.
Wilson, Robert McLachlan. *Colossians and Philemon.* ICC. London: Clark, 2005.
Wilson, Walter T. *The Hope of Glory: Education and Exhortation in the Epistle to the Colossians.* NovTSup 88. Leiden: Brill, 1997.
———. "The 'Practical' Achievement of Colossians: A Theological Assessment." *HBT* 20 (1998): 49-74.
Witherington, Ben. *Letters and Homilies for Hellenized Christians Volume 1: A Socio-Rhetorical Commentary on Titus, 1-2 Timothy and 1-3 John.* Downers Grove, Ill.: InterVarsity, 2006.
———. "Do Everything in the Name of God: Ethics and Ethos in Colossians." Pp. 303-33 in *Identity, Ethics, and Ethos in the New Testament.* Ed. Jan G. van der Watt. BZNW 141. Berlin: De Gruyter, 2006.
———. *The Letters to Philemon, the Colossians, and the Ephesians: A Socio-Rhetorical Commentary on the Captivity Epistles.* Grand Rapids: Eerdmans, 2007.
Witulski, Thomas. "Gegenwart und Zukunft in den eschatologischen Konzeptionen des Kolosser- und Epheserbriefes." *ZNW* 96 (2005): 211-42.
Wright, Nicholas Thomas. *The Epistles of Paul to the Colossians and Philemon: An Introduction and Commentary.* TNTC. Grand Rapids: Eerdmans, 1986.
———. "Poetry and Theology in Colossians 1.15-20." *NTS* 36 (1990): 444-68.
Wronka, S. "La proveniensa e il contesto del codice domestico di Col 3,18-4,1." *Analecta Cracoviensia* 36 (2004): 365-80.

Yamauchi, E. "The Scythians—Who Were They? And Why Did Paul Include Them in Colossians 3.11?" *Priscilla Papers* 21 (2007): 13–18.

Yates, Roy. "Colossians 2,14: Metaphor of Forgiveness." *Bib* 71 (1990): 248–59.

———. "Colossians 2.15: Christ Triumphant." *NTS* 37 (1991): 573–91.

———. "The Christian Way of Life: The Paraenetic Material in Colossians 3:1–4:6." *EvQ* 63 (1991): 241–51.

Yinger, Kent L. "Translating καταβραβευέτω ['Disqualify' NRSV] in Colossians 2:18." *BT* 54 (2003): 138–45.

Scripture Index

Old Testament

Genesis
1–2   51
1:26–27 (LXX)   149, 161
3:3 (LXX)   130
17:13 (LXX)   112

Exodus
4:22 (LXX)   65

Psalms
67:17 (LXX)   72
88:28 (LXX)   65
110:1   137

Hosea
2:13 (LXX)   122

Isaiah
29:13 (LXX)   130
43:25 (LXX)   118

Ezekiel
45:17 (LXX)   122
46:3 (LXX)   122

New Testament

Acts of the Apostles
12:12   192
12:25   192
13:13   192
15:36–40   192
15:37–39   192
19:29   191
20:4   191
27:2   191

Romans
5:20   117

1 Corinthians
5:3–5   97
16:17   84–85

Ephesians
1:23   110
3:19   110
6:21–22   2
6:22   2

Philippians
2:30   85

Colossians
1:1–2   16, 18, 32, 36, 37, 39–45, 48, 178, 188, 203, 208
1:1   5, 16, 31, 32, 33, 36, 39, 41, 42, 43, 44, 45, 79, 80, 88, 188, 195, 199, 203, 208
1:2   1, 4, 8, 16, 18, 31, 33, 35, 36, 39, 42, 44, 45, 47, 48, 49, 52, 53, 54, 55, 58, 70, 76–77, 81, 87, 146, 157, 160, 183, 188, 189, 190, 191, 200, 201, 202, 203, 204, 208, 209
1:3–14   16, 17–19, 20, 33, 36, 37, 47–61, 64, 177, 203, 207
1:3–9   17
1:3–4   18, 47–49, 57, 204
1:3   16, 17, 18, 33, 36, 47, 48, 49, 53, 55, 60, 61, 105, 155, 159, 165, 177, 178, 194, 207
1:4–8   17
1:4–5   52, 54, 60, 61
1:4   4, 8, 17, 18, 35, 47, 49, 50, 53, 54, 58, 59, 60, 70, 77, 79, 87, 94, 97, 115, 146, 156, 168, 208
1:5–7   193, 194, 197, 201, 202
1:5–6   18, 19, 48, 49–52, 54, 106, 203

COLOSSIANS (cont'd)

1:5 8, 17, 18, 30, 33, 34, 36, 47, 48, 50, 52, 53, 55, 58, 60, 61, 79, 86, 88, 139, 144, 146, 159, 164, 177, 178, 179, 183, 189, 199, 207
1:6 17, 19, 33, 47, 50, 51, 52, 53, 54, 55, 56, 57, 58, 61, 79, 86, 103, 127, 160, 178, 183, 189, 200, 201, 202
1:7–8 18, 19, 53–54, 203
1:7 8, 16, 17, 19, 32, 33, 47, 53, 54, 55, 61, 80, 81, 84, 86, 88, 104, 160, 189, 190, 193, 196, 197, 199, 202
1:8 17, 18, 19, 35, 47, 54, 55, 58, 59, 61, 94, 97, 146, 156, 160, 168
1:9–11 19, 54–57, 204
1:9–10 3, 34, 94, 95, 102, 146, 149, 178, 207
1:9 3, 17, 18–19, 32, 33, 35, 36, 47, 54, 55, 56, 57, 58, 61, 84, 89, 92, 97, 98, 106, 110, 146, 159, 160, 177, 178, 183, 194, 195, 196, 197, 202, 207, 209
1:10 3, 17, 19, 29, 34, 35, 36, 47, 56, 57, 61, 92, 103, 127, 143, 154, 155, 163, 164, 183
1:11–12 84
1:11 17–18, 19, 47, 56, 57, 61, 84, 88, 92, 140, 154
1:12–14 18, 19, 57–60, 204, 209
1:12 4, 8, 18, 33, 35, 36, 47, 57, 58, 60, 61, 70, 77, 81, 87, 104, 146, 152, 158, 165, 171, 177, 178, 204, 207
1:13–20 20
1:13–14 64, 192
1:13 18, 20, 35, 47, 58, 59, 60, 61, 64, 73, 94, 146, 152
1:14 4, 18, 47, 59, 60, 61, 117, 183
1:15–23 19–21, 22, 34, 36, 37, 63–81, 86, 163, 173, 204, 207
1:15–20 20, 63, 80, 81
1:15–17 20, 64–69, 80, 204
1:15–16 78, 150, 161
1:15 19, 20, 21, 63, 64, 65, 68, 70, 71, 72, 73, 108
1:16 19, 20, 21, 26, 34, 36, 63, 65, 66, 67, 68, 71, 72, 73, 74, 75, 80, 81, 110, 125, 137, 164, 173, 174, 175, 207
1:17 19, 20, 63, 68, 69, 71, 72
1:18–20 21, 69–73, 81, 204
1:18 19, 21, 26, 35, 63, 69, 70, 71, 73, 75, 77, 78, 81, 84, 86, 90, 98, 108, 110, 113, 115, 120, 123, 126, 131, 158, 198
1:19–22 75
1:19–20 74, 81
1:19 19, 63, 72, 73, 81, 108

1:20–22 78
1:20 19–20, 21, 27, 34, 36, 63, 73, 74, 75, 76, 78, 81, 137, 157, 164, 174, 175, 204, 207
1:21–23 80, 81
1:21–22 21, 75–78, 81, 86, 183, 204
1:21 8, 20, 29, 34, 36, 64, 76, 78, 81, 84, 116, 119, 163, 164, 207
1:22 4, 8, 20, 21, 22, 34, 35, 36, 64, 75, 76, 77, 78, 79, 81, 84, 90, 108, 113, 114, 119, 146, 152, 164, 207
1:23–28 180. 185
1:23 3, 5, 18, 20, 21, 22, 32, 34, 36, 64, 78–80, 81, 84, 86, 87, 88, 91, 96, 98, 103, 115, 164, 173, 174, 178, 180, 188, 199, 204, 207
1:24–2:5 21–23, 25, 34, 36, 37, 83–99, 102, 145, 204, 206
1:24–25 22, 84–86, 188, 189, 200, 204
1:24 7, 17, 21, 22, 32, 34, 36, 83, 84, 85, 86, 90, 93, 95, 96, 97, 98, 99, 108, 110, 113, 120, 123, 126, 131, 146, 158, 180, 196, 197, 198, 202, 206
1:25–28 180
1:25 21, 22, 30, 32, 34, 36, 83, 86, 87, 88, 91, 95, 96, 98, 146, 159, 179, 183, 199, 201, 202, 206
1:26–28 23, 87–90, 93, 184, 204
1:26–27 91, 96, 179, 185
1:26 4, 21, 23, 35, 36, 83, 87, 90, 93, 95, 98, 99, 138, 140, 146, 152, 159, 181, 189, 206
1:27–28 181
1:27 21, 22, 23, 83, 87, 88, 90, 93, 96, 97, 98, 99, 138, 139, 140, 144, 159, 189
1:28–2:1 93
1:28–29 93
1:28 3, 5, 21, 23, 34, 35, 36, 83, 89, 90, 91, 92, 93, 96, 98, 99, 104, 106, 145, 146, 156, 159, 179, 183, 194, 195, 202, 206, 209
1:29–2:1 94, 188, 204
1:29 22, 23, 83, 90–92, 99, 115, 194, 204
2:1–3 1, 95, 179, 185
2:1–2 95, 96, 99
2:1 8, 17, 22, 32, 34, 83, 92–93, 95, 96, 97, 99, 127, 190, 194, 195, 196, 197, 202
2:2 1, 22, 23, 35, 36, 83, 94, 95, 96, 127, 138, 140, 146, 149, 152, 156, 158, 159, 168, 190, 195, 206
2:2–3 23, 93–95, 97, 98, 99, 204
2:3 3, 4, 22, 23, 34, 83, 94, 95, 96, 106, 131, 133, 138, 159, 160, 183, 195, 202, 209
2:4–5 22, 95–98, 189, 204
2:4 22, 83, 95, 96, 98, 99, 105

Scripture Index

2:5   8, 22, 25, 34, 83, 96, 97, 98, 99, 102, 105, 115, 160
2:6–23   23–26, 27, 35, 37, 101–33, 135, 136, 204, 205
2:6–19   24
2:6–8   3, 25, 102–7, 128, 205
2:6–7   102, 103, 104, 107, 132, 170
2:6   3, 23, 25, 27, 34, 35, 37, 101, 104, 108, 109, 111, 113, 114, 115, 121, 126, 128, 129, 136, 143, 155, 164, 165, 167, 172, 174, 183, 199, 201, 202, 205, 209
2:7   23, 33, 35, 101, 103, 104, 108, 115, 121, 127, 146, 158, 178
2:8   8, 23, 25, 35, 101, 105, 106, 108, 110, 113, 120, 122, 128, 130, 132, 154, 160, 179, 183, 193, 194, 197, 198, 200, 201, 202
2:9–10   26, 108–10, 115, 120, 122, 123, 127, 131, 205
2:9   24, 25, 101, 108, 109, 110, 121, 132
2:10   24, 26, 101, 109, 110, 112, 113, 120, 121, 125, 126, 132
2:11–12   26, 111–15, 116, 193, 205
2:11   5, 8, 22, 24, 25, 26, 34, 101, 111, 112, 113, 114, 115, 116, 117, 120, 121, 126, 131, 132, 133, 148, 149, 161, 194, 201
2:12   5, 23, 24, 26, 35, 37, 101, 111, 112, 114, 115, 116, 121, 127, 128, 132, 135, 136, 137, 138, 143, 148, 205
2:13–14   26, 37, 115–20, 122, 205
2:13   8, 22, 24, 26, 34, 36, 101, 116, 117, 119, 122, 126, 132, 136, 138, 155, 157, 205
2:14   24, 26, 101, 117, 118, 119, 120, 129, 132
2:15–19   26, 120–28, 205
2:15   24, 26, 101, 120, 121, 125, 128, 132, 148
2:16–3:17   24, 102
2:16–19   122
2:16–18   137, 143
2:16   3, 8, 24, 27, 101, 122, 123, 124, 128, 133
2:17   24, 25, 101, 122, 123, 126, 128, 131, 132, 136
2:18   3, 22, 24, 26, 34, 101, 124, 125, 126, 127, 128, 130, 133, 154
2:19   24, 25, 26, 101–2, 126, 127, 128, 131, 133, 156, 158
2:20–23   25, 128–31, 205
2:20   5, 24, 25, 26, 27, 36, 37, 102, 128, 129, 131, 133, 135, 136, 138, 141, 205, 209
2:21–23   129

2:21–22   129, 131, 133, 137, 143
2:21   24, 102
2:22   24, 25, 35, 102, 128, 130, 131, 133, 136
2:23   3, 22, 24–25, 26, 30, 34, 102, 128, 131, 133, 136, 137, 143, 146, 154, 160, 179, 183, 202, 209
3:1–7   26–27, 28, 35, 37, 135–44, 147, 197, 205
3:1–2   3, 27, 136–38, 143
3:1   5, 26, 27, 35, 37, 135, 136, 137, 138, 139, 140, 141, 142, 143, 144, 205, 206, 209
3:2   26, 27, 135, 137, 139, 141, 144, 205
3:3   5, 27, 36, 37, 135, 136, 138–39, 140, 141, 143, 144, 205
3:4   4, 27, 36, 37, 135, 139–40, 141, 143, 144, 181, 205
3:5–7   27, 141–43, 209
3:5–6   206
3:5   3, 8, 27, 135, 141, 142, 147, 153, 155, 205
3:6   27, 135, 142
3:7   3, 8, 27, 28, 34, 35, 36, 37, 135, 136, 141, 142, 143, 147, 155, 183, 205, 206
3:8–16   28–29, 34, 36, 37, 145–62, 165, 206
3:8–9   3, 8, 28, 147–49, 161, 206
3:8   28, 145, 148, 153, 154, 157, 161
3:9   28, 35, 36, 145, 148, 149, 154, 155, 160, 161, 206
3:10   28, 35, 36, 145, 146, 149–50, 151, 152, 154, 161, 206
3:11   28, 145, 150–51, 154, 157, 161, 171, 173, 174, 175, 193, 206
3:12–17   3
3:12–16   164
3:12–14   167
3:12   4, 27, 28, 35, 36, 145, 146, 152–54, 155, 158, 160, 161, 167, 206
3:13–16   28, 154–61
3:13–14   154
3:13   28, 145, 155, 157, 159, 160, 161, 206
3:14   28, 35, 36, 145, 146, 154, 155, 156, 160, 162, 167, 206
3:15–16   157
3:15   28, 34, 36, 145, 146, 157, 158, 159, 160, 161, 162, 165, 178, 190, 206
3:16   3, 28, 30, 33, 34, 35, 36, 145, 146, 157, 159, 160, 161, 162, 164, 165, 179, 183, 190, 195, 200, 201, 202, 206, 209
3:17–4:1   29–30, 34, 36, 37, 163–75, 178, 207
3:17   29, 30, 33, 34, 36, 146, 163, 164–65, 166, 168, 170, 174, 178, 207

COLOSSIANS (cont'd)
3:18–4:1   8
3:18–23   3
3:18–21   29, 30, 165–69
3:18–19   166, 169, 175
3:18   29, 32, 163, 166, 167, 168, 170, 173
3:19   29, 163, 167, 168, 169, 173
3:20–21   168, 169, 175
3:20   29, 30, 32, 36, 163, 168, 169, 170, 173, 207
3:21   29, 30, 163, 168, 170, 173
3:22   22, 29, 30, 34, 36, 163, 164, 169–70, 171, 172, 173, 175, 190, 193, 207
3:23–4:1   29, 170–74
3:23–25   170, 174, 175
3:23   29, 34, 35, 163, 171, 172, 207
3:24   29, 163, 171, 172, 173, 174, 175
3:25   29, 163, 172
4:1–3   3
4:1   29, 30, 34, 36, 163, 164, 172, 173, 174, 175, 178, 193, 207
4:2–6   30, 31, 33, 36, 37, 177–85, 189, 207
4:2–4   182
4:2–3   30, 33, 178–80, 181, 182, 185, 200, 208
4:2   18, 30, 33, 36, 177, 178, 207
4:3–6   189
4:3–4   181, 184, 185, 200
4:3   7, 23, 30, 33, 36, 146, 177, 178, 179, 181, 182, 184, 185, 200, 207, 208
4:4   30, 177, 181–82, 185, 208
4:5–6   3, 30, 182–84, 185
4:5   3, 30, 34, 36, 177, 178, 183, 207, 209
4:6   30, 31, 33, 34, 36, 146, 177, 182, 183, 189, 201, 202, 207, 208
4:7–18   31–32, 36, 37, 187–202, 208
4:7–9   32, 188–91, 197, 201
4:7–8   2
4:7   16, 31, 32, 33, 36, 187, 188, 189, 190, 191, 197, 199, 208
4:8   1, 2, 31, 187, 190, 191
4:9   16, 31, 33, 36, 187, 188, 190, 193, 197, 198, 208
4:10–14   197
4:10–12   32, 191–95, 201
4:10–11   191, 197, 202
4:10   7, 31, 32, 187, 191, 192, 198, 208
4:11   31, 187, 192, 193, 194, 201
4:12–14   191
4:12   17, 19, 23, 31, 32, 33, 35, 36, 187, 188, 193, 194, 195, 196, 197, 198, 202, 208
4:13   8, 17, 31, 32, 187, 195–97, 202, 208
4:14   31, 32, 187, 192, 197, 198, 202, 208
4:15–18   3, 32, 36, 197–201
4:15–16   197
4:15   8, 16, 31, 33, 187, 188, 198, 201, 202, 208
4:16   2, 8, 31, 187, 198, 201, 202
4:17–18   199
4:17   8, 31, 32, 187, 199, 201, 202, 208
4:18   5, 7, 31, 32, 33, 36, 187, 188, 199, 200, 201, 202, 208, 209

2 TIMOTHY
4:10–11   197
4:11   192

PHILEMON
1:1–2   199
1:2   8
1:10–19   190
1:23–24   191
1:24   192, 197

1 PETER
5:13   192

Author Index

Aasgaard, Reidar, 42
Agnew, Francis H., 40
Aletti, Jean-Noël, 20, 64, 75, 87
Allan, John A., 4
Arnold, Clinton E., 8, 70
Attridge, Harold W., 8

Balch, David L., 166
Balz, Horst, 4
Barclay, John M. G., 107, 166
Barnett, Paul W., 40
Barth, Markus, 6, 57, 125
Basevi, Claudio, 63
Baugh, Steven M., 20
Bedale, Stephen, 70
Beetham, Christopher A., 8
Behr, J., 20
Benoit, Pierre, 57, 109
Berger, Klaus, 44
Bergmeier, Roland, 3
Beutler, Johannes, 42
Bevere, Allan R., 4, 9, 57, 58, 107, 122, 125, 139, 141, 142, 150, 152, 153, 155, 174
Bing, C. C., 80
Blanke, Helmut, 6, 57, 125
Blomberg, Craig L., 13
Bockmuehl, Markus N. A., 94, 181, 182
Borchert, Gerald L., 10
Botha, Pieter J. J., 10
Bouttier, Michel, 4
Breck, John, 15
Brouwer, Wayne, 14, 15
Bruce, Frederick Fyvie, 6, 49, 57, 68, 79, 80, 93, 113, 118, 122, 123, 126, 148, 156, 158, 167, 183, 191, 196, 197
Bujard, Walter, 5
Büchsel, Friedrich, 4
Bühner, Jan-Adolf, 39, 40

Cahill, Michael, 86

Campbell, Douglas A., 151
Cannon, George E., 10
Carlos Reyes, Luis, 20
Carr, Wesley A., 67
Carson, D. A., 5, 106
Carter, Warren, 10
Cassidy, Richard J., 7, 180, 200
Cervin, Richard S., 70
Christopher, G. T., 24, 102
Clarke, Andrew D., 42
Cole, H. R., 122
Craddock, Fred B., 69

Dautzenberg, Gerhard, 91
Delebecque, É., 135
DeMaris, Richard E., 8
DeSilva, David A., 14
Deterding, Paul E., 6, 18, 40, 43, 50, 53, 56, 57, 58, 66, 67, 76, 78, 79, 91, 93, 105, 106, 116, 123, 136, 153, 156, 164, 168, 184, 190, 192, 193, 195, 199, 200
Dewey, Joanna, 15
Drake, A. E., 198
Dübbers, Michael, 2, 24, 25, 57, 58, 64, 66, 68, 92, 108, 112, 114, 116, 119, 121, 124, 125, 129, 130, 138, 147, 148, 150, 152, 155, 156, 157
Dunn, James D. G., 1, 4, 6, 9, 17, 18, 19, 20, 24, 39, 40, 41, 42, 43, 44, 45, 48, 49, 50, 52, 53, 54, 55, 56, 57, 58, 59, 67, 68, 70, 71, 73, 74, 76, 77, 78, 79, 84, 87, 88, 89, 90, 92, 96, 97, 98, 103, 105, 106, 107, 108, 109, 111, 112, 113, 114, 116, 118, 119, 120, 121, 123, 124, 126, 129, 130, 131, 136, 137, 138, 139, 140, 141, 142, 147, 148, 149, 150, 153, 155, 156, 157, 158, 159, 160, 164, 165, 166, 167, 168, 169, 170, 171, 172, 173, 178, 179, 180, 182, 184, 189, 190, 192, 193, 195, 196, 197, 198, 199, 200

Elliger, Winfried, 4

Ellis, E. Earle, 5, 7, 192
Evans, Craig A., 9

Fatehi, Mehrdad, 4
Fee, Gordon D., 6, 17, 22, 28, 54, 58, 59, 64, 65, 70, 72, 92, 103, 137, 149, 157, 159, 160
Finlan, Stephen, 6, 59
Fossum, Jarl E., 64
Francis, Fred O., 9, 125

Garland, David E., 6, 9, 17, 41, 43, 44, 50, 51, 53, 57, 66, 67, 69, 70, 73, 74, 76, 78, 85, 86, 88, 110, 112, 119, 123, 124, 125, 126, 129, 151, 165, 167, 168, 169, 173, 182, 184, 192, 193, 195, 198, 200
Garuti, Paolo, 9, 63, 102
Gelardini, Gabriella, 16
Giesen, Heinz, 124
Gilfillan Upton, Bridget, 10
Goldenberg, D., 151
Gordley, Matthew E., 64
Gorman, Michael J., 6, 85
Goulder, Michael D., 9
Grudem, Wayne A., 70

Hackenberg, Wolfgang, 52
Harland, Philip A., 42
Harrington, Daniel J., 9
Harris, Murray J., 6, 16, 19, 22, 23, 26, 27, 52, 66, 67, 68, 69, 71, 72, 73, 74, 76, 77, 79, 85, 87, 88, 90, 91, 92, 96, 102, 103, 104, 105, 106, 107, 108, 109, 110, 113, 114, 116, 118, 120, 127, 128, 129, 136, 137, 138, 139, 140, 141, 142, 147, 149, 150, 151, 152, 155, 158, 164, 166, 169, 170, 172, 178, 179, 180, 183, 184, 191, 193, 196, 198, 200
Harrison, James R., 44
Hartman, L., 9, 20
Harvey, John D., 10
Hay, David M., 42, 51
Hearon, Holly E., 9
Heil, John Paul, 1, 10, 16
Helyer, Larry L., 63
Helyer, Larry R., 63, 65
Henderson, Suzanne Watts, 108, 166, 167
Hock, Andreas, 121
Hofius, Otfried, 63
Holbrook, F. B., 122
Holland, Tom, 65
Hooker, Morna D., 9
Hoppe, Rudolf, 75
House, H. Wayne, 8, 66

Jeremias, Joachim, 14
Johnson, Luke Timothy, 2, 6
Jones, P., 63
Jordaan, Pierre, 5, 166

Keesmaat, Sylvia C., 7
Kiley, Mark, 5
Kourie, Celia E. T., 4
Kremer, Jacob, 84, 85
Krentz, Edgar, 121
Kuhli, Horst, 64

Lähnemann, Johannes, 10
Lamp, Jeffrey S., 63
Langkammer, Hugolinus, 65
Lee, Michelle V., 16
Légasse, Simon, 72
Levison, John R., 135
Lieu, Judith M., 44
Lightfoot, Joseph Barber, 51
Lincoln, Andrew T., 166
Longenecker, Bruce W., 15
Luter, A. Boyd, 16, 44
Luttenberger, Joram, 117
Luz, Ulrich, 64
Lyonnet, Stansilas, 9

MacDonald, Margaret Y., 40, 123, 166, 171, 172
Maier, Harry O., 7
Maisch, Ingrid, 18, 52, 65, 87, 113
Man, Ronald E., 15
Martin, Ralph P., 67
Martin, Troy W., 9, 122, 123, 151
Matera, Frank J., 85
McCown, Wayne, 20
Merkel, Helmut, 73
Metzger, Bruce Manning, 17, 18, 19, 20, 22, 25, 27
Michel, Otto, 45
Moo, Douglas J., 5, 6, 106
Moser, Paul K., 39
Moule, Charles Francis Digby, 95
Mullins, Terrence Y., 48
Murphy-O'Connor, Jerome, 63, 197

Neugebauer, Fritz, 4
Nobbs, Alanna, 42
Nolland, John, 44

O'Brien, Peter Thomas, 3, 4, 6, 18, 24, 40, 41, 43, 44, 48, 49, 50, 53, 55, 56, 57, 58, 59, 60, 67, 69, 70, 71, 72, 73, 76, 77, 80, 86, 87, 89,

Author Index

90, 91, 92, 93, 94, 95, 96, 97, 102, 103, 104, 105, 106, 107, 110, 112, 116, 117, 118, 120, 121, 123, 124, 126, 131, 136, 137, 138, 142, 143, 147, 148, 149, 150, 151, 153, 155, 156, 158, 159, 160, 164, 165, 166, 168, 169, 170, 171, 172, 179, 180, 181, 182, 183, 184, 189, 190, 192, 193, 194, 195, 196, 198, 199, 200
Olbricht, Thomas H., 129
Ollrog, Wolf-Henning, 17, 192
Osiek, Carolyn, 166
Otero Lázaro, Tomás, 63
Overfield, P. D., 72

Pahl, Michael W., 86
Perriman, Andrew C., 85
Plümacher, Eckhard, 107
Porter, Stanley E., 4, 16, 147

Reicke, Bo, 1, 6, 7
Richards, E. Randolph, 2, 6, 10
Roberts, J. H., 9, 18
Robinson, John A. T., 7
Romanello, Stefano, 64
Rosner, Brian S., 142
Rowland, Christopher, 126
Royalty, Robert M., 9
Rusam, Dietrich, 107

Sand, Alexander, 126
Sappington, Thomas J., 9
Schneider, Gerhard, 108
Schubert, Paul, 48
Schweizer, Eduard, 73, 109
Seifrid, Mark A., 4
Shiell, William David, 10
Shiner, Whitney Taylor, 9
Shogren, Gary S., 60
Slater, Thomas B., 4
Smith, Ian K., 6, 8, 9, 65, 67, 68, 70, 73, 105, 107, 108, 111, 113, 114, 115, 117, 118, 119, 121, 124, 125, 126, 127, 128, 129, 136, 137, 139, 140, 141, 148, 152, 154, 160, 166, 173, 174
Son, Sang-Won, 123
Spicq, Ceslas, 44, 91
Standhartinger, Angela, 166
Sterling, Gregory E., 9, 67
Stettler, Christian, 9, 63

Still, Todd D., 6, 50
Stirewalt, Luther M., 6, 10
Stock, Augustine, 15
Sumney, Jerry L., 8, 9, 85
Swart, G. J., 139
Sweeney, J. P., 182, 185

Talbert, Charles H., 6
Thekkekara, M., 151
Thompson, Marianne Meye, 6, 7
Thomson, Ian H., 14, 24
Thornton, T. C. G., 122
Thurston, Bonnie B., 190
Tolmie, D. Francois, 10
Trainor, Michael, 64
Tripp, David, 72

Van Broekhoven, H., 9
van Kooten, George H., 63, 67
Vergeer, W. C., 123
Voelz, James W., 148

Walsh, Brian J., 7
Walter, Nikolaus, 118
Wedderburn, Alexander J. M., 4, 8
Welch, John W., 14
Wendland, Ernst R., 16
Wevers, John William, 112
Wilder, Terry L., 5
Wiles, Gordon P., 49
Williamson, L., 121
Wilson, Mark, 14
Wilson, Robert McLachlan, 4, 8, 9, 18, 19, 20, 41, 42, 43, 45, 48, 49, 54, 55, 56, 58, 60, 66, 69, 70, 74, 75, 80, 87, 88, 89, 91, 97, 115, 124, 126, 130, 140, 148, 153, 155, 157, 172, 173, 180, 181, 192, 198
Wilson, Walter T., 3, 51
Witherington, Ben, 5, 6, 165
Witulski, Thomas, 60
Wright, Nicholas Thomas, 6, 41, 43, 44, 55, 58, 63, 79, 87, 97, 102, 106, 109, 110, 112, 113, 117, 118, 123, 129, 131, 153, 154, 164, 171, 172, 179, 180, 184, 189, 195, 196, 201
Wronka, S., 166

Yamauchi, E., 151
Yates, Roy, 118, 121, 135, 154
Yinger, Kent L., 24

www.ingramcontent.com/pod-product-compliance
Lightning Source LLC
Chambersburg PA
CBHW032004220426
43664CB00005B/134